SUSTAINABILITY AND CORPORATE MECHANISMS IN ASIA

This is the first book to provide a comparative and critical analysis of why and how six corporate mechanisms – (1) sustainability reporting; (2) board gender diversity; (3) constituency directors; (4) stewardship codes; (5) directors' duty to act in the company's best interests; and (6) liability on companies, shareholders and directors – have been or can be used to promote sustainability in the four leading common law jurisdictions in Asia (Singapore, Hong Kong, India and Malaysia). A central challenge is whether and, if so, how the corporate mechanisms should be reconceptualised to promote sustainability in an environment that is characterised by controlling shareholders, particularly the government in state-owned enterprises. Because controlling shareholders are the norm for the majority of the world's companies, and state-owned enterprises play a significant role, this book has important insights on the problems and prospects of advancing sustainability in concentrated and mixed ownership jurisdictions.

ERNEST LIM is an associate professor at the Faculty of Law, National University of Singapore. He obtained his doctorate from Oxford. He has published widely on corporate law and governance. He practised corporate and securities law in New York and Hong Kong prior to entering academia. He is the author of *A Case for Shareholders' Fiduciary Duties in Common Law Asia* (Cambridge University Press 2019).

INTERNATIONAL CORPORATE LAW AND FINANCIAL
MARKET REGULATION

Corporate law and financial market regulation have major implications for how the modern economy is organized and regulated and for how risk is managed and distributed – domestically, regionally and internationally. This Series seeks to inform and lead the vibrant scholarly and policy debate in this highly dynamic area by publishing cutting-edge, timely and critical examinations of the most pressing and important questions in the field.

Series Editors

Professor Eilis Ferran, University of Cambridge
Professor Niamh Moloney, London School of Economics
and Political Science
Professor Howell Jackson, Harvard Law School

'This empirically and theoretically informed and contextually nuanced book deals with a highly topical issue in relation to corporations' sustainability and ESG obligations. It interrogates the corporate laws of common law Asian countries in order to tease out how the sustainability agenda is affecting these corporate laws. The book is clearly structured for comparative study, thoughtful and comprehensive in treatment. This is a must-have companion to those studying the impact of sustainability issues on corporate laws of Western jurisdictions.'

– Iris Chiu, Professor of Corporate Law and Financial Regulation, University College London Faculty of Laws

'Ernest Lim has written a uniquely important and informative book on sustainability in Asia. It sets out the case for sustainability, and the way in which it can be effectively implemented, with exceptional clarity and insight. It will be an invaluable guide for those interested in the principles, practices and policies that should guide the adoption of sustainability in Asia.'

– Colin Mayer, CBE, FBA, Peter Moores Professor of Management Studies, Saïd Business School, University of Oxford, and Academic Lead, British Academy Future of the Corporation Programme

'In this important contribution, Professor Ernest Lim shifts the academic debate about corporate sustainability from a focus on corporate actors and their behaviour to a focus on corporate governance and legal mechanisms. The book identifies six such mechanisms – sustainability reporting, board gender diversity, constituency directors, stewardship codes, director duties, and liability – and provides a comprehensive, clear and cogent analysis of their use in Hong Kong, India, Malaysia and Singapore. Professor Lim also draws broader lessons about these mechanisms for corporate governance, including the role of state-owned enterprises and controlling shareholders.'

– Frank Partnoy, Adrian A. Kragen Professor of Law, University of California, Berkeley, School of Law

'The obligations of businesses to play a leading role in addressing our global climate crisis are increasingly pressing. Yet the scope and contours of those obligations remain ill defined. Professor Lim's careful and thorough work brings precious clarity. His work will be helpful and enlightening to scholars, business leaders, governments and NGOs across Asia – and beyond.'

– Kent Greenfield, Professor of Law and Dean's Distinguished Scholar, Boston College Law School

SUSTAINABILITY AND CORPORATE MECHANISMS IN ASIA

ERNEST LIM
National University of Singapore

Shaftesbury Road, Cambridge CB2 8EA, United Kingdom

One Liberty Plaza, 20th Floor, New York, NY 10006, USA

477 Williamstown Road, Port Melbourne, VIC 3207, Australia

314–321, 3rd Floor, Plot 3, Splendor Forum, Jasola District Centre, New Delhi – 110025, India

103 Penang Road, #05–06/07, Visioncrest Commercial, Singapore 238467

Cambridge University Press is part of Cambridge University Press & Assessment, a department of the University of Cambridge.

We share the University's mission to contribute to society through the pursuit of education, learning and research at the highest international levels of excellence.

www.cambridge.org
Information on this title: www.cambridge.org/9781009376235

DOI: 10.1017/9781108658508

© Ernest Lim 2020

This publication is in copyright. Subject to statutory exception and to the provisions of relevant collective licensing agreements, no reproduction of any part may take place without the written permission of Cambridge University Press & Assessment.

First published 2020
First paperback edition 2023

A catalogue record for this publication is available from the British Library

ISBN 978-1-108-49451-9 Hardback
ISBN 978-1-009-37623-5 Paperback

Cambridge University Press & Assessment has no responsibility for the persistence or accuracy of URLs for external or third-party internet websites referred to in this publication and does not guarantee that any content on such websites is, or will remain, accurate or appropriate.

For Domin and my brothers

CONTENTS

List of Figures   *page* xv
List of Tables   xvi
Acknowledgements   xvii
List of Abbreviations   xviii

1 **Introduction and Overview**   1

  I Introduction   2
    A Terminology   4
    B Why Companies Should Pursue Sustainability   7
      1 Strategic Reason   7
      2 Ethical Reason   10

  II Rationales and Motivations   11
    A Significant, Recent Legal Developments in Common Law Asia   12
      1 Sustainability Reporting   12
      2 Gender Diversity on the Board of Directors   14
      3 Constituency Directors   15
      4 Stewardship Codes   16
      5 Directors' Duty to Act in the Best Interests of the Company   17
    B Common Law Asia Calls into Question Two Influential Theories   18
      1 Legal Origins   18
      2 Institutional Context   22

  III Factors that Drive Sustainability in Common Law Asia   25
    A Socio-economic Development Agendas of Governments   25
      1 Singapore   25
      2 Malaysia   27
      3 India   29
      4 Hong Kong   32

    B Rules of Stock Exchanges   33
    C Internationalisation of Companies   35
    D Rise of SRIs   36

IV Problems and Effects   39
    A Conflicts of Interest between the Government's Roles as Both Shareholder and Regulator   41
    B Political Interference and Extractions of Private Benefits of Control   43
    C Two Qualifications   45
        1 First Qualification: Public but Not Private Benefits of Control   46
        2 Second Qualification: Protect and Promote the State's Legitimacy   46

V Structure   50

2 Sustainability Reporting   55

I Structure and Contents of Reporting Requirements   57
    A Structure   57
        1 Comply or Explain   58
        2 Mandatory   67
    B Contents   69
        1 Materiality of ESG Factors   69
        2 Indicators   73
        3 India: BRRs and the CSR 2 Per Cent Spending Requirement   77

II Qualitative Evaluation of Sustainability Reports   83
    A Effect of Corporate Characteristics   83
        1 Singapore   83
        2 Malaysia   84
        3 India   85
    B Extent and Quality of Disclosures   86
        1 Singapore and Malaysia   86
        2 India   87
        3 Hong Kong   88
    C Qualitative Evaluation of the Sustainability Reports in Common Law Asia   89
        1 Hong Kong   92
        2 Singapore   94
        3 Malaysia   96
        4 India   96

  III Suggested Reforms 97
    A Oversight Mechanism 97
    B Sanctions 99

3 Board Gender Diversity 103

  I Rationales for Female Directors 104
    A Enhances Corporate Governance 105
    B Improves Firm Value 106
    C Equality Justifications 108
      1 Equality of Outcome 110
      2 Equality of Resources and Opportunity 111

  II Mechanisms to Promote Female Directors 115
    A Quota Requirement 115
    B Apply or Explain an Alternative 120
    C A Combined Approach: Monitoring Disclosure and 'Name and Shame' 124
    D Setting Targets 130

  III State-Owned Enterprises 133
    A Malaysia 134
    B Singapore 135
    C India 136
    D Hong Kong 136
    E SOEs with No Female Directors 137
    F Connected to the Government 137
    G Repeat Players 139

  IV Conclusion 140

4 Constituency Directors 142

  I German Co-determination 143
    A Costs and Benefits 145
      1 Costs 145
      2 Benefits 149
    B Adoption by Other Jurisdictions 152
      1 Singapore 153
      2 Malaysia 156
      3 Hong Kong 159
      4 India 161

  II Indian CSR Board Committee 162

  III Conclusion 168

5 Stewardship Codes   170

    I Emergence of Stewardship Codes   172

    II Stewardship Codes and Sustainability   175
        A Rationales   175
            1 Singapore   175
            2 Malaysia   176
            3 Hong Kong   180
        B Contents   180
        C Compliance Structure   183
        D Scope   185

    III Controlling Shareholders   188
        A How the Code Reinforces the Power of Controlling Shareholders   188
        B How Controlling Shareholders' Presence and Power Are Likely to Disincentivise Institutional Shareholders from Actively Engaging with the Company   189
            1 Formal Power   189
            2 Informal Power   193
        C Conflicts of Interest between the Controlling Shareholder (or Its Company) and the Institutional Shareholders   194

    IV Fiduciary Duties of Institutional Shareholders   196
        A First Interpretation   196
        B Second Interpretation   199
            1 The First View   199
            2 The Second View   202
        C Third Interpretation   202

    V Conclusion   204

6 Directors' Duty to Act in the Best Interests of the Company   206

    I Shareholder Primacy, Stakeholder Value, and Long-Term Value and Viability   208
        A Shareholder Primacy   208
        B Stakeholder Value   212
        C Long-Term Value and Viability   215

II Evaluation of the Law in the Four Asian Jurisdictions 217
   A India 217
   B Hong Kong 220
   C Singapore 223
   D Malaysia 225
   E Lessons 226

III Implications of Directors' Best Interest Duty for Corporate Governance Mechanisms 228
   A Sustainability Reporting 228
   B Stewardship Code 229
   C Constituency Directors 231

IV Conclusion 232

7 Liability of Companies, Shareholders and Directors 235

I Rationales for Limited Liability 237

II Existing Exceptions to Limited Liability 242
   A Distinguishing Limited Liability and Separate Legal Personality 243
   B Piercing the Corporate Veil 246
      1 Singapore and Hong Kong 247
      2 Malaysia 249
      3 India 250
   C Breach of Duty of Care by Parent Companies 252

III Proposed Exceptions to Limited Liability 261
   A Enterprise Liability 261
   B Liability on Shareholders of the Wrongdoing Company 264

IV My Proposal 267
   A Imposing Liability on the Controlling Shareholder 267
   B Liability in Networks 274

V Breach of Public Interest Legislations 277

VI Conclusion 282

8 Conclusion 284

Appendixes

Appendix 1 External Assurance   289

Appendix 2 Top Fifty Listed Companies in Each of the Four Jurisdictions   302

Appendix 3 Qualitative Assessment of Sustainability Reports   310

Appendix 4 Good Examples of Diversity Policy Disclosure   360

Appendix 5 Proportion of Female Directors   365

Bibliography   371
Index   394

FIGURES

3.1 Proportion of female directors in Singapore, Malaysia, India and Hong Kong (in %) (in the top fifty companies by market capitalisation) *page* 117
3.2 Proportion of female directors in Singapore, Malaysia, India and Hong Kong (in %) (among GLCs/SOEs in the top fifty companies by market capitalisation) 134
3.3 Proportion of female directors in Singapore, Malaysia, India and Hong Kong (in %) (among non-GLCs/SOEs in the top fifty companies by market capitalisation) 134
A5.1 Proportion of female directors to male directors in Singapore, Malaysia, India and Hong Kong:
  (a) Singapore 365
  (b) Malaysia 365
  (c) India 366
  (d) Hong Kong 366
A5.2 Proportion of female directors to male directors in the SOEs/GLCs in Singapore, Malaysia, India and Hong Kong:
  (a) Singapore 367
  (b) Malaysia 367
  (c) India 367
  (d) Hong Kong 368
A5.3 Proportion of female directors to male directors in the non-SOEs/GLCs in Singapore, Malaysia, India and Hong Kong:
  (a) Singapore 369
  (b) Malaysia 369
  (c) India 370
  (d) Hong Kong 370

TABLES

2.1 Extract from the BRR of Tata Consultancy Ltd *page* 79
5.1 Country distribution and summary statistics   192

ACKNOWLEDGEMENTS

I am tremendously grateful to the six referees – the three anonymous CUP readers and the three CUP series editors (Eilis Ferran, Niamh Moloney and Howell Jackson) – for their meticulous review and unequivocal support for this monograph. The careful reading and searching comments provided by the anonymous CUP readers have significantly improved the form and substance of the analysis. All errors remain my own.

Colleagues, friends and family members offered constructive feedback on the ideas and arguments in this book. The academics and students at the Center for Transnational Legal Studies at King's College London to whom I presented my draft chapters gave me valuable comments. Graham Ward, who was kind and hospitable, provided me with a stimulating and conducive working environment at Christ Church, Oxford. Lee Hsiang Hui provided constant encouragement. The ever efficient, responsive and solution-driven Joe Ng was a pleasure to work with. Kate Chan, Lim Boon Choon, Serene Chee, Stanley Tan and Lim Ke Jia provided indispensable research assistance. I thank each and every one of them. This project was supported by the Singapore Ministry of Education Academic Research Fund Tier 1 Grant (R241000177115).

I have endeavoured to state the law as it was known to me as of 1 July 2019.

ABBREVIATIONS

1MDB	1Malaysia Development Berhad
AUM	assets under management
BRR	business responsibility report
CBD	Council for Board Diversity
CEO	chief executive officer
CPSE	central public sector enterprise
CSR	corporate social responsibility
DAC	Diversity Action Committee
EES	economic, environmental and social
ESG	environmental, social and governance
EU	European Union
GLC	government-linked company
GRI-G4	Global Report Initiative Guidelines
HK CO	Hong Kong Companies Ordinance (Chapter 622)
HKEX LR	Hong Kong Stock Exchange Listing Rule
HKPRO	Hong Kong Principles of Responsible Ownership
HKSAR	Hong Kong Special Administrative Region
IN CA	India Companies Act 2013
IPO	initial public offering
KPI	key performance indicators
MCA	Ministry of Corporate Affairs, India
MCCG	Malaysian Code on Corporate Governance
MCII	Malaysian Code for Institutional Investors
MNC	multinational corporation
MSC	Malaysia Securities Commission
MSWG	Minority Shareholders Watch Group
MY CA	Malaysia Companies Act 2016 (Act 777)
NEP	New Economic Policy
NGO	non-government organisation
NTUC	National Trade Union Congress
PRC	People's Republic of China
PRI	Principles of Responsible Investments
PSU	public sector undertaking

R&D	research and development
SASAC	State-Owned Assets Supervision and Administration Commission
SEBI	Securities and Exchange Board of India
SEHK	Stock Exchange of Hong Kong
SG CA	Singapore Companies Act (Chapter 50) Revised edn 2006
SGX LR	Singapore Exchange Listing Rule
SOE	state-owned enterprise
SPFB	Stewardship Principles for Family Businesses
SRI	socially responsible investments
SSP	Singapore Stewardship Principles for Responsible Investors
UK	United Kingdom
UN	United Nations
UOB	United Overseas Bank Limited
US	United States

1

Introduction and Overview

I Introduction   2
   A Terminology   4
   B Why Companies Should Pursue Sustainability   7
      1 Strategic Reason   7
      2 Ethical Reason   10
II Rationales and Motivations   11
   A Significant, Recent Legal Developments in Common Law Asia   12
      1 Sustainability Reporting   12
      2 Gender Diversity on the Board of Directors   14
      3 Constituency Directors   15
      4 Stewardship Codes   16
      5 Directors' Duty to Act in the Best Interests of the Company   17
   B Common Law Asia Calls into Question Two Influential Theories   18
      1 Legal Origins   18
      2 Institutional Context   22
III Factors that Drive Sustainability in Common Law Asia   25
   A Socio-economic Development Agendas of Governments   25
      1 Singapore   25
      2 Malaysia   27
      3 India   29
      4 Hong Kong   32
   B Rules of Stock Exchanges   33
   C Internationalisation of Companies   35
   D Rise of SRIs   36
IV Problems and Effects   39
   A Conflicts of Interest between the Government's Roles as Both Shareholder and Regulator   41
   B Political Interference and Extractions of Private Benefits of Control   43
   C Two Qualifications   45
      1 First Qualification: Public but Not Private Benefits of Control   46
      2 Second Qualification: Protect and Promote the State's Legitimacy   46
V Structure   50

I Introduction

This is the first book to provide a comparative and critical analysis of why and how corporate governance and corporate law have been or can be used to promote and protect sustainability in the four common law jurisdictions in Asia, ie Singapore, Hong Kong, India and Malaysia. Based on theoretical, doctrinal and empirical research, I critically evaluate the rationales for, and effectiveness of, six corporate mechanisms, namely (1) sustainability reporting; (2) gender diversity on the board of directors; (3) constituency directors; (4) stewardship codes; (5) directors' duty to act in the best interests of the company; and (6) liability on companies, shareholders and directors. These six corporate mechanisms provide an analytic framework for understanding the role of corporate governance and corporate law in advancing (or thwarting) sustainability in jurisdictions other than those discussed in this book.

These six mechanisms will be evaluated in light of the distinctive contexts in the four common law Asian jurisdictions, specifically their ownership structures and institutional environment. This is because the majority of the listed companies there are dominated by controlling shareholders, particularly the government[1] in state-owned enterprises (SOEs), which wield significant and substantial power.[2] The pursuit of socio-economic agendas and social objectives by the government through SOEs has facilitated sustainability, and the government plays an important role in advancing this goal. However, the government as the controlling shareholder of the SOEs poses two key problems, namely, conflicts of interest between the government as the controlling shareholder on the one hand, and as the corporate regulator on the other, as well as political interference and extractions of benefits of control by the government. These problems may affect the corporate mechanisms for promoting sustainability. In short, a central challenge is whether, and, if so, how, the corporate mechanisms should be reconceptualised to promote sustainability in an environment that is characterised by controlling shareholders, governmental interference or state ownership of companies.

---

[1] The term 'government' does not necessarily refer to a unitary actor but may include complex, multi-layer networks of power in different regulatory departments, agencies and ministries involving different actors.

[2] Other than the government, the other dominant group of controlling shareholders in the four common law Asian jurisdictions consists of families. While there are more family-owned listed companies than listed SOEs, the latter wield more significant and substantial power and have greater impact on societies by virtue of the fact that their controller is the government. This explains the focus on governments and SOEs, which will be elaborated in subsequent parts of this chapter.

The analysis of the relationship between corporate mechanisms and sustainability, on the one hand, and governments and SOEs, on the other, using the four Asian jurisdictions as a case study, has broader policy and scholarly relevance and importance. First, the analysis will be relevant to other concentrated ownership jurisdictions seeking to promote sustainability. This is because controlling shareholders are the norm for a majority of the world's companies,[3] and SOEs constitute a significant proportion of companies among the Fortune Global 500 as well as in developing and to certain extent developed countries.[4] Second, while there is an emerging literature examining the costs and benefits of state capitalism in relation to sustainability,[5] there is little analysis of how this stream of literature is connected to the research on corporate governance and company law,[6] which have been deployed as legal strategies to promote sustainability. Finally, this book will expand the field of comparative corporate social responsibility (CSR)/sustainability research, which has been dominated by studies comparing the United States and Europe.

This chapter is divided into five parts. Part II explains the rationales and motivations for focusing on corporate mechanisms in the four common law jurisdictions in Asia. Part III analyses the factors that drive sustainability in these four Asian jurisdictions. Part IV discusses the problems arising from the government being the controller of SOEs

---

[3] OECD, OECD Corporate Governance Factbook 2019 (2019) at 17.
[4] PwC, 'State-Owned Enterprises: Catalysts for Public Value Creation?' (2017) at 9 12 (the study found that (1) the proportion of SOEs among the Fortune Global 500 has grown from 9 per cent in 2005 to 23 per cent in 2014; (2) 10.2 per cent of the Fortune 2,000 largest companies were majority-owned SOEs with ownership interests spread across thirty-seven countries; and (3) the top eight countries with the highest SOE shares (which include Malaysia, India and China) collectively accounted for more than 20 per cent of world trade) www.pwc.com/gx/en/psrc/publications/assets/pwc-state-owned-enterprise-psrc.pdf; Simon CY Wong, 'The State of Governance at State-Owned Enterprises' (2018) 40 *Private Sector Opinion* (IFC Corporate Governance Knowledge Publication) 3 www.ifc.org/wps/wcm/connect/b1adde06-267d-4d79-bfaf-62f17de51f4a/PSO40.pdf?MOD=AJPERES&CVID=m7T0xLQ; OECD, *The Size and Sectoral Distribution of State-Owned Enterprises* (OECD Publishing 2014).
[5] Nahee Kang and Jeremy Moon, 'Institutional Complementarity between Corporate Governance and Corporate Social Responsibility: A Comparative Institutional Analysis of Three Capitalisms' (2012) 10 *Socio-Economic Review* 85; Jeremy Moon, Nahee Kang and Jean-Pascal Gond, 'Corporate Social Responsibility and Government' in David Coen, Wyn Grant and Graham Wilson (eds), *Oxford Handbook of Business and Government* (Oxford University Press 2011) at ch 22.
[6] See eg Beate Sjåfjell and Benjamin J Richardson (eds), *Company Law and Sustainability* (Cambridge University Press 2015).

and how they may affect the corporate mechanisms for promoting sustainability. Part V sets out the structure of this book.

Before proceeding further, two preliminary points are made. First, I explain why I use the term 'sustainability' instead of 'corporate social responsibility'. Second, I defend a central assumption underlying this book, which is that it is good for companies to promote sustainability.

A   Terminology

Sustainability, instead of CSR,[7] is used in this book for the following reasons. To begin with, sustainability, rather than CSR, is the more widely used legal term in the common law Asian jurisdictions. It has been explicitly adopted in the listing rules in Singapore and Malaysia[8] and implicitly endorsed in Hong Kong[9] and India.[10] Given that the regulators and policy makers in common law Asia have generally adopted the term sustainability in formulating the rules and regulations,[11] and because this term has gained traction in the listed companies in the four countries, it is appropriate to use this term.

Equally important, although there is no conclusive meaning of sustainability, it is far less contested and controversial than CSR, a term that is afflicted with numerous and long-standing uncertainties.[12] A central

---

[7] See generally Andrew Crane, Dirk Matten, Abagail McWilliams, Jeremy Moon and Donald S Siegel (eds), *The Oxford Handbook of Corporate Social Responsibility* (Oxford University Press 2008); Kiyoteru Tsutsui and Alwyn Lim (eds), *Corporate Social Responsibility in a Globalizing World* (Cambridge University Press 2015).

[8] SGX-ST, Listing Rules, Practice Note 7.6, Sustainability Reporting Guide (2016); Bursa Malaysia, Sustainability Reporting Guide (2015).

[9] While Hong Kong uses the term Environmental, Social and Governance (ESG) Reporting Guide, it has relied extensively on the fact that other stock exchanges have implemented sustainability reporting when it sought to justify changing the regime from a purely voluntary to a comply or explain basis: see Hong Kong Exchanges and Clearing Limited, Consultation Paper: Review of the Environmental, Social and Governance Reporting Guide (July 2015).

[10] The top 100 listed companies by market capitalisation in India are required to disclose 'Business Responsibility Reports' under the listing rules. The contents of such a report are based on ESG considerations and the National Voluntary Guidelines on Social, Environmental and Economic Responsibilities of Business, the latter of which make specific and repeated references to sustainability, and not CSR: see Securities and Exchange Board of India, Business Responsibility Reports, CIR/CFD/DIL/8/2012 (13 August 2012) paras 2 and 3.

[11] But note that in India, s 135 of the Companies Act 2013 uses the term CSR.

[12] See eg Jean-Pascal Gond and Jeremy Moon, 'Corporate Social Responsibility in Retrospect and Prospect: Exploring the Life-Cycle of an Essentially Contested Concept' in Jean-Pascal Gond and Jeremy Moon (eds), *Corporate Social Responsibility: A Reader*, vol 1 (Routledge 2011); Frank GA De Bakker, Peter Groenewegen and Frank Den Hond,

and persistent debate in the CSR literature is whether companies' compliance with laws constitutes CSR or whether CSR refers only to actions taken on a voluntary basis, ie above and beyond legal compliance. Another outstanding issue in CSR is whether companies are engaging in CSR if they are merely addressing the externalities they have caused (such as environmental damage, human rights abuses and systemic risks to the economy). The uncertainties have led to a proliferation of confusing terminologies such as 'corporate business responsibility' and 'corporate responsibility' with some commentators advocating the use of these terms instead of CSR,[13] the latter of which has been regarded by some as not materially different from corporate philanthropy. Others, however, argue that CSR should encompass both legal compliance and voluntary actions.[14] Another unresolved issue is whether companies should engage in strategic/instrumental CSR (defined as promoting the interests of non-shareholders only if doing so maximises share price or profitability), or ethical/intrinsic CSR (defined as promoting the interests of non-shareholders because these interests are morally worthy in themselves of protection, even if doing so does not increase shareholder value).[15] Given that CSR carries with it substantial political, legal and social baggage, it is not unwise to adopt a different terminology.[16] Unsurprisingly, it has been said that the controversies surrounding the definition of CSR have impeded empirical research in that area.[17]

'A Bibliometric Analysis of 30 Years of Research and Theory on Corporate Social Responsibility and Corporate Social Performance' (2005) 44 *Business and Society* 283.

[13] Céline Gainet, 'Exploring the Impact of Legal Systems and Financial Structures on CR' (2010) 95 *Journal of Business Ethics* 195 at 197.

[14] Tom Campbell, 'The Normative Grounding of Corporate Social Responsibility: A Human Rights Approach' in Doreen McBarnet, Aurora Voiculescu and Tom Campbell (eds), *The New Corporate Accountability: Corporate Social Responsibility and the Law* (Cambridge University Press 2007) at 534–42.

[15] David Million, 'CSR and Environmental Sustainability' in Beate Sjåfjell and Benjamin J Richardson (eds), *Company Law and Sustainability: Legal Barriers and Opportunities* (Cambridge University Press 2015) at 41–76.

[16] To clarify, not adopting the term CSR does not imply that the literature in that area is not valuable. On the contrary, as I will show, the recent empirical and finance literature on the correlation between firm value and corporate governance, on the one hand, and CSR, on the other, can illuminate the analysis of the question of why the listed companies in the four common law Asian countries should pursue sustainability.

[17] Cynthia Williams and Ruth V Aguilera, 'Corporate Social Responsibility in a Comparative Perspective' in Andrew Crane, Dirk Matten, Abagail McWilliams, Jeremy Moon and Donald S Siegel (eds), *The Oxford Handbook of Corporate Social Responsibility* (Oxford University Press 2008) at 453.

While there is no definitive understanding of sustainability, one widely cited definition, endorsed by the Malaysian and Singapore sustainability reporting guides, is that found in the Brundtland Report, which defines sustainable development as 'development that meets the needs of the present without compromising the ability of future generations to meet their own needs'.[18] When operationalised in the context of listed companies, sustainability is understood in this book to refer to the responsibilities of companies for the impacts that they cause to societies and the actions that should be taken by them to address these impacts, which include but are not limited to giving effect to environmental, social and governance (ESG)[19] as well as human rights considerations in their business operations and core strategies. This is consistent with the definition of sustainability provided by the United Nations Global Compact, which is 'a company's delivery of long-term value in financial, social, environmental and ethical terms'.[20] Sustainability, as defined here, includes both voluntary actions and actions that are mandated by the law.

Having clarified the terminology, the last preliminary question which we need to address is why companies should pursue sustainability. There are two main reasons. The first is strategic and the second ethical. The first and second reasons are also known as instrumental and intrinsic justifications.

---

[18] World Commission on Environment and Development, 'Our Common Future' (1987) para 1.

[19] Adoption of ESG factors is important because it can: provide an effective risk management framework; provide a new lens for strategy development and growth opportunities; and address the demands of stakeholders such as customers, employees and investors: see Brandon Boze, Margarita Krivitski, David F Larcker, Brian Tayan and Eva Zlotnicka, 'The Business Case for ESG' (23 May 2019), Rock Center for Corporate Governance at Stanford University Closer Look Series: Topics, Issues and Controversies in Corporate Governance No. CGRP-77, https://ssrn.com/abstract=3393082. There are variations in the ESG definition in the listing rules in the common law Asian jurisdictions. But, generally, environmental includes climate change, greenhouse gas emissions and resource depletion. Social includes working conditions, local communities, health and safety, employee relations, diversity, labour standards, supply chain management, product responsibility and anti-corruption. Governance, which includes executive pay, board diversity and corruption, has been partially subsumed under social considerations (with the exception of executive pay) in Singapore's and Hong Kong's listing rules. Malaysia's listing rules exclude governance considerations because there are specific requirements related to corporate governance in the listing rules and corporate governance codes. Malaysia's listing rules replaced governance with economic considerations, the latter of which refers to the company's economic impacts on its stakeholders at local, national and global levels. So, instead of ESG, it is called EES (economic, environmental and social) in Malaysia (Bursa Malaysia, Sustainability Reporting Guide (2015)).

[20] United Nations, Global Compact (2013) at 6.

I INTRODUCTION

B Why Companies Should Pursue Sustainability

1 Strategic Reason

There is evidence of the benefits of promoting sustainability. This is also known as the business case for sustainability. First, it can strengthen the company's risk management because, by proactively identifying and addressing the risks, companies are in a better position to reduce the adverse impact of these risks on their businesses. For example, one study has found that companies that focus on material sustainability risks have financially outperformed other companies by 3 per cent to 8 per cent.[21]

Second, companies that have good sustainability disclosure and practices have enhanced their reputation among their investors and stakeholders.[22] After all, studies have shown that 70 per cent to 80 per cent of a company's market value is based on intangibles such as reputation and goodwill.[23] Conversely, failure to pre-empt or address serious sustainability problems (including but not limited to environmental catastrophes and egregious human rights abuses in supply chain) can have an adverse and material impact on companies' reputation.

Third, there is a correlation between promoting sustainability and firm innovation.[24] Attention to sustainability considerations can spur companies to explore business opportunities, as evidenced, for instance, in sustainability driven products and services. General Electric's Ecomagination Initiative is a prominent example. One study found that companies issued more patents after the directors considered the interests of stakeholders because this allowed for greater experimentation within companies.[25]

---

[21] Mozaffar Khan, George Serafeim and Aaron Yoon, 'Corporate Sustainability: First Evidence on Materiality' (2016) 91 *Accounting Review* 1697; Lawrence Loh, Thomas Thomas and Yu Wang, 'Sustainability Reporting and Firm Value: Evidence from Singapore-Listed Companies' (2017) 9 *Sustainability* 1 (concluding that sustainability reporting is positively related to a firm's market value and that this relationship is independent of sector or firm status such as government-linked companies and family businesses).

[22] Ernst & Young and Boston College Centre for Corporate Citizenship, Value of Sustainability Reporting (2013) at 3.

[23] See eg Robert G Eccles, Scott C Newquist and Roland Schatz, 'Reputation and Its Risks' (2007) *Harvard Business Review* https://hbr.org/2007/02/reputation-and-its-risks.

[24] Ram Nidumolu, CK Prahalad and MR Rangaswami, 'Why Sustainability Is Now the Key Driver of Innovation' (2009) *Harvard Business Review* https://hbr.org/2009/09/why-sustainability-is-now-the-key-driver-of-innovation.

[25] See Caroline Flammer and Aleksandra Kacperczk, 'The Impact of Stakeholder Orientation on Innovation: Evidence from a Natural Experiment' (2014) http://papers.ssrn.com/sol3/papers.cfm?abstract_id=2353076.

Fourth, promoting sustainability can enhance access to capital. Investors take into account a company's commitment to sustainability in their investment decisions. For example, the global sustainable investment market increased by 61 per cent to US$21.4 trillion from 2012 to 2014.[26] In Asia, there was an increase in responsible investment by 32 per cent during that period.[27] Further, as of 31 March 2017, there were 1,713 institutions managing over US$45 trillion in assets who were signatories to the UN Principles for Responsible Investment (PRI), under which they were required to incorporate ESG considerations into their investment decisions.[28] In addition, the Carbon Disclosure Project, which works with 2,000 worldwide companies to collate and analyse data on companies' greenhouse gas emissions, is supported by institutional investors holding over US$92 trillion in assets.[29] Unsurprisingly, one comprehensive study that has surveyed the field found that 90 per cent of the literature demonstrates that companies with good sustainability regimes have lower cost of capital and thus improved access to capital.[30]

Finally, there are studies showing that there is a correlation between sustainability practices and firm value. For instance, one study found that indices with companies that adhere to ESG practices generally performed on par with the benchmark index at different periods.[31] A comprehensive study found that integrating ESG into the investment process had a positive impact on 65 per cent of companies in emerging markets as compared to 38 per cent in developed markets.[32] Another study found that there is a positive and significant correlation between the sustainability performance of major companies in Asia and share price.[33]

---

[26] Bursa Malaysia, Sustainability Reporting Guide (2015) at 12.
[27] Association for Sustainable and Responsible Investment in Asia, 2014 Asia Sustainable Investment Review (2014).
[28] UN Principles for Responsible Investment www.unpri.org/annual-report-2018.
[29] Carbon Disclosure Project, Catalyzing Business and Government Action www.cdp.net/en-US/Pages/About-Us.aspx.
[30] See Gordon L Clark, Andreas Feiner and Michael Viehs, 'From the Stockholder to the Stakeholder: How Sustainability Can Drive Financial Outperformance' (2015) http://papers.ssrn.com/sol3/papers.cfm?abstract_id=2508281.
[31] Bessemer Trust, *Integrating Value and Your Investments* (2018).
[32] Deutsche Bank, 'ESG and Financial Performance: Aggregated Evidence from More than 2000 Empirical Studies' (14 January 2016) www.db.com/newsroom_news/2016/ghp/esg-and-financial-performance-aggregated-evidence-from-more-than-200-empirical-studies-en-11363.htm.
[33] Yan Leung Cheung, Weiqiang Tan, Hee-Joon Ahn and Zheng Zhang, 'Does Corporate Social Responsibility Matter in Asian Emerging Markets' (2010) 92 *Journal of Business*

A further recent study found that 80 per cent of the literature shows that good sustainability practices are strongly correlated with share price.[34] A recent study of 116 listed companies (which include 38 firms listed on the Stock Exchange of Hong Kong) confirmed the view that sustainability engagement (as evidenced in sustainability disclosure) is significantly and positively associated with financial performance.[35]

In short, not only are there studies that show that good sustainability practices lead to improved innovation, operating performance and share price,[36] but there is also a study showing that companies with good corporate governance engage in sustainability conduct.[37] And the study rebuts the criticism that sustainability is associated with poor corporate governance.[38]

That said, there are commentators that have argued that boards and management pursue sustainability to enrich themselves at the shareholders' expense[39] and that the pursuit of sustainability practices by the

---

Ethics 401; Priyanka Garg, 'CSR and Corporate Performance: Evidence from India' (2016) 43 *Decision* 333 at 341–3.

[34] See Gordon L Clark, Andreas Feiner and Michael Viehs, 'From the Stockholder to the Stakeholder: How Sustainability Can Drive Financial Outperformance' (2015) http://papers.ssrn.com/sol3/papers.cfm?abstract_id=2508281. A study of the listed companies in Hong Kong found that markets react positively to ESG initiatives, but less positively to companies' being included in sustainability indexes or rankings by the companies; this is because companies did not explain, and investors did not appreciate, the impact of these investments on the companies' financial performance: Kar Yee Lo and Calvin Lee Kwan, 'The Effect of Environmental, Social, Governance and Sustainability Initiatives on Stock Value: Examining Market Response to Initiatives Undertaken by Listed Companies' (2017) 24 *Corporate Social Responsibility and Environmental Management* 606 at 615. But one study found that sustainability practices are positively correlated with both return on capital and expectations of future performance only if these practices are strategic rather than common: Ioannis Ioannou and George Serafeim, 'Corporate Sustainability: A Strategy?' (1 January 2019). Harvard Business School Accounting & Management Unit Working Paper No. 19-065 https://ssrn.com/abstract=3312191.

[35] Cornelia Beck, Geoffrey Frost and Stewart Jones, 'CSR Disclosure and Financial Performance Revisited: A Cross Country Analysis' (2018) 43 *Australian Journal of Management* 517 at 530–1.

[36] See eg Xin Deng et al, 'Corporate Social Responsibility and Stakeholder Value Maximization: Evidence from Mergers' (2013) 110 *Journal of Financial Economics* 87; Elroy Dimson, 'Active Ownership' (2015) 28 *Review of Financial Studies* 3225.

[37] See eg Allen Ferrell, Hao Liang and Luc Renneboog, 'Socially Responsible Firms' (2016) 122 *Journal of Financial Economics* 585.

[38] Ibid.

[39] See eg Ing-Haw Cheng, Harrison G Hong and Kelly Shue, 'Do Managers Do Good with Other Peoples' Money?' (2011) Chicago Booth Research Paper No. 12-47 https://ssrn.com/abstract=1962120; Ronald W Masulis and Syed Walid Reza, 'Agency Problems of Corporate Philanthropy' (2015) 28 *Review of Financial Studies* 592.

board can be time-consuming and distract them from fulfilling their core duties.[40] However, the literature overall demonstrates that promoting sustainability/CSR is consistent with maximisation of shareholder value.[41]

2 Ethical Reason

The second reason why companies should pursue sustainability is that it is a morally good thing to do. It is telling that in the National Voluntary Guidelines on Social, Environmental and Economic Responsibilities of Business, issued by India's Ministry of Corporate Affairs (MCA), and which subsequently inspired the promulgation of the mandatory business responsibility reporting requirement, the Union Minister said that '[b]usiness involvement in social welfare and development has been a tradition in India'[42] stretching all the way back to Mahabharata[43] and the Arthashastra.[44] He also said that many Indian businessmen were influenced by Ghandi's idea of trusteeship to contribute to the betterment of society. Interestingly, he rejected the idea that it is a Western import. Before one dismisses these statements as a politician's rhetoric, there is substantial literature demonstrating that in India, corporate sustainability practices are grounded in Hinduism.[45] Moreover, a survey of the directors and senior officers of sixteen listed companies in India consisting of different industries found that while the participants justified the companies' sustainability actions on the basis of both

---

[40] Michael Jensen, 'Value Maximisation, Stakeholder Theory and the Corporate Objective Function' (2010) 22 *Journal of Applied Corporate Finance* 32.

[41] See eg Allen Ferrell, Hao Liang and Luc Renneboog, 'Socially Responsible Firms' (2016) 122 *Journal of Financial Economics* 585; Alex Edmans, 'Does the Stock Market Fully Value Intangibles? Employee Satisfaction and Equity Prices' (2011) 101 *Journal of Financial Economics* 621; Xin Deng, Jun-koo Kang and Buen Sin Low, 'Corporate Social Responsibility and Stakeholder Value Maximization: Evidence from Mergers' (2013) 110 *Journal of Financial Economics* 87.

[42] Ministry of Corporate Affairs, National Voluntary Guidelines on Social, Environmental and Economic Responsibilities of Business (2011) at 1 www.mca.gov.in/Ministry/latest news/National_Voluntary_Guidelines_2011_12jul2011.pdf.

[43] Mahabharata is one of the two major Sanskrit epics in India. See *The Mahabharata* (John D Smith tr, Penguin 2009).

[44] Arthashastra is an ancient Indian treatise on economic policy and military strategy. See N Siva Kumar and US Rao, 'Guidelines for Value Based Management in Kautilya's Arthashastra' (1996) 15 *Journal of Business Ethics* 415.

[45] See eg the copious literature cited in Balakrishnan Muniapan, 'The Roots of Indian Corporate Social Responsibility (CSR) Practice from a Vedantic Perspective' in Kim Cheng Patrick Low, Samuel O Idowu and Sik Liong Ang (eds), *Corporate Social Responsibility in Asia: Practice and Experience* (Springer 2014) at ch 2.

strategic and ethical justifications, the latter were given greater weight by the participants.[46] Further, there are studies showing that in Malaysia, which is a predominantly Muslim society, the pursuit of sustainability is justified on the basis of and is traceable to Islam.[47] And there are studies showing that sustainability practices in Singapore and Hong Kong, the population of which consist predominantly of Chinese, can be justified on the basis of Confucianism.[48] In short, the communitarian and collectivist religious and cultural norms in the four common law Asian jurisdictions provide an ethical basis for the pursuit of sustainability.

In light of the above two justifications for companies to pursue sustainability, the next question is whether there are corporate law and governance mechanisms that have been or can be used to promote sustainability in the four common law Asian jurisdictions. As I show in Section II, the corporate mechanisms of sustainability reporting, board gender diversity, constituency directors and directors' duties have been deployed in various ways by the different jurisdictions in Asia to promote sustainability. This provides the first rationale for writing this book.

II Rationales and Motivations

There is literature on the role of public international law, anti-corruption law, trade law and human rights law in supporting or undermining sustainability in different countries, but less has been written about the role of comparative corporate law and governance.[49] While there is literature on the relationship between company law and sustainability,[50] there is little analysis of the common law jurisdictions in Asia. However, it is

---

[46] Ganga S Dhanesh, 'Why Corporate Social Responsibility? An Analysis of Drivers of CSR in India' (2015) 29 *Management Communication Quarterly* 114.

[47] See eg Abbas Zaidi and Kim Cheng Patrick Low, 'The Koranic Discourse on Corporate Social Responsibility' in Kim Cheng Patrick Low, Samuel O Idowu and Sik Liong Ang (eds), *Corporate Social Responsibility in Asia: Practice and Experience* (Springer 2014) at ch 6.

[48] See eg Kim Cheng Patrick Low and Sik Ang, 'Confucian Ethics, Governance and Corporate Social Responsibility' (2013) 8 *International Journal of Business and Management* 30.

[49] See eg Jennifer A Zerk, *Multinationals and Corporate Social Responsibility: Limitations and Opportunities in International Law* (Cambridge University Press 2011); Adefolake O Adeyeye, *Corporate Social Responsibility of Multinational Corporations in Developing Countries: Perspectives on Anti-Corruption* (Cambridge University Press 2012); Phillip Paiement, *Transnational Sustainability Laws* (Cambridge University Press 2017).

[50] See eg Beate Sjåfjell and Benjamin J Richardson (eds), *Company Law and Sustainability: Legal Barriers and Opportunities* (Cambridge University Press 2015).

important to rectify this for two reasons. First, there have been significant, recent legal developments in the area of sustainability in the four common law Asian jurisdictions that have received insufficient scholarly attention. Second, these four jurisdictions call into question two influential theories – legal origins and institutional context – that have shaped the discourse on sustainability.

A Significant, Recent Legal Developments in Common Law Asia

1 Sustainability Reporting

It has been widely recognised that a company's financial information alone provides an insufficient basis for stakeholders to form an informed view as to the present and future conditions of the company and the impacts of companies' business operations. Shareholders and stakeholders are increasingly interested to know whether and how companies have integrated sustainability considerations in their businesses, as well as how companies have been managing sustainability-related risks. As a result, many jurisdictions subject listed companies to some sort of requirement to publish sustainability reports, which in a narrow sense refers to the 'publication of environmental, social and governance (ESG) information in a comprehensive and strategic manner that reflects the activities and outcomes across these three dimensions of an organisation's performance'.[51]

For example, the 2014 EU Directive requires large listed companies, on a comply or explain basis, to disclose information on their policies and the actions they have taken with respect to social and employee related matters, environmental matters, diversity, human rights and anti-corruption matters.[52] In the UK, since 2013, all large and medium-sized companies are required to provide a strategic report which includes information on environmental matters, employees, social, community and human rights issues.[53]

---

[51] Singapore Exchange, Guide to Sustainability Reporting for Listed Companies (2011) para 2.3 http://rulebook.sgx.com/net_file_store/new_rulebooks/s/g/SGX_Sustainability_Reporting_Guide_and_Policy_Statement_2011.pdf.

[52] Directive 2014/95/EU of the European Parliament and of the Council of 22 October 2014, amending Directive 2013/34/EU as regards disclosure of non-financial and diversity information by certain large undertakings and groups, 2014 O.J. (L330) 1.

[53] Companies Act 2006 (Strategic Report and Directors' Report) Regulations 2013, ss 414A–414C.

In Singapore, with effect from the financial year ending 31 December 2017, listed companies are required to publish a sustainability report on a comply or explain basis.[54] The report has to contain: the material ESG factors; the company's policies, practices and performance in relation to the ESG factors; the targets for each ESG factor; a reporting framework to guide the disclosure; and a board statement that the board has considered sustainability issues as part of its strategic formulation, determined the material ESG factors and overseen the management and monitoring of the material ESG factors. In Hong Kong, with effect from the financial year starting 1 January 2016, companies have to disclose on a comply or explain basis whether they have complied with the ESG reporting guide, which comprises a general disclosure section (pertaining to the company's policies and whether they have complied with the relevant laws and regulations) and a key performance indicator section (which requires companies to demonstrate how they have performed).[55]

By contrast, in Malaysia and India, the reporting requirement is of a mandatory instead of a comply or explain nature. In Malaysia, large companies (with effect from the financial year ending 31 December 2016) and other companies (with effect from the financial year ending 31 December 2017) must publish a sustainability statement consisting of: the material economic, environmental and social risks and opportunities (the 'sustainability matters'); the governance structure that has been put in place to manage the sustainability matters; policies related, and actions taken, to deal with these matters; and indicators which demonstrate how companies have managed these matters.[56] In India, as of 31 March 2012, the top 100 companies by market capitalisation must include business responsibility reports (BRRs), in which they have to describe the initiatives taken by them from an environmental, social and governance perspective, in their annual reports.[57] And with effect from 1 April 2014, companies are required under s 135(3)(a) of the Indian Companies Act 2013 to form a CSR board committee which is

---

[54] SGX Listing Rule 711A; SGX-ST Listing Rules, Practice Note 7.6, Sustainability Reporting Guide para 6.1.
[55] HKEX Main Board Listing Rules, LR 13.91.
[56] Bursa Malaysia, Amendments Relating to Sustainability Statement in Annual Reports paras 6.2–6.4.
[57] Securities and Exchange Board of India, Business Responsibility Reports, CIR/CFD/DIL/8/2012 (13 August 2012) para 5.

responsible for formulating and disclosing a CSR policy, the latter of which has to provide for the activities to be undertaken by the company.[58]

While there is literature on section 135 of the Indian Companies Act 2013, there is little analysis of the other three Asian jurisdictions, let alone a comparative analysis. I will critically evaluate the structure and substance of the sustainability/ESG reporting requirements in the four Asian jurisdictions and analyse the actual disclosures produced by the companies.

2 Gender Diversity on the Board of Directors

It has been said that having more woman directors will improve the board's decision-making process because women bring varied and new perspectives and they have better understanding of the needs of female employees and customers, the result of which is that better board decisions will be taken. Another rationale is that having a diverse board will attract more investments because board diversity is one of the key considerations that investors take into account as part of their socially responsible investment (SRI) strategies.

In India, s 149(1) of the Companies Act 2013 imposes a mandatory requirement on all listed companies to have at least one female director. There is no quota requirement in the other three Asian jurisdictions; nor is there one in the UK, which merely requires companies with a premium listing to report on diversity policy, including gender. But there are non-quota approaches taken by the other three common law jurisdictions that vary in their rigour.

The 2017 Malaysian Code on Corporate Governance (MCCG) requires all listed companies to disclose their 'policies on gender diversity, its targets and measures to meet those targets. For Large Companies,[59] the board must have at least 30% women directors.'[60] By contrast, the 2018 Singapore Code of Corporate Governance merely requires the board to have 'appropriate balance and mix of skills, knowledge, experience, and other aspects of diversity such as gender and age, so

---

[58] Section 135(5) also requires companies, but on a comply or explain basis, to spend at least 2 per cent of their average net profits made during the three immediately preceding financial years, in pursuance of their CSR policy.

[59] Para 2.6: 'Large Companies are: "Companies on the FTSE Bursa Malaysia Top 100 Index; or Companies with market capitalisation of RM2 billion and above, at the start of the companies' financial year."'

[60] Para 4.4.

as to avoid groupthink and foster constructive debate'. The company has to merely disclose its 'board diversity policy and progress made towards implementing the board diversity policy' in the annual report. That said, Singapore has set a target of having 20 per cent female directors on boards by 2020.[61] Of all the four Asian jurisdictions, Hong Kong's regulatory approach is the least progressive with regard to board gender diversity. The Corporate Governance Code merely requires the nomination committee of a listed company to have a policy regarding diversity on a comply or explain basis.[62]

The reasons provided by the governments in the Asian jurisdictions for having more female directors and the mechanisms for doing so are subject to little scrutiny. Further, while there are some data on the percentage of female directors in Malaysia and Singapore, there appear to be none in relation to India and Hong Kong. In this book, not only do I engage in a critical, normative examination of the rationales and mechanisms for having more female directors in these jurisdictions, I also present and analyse the data on the percentage of female directors in a selected number of companies.

3 Constituency Directors

The broad version of constituency directors refers to directors being appointed by (or who are representatives of) non-shareholders to protect the latter's interests. But in the narrow version, the constituency directors are not appointed by non-shareholders; they refer to a committee of directors who are authorised by the statute to promote the interests of specific constituencies.

Many countries in the EU (with the exception of the UK, Italy and others) have constituency directors in the broad sense as they give employees the right to appoint directors.[63] A number of European jurisdictions require that directors appointed by employees constitute one-third of the board.[64] Notably, in Germany, it is a requirement for companies with over 2,000 Germany based employees to have 50 per cent of the supervisory board consist of employee directors.[65] Under the 2018

---

[61] Grace Fu, 'More Gender Diversity in Boards', Singapore Institute of Directors' Final Launch of Corporate Governance Guides for Boards and Board Committees (2017).
[62] HKEX LR Appendix A.5.6.
[63] See www.worker-participation.eu/.
[64] See eg Austria, Denmark, Luxembourg and Hungary: Alice Conchon, Board-Level Employee Representation Rights in Europe: Facts and Trends, European Trade Union Institute Report No. 121 (2011) www.etui.org.
[65] Mitbestimmungsgestz, ss 1, 7.

UK Corporate Governance Code, the board is required, on a comply or explain basis, to engage with the workforce through one or more of the following methods: a director appointed from the workforce; a formal workforce advisory panel; or a designated non-executive director.[66]

While none of the four common law Asian jurisdictions have constituency directors in the broad sense, India has constituency directors in the narrow sense. Under s 135 of the Indian Companies Act 2013, the boards of companies of certain net worth or turnover[67] are required, with effect from 2015, to form a CSR committee. Not only is this committee required to formulate and disclose the company's CSR policy, but it is also required to ensure that the company spends, in every financial year, at least 2 per cent of the average net profits of the company made during the three immediately preceding financial years, in pursuance of its CSR policy, and should the company fail to spend such amount, the board is required to give reasons for not spending the amount in its annual report. There are numerous criticisms of s 135, which will be appraised in this book. But there appears to be no examination of the broader and more interesting issue of whether Singapore, Hong Kong and Malaysia should have constituency directors (either in its broad or narrow version) in order to promote sustainability. In Chapter 4, I present a critique of the merits and deficiencies of constituency directors, situating the analysis in light of the distinct political economy in each of the four jurisdictions.

4 Stewardship Codes

An increasing number of jurisdictions have standards of conduct for institutional shareholders that are inspired by the UK Stewardship Code[68] and the EU Shareholder Rights Directive.[69] Hong Kong launched the Principles of Responsible Ownership (HKPRO) in 2016, Malaysia launched the Malaysian Code for Institutional Investors (MCII) in 2014 and the Singapore Stewardship Principles for Responsible Investors (SSP) were issued in 2016. India has codes that apply to insurance

---

[66] See Principle 1, provision 5.
[67] The Act applies to every company having net worth of rupees five hundred crore or more, or turnover of rupees one thousand crore or more or a net profit of rupees five crore or more during any financial year.
[68] 2012 UK Stewardship Code (a revised version is scheduled to be issued in July 2019).
[69] Directive (EU) 2017/828 of the European Parliament and of the Council of 17 May 2017 amending Directive 2007/36/EC as regards the encouragement of long-term shareholder engagement.

companies,[70] mutual funds and pension funds,[71] and has been considering having a stewardship code that applies to all institutional shareholders.

The stewardship codes stress the vital role played by institutional shareholders in the global economy and in the corporate governance of companies. All the stewardship codes have a number of principles under which institutional shareholders are urged to monitor and engage with their investee companies and to have policies on stewardship, voting and managing conflicts of interest. The importance of sustainability is repeatedly emphasised in the SSP and the MCII and, to some extent, the HKPRO. Institutional shareholders are urged to incorporate ESG considerations into their investment decision-making process, as well as to engage with their investee companies on ESG issues.

An important but neglected question is whether the SSP, the HKPRO and the MCII are effective in promoting sustainability. After all, these codes are soft law: they are not legally binding and failure to adhere to them attracts no sanctions or penalties whatsoever. Further, institutional investors face free rider and collective action problems. Crucially, these codes do not apply to controlling shareholders.

5 Directors' Duty to Act in the Best Interests of the Company

Another significant, recent development concerns the doctrine of directors' duties, specifically whether directors can promote the interests of non-shareholders. For example, s 166(2) of the Indian Companies Act 2013 states: 'A director of a company shall act in good faith in order to promote the objects of the company for the benefit of its members as a whole, and in the best interests of the company, its employees, the shareholders, the community and for the protection of environment.' It is remarkable that this provision specifically requires directors to act in, and not merely to consider, the interests of non-shareholders, ie employees, community and environment. By contrast, s 172 of the UK Companies Act, which is a codified version of the common law duty to act in good faith in the company's best interests, makes it clear that directors have to act for shareholders' benefit and in doing so have regard for the interests of employees, customers, suppliers, community, environment, etc. It is clear

---

[70] Insurance Regulatory and Development Authority, Guidelines on Stewardship Code for Insurers in India (22 March 2017).

[71] Securities and Exchange Board of India, Master Circular for Mutual Funds (31 December 2010) paras 6.15–6.18 www.sebi.gov.in/sebi_data/attachdocs/1295932761762.pdf; Pension Fund Regulatory and Development Authority, Common Stewardship Code (PFRDA/2018/01/PF/01, 4 May 2018).

that under s 172, directors merely have to consider the interests of non-shareholders and they are required to do so only if it benefits the shareholders. That is, taking into account the interests of non-shareholders is merely a means to promote the end, ie to benefit shareholders.

Although Singapore, Malaysia and Hong Kong do not have any statutory provision that is comparable to India's s 166(2) or the UK's s 172, there is legal support for the argument that under the Singapore and Malaysian law governing directors' duty to act in the company's best interests, directors of solvent companies are permitted not only to consider but also to act in the interests of non-shareholders. There are also authorities for the proposition that directors can prefer the interests of the company over those of the shareholders where the interests of the former conflict with the latter. But what is the relationship between these laws and their normative justifications – shareholder primacy, stakeholder value and long-term value and viability? And what is the relationship between the laws and their underlying theories, on the one hand, and the SOEs and their controlling shareholder, on the other? To what extent does the presence of the controlling shareholder impede or facilitate the best interest duty? This book will address these issues.

Having examined the first motivation for writing this book, ie there are five significant, recent legal developments on sustainability in the common law Asian jurisdictions, I now turn to the second reason, ie an analysis of these four Asian countries calls into question a pervasive view in the sustainability and CSR literature concerning legal origins and institutional theory.

B Common Law Asia Calls into Question Two Influential Theories

1 Legal Origins

A comprehensive study of 23,000 companies from 114 countries (which include the 4 Asian common law jurisdictions) found that there is a strong correlation between a country's legal origin and a company's environmental and social ratings.[72] Companies from civil law origins have higher environmental and social ratings than those from common law countries because of legal origins. According to the legal origins theory,[73] common law origin

---

[72] Hao Liang and Luc Renneboog, 'On the Foundations of Corporate Social Responsibility' (2017) 72 *Journal of Finance* 853.
[73] Rafael La Porta, Florencio Lopez-de-Silanes and Andrei Shleifer, 'The Economic Consequence of Legal Origins' (2008) 46 *Journal of Economic Literature* 285;

countries emphasise private market outcomes and subscribe to shareholder primacy theory which prioritises shareholders' rights and interests. There is thus less state intervention and, as compared to civil law countries, common law countries rely more on ex post sanctions rather than ex ante rules,[74] an example of which is that directors are subject to fewer ex ante restrictions but their behaviour is constrained by ex post judicial sanctions. The thinking is that acting in the interests of shareholders will result in aggregate social welfare, benefitting the society and economy.[75]

By contrast, a civil law origin is characterised by extensive state intervention in the economy and politics through ex ante rules and regulation, and the interests of stakeholders are favoured.[76] These countries have stronger unions and more laws that are protective of employees.[77] They also have laws that are more protective of consumer rights. In short, civil law countries have stronger regulatory protection of stakeholders' interests. These laws protecting stakeholders may be driven in part by social preferences from citizens, consumers and shareholders.[78] These preferences in turn have an impact on the sustainability conduct of companies.

The implications of the legal origin theory for sustainability are twofold.[79] First, as directors are more likely to be sued by shareholders in common law than in civil law countries, they are less likely to promote sustainability.[80] This is because of the ex post rights conferred on

---

Simeon Djankov, Rafael La Porta, Florencio Lopez-de-Silanes and Andrei Shleifer, 'The Law and Economics of Self-Dealing' (2008) 88 *Journal of Financial Economics* 430.

[74] Ibid; James D Cox and Randall S Thomas, 'Common Challenges Facing Shareholder Suits in Europe and the United States' (2009) 6 *European Company and Financial Law Review* 348.

[75] Reiner Kraakman, John Armour, Paul Davies et al, *The Anatomy of Corporate Law: A Comparative and Functional Approach* (3rd edn, Oxford University Press 2017) at 22-4.

[76] Franklin Allen, Elena Carletti and Robert Marquez, 'Stakeholder Governance, Competition and Firm Value' (2015) *Review of Finance* 1315; Michael Magill, Martine Quinzii and Jean-Charles Rochet, 'A Theory of the Stakeholder Corporation' (2015) 83 *Econometrica* 1685.

[77] Rafael La Porta, Florencio Lopez-de-Silanes and Andrei Shleifer, 'The Economic Consequence of Legal Origins' (2008) 46 *Journal of Economic Literature* 285; Simeon Djankov, Rafael La Porta, Florencio Lopez-de-Silanes and Andrei Shleifer, 'The Law and Economics of Self-Dealing' (2008) 88 *Journal of Financial Economics* 430.

[78] See eg Roland Bénabou and Jean Tirole, 'Individual and Corporate Social Responsibility' (2010) 77 *Econometrica* 1.

[79] Hao Liang and Luc Renneboog, 'On the Foundations of Corporate Social Responsibility' (2017) 72 *Journal of Finance* 853 at 857-8, 894-7.

[80] Brian Cheffins and Bernard Black, 'Outside Director Liability across Countries' (2006) 84 *Texas Law Review* 1385; Martin Gelter, 'Why Do Shareholder Derivative Suits Remain Rare in Continental Europe?' (2012) 37 *Brooklyn Journal of International Law* 843.

shareholders in common law countries. In other words, the risk of litigation will disincentivise directors to give effect to environmental and social considerations beyond what the law requires them to do. Second, because directors in civil law countries are insulated from pressures from short-term shareholders as compared to common law countries, they have more freedom to promote sustainability.[81] One important reason lies with the supermajority requirements in the corporate constitutions of companies from civil law countries.

However, an analysis of the four common law Asian jurisdictions calls into question the characterisation of countries that are of common law origins, as well as the implications of the legal origins theory.

While the four Asian jurisdictions are common law based, they are characterised by greater state intervention in the economic, social, political and legal realm than the United States and the UK. One clear example can be found in state-owned enterprises (SOEs) (also known as government-linked companies (GLCs)), of which the government is the controlling shareholder. These SOEs wield significant and substantial economic, political and social power in the four common law Asian jurisdictions.[82] They constitute a significant percentage of the market capitalisation in the four jurisdictions.[83] Many of these SOEs do not have shareholder value maximisation as their primary objective but have

---

[81] Martijn Cremers and Simone M Sepe, 'The Shareholder Value of Empowered Boards' (2016) 68 *Stanford Law Review* 1.

[82] See eg and generally OECD, 'SOEs in India's Economic Development' in *State-Owned Enterprises in the Development Process* (OECD Publishing 2015) https://doi.org/10.1787/9789264229617-7-en; Cheng Han Tan, Dan W Puchniak and Umakanth Varottil, 'State-Owned Enterprises in Singapore: Historical Insights into a Potential Model for Reform' (2015) 28 *Columbia Journal of Asian Law* 61; Edmund Terence Gomez and KS Jomo, *Malaysia's Political Economy: Politics, Patronage, and Profits* (2nd edn, Cambridge University Press 1999); Lin Lin-Wen and Curtis J Milhaupt, 'We Are the (National) Champions: Understanding the Mechanisms of State Capitalism in China' (2013) 65 *Stanford Law Review* 697; Ram Kumar Mishra, 'Role of State-Owned Enterprises in India's Economic Development', OECD Workshop on State-Owned Enterprises in the Development Process (4 April 2014) www.oecd.org/daf/ca/Workshop_SOEsDevelopmentProcess_India.pdf.

[83] For eg, in Hong Kong, SOEs constitute about 20.1 per cent of the listed companies in Hong Kong, including eleven out of the top thirty companies by market capitalisation. All the SOEs account for 40 per cent of total market capitalisation of listed companies on the Main Board of SEHK. In Malaysia, one study founds that 38 per cent of the fifty largest listed companies by market capitalisation had one dominant shareholder (who held more than 40 per cent control); 85 per cent of these fifty companies were SOEs. A study of the top 150 listed companies by market capitalisation showed that the government held an average of 55.23 per cent of the shares in SOEs. In India, while PSUs in India accounted for 0.19 per cent of the total companies, they constituted 25 per cent of the paid-up

political and social goals such as equitable distribution and societal welfare.[84] Although one cannot say that these four common law Asian jurisdictions have strong protection for stakeholders like the civil law countries, they do not rely as much on private market outcomes as compared to the United States and the UK.[85] Further, although the corporate laws of Asian jurisdictions are derived from or inspired by UK law, it is not clear that they subscribe to shareholder primacy theory or the enlightened shareholder value (with the exception of Hong Kong). India manifestly does not, as explained above. While there is some support for shareholder primacy theory in Singapore and Malaysian case law, there is also support for a nuanced, context-dependent approach in which directors can prefer the interests of the solvent company over those of shareholders, as discussed above. Accordingly, the four common law Asian jurisdictions, two of which are among the world's leading financial centres (Hong Kong and Singapore)[86] and one of which is the world's sixth and soon to be the fifth largest economy (India),[87] do not fit, and may even challenge, the legal origins theory. This makes an analysis of these jurisdictions interesting and important.

The two implications of legal origins for sustainability are also questionable. While it is true that there is higher risk of shareholder litigation in common law than civil law countries because of the 'law on the books',

---

capital, equivalent to 15 per cent of the GDP. In another study, PSUs accounted for 23 per cent of the market capitalisation. In Singapore, 26 of the 100 largest companies are controlled by the Singapore government. The Singapore government through the Ministry of Finance (MOF) owns Temasek Holdings Pte Ltd, which in turn controls twenty-three of Singapore's largest listed companies – the GLCs. These twenty-three companies accounted for 37 per cent of Singapore's total market capitalisation. See Ernest Lim, *A Case for Shareholders' Fiduciary Duties in Common Law Asia* (Cambridge University Press 2019) at 47–64.

[84] Michael Carney and Edo Andriesse, 'Malaysia: Personal Capitalism' in Michael A Witt and Gordon Redding (eds), *The Oxford Handbook of Asian Business Systems* (Oxford University Press 2014) at 145–51. But the GLCs in Singapore, unlike those in the other three Asian jurisdictions, take a commercial, profit-oriented approach: see Grant Kirkpatrick (Consultant for OECD Secretariat), 'Managing State Assets to Achieve Development Goals: The Case of Singapore and Other Countries in the Region', OECD Workshop on State-Owned Enterprises in the Development Process (2014) at 7; Temasek, *Temasek Review* (2017) at 12.

[85] See generally Witt and Redding, ibid.

[86] See the March 2018 Global Financial Centres Index (GFCI) which ranks the most attractive financial hubs worldwide: the top four are London, New York, Hong Kong and Singapore www.longfinance.net/Publications/GFCI23.pdf.

[87] Salvatore Babones, 'India Is Poised to Become the World's Fifth Largest Economy, But It Can't Stop There', *Forbes* (27 December 2017).

it does not follow that this is the case in 'law in action'. For a start, there appear to be fewer than twenty cases of derivative action and oppression/unfair prejudice claim involving listed companies in all the four Asian jurisdictions combined.[88] It is questionable whether shareholder litigation poses a credible threat to directors' promotion of sustainability, particularly if doing so is consistent with long-term shareholders' interests, or is consistent with the purposes of companies, especially SOEs. With regard to the second implication, given that the majority of the listed companies in the four Asian countries are owned by controlling shareholders comprising the government and families, they are less susceptible to the sort of short-term pressure as compared to dispersed ownership companies in the United States and the UK. If that is the case, these companies should be engaging in more sustainability and hence have higher sustainability ratings than US and UK companies, but one study has suggested otherwise.[89]

In short, the four common law Asian jurisdictions call into question the legal origins theory and its implications for sustainability, which makes it worthwhile to examine the laws and practices in these jurisdictions.

2 Institutional Context

Common law Asia also poses a puzzle to a highly influential theory that argues that differences in institutions (broadly defined as formal

---

[88] As of 2017, there appear to be four derivative actions in Hong Kong (*Waddington Ltd v Chan Chun Hoo Thomas* [2013] HKEC 2013; *Yu Yuchuan v China Shanshui Investment Co Ltd* [2015] HKEC 437; *Hong Kong Zhongxing Group Company v Grand Field Group Holdings* [2014] HKCU 2729; *Veron International v RCG Holdings* [2015] HKCFI 1246 (unreported)), and one in each of Malaysia (*Dato' Low Tuck Choy v Datuk Lye Ek Seang* [2016] AMEJ 0671), India (*Northern Projects Limited v Blue Coast Hotels and Resorts Limited* 2007 Indlaw CLB 7) and Singapore (*Chua Swee Keng v E3 Holdings* [2015] SGHC 22). As of 2017, there appear to be four cases of oppression/unfair prejudice actions involving listed companies in Hong Kong (*Luck Continent Ltd v Cheng Chee Tock Theodore* [2013] 4 HKLRD 181; *Yu Yuchuan v China Shanshui Investment Co Ltd* [2015] HKEC 437; *Passport Special Opportunities v Esun Holdings* [2011] 4 HKC 62; *Able Success Asia v China Packaging Group Company Limited* [2014] HKCU 1316), one in Singapore (*Kingboard Chemical Holdings v Annuity and Life Reassurance* CA 24 of 2015 (Supreme Court, Bermuda) concerning an SGX-listed company; the action succeeded in the High Court of Singapore but was overturned on appeal in Bermuda), one in Malaysia (*Kang Choon Leu @ Kang Chee Sim v Wintoni Group Berhad* [2016] AMEJ 1264) and two in India (*Morgan Ventures Limited v Blue Coast Hotels and Resorts Limited* [2010] 155 Comp Cas 431; *Union of India (UOI) v Satyam Computer Services Ltd* [2009] 148 Comp Cas 252).

[89] Hao Liang and Luc Renneboog, 'On the Foundations of Corporate Social Responsibility' (2017) 72 *Journal of Finance* 853.

governance and rules as well as informal incentives and values) between Europe and the United States explain why companies in the United States are more explicitly committed to CSR, in the sense of voluntary adoptions and explicit articulations of CSR policies and practices, as compared to companies in Europe which have been implicit about their CSR initiatives.[90] According to this institutional theory, in Europe, the state plays a strong and active role in regulating economic and social matters in relation to, for example, employees' welfare through state health and pension programmes and policies. Further, continental European company law takes a stakeholder value approach, which protects the interests of employees, examples of which include the German co-determination model. Thus, there is less incentive for companies to explicitly articulate their CSR policies and practices, given that CSR is already embedded in the institutional system in which companies operate. By contrast, in the United States, there is comparatively less government regulation, market-based solutions are prioritised, and corporate law and practice generally adopt a shareholder primacy approach. There are therefore more opportunities for companies to be explicit about their role in CSR.

Although the authors confine their analysis to Europe and the United States, an interesting question is whether their institutional theory can explain the situation in common law Asia. In Singapore, Malaysia and India, the extent of governmental intervention in economic, social and political matters is far more extensive and pervasive than in the United States and the UK, as evidenced, for example, in the SOEs which provide employment as well as essential goods and services.[91] In addition, the SOEs in general play an important social role by pricing goods below market rate, redistributing income and taking on redundant workers.[92] In relation to corporate law, India adopts a pluralist stakeholder approach, and Singapore and Malaysian law can be interpreted as having

---

[90] Dirk Matten and Jeremy Moon, '"Implicit" and "Explicit" CSR: A Conceptual Framework for a Comparative Understanding of Corporate Social Responsibility' (2008) 33 *Academy of Management Review* 404.

[91] Michael A Witt and Gordon Redding (eds), *The Oxford Handbook of Asian Business Systems* (Oxford University Press 2014); see generally Mariana Pargendler, Aldo Musacchio and Sérgio G. Lazzarini, 'The Puzzle of Private Investment in State Controlled Firms', Harvard Business School BGIE Unit Working Paper No. 13-071 (2013) https://papers.ssrn.com/sol3/papers.cfm?abstract_id=2217627; Aldo Musacchio and Sérgio G Lazzarini, 'Leviathan in Business: Varieties of State Capitalism and Their Implications for Economic Performance' (2012) https://papers.ssrn.com/sol3/papers.cfm?abstract_id=2070942.

[92] Ibid.

a context-dependent approach that permits interests of non-shareholders to be considered and even promoted (as discussed above). Thus, according to this institutional explanation, there should be fewer explicit commitments to CSR in companies in common law Asia, because the institutions in these Asian jurisdictions already facilitate CSR. But this is not what I have observed in the sustainability/CSR reports of the listed SOEs in the four Asian jurisdictions.

In relation to the non-SOEs, ie the family-owned companies and certain financial institutions, given that they operate within the political and social context of strong government authority and extensive state regulation, one would also expect less explicit CSR. In short, based on the authors' institutional theory, implied CSR ought to be the norm in common law Asia.

But this is not what I have found. Based on an original empirical analysis of the avowed corporate purposes of the top thirty listed companies by market capitalisation in each of the four common law Asian jurisdictions, an average of about 40 per cent of the companies adopt a stakeholder value approach and are explicitly committed to CSR/sustainability.[93] This suggests that this institutional theory is less persuasive in explaining the situation in common law Asia, which in turn makes it interesting and worthwhile to explore whether there are other institutional or even non-institutional reasons that can explain the explicit commitments to sustainability in common law Asia.

I suggest that there are three reasons why there are explicit commitments to promote sustainability by the companies in the four Asian jurisdictions. The first is the rules of the stock exchanges. To increase their competitiveness and enhance their international reputation, the stock exchanges in these four Asian jurisdictions have issued rules requiring companies to comply with sustainability practices. Second, the rise of SRIs spearheaded by leading institutional shareholders has influenced companies to undertake sustainability initiatives. The third reason is the increased internationalisation of companies. These three reasons, together with the socio-economic development agendas of the SOEs, can also explain why the companies in the four Asian jurisdictions, which are common law based, have been actively pursuing sustainability; this is contrary to the legal origins theory (discussed earlier) which posits that companies in common law countries engage in less sustainability

---

[93] Ernest Lim, *A Case for Shareholders' Fiduciary Duties in Common Law Asia* (Cambridge University Press 2019) at 510.

than those in civil law countries. Finally, these three reasons are also the drivers of sustainability in the four Asian jurisdictions, which will be elaborated in Section III.

III Factors that Drive Sustainability in Common Law Asia

Understanding what has driven the explicit adoption of sustainability by these companies in the four common law Asian jurisdictions could help us to evaluate the existing corporate mechanisms for promoting sustainability and to make suitable reforms. I suggest that there are four main drivers: (1) the socio-economic development agendas in the four countries; (2) the reform and issuance of sustainability reporting rules by the stock exchanges in the Asian jurisdictions; (3) increased internationalisation of companies; and (4) the rise of SRIs. To be clear, these drivers of sustainability are not manifested in the same way or to the same degree in these four Asian jurisdictions, in light of the variations in institutional contexts within each jurisdiction.

A Socio-economic Development Agendas of Governments

The socio-economic development agendas of the government of the jurisdiction in which the companies operate have an important influence over the sustainability actions taken by the companies. This is particularly so for two reasons. First, as discussed above, the controlling shareholder of a significant number of companies in the four Asian jurisdictions – known as SOEs or GLCs – is the government (or a company owned by or affiliated with the government). Second, the government, at least in Malaysia, India and Singapore, has stated that the SOEs play an important political, social and economic role, a role that clearly extends beyond profit maximisation.

1 Singapore

The creation and success of the GLCs were inextricably tied to the success and legitimacy of the Singapore government.[94] After Singapore was separated from Malaysia, the government set up GLCs (including but not limited to the Development Bank of Singapore, Singapore Airlines,

---

[94] Cheng-Han Tan, Dan W Puchniak and Umakanth Varottil, 'State-Owned Enterprises in Singapore: Historical Insights into a Potential Model for Reform' (2015) 28 *Columbia Journal of Asian Law* 61.

Singapore Technologies Engineering) to advance industrial growth, generate employment, boost GDP and promote political allegiance. To date, the Singapore government regards successful economic performance, in which the GLCs play a critical role, as central to its political viability. Temasek Holdings Pte Ltd, which is the controlling shareholder of the GLCs, leaves the decision-making to the boards of the respective GLCs, which are commercially run with a view to long-term profit maximisation.[95] There are studies showing that the GLCs have a higher rate of return on equity and assets than non-GLCs in Singapore.[96]

What implication does this have for the sustainability policies and practices of the Singapore GLCs? I suggest that there are at least three. First, sustainability actions taken by the GLCs are likely to be consistent with long-term profit maximisation. In other words, sustainability actions that do not result in enhancement of long-term share price are unlikely to be pursued. Second, given that the GLCs play a key role in the Singapore government's strategy to maintain and generate employment, among the ESG considerations that will be taken into account by the GLCs, social considerations, particularly those that relate to employment, are likely to have greater salience than environmental considerations. However, the protection of employees' interests is subordinated to the overriding goal of advancing economic growth, a key strategy of which is to produce a capable but docile workforce. As for economic and governance considerations, they will be important insofar as they impact on long-term profit maximisation and reputation. Finally, because the GLCs are generally[97] free from corruption and appear to be generally operated efficiently, the risk that either the board or the controlling shareholder of GLCs (ie Temasek) will exploit the sustainability mechanisms for its own benefit at the expense of the company is minimised. This implies that,

---

[95] Ibid.

[96] James S Ang and David K Ding, 'Government Ownership and the Performance of Government-Linked Companies: The Case of Singapore' (2006) 16 *Journal of Multinational Financial Management* 64 at 85–6; Carlos D Ramirez and Ling Hui Tan, 'Singapore, Inc. Versus the Private Sector: Are Government-Linked Companies Different?', IMF Working Paper No. WP/o3/156 (2003) www.imf.org/external/pubs/ft/wp/2003/wp03156.pdf.

[97] But note that the GLC Keppel Offshore & Marine was fined US$422 million in 2016 for bribing government officials in Brazil in exchange for business deals: www.straitstimes.com/business/companies-markets/elaborate-scheme-used-to-disguise-bribes-us-attorney; www.straitstimes.com/business/companies-markets/keppel-om-to-pay-us422m-in-fines-to-settle-bribery-probe.

among the four Asian jurisdictions, GLCs in Singapore are in the best position to utilise the corporate mechanisms to promote sustainability. Whether and the extent to which they will do so will be analysed in subsequent chapters.

However, the use of GLCs to promote the economic development of the state is only part of the story. Another crucial aspect of the government's strategy is the reliance on foreign multinational corporations (MNCs) to set up businesses in Singapore.[98] To attract and retain MNCs and foreign businesses, the government has to ensure that the laws, regulations and infrastructure in Singapore are conducive for foreign investment. This has resulted in the implementation not only of global financial standards and minority shareholder protection laws but also of openness and acceptance of best business practices, which would include sustainability policies and practices, either already adopted by the MNCs or issued by international bodies.

2 Malaysia

Regarding the GLCs in Malaysia, the creation of the GLCs is a central affirmative action strategy of the government to foster entrepreneurialism in the indigenous Malays (the Bumiputera).[99] This was part of the wider New Economic Policy (NEP) implemented in 1971 that provided, among other things, preferential treatment to Malays, who constitute the majority of the population.[100] One of the rationales of this policy was to contain the economic power of the ethnic Chinese, who, although in the minority, controlled a significant part of the economy.[101] The government set up a number of GLCs to implement the NEP. The controlling shareholders of the GLCs comprise largely investment and pension

---

[98] Richard W Carney, 'Singapore: Open State-Led Capitalism' in Michael A Witt and Gordon Redding (eds), *The Oxford Handbook of Asian Business Systems* (Oxford University Press 2014) at 193.

[99] Michael Carney and Edo Andriesse, 'Malaysia: Personal Capitalism' in Michael A Witt and Gordon Redding (eds), *The Oxford Handbook of Asian Business Systems* (Oxford University Press 2014) at 146–50; Joel David Moore, *Varieties of Capitalism in Southeast Asia* (Springer 2017) at 120.

[100] Takashi Torii, 'The New Economic Policy and the United Malays National Organisation, with Special Reference to the Restructuring of the Malaysian Society' (2007) 35 *Developing Economies* 209; AB Shamsul, 'The Economic Dimension of Malay Nationalism: The Socio-historical Roots of the New Economic Policy and Its Contemporary Implications' (1997) 35 *Developing Economies* 240; Pek Koon Heng, 'The New Economic Policy and the Chinese Community in Peninsula Malaysia' (1997) 35 *Developing Economies* 262.

[101] Ibid.

funds, such as Permodalan Nasional Bhd, Khazanah Nasional Bhd and Employee Provident Fund, the main objective of which was to accumulate and redistribute wealth to the Malays by owning the shares on behalf of the Malays and to sell the shares to them at an appropriate time. However, not only has the aim of producing a Malay entrepreneurialism class been unsuccessful, but there are also studies demonstrating corruption, cronyism and inefficiencies in the GLCs.[102] The notorious case of 1MDB, a GLC from which the former Prime Minister, Najib Razak, siphoned funds to himself and his allies, is one egregious manifestation of these problems.[103] The current government recognises part of these problems and has taken preliminary steps to make the GLCs more profitable by attempting to reform the executive compensation structure.[104] But, given the deep-seated nature of the problems afflicting GLCs, the reforms would have to be structural, systematic and long term.

The implications for corporate sustainability are twofold. First, the GLCs in Malaysia will continue to be used as state mechanisms to promote affirmative action for the Malays and to address socio-economic development challenges such as income inequality and infrastructure development. Thus, addressing environmental considerations such as climate change and greenhouse gas emissions is unlikely to be of paramount importance. More resources will be naturally channelled towards the socio-economic development agenda. Hence, any assessment of the sustainability disclosure by the Malaysian GLCs has to be carried out in this light.

Second, in light of the corruption and cronyism in the GLCs, there is a serious risk that the controlling shareholders or the directors (under the

---

[102] Michael Carney and Edo Andriesse, 'Malaysia: Personal Capitalism' in Michael A Witt and Gordon Redding (eds), *The Oxford Handbook of Asian Business Systems* (Oxford University Press 2014) at 146–50; Simon Johnson and Todd Mitton, 'Cronyism and Capital Controls: Evidence from Malaysia' (2003) 67 *Journal of Financial Economics* 351; Puan Yatim, Pamela Kent and Peter Clarkson, 'Governance Structures, Ethnicity, and Audit Fees of Malaysian Listed Firms' (2006) 21 *Managerial Auditing Journal* 757; Ferdinand A Gul, 'Auditors' Response to Political Connections and Cronyism in Malaysia' (2006) 44 *Journal of Accounting Research* 931; Jayant Menon, 'Government-Linked Companies: Impacts on the Malaysian Economy', Policy IDEAS No. 45 (December 2017).
[103] The most comprehensive analysis to date can be found in the *Wall Street Journal* http://graphics.wsj.com/1mdb-decoded/; www.wsj.com/articles/1mdb-trial-against-former-malaysian-prime-minister-najib-begins-11554297619.
[104] Bernama, '"Days of GLC Top Execs Getting Fat Salaries Over," Says PM' *New Straits Times* (5 March 2019) www.nst.com.my/news/nation/2018/07/388989/days-glc-top-execs-getting-fat-salaries-over-says-pm.

control of the controller) will use the corporate mechanisms such as that of sustainability reporting to effect cosmetic changes to improve corporate image at best, or to enrich themselves at the expense of other shareholders and stakeholders at worst. In other words, the pursuit of sustainability initiatives is a reflection of conflicts of interest between controlling shareholders (and the board under its control), on the one hand, and the company, minority shareholders and stakeholders, on the other hand. For example, the board (on its own or at the controller's behest) may cause the company to donate money to charitable organisations that have connections with the board or the controller.[105] Or the controlling shareholder or the board of the GLC could engage in unprofitable business transactions to benefit themselves under the guise of promoting sustainability (broadly defined). For example, the former Prime Minister of Malaysia, Najib Razak, who has been charged with corruption (in connection with tunnelling money out of 1MDB), directed the Employees Provident Fund, the controlling shareholder of the GLC Malaysian Airlines Berhad, to purchase aircraft worth US $3 billion to US $4 billion from the United States for the avowed purpose of promoting national interest by enhancing the relationship between the United States and Malaysia.[106] This was despite the fact that Malaysian Airlines (which was previously declared bankrupt) had been making severe losses and trying to cut cost.[107]

3 India

The SOEs in India, also known as public sector enterprises or public sector undertakings (PSUs), have played a pivotal role in the economic and social development of India since independence.[108] These PSUs include, but are not limited to, aircraft, shipping, oil, coal and gas, railways, utilities, telecommunications, technological and housing companies.[109] Importantly, the Indian government has also accorded greater importance to the PSUs than private enterprises in its industrialisation strategy and

---

[105] Ronald W Masulis and Syed Walid Reza, 'Agency Problems of Corporate Philanthropy' (2015) 28 *Review of Financial Studies* 592.
[106] Jayant Menon, 'Government-Linked Companies: Impacts on the Malaysian Economy', Policy IDEAS No. 45 (December 2017) at 13.
[107] Ibid.
[108] Ram Kumar Mishra, 'Role of State-Owned Enterprises in India's Economic Development', OECD Workshop on State-Owned Enterprises in the Development Process (4 April 2014).
[109] Ibid.

economic policy for the following reasons.[110] To begin with, the government would like to retain control over companies that have strategic importance (such as large infrastructure, oil and gas, and telecommunication firms). Next, the Indian constitution specifically states that India is a 'socialist secular democratic republic' and requires the state to use the resources to promote the common good.[111] Crucially, since 1955, the main developmental strategy and policy of India was to establish a socialist state by promoting self-reliant economic growth (mainly through import substitution industrialisation) and eradicating poverty, although certain sectors of the economy were gradually liberalised and deregulated.[112] However, similar to the GLCs in Malaysia, the PSUs in India are afflicted with corruption, cronyism and inefficiencies. There are several explanations for this phenomenon. A key explanation is that the risk of side-payments is particularly high, especially in oil, gas and mining SOEs where the allocation of licences is subject to opaque and cumbersome bureaucratic complexity.[113] Thus, the SOEs provide licences, permissions and rights to third parties (who are connected to the directors/management and controller) in exchange for bribes.

There are at least three implications for corporate sustainability. First, given that India is a socialist state, it has adopted a stakeholder-based approach in its corporate law. Thus, promoting sustainability in the sense of benefitting a variety of stakeholders will be a dominant objective in the SOEs. Unlike the GLCs in Singapore in which sustainability initiatives have to be consistent with long-term shareholder value maximisation, it is suggested that, by contrast, the Indian PSUs will prioritise sustainability over maximisation of share price or profits. It may be queried why the government as the controlling shareholder of the PSUs would want to prioritise sustainability actions over maximisation of profit or share price as this will hurt its interests given that it owns the bulk of the shares. There are two possible explanations. First, while promoting sustainability may reduce share price or profitability in the short term, it will eventually

---

[110] Ibid.
[111] The Constitution of India, Preamble.
[112] Ram Kumar Mishra, 'Role of State-Owned Enterprises in India's Economic Development', OECD Workshop on State-Owned Enterprises in the Development Process (4 April 2014).
[113] Sandip Sukhtankar and Milan Vaishnav, 'Corruption in India: Bridging Research Evidence and Policy Options' (2014–5) *India Policy Forum* 193 at 202. For example, the Comptroller and Auditor General of India alleged that the government allocated coal blocks to private companies from 2004 to 2009 without a competitive auction process. Many of these private companies are either owned by or connected to the politicians.

lead to long-term improvement in corporate performance. Second, even if it does not result in long-term improvement, the government as the controlling shareholder may extract private benefits of control that outweigh the reduction in share price. For example, when the PSUs pursue corporate philanthropy, the government may reap non-pecuniary gains (such as enhanced reputation) or pecuniary gains when the PSUs transact with other companies that are affiliated with the government.

An interesting question then is, in light of India's socialist and stakeholder value approach to governance, whether the SOEs in India have better sustainability disclosures than non-SOEs, and whether they have more female directors than non-SOEs. Another question is whether there are more or better sustainability disclosures (or more female directors) in Indian SOEs as compared to the SOEs in the other three jurisdictions which are not socialist in nature. I discuss these issues in Chapters 2 and 3, respectively.

The second implication is that, in view of the uniquely socialist character of India, which explains the existence of the (narrow) version of constituency directors, there are difficulties with transplanting such a version to the other three Asian jurisdictions. In other words, not only can path dependency help us to explain the existence and effectiveness of a corporate sustainability mechanism, but it can also explain whether and the extent to which the mechanism should or could be adopted by other jurisdictions.

The final implication is that, similar to Malaysia, there is a heightened risk that the controlling shareholder or the board which is under its control will use the corporate mechanisms such as sustainability reporting, board gender diversity and directors' duties to advance its own interests at the expense of the company and other shareholders. The risk is arguably more pronounced in India because promoting sustainability is explicitly mandated by the Indian Companies Act as evidenced in the requirement to promote corporate philanthropy: the requirement to spend 2 per cent of net profits on effecting CSR policy (under s 135(5)) and the requirement to protect the interests of employees, community and environment (under s 166(2)). For example, there is the concern that, on the pretext of complying with the requirement to pursue philanthropy under s 135(5), companies may channel funds to charitable organisations which in turn funnel part of the money back to the controller or the board.[114] A less extreme form of extraction of

---

[114] Dhammika Dharmapala and Vikramaditya S Khanna, 'The Impact of Mandated Corporate Social Responsibility: Evidence from India's Companies Act of 2013' (2018) at 21 https://papers.ssrn.com/sol3/papers.cfm?abstract_id=2862714.

personal gains is when the controller or the board engages in corporate philanthropy to satisfy its personal preferences that do not benefit the minority shareholders or other stakeholders.[115]

4 Hong Kong

The situation in Hong Kong is different from the other three Asian jurisdictions in the sense that the corporate sustainability practices and policies of the listed companies, especially the PRC SOEs listed in Hong Kong (which account for 40 per cent of the total market capitalisation on the main board of the Stock Exchange of Hong Kong[116]), are not determined by the socio-economic development agenda of the Hong Kong government. But it would be correct to say that the sustainability policies and practices of PRC SOEs listed in mainland China and Hong Kong are inextricably tied to the socio-economic development agenda of the PRC government (more accurately known as the Communist Party of China).[117]

In other words, while it would be correct to say that one of the rationales of the PRC government in having its SOEs listed on the Stock Exchange of Hong Kong is to promote the financial development of Hong Kong and to advance greater integration between the economies of Hong Kong and China,[118] the Chinese SOEs in Hong Kong play a less pivotal and defining role in the socio-economic development of Hong Kong than the SOEs in the other three Asian jurisdictions. The governments in the other three Asian jurisdictions have deployed SOEs as a central mechanism for 'nation building' and industrialisation. But the Chinese SOEs listed in Hong Kong have not been a pivotal strategy of the PRC government to promote Hong Kong's socio-economic development. Rather, the socio-economic development of Hong Kong has been largely driven by private commercial entrepreneurialism, with relatively limited intervention from the colonial government (prior to Hong Kong's handover to the PRC) or Hong Kong

---

[115] Ronald W Masulis and Syed Walid Reza, 'Agency Problems of Corporate Philanthropy' (2015) 28 *Review of Financial Studies* 592.

[116] HKEX China Dimension www.hkex.com.hk/eng/stat/smstat/chidimen/cd_mc.htm.

[117] Peter S Hofman, Jeremy Moon and Bin Wu, 'Corporate Social Responsibility under Authoritarian Capitalism: Dynamics and Prospects of State-Led and Society-Driven CSR' (2017) 56 *Business & Society* 651; ChungMing Lau, Yuan Lu and Qiang Liang, 'Corporate Social Responsibility in China: A Corporate Governance Approach' (2016) 136 *Journal of Business Ethics* 73.

[118] David Donald, Jiangyu Wang and Jefferson P VanderWolk, *A Financial Center for Two Empires: Hong Kong's Corporate, Securities and Tax Laws in Its Transition from Britain to China* (Cambridge University Press 2014) at 228–9.

III FACTORS DRIVING SUSTAINABILITY COMMON LAW ASIA 33

and the PRC government (after the handover).[119] It is not inaccurate to describe Hong Kong's economy as much more laissez-faire than those of the other three Asian jurisdictions. For example, the Heritage Foundation has consistently rated Hong Kong's economy as the freest in the world.[120]

While the sustainability policies and practices of the listed companies in Hong Kong are not driven by the socio-economic development agenda of the Hong Kong government, they are driven in part by law, primarily the rules issued by the stock exchange, which will be examined in Section III(B).

B Rules of Stock Exchanges

The second factor that has, in part, driven the sustainability actions of the listed companies are the rules issued by stock exchanges. When the Stock Exchange of Hong Kong (SEHK) was considering whether to amend its ESG disclosure rules to make them robust and to amend them from a voluntary to a comply or explain basis, the SEHK stated in the consultation paper that its role as a leading stock exchange is to promote an orderly, fair and informed market, the last of which requires financial and non-financial information to be disclosed.[121] The SEHK cited evidence of the requirement to produce ESG disclosure from other stock exchanges and regulatory authorities in diverse jurisdictions such as those from mainland China, the UK, the EU, the United States, Australia and Taiwan.[122] The implication was that the SEHK should not fall behind other stock exchanges in terms of best practices, and that failure to amend the ESG rules could have an adverse impact on the SEHK's reputation and, thus, on the financial and economic development of Hong Kong.

This is not surprising because Hong Kong is an international financial centre with the fifth largest stock exchange in the world and the third largest in Asia (after Japan and Shanghai).[123] Thus, corporate

---

[119] Gordon Redding, Gilbert YY Wong and William K Leung, 'Hong Kong: Hybrid Capitalism as Catalyst' in Michael A Witt and Gordon Redding (eds), *The Oxford Handbook of Asian Business Systems* (Oxford University Press 2014) at 37–8.
[120] www.heritage.org/index/country/hongkong.
[121] Hong Kong Exchanges and Clearing Limited, Consultation Paper on Review of the Environmental, Social and Governance Reporting Guide (July 2015) para 5.
[122] Ibid at 7–11.
[123] Vikas Shukla, 'Top 10 Largest Stock Exchanges in the World by Market Capitalization' (19 February 2019) *Value Walk* www.valuewalk.com/2019/02/top-10-largest-stock-exchanges/.

sustainability disclosure rules will inevitably be impacted by external pressure, namely, the sustainability disclosure rules from other leading stock exchanges around the world. The need to maintain and enhance its standing as a competitive stock exchange is not only an important consideration in Hong Kong's decision to reform and implement its sustainability disclosure rules, but it also applies to the other three Asian jurisdictions. After all, other than the SEHK, the Bombay Stock Exchange is among the world's top ten stock exchanges[124] and Bursa Malaysia is one of the top twenty-five stock exchanges by market capitalisation in the world.[125] Further, as of 2017, the SEHK and the National Stock Exchange of India were ranked among the top five stock exchanges in the world in terms of the number of initial public offerings (IPOs), surpassing Nasdaq and the New York Stock Exchange.[126]

Similarly, the Malaysian stock exchange, Bursa Malaysia, issued sustainability reporting rules in response to the fact that companies have gained a deeper understanding of sustainability and its importance to their business and operations and that stakeholders are increasingly interested in the sustainability impacts of the companies' business. Bursa Malaysia recognised that it performs an important function in promoting the long-term competitiveness of the market and, thus, it was vital to introduce sustainability reporting rules.

Another reason for the development and issuance of sustainability rules is that the stock exchanges in the four Asian common law jurisdictions committed themselves to improving sustainability disclosure and to pursuing sustainability initiatives when they joined the United Nations-backed Sustainable Stock Exchanges Initiative.[127]

The argument that the rules of the stock exchanges play an important role in promoting corporate sustainability is consistent with a widely cited empirical study on sustainability reporting rules issued by the stock exchanges in South Africa, China and Malaysia (as well as those issued by the legislature in Denmark).[128] The study found that these reporting rules have led to a significant and positive increase in sustainability disclosures in the listed companies of these four countries. Specifically, the authors

---

[124] Ibid.
[125] OECD, OECD Corporate Governance Factbook 2019 (2019) at 19.
[126] Ibid at 21.
[127] www.sseinitiative.org/sse-partner-exchanges/list-of-partner-exchanges/.
[128] Ioannis Ioannou and George Serafeim, 'The Consequences of Mandatory Corporate Sustainability Reporting' (1 May 2017) Harvard Business School Research Working Paper No. 11-100 https://ssrn.com/abstract=1799589.

found that companies that did and those that did not disclose sustainability information prior to the reporting rules increased their disclosure after the rules were issued. Further, they found that companies, on average, are more likely to obtain assurance for their sustainability disclosures and more likely to adopt the Global Reporting Initiative Guidelines. This is because the companies that were already voluntarily producing sustainability disclosure prior to the issuance of reporting rules by the stock exchange would want to distinguish themselves from those companies that started to produce disclosure in response to the rules. After all, studies have shown that higher sustainability disclosures enhance a company's reputation and improve its access to finance.[129]

In addition to the rules issued by stock exchanges, I suggest that there are two other factors that provide a more complete account for the increase in sustainability practices of the listed companies: internationalisation of companies and the rise of SRIs.

C Internationalisation of Companies

It has been argued that globalisation, associated with the liberalisation and proliferation of trade and investment, and the adoption of multilateral agreements have had an impact on companies' adoption of sustainability policies and practices.[130] Domestic companies which are exposed to the sustainability policies and practices of foreign companies may adopt some of them, or foreign companies may require the domestic Asian companies to adopt sustainability policies as one of the conditions for trading and investment. There are several aspects of globalisation that may result in an increase in sustainability reporting. One aspect could be the relation between foreign direct investments and sustainability reporting.[131] The other could be the level of trading between the Asian jurisdictions and their Western counterparts. A third could be the international reach of the companies. For example, there are companies that are headquartered in the country in question but have business

---

[129] n 21–36 and accompanying text.
[130] Colin Higgins and Philippe Debroux, 'Globalization and CSR in Asia' (2009) 8 *Asian Business and Management* 125; Andreas Georg Scherer and Guido Palazzo, 'The New Political Role of Business in a Globalized World: A Review of a New Perspective on CSR and Its Implications for the Firm, Governance, and Democracy' (2011) 48 *Journal of Management Studies* 899.
[131] See eg Azlan Amran and AKS Nabiha, 'Corporate Social Reporting in Malaysia: A Case of Mimicking the West or Succumbing to Local Pressure' (2009) 5 *Social Responsibility Journal* 358.

operations in other countries or export to other countries ('international companies'). By contrast, there are companies that are headquartered in the country in question and have business only within that country ('domestic companies').

An empirical study of the sustainability disclosures on the websites of the top fifty companies by market capitalisation in seven Asian countries including Singapore, Malaysia and India made three findings.[132] First, while there is some correlation between foreign direct investment and sustainability reporting, it is not strong. Singapore has relatively high foreign direct investment but average sustainability reporting, whereas India has relatively low foreign investment but high sustainability reporting. Second, there is no positive association between level of trading and sustainability reporting. The third finding is that international companies – companies with overseas businesses – correlate with higher sustainability reporting, which supports the claim that globalisation furthers sustainability. The study suggests that there are three possible explanations for this finding. International companies are likely to have different kinds of stakeholder who will engage with them with respect to sustainability issues. Moreover, international companies will care about their reputation in the international market. Finally, such companies are more likely than domestic companies to be influenced by international norms on sustainability/CSR such as the UN Global Compact, the UN PRI and the Global Reporting Initiative.

D Rise of SRIs

SRIs have become very important in Europe and the United States and increasingly in Asia. In Europe, the total assets for SRIs increased to US $12.04 trillion, which represented a growth of 12 per cent from 2014 to 2016.[133] Fifty-three per cent of assets under management (AUM) in Europe now deploy SRI strategies.[134] In the United States, AUM for SRIs increased from US $6.57 trillion in 2014 to US $8.72 trillion in 2016, which represents an increase of 33 per cent.[135] Further, US $8.1

---

[132] Wendy Chapple and Jeremy Moon, 'Corporate Social Responsibility (CSR) in Asia: A Seven Country Study of CSR Website Reporting' (2005) 44 *Business and Society* 415.

[133] Global Sustainable Investment Alliance, 2016 Global Sustainable Investment Review (2016) at 12 www.gsi-alliance.org/wp-content/uploads/2017/03/GSIR_Review2016 .F.pdf.

[134] Ibid at 7.

[135] Ibid at 4.

trillion AUM are held by institutional shareholders who based their investment decision-making process on ESG criteria.[136] In Asia, while SRIs lag behind Europe and the United States, they are on the rise. AUM that deploy sustainability investment strategies increased by 32 per cent between 2012 and 2014 and since 2014 by 16 per cent.[137] As of 2016, there were US $52.1 billion AUM applying sustainability investment strategy criteria.[138]

Notably, since the launch of the PRI network by the United Nations in 2006, there have been 1,449 reporting signatories (comprising investment managers and asset owners) accounting for more than US$89 trillion in AUM as of 2018.[139] By signing up to the PRI, the signatories have expressed their commitment to incorporate sustainability criteria into their investment analysis and decisions and to influence their investee companies to produce sustainability disclosures. Importantly, a significant number of the top five shareholders in the top fifty listed companies in each of the four common law Asian jurisdictions are also signatories to the PRI.[140] These top five shareholders who are signatories include but are not limited to some of the largest and most influential mutual, pension and investment funds such as BlackRock, Vanguard and State Street, as well as sovereign wealth funds such as the Norwegian Government Pension Fund and Malaysia's Khazanah Nasional Berhad. Further, in recognition of the important role that SRIs play in Asia, particularly in China, Singapore and Malaysia, the PRI employed its first-ever head of China to promote sustainability in China and other Asian jurisdictions.[141]

Investors who pursue SRIs are motivated by the fact that SRIs generate higher financial returns; SRIs enhance their reputation; and they have strong pro-social preferences.[142] The sustainability policies and practices

---

[136] Ibid.
[137] Ibid.
[138] Ibid.
[139] UN Global Compact, Principles for Responsible Investment, Annual Report 2018 www.unpri.org/Uploads/z/b/u/pri_ar2018_761642.pdf. In addition to PRI, the proliferation and adoption of international standards (such as the Global Reporting Initiative, OECD Guidelines for Multinational Enterprises and the UN Global Compact) also have an impact.
[140] Principles for Responsible Investment, Signatories www.unpri.org/signatories.
[141] UN Global Compact, Principles for Responsible Investment, Annual Report 2018 www.unpri.org/Uploads/z/b/u/pri_ar2018_761642.pdf.
[142] Arno Riedl and Paul Smeets, 'Why Do Investors Hold Socially Responsible Mutual Funds?' (2017) 72 *Journal of Finance* 2505.

of the companies are impacted by SRIs in three main ways.[143] First, socially responsible investors can and have invested in companies that meet their SRI criteria. Such investments include theme/asset-based investments (related to sustainability, examples of which are green technology, clean energy and sustainable agriculture) and impact investments (which are directed at companies with clear social or environmental purpose). This will incentivise companies not only to consider but also to give effect to ESG considerations in their business strategies and operations. Second, socially responsible investors can and have undertaken different types of screening of companies, such as negative/exclusionary screening, which entails divestments from companies that flout the investors' SRI criteria, as well as positive/best practice screening, which results in investments in companies that outperform their peers in ESG ranking. Exclusionary screening can act as credible deterrence when the divestments are of a significant amount or the shares are of a specialised nature. Positive screening can act as incentive for companies to comply with ESG disclosure rules and to adhere to best practices. Third, socially responsible investors can press for changes in the company through formal means (such as requisitioning general meetings, voting for or against directors and business transactions and pursuing litigation) and informal ways (such as private communication with the company). That said, the effectiveness of the impact of SRIs depends on factors such as the type of investor (whether they are passive or activist), their portfolio structure (ie the extent of the diversification of investments), the resources available to investors and the extent of any free rider and collective action problems.

Separately but connectedly, the rise of sustainability investments has recently led to a surge in demand for green stocks and bonds. The Hong Kong and Singapore governments have taken action to promote their respective countries as regional hubs for green finance such as green bond schemes and tax incentives.[144] There is an increasing investor demand for green bonds issued by companies listed in Singapore and Hong Kong.[145] In 2018, UBS launched its first green investment portfolio

---

[143] Benjamin Richardson, 'Financial Markets and Socially Responsible Investing' in Beate Sjåfjell and Benjamin J Richardson (eds), *Company Law and Sustainability: Legal Barriers and Opportunities* (Cambridge University Press 2015) at 232–55.

[144] Oliver Wyman and AVPN, *Driving ESG Investing in Asia: The Imperative for Growth* (Marsh & McLennan Companies' Asia Pacific Risk Center 2018) at 11–12.

[145] 'Demand for Green Bonds Set to Soar in Asia' *Straits Times* (8 June 2018) www.straitstimes.com/business/demand-for-green-bonds-set-to-soar-in-asia.

in Asia based in Hong Kong to cater to investors' demand for green stocks and bonds.[146] In 2017, Manulife Financial Corp issued and listed a US $500 million green bond, and in 2018, Indonesia's Star Energy Geothermal listed a US$580 million amortising green project bond and the Indian Renewable Energy Development Agency listed a US $387 million green bond, all on the Singapore Exchange. In 2018, the World Bank issued and listed a HK$1 billion green bond on the SEHK,[147] which remains the world's largest sovereign green bond issuance programme. There have been more than thirteen green bonds issued and listed on the SEHK, accounting for more than US$5 billion.[148]

Government promotion of ESG investments in Hong Kong, Singapore and Malaysia has to be seen in light of the other actions taken such as the recent reforms made to the stock exchange rules concerning ESG disclosure, the promoting of board gender diversity as well as the issuance of stewardship codes. However, while these governments have played an important role in promoting sustainability initiatives, there are issues associated with government intervention, particularly in SOEs, which will be examined next.

IV Problems and Effects

It is important to engage with the issue of the effect of controlling shareholders, particularly the government[149] and SOEs, on the corporate mechanisms for promoting sustainability.[150] This is because the four common law jurisdictions in Asia are concentrated ownership

---

[146] Enoch Yiu, 'UBS Introduces First Pure Green Investment Portfolio in Asia' *SCMP* (20 July 2018) www.scmp.com/business/companies/article/2140784/ubs-introduces-first-pure-green-investment-portfolio-asia.

[147] The World Bank, 'World Bank Issues Its First Hong Kong Dollar Green Bond' (16 April 2018) www.worldbank.org/en/news/press-release/2018/04/16/world-bank-issues-first-hong-kong-dollar-green-bond.

[148] Enoch Yiu, 'HK$100 Billion Green Bond Plan to Establish Hong Kong as Global Hub, Says Monetary Authority' *SCMP* (11 June 2018) www.scmp.com/business/banking-finance/article/2150260/hk100-billion-green-bond-plan-establish-hong-kong-global.

[149] Jean-Pascal Gond, Nahee Kang and Jeremy Moon, 'The Government of Self-Regulation: On the Comparative Dynamics of Corporate Social Responsibility' (2011) 40 *Economy and Society* 640 examines the relationship between government and CSR, but no mention is made of the role of the government in state-owned enterprises; nor is there any analysis of the four common law Asian countries.

[150] The literature is scant but see Fathilatul Zakimi Abdul Hamid, Ruhaya Atan and Md Suhaimi Md Saleh, 'A Case Study of Corporate Social Responsibility by Malaysian Government Link Company' (2014) 164 *Procedia – Social and Behavioral Sciences* 600; Ruhaya Atan and Noraida Mohd Razali, 'CSR Reporting by Government Linked

jurisdictions, that is, the majority of the listed companies are controlled either by the government or by families. I focus on the government and SOEs rather than families for two reasons. As discussed earlier, first, the SOEs wield significant and substantial economic, political and social power in the four common law Asian jurisdictions. These SOEs are ranked among the top listed companies by market capitalisation in all the four jurisdictions.[151] And they provide not only crucial financing for long-term, complex projects, but also financial stability to the economy particularly in times of crisis. The SOEs also control and manage the key infrastructure, energy and public utilities systems as well as the provision of vital financial and technological services.[152] Further, not only are they responsible for providing employment as well as products and services (like most companies), but they also take a lead role in income redistribution, preventing redundancy, and keeping prices below market rate.[153] In short, because of listed SOEs' economic, political and social objectives, they play a vital role in creating and delivering value to the public, while having to be run competitively and profitably as they are listed companies.

Nevertheless, there are at least three problems that are usually associated with SOEs.[154] First, there may be conflicts between the political and social objectives of SOEs and profit maximisation.[155] Second, there may be conflicts of interest between the government's role as a shareholder and its role as a regulator.[156] Finally, there are the concerns arising from political interference and extractions of private benefits of control by the government.[157] The latter of these two problems may have an impact on the corporate mechanisms for promoting sustainability.

Companies and Their Corporate Attributes' (2013) 7 *Australian Journal of Basic and Applied Sciences* 163.

[151] n 83.
[152] Michael A Witt and Gordon Redding (eds), *The Oxford Handbook of Asian Business Systems* (Oxford University Press 2014).
[153] Ibid.
[154] See eg Andrei Shleifer and Robert W Vishny, *The Grabbing Hand: Government Pathologies and Their Cures* (Harvard University Press 2002).
[155] Aldo Musacchio and Sergio G Lazzarini, *Reinventing State Capitalism: Leviathan in Business, Brazil and Beyond* (Harvard University Press 2014).
[156] Marina Pargendler, 'State Ownership and Corporate Governance' (2012) 80 *Fordham Law Review* 2917.
[157] See eg Ronald J Gilson, 'Controlling Shareholders and Corporate Governance: Complicating the Comparative Taxonomy' (2006) 119 *Harvard Law Review* 1641.

IV PROBLEMS AND EFFECTS

A Conflicts of Interest between the Government's Roles as Both Shareholder and Regulator

The conflicts of interest between the government as the controlling shareholder and the government as the corporate regulator may arise in two ways. First, where the SOEs fail to comply with the corporate governance norms and rules for promoting sustainability, there is a risk that the government, as the corporate regulator, may not enforce the rules against the delinquent SOEs. For example, regarding the mechanism of sustainability reporting, where SOEs have failed to comply with the mandatory requirements (such as those in Malaysia and India), or where they have failed to provide adequate explanation for failing to comply (such as in Hong Kong and Singapore), it is questionable whether, and, if so, the extent to which, the government, as the regulator, will effectively hold the SOEs accountable. Further, it is not clear that the two key assumptions underlying the comply or explain mechanism – that shareholders lack information but, with the disclosure provided by the company, will monitor and discipline the directors and managers for failing to comply or for poor explanation – are applicable to SOEs. This is because, first, controlling shareholders will have access to or be in possession of material information (unlike shareholders in a dispersed ownership jurisdiction) and, second, they are unlikely to discipline the directors given that the directors are unlikely to violate the reporting requirements without first obtaining the acquiescence of the controller, as it wields the power of dismissal and appointment over them. Similarly, where the SOEs have failed to comply with the law governing diversity disclosure or female directors, it is not clear that the government as the regulator will take action against the SOE. It may be said, however, that these SOEs will eventually comply with the requirements because failure to do so will adversely affect their reputation, which may reduce their share price and hence ultimately harm the interests of the government as the controller. This is possible, but it would depend, among other things, on whether the cost of compliance is not exceeded by the benefits of 'getting away with' not complying, as well as whether and to what extent the government will bring enforcement actions against the companies it owns.

The second way in which the conflict may arise is this. There is the risk that, to protect its interest as the controlling shareholder of SOEs, the government, as the regulator, may either not promulgate certain rules/norms because doing so may adversely affect its interest or resist legal reforms that constrain its powers.[158] For example, as will be elaborated in Chapter 2, a significant problem with the corporate governance tool of sustainability reporting is the lack of mechanisms to monitor and audit the quality of the disclosures. All factors being equal, it seems doubtful if the government will initiate reforming the rules to require companies including SOEs to be subject to independent audit and verification. Regarding the mechanism of constituency directors, the government as the regulator may be disinclined to reform the law so as to allow directors to be appointed or nominated by employees because this will dilute their power, and the reform may jeopardise the pro-employer economic policies set by the government in Singapore and Hong Kong. With respect to the mechanism of imposing liability on shareholders for the torts committed by the subsidiary, I argue that, although there are strong legal and moral justifications for requiring the government as the controlling shareholder of the SOE to compensate the tort victims of its subsidiary, such a legal reform may be resisted by the government.

Thus, in view of the problem of conflicts of interest and the potential objections from the state to proposed legal reforms to the corporate mechanisms that will curtail its power, I make several suggestions, which will be elaborated in the subsequent chapters. For instance, with respect to sustainability reporting, I suggest that having an independent, third-party private entity verify and assess the sustainability reports (provided that issues concerning the independence of that entity are addressed) is preferable to having a governmental body do so. With respect to constituency directors, I suggest that a reformed version of India's CSR board committee will be more acceptable to the government and SOEs than the German co-determination model. As for stewardship codes (which currently apply to only institutional investors), I suggest that, should they be reformed to apply to controlling shareholders, the compliance structure of the codes ought to be comply or explain (despite its flaws) and not optional, let alone mandatory. Finally, regarding the redress mechanism for victims of

---

[158] On the subject of those who wield political and economic power opposing positive reforms, see Mancur Olson, *The Rise and Decline of Nations* (Yale University Press 1982); Raghuram G Rajan and Luigi Zingales, 'The Great Reversals: The Politics of Financial Development in the Twentieth Century' (2003) 69 *Journal of Financial Economics* 5. See also Lucian A Bebchuk and Mark J. Roe, 'A Theory of Path Dependence in Corporate Ownership and Governance' (1999) 52 *Stanford Law Review* 127 at 157–60; Lucian A Bebchuk and Zvika Neeman, 'Investor Protection and Interest Group Politics' (2010) 23 *Review of Financial Studies* 1089; Mariana Pargendler, 'State Ownership and Corporate Governance' (2011) 80 *Fordham Law Review* 2917 at 2921–2.

tortious acts committed by a subsidiary, I argue, contrary to other commentators, that statutory strict liability should not be imposed; rather, it should be statutory fault-based liability subject to a reverse burden of proof.

B Political Interference and Extractions of Private Benefits of Control

A recurring problem is that governments interfere in the business and operations of SOEs to pursue personal and political agendas with little regard for the long-term commercial success of companies.[159] In other words, governments extract private benefits of control, to the detriment of the companies, minority shareholders and stakeholders. In addition, governments can use SOEs to provide benefits to other persons for political gains.[160] Governments can extract not only private financial gains but also non-pecuniary ones such as political influence and prestige, as well as gains deriving from corruption.[161] For instance, there is extensive literature showing that the controlling shareholder of the Chinese SOEs listed in Hong Kong, ie the State-Owned Assets Supervision and Administration Commission (SASAC), not only engages in value-destroying related party transactions but the politicians controlling SASAC also benefitted from non-financial gains such as patronage and promotion.[162] As for the Malaysian GLCs, there are studies showing that the politicians have used them for their own personal and political gains.[163] There are also cases of the government as the

---

[159] Andrei Shleifer and Robert W Vishny, *The Grabbing Hand: Government Pathologies and Their Cures* (Harvard University Press 2002); Mara Faccio, 'Politically Connected Firms' (2006) 96 *American Economic Review* 369; Anne O Krueger, 'Government Failures in Development' (1990) 4 *Journal of Economic Perspectives* 9.

[160] Ibid.

[161] Lin Li-Wen and Curtis J Milhaupt, 'We Are the (National) Champions: Understanding the Mechanisms of State Capitalism in China' (2013) 65 *Stanford Law Review* 697.

[162] Curtis J Milhaupt, 'Chinese Corporate Capitalism in Comparative Context' in Weitseng Chen (ed), *The Beijing Consensus? How China Has Changed the Western Ideas of Law and Economic Development* (Cambridge University Press 2017) at ch 11; Yan-Leung Cheung, P Raghavendra Rau and Aris Stouraitis, 'Tunnelling, Propping, and Expropriation: Evidence from Connected Party Transactions in Hong Kong' (2006) 82 *Journal of Financial Economics* 343; Shu-Yun Ma, 'Role of the State in Chinese Enterprises Listed in Hong Kong' (2002) 15 *Pacific Review* 279.

[163] Michael Carney and Edo Andriesse, 'Malaysia: Personal Capitalism' in Michael A Witt and Gordon Redding (eds), *The Oxford Handbook of Asian Business Systems* (Oxford University Press 2014) at 146–50.

controlling shareholder of the Indian PSUs extracting private benefits of control by misusing corporate assets or diverting resources from the companies.[164] In these SOEs, the directors and officers who are appointed by the government are often expected to do the latter's bidding and, in turn, receive favours from the government,[165] which are examples of cronyism.[166]

After all, the power of appointment, re-appointment and dismissal of directors (including independent directors) lies with the government as the controlling shareholder. Further, directors can be dismissed any time without cause despite anything in the company's constitution or agreement.[167] Moreover, it is common in SOEs for the government to appoint its associates or nominees to be on the board or management. The government as the controller wields not just formal power over the directors but also informal power in the sense of the influence that it exerts over them. Thus, directors and the management are unlikely to do anything that will have a material adverse effect on the interests of the government without first consulting it. In addition, because the directors

---

[164] See eg R Jagannathan, 'Why Only CIL? Here Are 9 Other PSU Boards Investors Can Sue' *First Post* (20 December 2014) www.firstpost.com/business/why-only-cil-here-are-9-other-psu-boards-investors-can-sue-241950.html; Sarita Singh and Himangshu Watts, 'Corruption, Inefficiency Eat 25% of CIL Output: Sriprakash Jaiswal' *Economic Times* (19 October 2011) http://economictimes.indiatimes.com/industry/energy/power/corruption-inefficiency-eat-25-of-cil-output-sriprakash-jaiswal/articleshow/10407210.cms?intenttarget=no.

[165] S Subramanian, 'A Comparison of Corporate Governance Practices in State-Owned Enterprises and Their Private Sector Peers in India' (2016) 5 *IIM Kozhikode Society & Management Review* 200; Jayanth Rama Varma, 'Corporate Governance in India: Disciplining the Dominant Shareholder' (1997) 9 *IIMB Management Review* 5; Edmund Terence Gomez and KS Jomo, *Malaysia's Political Economy: Politics, Patronage and Profits* (2nd edn, Cambridge University Press 1999); Mingyi Hung, TJ Wong and Tianyu Zhang, 'Political Considerations in the Decision of Chinese SOEs to List in Hong Kong' (2012) 53 *Journal of Accounting and Economics* 435 at 439.

[166] In the crony capitalism index formulated by The Economist, Malaysia, Singapore and India are among the top ten most cronyistic countries in the world, ranking two, four and nine, respectively, out of twenty-two countries. While there is no separate ranking for Hong Kong, it is subsumed by the index under China, which is ranked eleven: see The Economist, 'Comparing Crony Capitalism Around the World: The Economist's Crony-Capitalism Index' (5 May 2016) www.economist.com/graphic-detail/2016/05/05/comparing-crony-capitalism-around-the-world.

[167] HKCO, s 462; SG CA, s 152; MY CA, s 206(2); IN CA, s 169. Although directors can be removed by ordinary resolution in India, the Indian Companies Act does not contain the language that appears in the companies legislations of the other three jurisdictions which states that directors can be removed notwithstanding anything in the company's constitution or in any agreement between the company and him.

and officers of the SOEs are dependent on the government for promotion and other favours, they are unlikely to defy it.

Governments' interference in SOEs, extractions of private benefits of control as well as legal and political powers over the boards have implications for the corporate mechanisms for promoting sustainability.

For example, regarding the mechanism of board gender diversity, there is the concern that female directors may not be appointed on the basis of merit but on the basis of political connection. Even if that is not the case, there is still the concern as to whether they are willing and able to monitor and challenge the controlling shareholder. This calls into question the persuasiveness of a central rationale for having female directors – they improve corporate governance. With respect to stewardship codes, the government may use the code as a tool to entrench its power while using it as a device to signal its ostensible commitment to good corporate governance. This is because the code applies not to controlling shareholders but to institutional investors (who are in the minority) and these investors are unlikely to monitor and challenge the controlling shareholder where they have or wish to have business relationships with the controller or the company. As for the mechanism of directors' duties to act in the company's best interests, even if the law permits or requires directors to promote the interests of stakeholders, there is the concern that directors will still prioritise the interests of the (controlling) shareholder (by maximising profits or share price) where the interests of the controller conflict with those of stakeholders.

C Two Qualifications

However, two qualifications should be made. First, while governments will extract benefits of control from SOEs, these are not always or necessarily private, ie not to the detriment of the company, minority shareholders and other stakeholders.[168] Second, in light of the importance of their being perceived as legitimate, governments as the controlling shareholders can play an important role in promoting sustainability, but the extent of which remains questionable.

---

[168] Dan W Puchniak, 'Multiple Faces of Shareholder Power in Asia: Complexity Revealed' in Jennifer G Hill and Randall S Thomas (eds), *Research Handbook on Shareholder Power* (Edward Elgar 2015) at 529.

1 First Qualification: Public but Not Private Benefits of Control

Regarding the first qualification, consider the case of the Singapore GLCs. Temasek Holdings Private Limited is the controlling shareholder of many of Singapore's largest listed companies. Unlike the SOEs in Hong Kong, India and Malaysia, there is far less political interference by the Singapore government in the SOEs, as the SOEs are intended to be commercially run with a view towards long-term profit maximisation.[169] This is because the political legitimacy of the ruling government in Singapore depends to a significant extent on the country's economic performance, in which the SOEs play an important role.[170] In light of this, the government, through Temasek, is incentivised to ensure that the SOEs are financially strong and well-managed. In this sense, Temasek does extract political benefits of control by virtue of being the controller of some of the most influential, powerful and profitable companies in Singapore. But such control is not at the expense of the company, minority shareholders and stakeholders. Rather, it is the reverse. The generally strong corporate performance benefits the minority shareholders and stakeholders.[171]

This has implications for the corporate mechanisms for promoting sustainability. For example, given that the government takes the view that board gender diversity will improve corporate performance, Temasek as the controlling shareholder will be incentivised to appoint one or more female directors in its investee companies. This partly explains why SOEs in Singapore on average have a higher percentage of female directors than non-SOEs (as discussed in Chapter 3). Similarly, because the government shares the view that better ESG disclosure is associated with improved corporate governance, one would expect that the SOEs will generally have better disclosures than non-SOEs. This seems to be borne out in reality (as discussed in Chapter 2).

2 Second Qualification: Protect and Promote the State's Legitimacy

Given that governments as controlling shareholders will have more power and resources to monitor and discipline SOEs, and because of

---

[169] Cheng-Han Tan, Dan W Puchniak and Umakanth Varottil, 'State-Owned Enterprises in Singapore: Historical Insights into a Potential Model for Reform' (2015) 28 *Columbia Journal of Asian Law* 61 at 86–91.
[170] Ibid.
[171] n 96.

their significant and substantial impacts on the four Asian jurisdictions, it is not unreasonable to expect the governments acting through SOEs to play a more active role in promoting sustainability as compared to non-SOEs,[172] the latter of which are essentially commercial, profit-driven companies.

Arguably more importantly, because SOEs may wish to be perceived as 'role models', it is not unreasonable to expect SOEs to engage in more sustainability activities than non-SOEs. For example, it has been found that the government has exerted influence on Chinese SOEs to publish sustainability reports[173] and that SOEs in Malaysia produce more sustainability disclosures than non-SOEs.[174]

Central to this idea of 'role models' is legitimacy theory – 'a condition or status which exists when an entity's value system is congruent with the values system of the larger social system of which the entity is a part'[175] – which provides an explanation as to why SOEs, despite the problems of conflicts of interests, extractions of private benefits of control, and corruption, will not abandon or minimise their role in promoting sustainability. This is because the government and the SOEs see the need to maintain and defend their legitimacy, which will act as a constraint against persistent or egregious wrongdoing. Legitimacy theory is tied to the idea that organisations seek to ensure that the values implied by or associated with their actions are consistent with the norms of the society of which they form a part. There is organisational legitimacy where these

---

[172] For eg states should take additional steps to prevent human rights abuses by SOEs. See UN Working Group on Business and Human Rights, 'Leading by Example: The State, State-Owned Enterprises, and Human Rights' (2016) www.ohchr.org/EN/HRBodies/HRC/RegularSessions/Session32/Documents/ExSummary-WGBHR-SOE_report-HRC32.pdf; OECD Guidelines on Corporate Governance of State-Owned Enterprises (2015) www.bicg.eu/wp-content/uploads/2017/07/OECD-2015.pdf.

[173] ChungMing Lau, Yuan Lu and Qiang Liang, 'Corporate Social Responsibility in China: A Corporate Governance Approach' (2016) 136 *Journal of Business Ethics* 73 at 78.

[174] NA Mohamed Ghazali, 'Ownership Structure and Corporate Social Responsibility Disclosure: Some Malaysian Evidence' (2007) 7 *Corporate Governance* 251 at 261; Azlan Amran and S Susela Devi, 'The Impact of Government and Foreign Affiliate Influence on Corporate Social Reporting: The Case of Malaysia' (2008) 23 *Managerial Auditing Journal* 386.

[175] CK Lindblom, 'The Implications of Organizational Legitimacy for Corporate Social Performance and Disclosure', Paper Presented at the Critical Perspectives on Accounting Conference, New York NY at 2; see also Matthew V Tilling and Carol A Tilt, 'The Edge of Legitimacy Voluntary Social and Environmental Reporting in Rothmans' 1956–1999 Annual Reports' (2010) 23 *Accounting, Auditing and Accountability Journal* 55; Walter Aerts and Denis Cormier, 'Media Legitimacy and Corporate Environmental Communication' (2009) 34 *Accounting, Organisations and Society* 1.

two value systems are consistent and do not compete or conflict.[176] Once companies are incorporated, they have to maintain their legitimacy not only by pursuing acceptable actions but also by actively responding to adverse social and economic situations such as environmental disasters or financial crises. For example, a study of Malaysian companies found that there were more disclosures subsequent to the Asian financial crisis.[177] Another study found that Australian companies produced more sustainability disclosures after the occurrence of major social incidents.[178] If companies have to maintain and defend their legitimacy, then there is a greater need for SOEs to do so because their corporate objectives lie primarily and predominantly in the pursuit of social and economic ends (as discussed earlier in Section III(A)) and in light of the fact that their controller is the government, which has the prime responsibility for advancing the common good.

The process through which the government seeks to preserve and enhance its legitimacy through the promotion of sustainability can be further explained using this framework, namely, (i) sustainability as endorsed by government; (ii) sustainability as facilitated by government; (iii) sustainability as a partnership with government; and (iv) sustainability as mandated by government.[179] In the first category, the government provides political support through campaigns, websites, rhetoric and awards. In the second category, the government provides incentives to companies to pursue sustainability through tax incentives, subsidies, public procurement policies, etc. In the third category, the government collaborates with business organisations to produce and disseminate knowledge and to develop and maintain standards and guidelines. In the last category, the government imposes rules and regulations on companies.

For instance, the Malaysian government has launched a strategic framework – the Silver Book – to guide GLCs in their sustainability

---

[176] John Dowling and Jeffrey Pfeffer, 'Organizational Legitimacy: Social Values and Organizational Behavior' (1975) 18 *Pacific Sociological Review* 122.

[177] RM Haniffa and TE Cooke, 'The Impact of Culture and Governance on Corporate Social Reporting' (2005) 24 *Journal of Accounting and Public Policy* 391.

[178] Craig Deegan, Micheala Rankin and Peter Voght, 'Firms' Disclosure Reactions to Major Social Incidents: Australian Evidence' (2000) 24 *Accounting Forum* 101.

[179] Jean-Pascal Gond, Nahee Kang and Jeremy Moon, 'The Government of Self-Regulation: On the Comparative Dynamics of Corporate Social Responsibility' (2011) 40 *Economy and Society* 640 at 647; Jette Steen Knudsen and Jeremy Moon, *Visible Hands: Government Regulation and International Business Responsibility* (Cambridge University Press 2017) at 48.

contributions; this falls under the first and third categories.[180] It has also been found that there is more corporate sustainability disclosure after this regulatory initiative by the government.[181]

With respect to the corporate mechanism of board gender diversity, the third category (ie sustainability as partnership with government) is relevant because the government (such as that in Singapore and Malaysia) has collaborated with business organisations and NGOs to advocate for more female directors. The mechanism of stewardship codes also shows the relevance of the first and third categories. The first category (ie sustainability as endorsed by the government) is relevant because the Monetary Authority of Singapore and the Singapore Exchange support the Singapore Stewardship Principles for Responsible Investors. The third category (ie sustainability as a partnership with government) is relevant because leading Malaysian GLCs (which are controlled by the government) were part of the group that included industry participants that formulated the Malaysian Code for Institutional Investors. The mechanism of constituency directors provides an example of the fourth category (sustainability as mandated by government). For example, India's companies statute requires companies to have a specially constituted board committee to formulate and disclose their CSR policies and the law further requires companies to spend at least 2 per cent of their net profits to implement these policies. Finally, the mechanism of directors' best interest duty also illustrates how sustainability is mandated by the government because India's companies legislation requires directors to act in the interests of not only shareholders but also stakeholders, namely, employees, the community and the environment.

Nevertheless, although SOEs can promote and protect their legitimacy through the pursuit of sustainability actions using the corporate mechanisms, they can also use these mechanisms to give the appearance of advancing sustainability. In other words, the government or the SOEs can change the perceptions of the relevant stakeholders but without effecting any meaningful or substantive change in their own behaviour. For example, an SOE can produce boilerplate and uninformative

---

[180] Putrajaya Committee on GLC High Performance, Catalysing GLC Transformation: Silver Book: Achieving Value through Social Responsibility (2007) www.oecd.org/daf/ca/corporategovernanceofstate-ownedenterprises/40792845.pdf. The Silver Book provides GLCs with detailed methodologies, processes and principles in order to guide GLCs to make proactive and strategic social contributions.

[181] Elinda Esa and Nazli Anum, 'Corporate Social Responsibility and Corporate Governance in Malaysian Government-Linked Companies' (2012) 12 *Corporate Governance* 292 at 294.

sustainability disclosures that give the appearance of complying with the letter but not the spirit of the regulations. Or an SOE can appoint one female director not because it genuinely believes in the importance of gender diversity but merely to comply with the law or to avoid criticisms. Or the government as a controller of SOEs and as a regulator can actively support stewardship codes knowing full well that they are not effective in curbing extractions of private benefits of control or conflicts of interest. I discuss these examples in detail in the subsequent chapters.

Finally, in view of the problems of lack of transparency and accountability as well as corruption[182] that are often associated with the government as the controlling shareholder in the SOEs in Malaysia, India and Hong Kong (with the arguable exception of Singapore), the expectation that the government and the SOEs could play an effective role in promoting sustainability through the corporate mechanisms remains a challenge. I will suggest possible reforms to the corporate mechanisms in subsequent chapters.

V Structure

This book critically evaluates the effectiveness of four corporate governance mechanisms for promoting sustainability – sustainability reporting (Chapter 2), board gender diversity (Chapter 3), constituency directors (Chapter 4) and stewardship codes (Chapter 5) – followed by that of two corporate law mechanisms, namely, directors' duty to act in good faith in the best interests of the company (Chapter 6) and the judicial and statutory imposition of liability on companies, shareholders and directors (Chapter 7) in Hong Kong, Singapore, India and Malaysia. The analysis is shaped by two salient features in these four jurisdictions, namely, all four are based on the common law, and SOEs, of which the government is a controlling shareholder, have important implications for the use of the corporate mechanisms in promoting sustainability.

Chapter 2 first critiques the structure and contents of the sustainability reporting rules. Regarding the structure, I examine the merits of comply or explain and mandatory requirements, bearing in mind a significant characteristic of listed companies in the four common law Asian jurisdictions, ie the presence of SOEs and the government (or a government-linked company) as their controlling shareholder. As for the contents,

---

[182] OECD, *State-Owned Enterprises and Corruption: What Are the Risks and What Can Be Done?* (OECD Publishing 2018).

V STRUCTURE

I analyse two key features of the reporting rules in Singapore, Malaysia and Hong Kong, namely, the materiality of the ESG factors and the indicators for giving effect to the factors. Then I assess the contents of India's BRRs, which are very different from the reporting requirements in the other three Asian jurisdictions.

Subsequently, based on hand-collected data from the sustainability reports of 200 listed companies in the four Asian jurisdictions (ie the top fifty listed companies by market capitalisation in each of Singapore, Hong Kong, Malaysia and India)[183] for the financial year ending December 2017, I critically evaluate the extent and quality of the disclosures. The empirical analysis also indicates a breakdown of the companies by SOEs versus non-SOEs.

Finally, I conclude by proposing solutions to two major problems with the sustainability reporting requirements in all four Asian jurisdictions – the lack of verification or oversight and the absence of sanctions.

Chapter 3 begins by interrogating the rationales provided by the authorities in the four Asian jurisdictions for having female directors, namely, that they improve corporate governance and firm value. I show that evidence in support of these touted benefits is not unequivocal and I argue that these rationales, which are based on utilitarian arguments, are necessary but insufficient. They should be supplemented with intrinsic/ethical justifications based on equality.

I then critically evaluate the effectiveness of four measures that have been taken in these four Asian jurisdictions to increase the number of female directors: imposing a quota; applying or explaining an alternative (requiring companies to apply the code or, if they choose not to do so, demonstrate how their alternative measures will give effect to the code); adopting a combined approach consisting of monitoring disclosure and 'name and shame'; and, finally, setting targets.

Subsequently, using hand-collected data from the annual reports of 200 listed companies in the four Asian jurisdictions for the financial year 2017 to 2018 (the reports of the top fifty listed companies by market capitalisation in each of the four countries), I conduct an empirical analysis to ascertain the percentage of female directors, with

---

[183] Based on hand-collected data, the top fifty companies in each of Singapore, Malaysia, Hong Kong and India account for 78 per cent, 72 per cent, 65 per cent and 58 per cent of the total market capitalisation in each of the respective jurisdictions as of 1 August 2018. Given that market capitalisation evidences the size and impact of companies, the data drawn from these top fifty companies show the practices of some of the most important companies in these jurisdictions.

a breakdown by SOEs versus non-SOEs, in each of the four jurisdictions. I also offer explanations for the rankings. I then consider certain specific issues raised by SOEs and the government as the controller such as the risk that the female directors may be appointed on the basis not of merit but of political connection, and the problem of repeat players (the same women holding multiple directorships).

Chapter 4 critically analyses two versions of constituency directors for the purpose of understanding whether this mechanism can and should be used to promote sustainability in the Asian jurisdictions. The broad version is that directors are appointed by employees, the most well-known example of which is the German co-determination model. The narrow version is the one adopted in India, under which a committee of directors, although not appointed by employees or other stakeholders, is specifically constituted by the board and required by the companies legislation to promote CSR. Neither the UK nor the other three Asian jurisdictions (ie Singapore, Hong Kong and Malaysia) have constituency directors, whether the broad or narrow version. I evaluate the costs and benefits of these two versions of constituency directors for the purpose of considering whether Singapore, Hong Kong and Malaysia should have constituency directors, specifically taking into account the issue of SOEs and the government as the controlling shareholder.

Chapter 5 critically examines whether stewardship codes are an effective mechanism for promoting sustainability. I begin by explaining why and how the stewardship codes came about. I then critically analyse the rationales, contents, compliance structure and scope of the codes in Singapore, Malaysia and Hong Kong (but not in India because it does not have an overarching stewardship code that applies to all institutional investors unlike the other three jurisdictions, although it has codes that apply to mutual funds and insurance companies).

After that, I examine the effect of the controlling shareholders on the codes by showing: first, how the code reinforces the power of controlling shareholders; second, that the controllers will disincentivise institutional shareholders from actively engaging with the company; and, finally, the conflicts of interest between the controlling shareholder (or its company) and the institutional investors. Next, I demonstrate that the institutional investors' different interpretations of the fiduciary duties that they owe to their clients/beneficiaries will have an important bearing on the promotion of sustainability. Finally, I conclude by suggesting reforms to the codes.

Chapter 6 analyses the first corporate law mechanism, namely, directors' best interest duty. I examine whether the law governing the duty of directors to act in the best interests of the company in each of the four Asian jurisdictions is an effective mechanism to promote sustainability. I begin by analysing three normative justifications underlying the best interest duty – shareholder primacy, stakeholder value, and long-term value and viability. I then examine how these theories are consistent with and reflected in the laws of the four Asian jurisdictions. Importantly, I evaluate the pros and cons of the laws in each of the four jurisdictions and I argue that the long-term value and viability theory of the company, which finds support in the Singapore and Malaysian law, provides a better approach for directors to promote sustainability than the shareholder primacy approach (reflected in Hong Kong law) or the stakeholder approach (espoused by Indian law). One key point that I emphasise in this chapter is that it is important to evaluate the theories and laws on the directors' best interest duty in light of the concentrated ownership structure of the listed companies, specifically, the powers, actions and motivations of the controlling shareholders (including the government) because they will have a bearing on how directors discharge their duties. Subsequently, I show that the best interest duty has implications for the effectiveness of three corporate governance mechanisms, namely, sustainability reporting, stewardship code and constituency directors, and that these mechanisms will in turn affect the best interest duty. I conclude by considering the factors that affect the effectiveness of the mechanism of the best interest duty.

Chapter 7 analyses the third corporate law mechanism, namely, judicial and legislative imposition of liability on shareholders, companies as well as directors and officers for the wrongs committed by the companies and their insiders. This chapter is divided into two principal parts. The first critically analyses the existing and proposed redress mechanisms for claimants to whom the defendant subsidiary has caused harm but to whom it is unable to provide compensation (because it is undercapitalised or insolvent). I begin by examining the rationales for the limited liability principle and I argue that the rationales do not apply to the situation of claimants seeking redress from the parent company (or other shareholders) as a result of the harms caused to them by the subsidiary. I then distinguish between exceptions to the limited liability principle and piercing the corporate veil and I argue that the former does not entail the latter. Next, I evaluate the existing redress mechanisms such as judicial piercing of the corporate veil and judicial imposition of duty of care, and the proposed mechanisms such as statutory enterprise liability (which renders the entire corporate group liable) and statutory strict liability on the shareholders of the wrongdoing subsidiary. I also examine the mechanism for addressing harms caused not by entities within the traditional corporate group structure but by networks. Finally, taking into account the fact that the majority of the listed companies consist of controlling shareholders, of which the government plays a critical role in the SOEs, I make the case for a statutory fault-based liability subject to a reverse burden of proof to be imposed on the controlling shareholder of the SOEs.

The second principal part of this chapter analyses the public interest legislations such as those pertaining to environmental protection, occupational safety, as well as health and operation of factories that impose liability on companies as well as their directors and officers. I first assess the structure of liability, namely, who bears the burden of proving the guilt of the directors and officers, and then I consider issues related to enforcement.

Chapter 8 concludes by setting out the main contributions of this book to the literature on sustainability, CSR and corporate governance.

2

Sustainability Reporting

I   Structure and Contents of Reporting Requirements   57
   A   Structure   57
      1   Comply or Explain   58
      2   Mandatory   67
   B   Contents   69
      1   Materiality of ESG Factors   69
      2   Indicators   73
      3   India: BRRs and the CSR 2 Per Cent Spending Requirement   77
II   Qualitative Evaluation of Sustainability Reports   83
   A   Effect of Corporate Characteristics   83
      1   Singapore   83
      2   Malaysia   84
      3   India   85
   B   Extent and Quality of Disclosures   86
      1   Singapore and Malaysia   86
      2   India   87
      3   Hong Kong   88
   C   Qualitative Evaluation of the Sustainability Reports in Common Law Asia   89
      1   Hong Kong   92
      2   Singapore   94
      3   Malaysia   96
      4   India   96
III   Suggested Reforms   97
   A   Oversight Mechanism   97
   B   Sanctions   99

All the four common law jurisdictions in Asia – Singapore, Hong Kong, Malaysia and India – have imposed sustainability reporting requirements on listed companies. In Hong Kong, listed companies are required with effect from the financial year starting 1 January 2016 to disclose whether they have complied with the ESG reporting guide.[1] In Malaysia, large listed companies must publish a sustainability report with effect from the financial year ending 31 December 2016, and other listed companies 31 December 2017.[2] In Singapore, the rules require companies to publish the reports with effect from the financial year ending 31 December 2017.[3] In India, the top 100 companies by market capitalisation must publish BRRs with effect from March 2012.[4] Further, in India, with effect from 1 April 2014, companies are required to disclose their CSR policy and they are required to spend at least 2 per cent of their net profits on the activities stated in that policy.[5]

The stock exchanges of Singapore, Hong Kong and Malaysia have provided two principal rationales for sustainability reporting. First, in light of investors' expectations that companies should be managed in a sustainable manner because of the impacts that companies have on the economy, environment and society, companies should supplement their disclosure of financial information with sustainability reports.[6] The disclosure of financial and non-financial information will thus enable investors to develop a better assessment of the financial performance and business operations of the company. Second, sustainability reporting will enhance the value of companies because it will improve risk management, facilitate access to capital, enhance reputation, promote innovation, increase investments and attract talents.[7] A third rationale, which is distinct from the first and second, is that provided by the Securities Exchange Board of India,

---

[1] Hong Kong Exchanges and Clearing Limited, Consultation Conclusions: Review of the Environmental, Social and Governance Reporting Guide (December 2015) para 10. The comply or explain requirement with respect to the indicators under the environmental factor became effective only for issuers' financial year commencing on or after 1 January 2017.

[2] Bursa Malaysia, Appendix 1, Amendments Relating to Sustainability Statements in Annual Reports para 6.4.

[3] SGX Listing Rule 711A; SGX-ST Listing Rules, Practice Note 7.6, Sustainability Reporting Guide para 6.1.

[4] Securities and Exchange Board of India, Business Responsibility Reports, CIR/CFD/DIL/8/2012 (13 August 2012); Business Responsibility Reports – Frequently Asked Questions (FAQs) www.bseindia.com/downloads1/BRR_FAQs%2010052013.pdf.

[5] Ministry of Corporate Affairs, Government of India, Clarifications with Regard to Provisions of Corporate Social Responsibility under s 135 Companies Act 2013, General Circular No. 21/2014 (18 June 2014).

[6] Bursa Malaysia Sustainability Reporting Guide (2015) at [2.3]; Hong Kong Exchanges and Clearing Limited, Consultation Paper: Review of the Environmental, Social and Governance Reporting Guide (July 2015) para 51; SGX-ST Listing Rules, Practice Note 7.6, Sustainability Reporting Guide paras 2.1–2.2.

[7] Bursa Malaysia Sustainability Reporting Guide (2015) paras 2.3.1–2.3.6; Hong Kong Exchanges and Clearing Limited, Consultation Paper: Review of the Environmental,

I STRUCTURE & CONTENTS OF REPORTING REQUIREMENTS 57

namely, that because companies are accountable not only to shareholders 'but also to the larger society which is also its stakeholder',[8] they need to pursue responsible business practices to protect the interests of the society and the environment. The need to protect and promote the interests of stakeholders was also a key motivation.

Apart from the differences in rationales, there are two main differences in the sustainability reporting requirements in the four jurisdictions. The first lies in the structure, that is, whether it is of a comply or explain nature or mandatory, and the second concerns the specific contents of the disclosure requirements. Section I of this chapter critiques the structure and contents. Section II first summarises the literature on the effects of corporate characteristics on the extent of disclosures and then provides a qualitative analysis of the sustainability disclosures (drawn from the publicly disclosed reports) of the top fifty listed companies in each of the four common law Asian jurisdictions. Finally, Section III discusses the reforms that should be made to the reporting requirements.

I Structure and Contents of Reporting Requirements

A Structure

Two major regulatory techniques have been adopted with regard to the disclosure requirements. The first is comply or explain, that is, companies are required to comply with the rules, but if they choose not to do so, they are required to provide an explanation. The second, of course, is to make it mandatory for companies to comply. The sustainability reporting rules issued by the Singapore Exchange[9] and the SEHK[10] are of a comply or explain nature. By contrast, they are mandatory under Bursa Malaysia[11] listing rules and the SEBI regulations with respect to BRRs.[12] Additionally, the Indian Companies Act provides that companies have to contribute at least 2 per cent of their net profits to activities stated in their CSR policy, but this expenditure requirement is not mandatory; should companies fail to comply with it, they have only to give an explanation.[13]

Social and Governance Reporting Guide (July 2015) paras 57–66; SGX-ST Listing Rules, Practice Note 7.6, Sustainability Reporting Guide para 2.2.
[8] SEBI, Business Responsibility Reports (CIR/CFD/DIL/8/2012) (13 August 2012) para 1.
[9] SGX Exchange LR 711B(2).
[10] HKEX Appendix 27 Environmental, Social and Governance Reporting Guide para 2.
[11] Bursa Malaysia Listing Requirements, Appendix 9C, Part A paras 9.45(2), 29.
[12] SEBI, Business Responsibility Reports (CIR/CFD/DIL/8/2012) (13 August 2012) para 5a.
[13] S 135(5) IN CA.

1 Comply or Explain

In critiquing these two regulatory techniques, it is important to first understand the aim of the comply or explain mechanism, which is essentially to allow shareholders to decide whether the explanation given by the company for not complying is satisfactory and, if not, to take action.[14] In other words, the onus is on the shareholders and not the regulators to assess the adequacy of the disclosure. The comply or explain mechanism seeks to strike a balance between those who oppose governmental regulation (particularly mandatory rules), on the one hand, and those who want to use sustainability reporting specifically and corporate governance generally to effect social changes, on the other.[15] The comply or explain mechanism also suits those who prefer lighter, reflexive regulation that is responsive to evolving contexts, as well as those who take the view that non-state actors should be involved in the monitoring of corporations.

The origins of the comply or explain mechanism are found in the 1992 UK Report of the Committee on the Financial Aspects of Corporate Governance, known as 'the Cadbury Report', which issued the first corporate governance code.[16] A lynchpin of the code is that companies are required to comply with it, but should companies choose not to do so, they have to give an explanation. The idea is twofold. First, given the considerable variations in the types of companies and their businesses, imposing a mandatory rule is inappropriate, which is a rejection of the one size fits all approach.[17] Second, it is up to the shareholders and the market, and not the government, to monitor and if necessary discipline the company for failing to provide a satisfactory explanation. The implication is that directors are accountable to shareholders and that the latter, who care about the share price, will take appropriate action against the board if they wish to.[18]

---

[14] Andrew Keay, 'Comply or Explain in Corporate Governance Codes: In Need of Greater Regulatory Oversight?' (2014) 34 *Legal Studies* 279 at 280.
[15] Mariana Pargendler, 'The Corporate Governance Obsession' (2016) 42 *Journal of Corporation Law* 359 at 366.
[16] https://ecgi.global/sites/default/files//codes/documents/cadbury.pdf.
[17] Sridhar R Arcot and Valentina G Bruno, 'One Size Does Not Fit All, After All: Evidence from Corporate Governance' (2007) 4 *Journal of Empirical Legal Studies* 1041.
[18] Amama Shabbir, 'To Comply or Not to Comply: Evidence on Changes and Factors Associated with the Changes in Compliance with the UK Code of Corporate Governance' (18 March 2008) http://papers.ssrn.com/sol3/papers.cfm?abstract_id=1101412.

There have been extensive criticisms of the comply or explain mechanism. For example, it has been found that shareholders are passive or indifferent to the poor quality of the explanation. Another objection is that companies who have failed to comply do not provide any explanation. And even if they do, the explanation is boilerplate and uninformative, and it is being repeated year to year.[19] For example, one study found that 20 per cent of companies furnished no explanation for failing to comply.[20] A later study found that 15 per cent of UK companies failed to give any explanation for not following the corporate governance code.[21]

a Suitable to Be Transplanted to Concentrated Ownership Jurisdictions with SOEs? However, there is another major concern that has eluded the commentators, which is whether the comply or explain mechanism, developed and applied in the context of the UK, a dispersed ownership jurisdiction, is suitable for transplantation to the four Asian countries, which are concentrated ownership jurisdictions consisting of SOEs. There are three reasons for this concern.

First, the fundamental premise of the comply or explain mechanism, as originated and developed in the UK, is that where the board has provided an explanation for non-compliance, shareholders will be able to make an informed assessment of the non-compliance, and will be willing and able to monitor and even discipline the board. But in concentrated ownership jurisdictions with SOEs, such as those in the common law Asian countries, where there is evidence of interference by the government in the affairs of the companies,[22] it seems unlikely that directors will either not explain or give a poor explanation for not complying, unless acquiescence (or even consent) has been sought from the controlling shareholder, the government. Further, even if there was no acquiescence, it is not likely for the government to take action against the board for its failure to provide any explanation or failure to provide satisfactory

---

[19] Sridhar Arcot and Valentina Bruno, 'In Letter but Not in Spirit: An Analysis of Corporate Governance in the UK' (May 2006) http://ssrn.com/abstract=819784.

[20] Sridhar Arcot, Valentia Bruno and Antoine Faure-Grimaud, 'Corporate Governance in the UK: Is the Comply or Explain Approach Working?' (2010) 30 *International Review of Law and Economics* 193.

[21] David Seidl, Paul Sanderson and John Roberts, 'Applying "Comply-or-Explain": Conformance with Codes of Corporate Governance in the UK and Germany', Centre for Business Research, University of Cambridge, Working Paper 389 (June 2009) www.cbr.cam.ac.uk/fileadmin/user_upload/centre-for-business-research/downloads/working-papers/wp389.pdf.

[22] See Chapter 1, Section IV(B).

explanation if doing so will adversely affect the government's interests. For example, suppose that the board decides either not to provide any explanation or to provide a boilerplate one for not complying with certain environmental regulations stipulated by the sustainability reporting rules. It is not likely that the government will discipline the directors for their decision, particularly if the provision of an explanation or a more detailed one is likely to cause embarrassment to the government.

Moreover, the assumption underlying the comply or explain mechanism – that shareholders do not have information on the company's failure to comply, which is why the board has to furnish the explanation – while true for shareholders in dispersed ownership jurisdictions such as the UK, is unlikely to be true in the Asian SOEs. In the four Asian jurisdictions, the government as the controller usually appoints directors who currently or used to work for the government, or who are connected to the government.[23] In short, many of these directors either are or were civil servants and politicians. Thus, the government as the controller would be in possession of, or at the very least have access to, material information that is likely to include that which is related to the company's failure to comply with the law.

Second, the comply or explain mechanism, which originated in the UK, a shareholder primacy jurisdiction, assumes that shareholders are motivated by the maximisation of profits or share price, and thus will evaluate the explanations provided by the board and take appropriate action. But as discussed in Chapter 1, SOEs do not have maximisation of share price or profits as their sole or primary corporate objective; they also have social, economic and political aims. Thus, whether the government as the controlling shareholder would have the incentive to take any action if the board provides either no or poor explanation depends on whether doing so would be aligned with its political and social objectives and interests. But it may be argued that in the context of sustainability reporting, there should be an alignment as the government would want to

---

[23] On PRC SOEs, see eg Mingyi Hung, TJ Wong and Tianyu Zhang, 'Political Considerations in the Decision of Chinese SOEs to List in Hong Kong' (2012) 53 *Journal of Accounting and Economics* 435 at 439, 447; on Malaysia SOEs, see eg Edmund Terence Gomez and KS Jomo, *Malaysia's Political Economy: Politics, Patronage and Profits* (2nd edn, Cambridge University Press 1999); on Indian SOEs, see eg S Subramanian, 'A Comparison of Corporate Governance Practices in State-Owned Enterprises and Their Private Sector Peers in India' (2016) 5 *IIM Kozhikode Society & Management Review* 200 at 204–6; on Singapore GLCs, see eg Dan W Puchniak and Luh Luh Lan, 'Independent Directors in Singapore: Puzzling Compliance Requiring Explanation' (2017) 65 *American Journal of Comparative Law* 265 at 313, 315.

ensure that a credible explanation is given for non-compliance. After all, the social objectives and reputations of the SOEs are at stake. This is theoretically correct. But the reality is more complex. While SOEs have an incentive to comply with the sustainability reporting requirements, they have also flouted them by either not providing any explanation or furnishing a boilerplate one, as will be elaborated in Section II(C) where I discuss my empirical findings. There are several possible explanations for this. One is that the SOEs may take the view that they can get away with a poor explanation particularly if they control the key resources in the country such as telecommunications, utilities as well as oil and gas. In other words, the effect of a drop in share price or any reputational damage is not likely to be consequential. Another is that civil society and other stakeholders may not be effective in holding them to account for their failure to comply. Moreover, nothing in the sustainability reporting rules provides for any enforcement measures to be taken against the company for failing to provide any explanation or for providing inadequate information.

Third and finally, the comply or explain mechanism rests on the stark and questionable dichotomy between 'regulation' by shareholders and regulation by the state. For example, supporters of the comply or explain mechanism have rejected the suggestion of allowing the state to monitor the quality of the explanation as this will usurp shareholders' right to do so.[24] But this objection is no longer persuasive when both the state and the shareholder are one and the same person, as is the case with SOEs. The concern with allowing the state to assess the quality of the explanation is no longer that of taking away shareholders' right to do so; rather, it lies with conflicts of interest between the state as the regulator and the state as the controller of the SOEs. This problem has not been addressed by proponents of comply or explain who are critical of state regulation. Nor has it been considered by those who advocate giving power to the state to monitor the quality of the board's explanation.

b No Guidelines to the Explanation Another problem is that no guidelines have been provided by SEHK or the Singapore Exchange as to what is considered an adequate or satisfactory explanation for non-compliance with the sustainability reporting rules. Likewise, the MCA

---

[24] Financial Reporting Council, Response to the European Commission Green Paper on the EU Corporate Governance Framework (2011) at 5; Financial Reporting Council, What Constitutes an Explanation under Comply or Explain? (2012).

has not furnished any guidelines on what ought to be included in the explanation should companies fail to comply with the 2 per cent expenditure requirement. As I elaborate in Section II(C) on empirical evidence, there are a number of SOEs (as well as non-SOEs) that have either failed to provide any explanation or provided cursory and not meaningful ones.

Because a critical feature of comply or explain is the latter aspect, regulators should have at least tried to come up with some recommendations as to what ought to be included in the explanation, while bearing in mind that there is no 'one size fits all' recommendation, and taking into account the dangers of box-checking. But there appear to be no recommendations or guidelines. It may be argued, however, that the point of the comply or explain mechanism, as originally conceived of and applied in the UK, is to let the shareholders and markets decide what is an acceptable or satisfactory explanation and respond accordingly; the point is not to let an external body such as a regulator decide. That said, letting shareholders decide is not inconsistent with the provision of a set of recommended guidelines.

c **Potential Difficulties in Holding SOEs to Account** It may be difficult for the regulators to hold SOEs to account when they do not provide any explanations or provide poor explanations for their failure to comply. This is because the relevant regulatory bodies may be subject to interference or influence by the government, which is also a controlling shareholder (or the ultimate controller) of the SOEs or is connected to the controller of the SOEs. For example, where the regulator is the stock exchange, it is in turn regulated by a government entity that exercises control or influence over it.[25] Further, the government (or companies that are controlled by or affiliated with it) could own shares in the regulator or have control rights over it. For example, although SEHK is wholly owned by Hong Kong Exchanges and Clearing Limited in which the government owns fewer than 6 per cent shares,[26] the government has the right to appoint up to eight directors in SEHK.[27] Moreover, where the

---

[25] For example, the Singapore Exchange is regulated by the Monetary Authority of Singapore. The Stock Exchange of Hong Kong, however, is regulated by the Hong Kong Securities and Futures Commission, which is independent of the government: see Securities and Futures Commission, 'Our Role' www.sfc.hk/web/EN/about-the-sfc/our-role/. But note that the Hong Kong Chief Executive appoints the chairperson and commissioners of the SFC.

[26] See HKEX 2016 Annual Report at 64 www.hkexnews.hk/listedco/listconews/SEHK/2017/0320/LTN20170320225.pdf.

[27] Securities and Futures Ordinance (Cap 571), ss 77(1), (5).

regulator is the government itself, it is doubtful whether it would challenge the SOEs on their inadequate explanations. Thus, if the SOEs come up with an explanation that they deem adequate for their non-compliance or if they do not even provide any explanation, it is questionable whether and, if so, to what extent the regulator would hold them accountable.

d No Third-Party or Independent Assessment There is no third-party or independent monitoring or oversight, let alone verification or audit, to ascertain and assess the quality and reliability of the explanation where there is no compliance, let alone the quality of the disclosure (assuming that the companies claim they have complied). This not only further highlights the issue with the comply or explain mechanism but also increases the risk that the sustainability report will become a public relations or greenwashing[28] exercise.

The objection to having third-party verification or audit is that this will stymie any dialogue among the companies, the markets and the NGOs because it will shift power to the audit industry or the organisation in charge of the verification.[29] This objection is premised on two assumptions, both of which are questionable. The first assumption is that the sustainability reports provided by companies are sufficiently detailed and clear such that the markets and the NGOs can evaluate the reports for themselves for the purpose of forming an informed view of the companies. The second assumption is that the markets and the NGOs are active and effective in holding companies accountable for their disclosures.

With respect to the first assumption, my empirical analysis in Section II(C) (a detailed version of which can be found in Appendix 3) shows that the sustainability reports furnished by the companies in the four common law Asian jurisdictions[30] are often inadequate and generic, and that

---

[28] Beate Sjåfjell, 'Dismantling the Legal Myth of Shareholder Primacy: The Corporation as a Sustainable Market Actor' (2017), University of Oslo Faculty of Law Research Paper No. 2017-03, at 12-13 https://papers.ssrn.com/sol3/papers.cfm?abstract_id=2912141.

[29] Patrick C Leyens, 'Corporate Social Responsibility in European Union Law: Foundations, Developments, Enforcement' in Jean J du Plessis, Umakanth Varottil and Jeroen Veldman (eds), *Globalisation of Corporate Social Responsibility and Its Impact on Corporate Governance* (Springer 2018) at 172.

[30] The findings of my analysis of the companies in India are consistent with those of the existing studies: see eg KPMG, India's CSR Reporting Survey (2015) https://assets.kpmg.com/content/dam/kpmg/pdf/2016/03/KPMG-CSR-Survey2015.pdf; Umakanth Varottil, 'Analysing the CSR Reporting Requirements under Indian Company Law' in Jean J du Plessis et al (ibid) at 245-8.

a number of companies which failed to comply provided either no explanations or inadequate ones. Thus, it is highly questionable whether the explanations (or lack thereof) enable the market or the NGOs to form an informed view or to carry out any meaningful evaluation.

Regarding the second assumption, there appear to be no event studies demonstrating that the lack of or the inadequacy of explanations provided by companies (in Hong Kong or Singapore) as a result of their failure to comply with the reporting rules has triggered an abnormal drop in the share price.[31] Nor is there evidence that good explanations have been rewarded with increased share price. After all, if the information provided is of a cursory or boilerplate nature, it is unlikely to elicit any unusual stock market reaction. To put it another way, unless there are special circumstances that warrant the explanation or unless the explanation is in response to special circumstances such as environmental catastrophes, serious human rights abuses in the supply chain or egregious violations of health and safety regulations, it is unlikely that the market or the NGO will actively monitor or even discipline the companies for their inadequate explanation (or lack thereof).

Of course, it may be argued that that there are studies showing positive and significant associations between sustainability disclosures and share price, as discussed in Chapter 1. However, there are also studies showing otherwise. For example, a study of US companies found that there is insignificant stock market reaction to companies' disclosure of environmental business strategies, recycling and renewable energy.[32] Further, a study of seventeen listed companies in Hong Kong in the period 2010–12 found that although there is positive market reaction to disclosure of ESG initiatives by companies, the evidence is weak.[33]

---

[31] Cf. One study found that there was a decline of 2.6 per cent to 3.3 per cent in the share price of companies when the Indian authorities first announced in 2010 that companies would be subject to the mandatory requirement to spend at least 2 per cent of profits on CSR activities: Dhammika Dharmapala and Vikramaditya S Khanna, 'The Impact of Mandated Corporate Social Responsibility: Evidence from India's Companies Act of 2013' (2016) https://papers.ssrn.com/sol3/papers.cfm?abstract_id=2862714. But note that the 2 per cent mandatory requirement was eventually dropped in favour of comply or explain in the actual statutory provision.

[32] Brian W Jacobs, Vinod R Singhal and Ravi Subramanian, 'An Empirical Investigation of Environmental Performance and the Market Value of the Firm' (2010) 28 *Journal of Operations Management* 430 at 439.

[33] Kar Yee Lo and Calvin Lee Kwan, 'The Effect of Environmental, Social, Governance and Sustainability Initiatives on Stock Value: Examining Market Response to Initiatives Undertaken by Listed Companies' (2017) 24 *Corporate Social Responsibility and Environmental Management* 606 at 615.

Conversely, unless a disclosure shows that the company has achieved certain environmental milestones such as being certified ISO 14001, the stock market will not react positively.[34]

That said, there is also one study showing that stock prices fell in response to the announcement of negative ratings – provided by India's leading environmental NGO – of the environmental performance of Indian companies.[35] It may be argued that this study supports the claim that stock markets are not indifferent to the environmental performance of companies. However, what this study does show is that stock markets do react to independent, third-party assessments of companies' environmental performance. But where there is no such assessment but mere disclosures by companies, it is open to doubt whether these correlate with any significant changes in the companies' share price. This suggests that it is important to have independent, third-party assessments of companies' sustainability disclosures.

In any event, although the majority of studies show that sustainability disclosures are associated with significant changes in share price, the disclosures do not differentiate between those issued pursuant to mandatory rules and those issued pursuant to comply or explain.[36] Nor, as mentioned earlier, are there studies that have established correlations between share price and the explanations furnished by companies for their failure to comply. This is important because recall that the point of this discussion is to call into question an assumption underlying the objection to the imposition of the requirement to have third-party, independent assessment, namely, that markets can provide an effective

---

[34] Brian W Jacobs, Vinod R Singhal and Ravi Subramanian, 'An Empirical Investigation of Environmental Performance and the Market Value of the Firm' (2010) 28 *Journal of Operations Management* 430 at 438.

[35] Shreekant Gupta and Bishwanath Goldar, 'Do Stock Markets Penalize Environment-Unfriendly Behavior? Evidence from India' (2005) 52 *Ecological Economics* 81.

[36] See eg Cornelia Beck, Geoffrey Frost and Stewart Jones, 'CSR Disclosure and Financial Performance Revisited: A Cross Country Analysis' (2018) 43 *Australian Journal of Management* 517 at 530–1; Lawrence Loh, Thomas Thomas and Yu Wang, 'Sustainability Reporting and Firm Value: Evidence from Singapore-Listed Companies' (2017) 9 *Sustainability* 1; Gordon L Clark, Andreas Feiner and Michael Viehs, 'From the Stockholder to the Stakeholder: How Sustainability Can Drive Financial Outperformance' (2015) http://papers.ssrn.com/sol3/papers.cfm?abstract_id=2508281; Jyothika Grewal, Edward J Riedl and George Serafeim, 'Market Reaction to Mandatory Nonfinancial Disclosure' (2019) 65 *Management Science* 2947 (finding that ESG disclosure requirements lead to net benefits for firms that have made investments to improve ESG-related performance and disclosure).

mechanism to hold companies accountable for their lack of explanations or inadequate ones in connection with their failure to comply.

That said, it may be argued that it is not necessary for the listing rules to impose a requirement on companies to submit their disclosures to external assessment or verification. This is because companies who have been voluntarily producing sustainability disclosures prior to the issuance of the reporting rules by the stock exchanges would want to differentiate themselves from those companies that have not been producing sustainability disclosures prior to the reporting rules but will do so after the rules come into effect. In other words, there is a greater need for the former companies to signal that they are good corporate citizens and to show that they are not greenwashing. An important differentiating or signalling technique is subjecting the disclosures to assurance by auditing firms. Thus, one study has found that the reporting rules increase the likelihood of companies voluntarily incurring the cost to receive assurances from auditing firms.[37] But this study does not distinguish between the rules that are mandatory and those that are comply or explain in arriving at this finding. Instead, the study combines both types of rules in its empirical analysis. But it is important to make this distinction because it will have a bearing on whether companies will seek assurance. This is because if the rules are mandatory (such as those imposed by Bursa Malaysia), there will be a greater need for companies that have been voluntarily issuing sustainability reports prior to the rules to differentiate themselves from companies that have not been doing so by obtaining assurance, given that the mandatory rules require all listed companies to produce the report. In other words, companies that have been voluntarily issuing sustainability reports no longer have the competitive edge as they can no longer show in any significant way that they are good corporate governance citizens because the rules now require all listed companies to issue the reports. However, if the rules are comply or explain, then companies that have not been issuing any sustainability reports prior to the rules can 'get away with it' to some extent because they have the option of providing a boilerplate explanation for their failure to comply with the reporting requirements. This means that there is a less pressing need for companies that have already been voluntarily issuing sustainability reports to obtain assurance.

---

[37] Ioannis Ioannou and George Serafeim, 'The Consequences of Mandatory Corporate Sustainability Reporting', Harvard Business School Research Working Paper No. 11-100 at 13, 21 https://ssrn.com/abstract=1799589.

I STRUCTURE & CONTENTS OF REPORTING REQUIREMENTS 67

Nevertheless, one study of the top 100 listed companies by market capitalisation in four Asian jurisdictions (Indonesia, Malaysia, Singapore and Thailand) found that extremely few companies have obtained external assurances for their sustainability disclosures: there are only four of such companies in each of Singapore and Indonesia, nine in Malaysia and thirteen in Thailand.[38] This shows that it is necessary to consider whether there should be a requirement for companies to subject their disclosures to external, independent assessment. In a separate study that I conducted on the top fifty listed companies in each of Singapore, Hong Kong, Malaysia and India, it was found that only 31.58 per cent, 37.5 per cent, 20 per cent and 14.29 per cent of the companies, respectively, have obtained assurance for their sustainability disclosures.[39]

2 Mandatory

The second regulatory technique that has been used to subject companies to sustainability disclosures is to make the rules compulsory; companies must comply. Should they fail to do so, they will be in breach of the rules. Unlike the comply or explain mechanism, companies are not given an option to provide an explanation if they are unwilling or unable to comply. Malaysia and India have adopted the mandatory technique, unlike Hong Kong and Singapore.

There are five advantages to the mandatory technique over comply or explain. First, it avoids the problem of poor or inadequate explanations that companies are susceptible of providing should they be unwilling or unable to comply. Second, there is arguably a greater reputational cost associated with the breach of a mandatory rule as compared to a comply or explain rule. Allowing companies to explain their failure to comply implies that the law does not regard failure to comply with the rules as a problem, only failure to furnish an explanation. Thus, failure to comply should not result in any adverse reputational consequences unless it is also accompanied by a failure to explain. Third, the mandatory technique may provide a more effective focal point for the purpose of mobilising stakeholders and NGOs. This is because these constituencies can more effectively hold companies by pointing out that companies have failed to comply with the reporting requirements. However, if it is comply or

---

[38] Lawrence Loh, Nguyen Thi Phuong, Isabel Sim, Thomas Thomas and Wang Yu, 'Sustainability Reporting in ASEAN: State of Progress in Indonesia, Malaysia, Singapore and Thailand' (2015) at 10 https://bschool.nus.edu.sg/cgio/wp-content/uploads/sites/7/2018/10/ACN-CGIO-Sustainability-Reporting-in-ASEAN-2016.pdf.
[39] See Appendix 1.

explain, in deciding whether to criticise the companies and demand remedial measures to be taken, these constituencies have to assess the adequacy of the explanation provided by companies, on which reasonable minds will differ, or at least will differ more significantly as compared to assessing whether companies have failed to comply with a mandatory reporting requirement. Fourth, having mandatory rules demonstrates greater commitment and seriousness on the part of the stock exchange to promote sustainability, whereas comply or explain may send a mixed signal. Finally, a study found that having a mandatory sustainability reporting requirement has significantly increased the disclosures published by companies since the regulations were issued.[40] But this study includes comply or explain as part of what it considers a mandatory requirement. Thus, this study by itself does not tell us whether mandatory reporting is more effective than comply or explain.

However, despite the advantages of the mandatory requirement, and notwithstanding the problems with comply or explain, it does not follow that Singapore and Hong Kong should adopt a mandatory requirement such as that in Malaysia. After all, there are benefits to comply or explain. Consider three of them. First, where there is a high level of uncertainty, comply or explain may work better. For example, given that the impact of the sustainability reporting rules on the cost of the company's business remains uncertain, and that the effect of the rules on the actual sustainability practices remain inconclusive, and in view of the objections from companies, a stock exchange may decide to start off by having comply or explain, before deciding whether to switch to mandatory rules. Further, comply or explain allows for experimentation and adaptation. It is preferable to begin the reporting requirements by first adopting comply or explain and, should that not work, then switching to mandatory rules. But it does not reflect well on the stock exchange if it begins by having mandatory rules and then, assuming that they do not work, changes to comply or explain. Second, comply or explain allows for flexibility in implementation. It takes into account the fact that there are companies that may not have the resources to implement all the reporting rules, and thus permitting them to explain their inability to comply is a more sensible approach. Finally, comply or explain acts as a compromise

---

[40] Ioannis Ioannou and George Serafeim, 'The Consequences of Mandatory Corporate Sustainability Reporting', Harvard Business School Research Working Paper No. 11-100 at 21 https://ssrn.com/abstract=1799589.

I STRUCTURE & CONTENTS OF REPORTING REQUIREMENTS 69

between having mandatory requirements or nothing. It is a sensible compromise between those who oppose intrusive government intervention (such as imposing mandatory rules) and those who want to effect social changes through companies.

Thus, whether a jurisdiction should adopt comply or explain or a mandatory regime requires a nuanced cost–benefit analysis, which would also include an evaluation of the issue of whether having mandatory rules produces better disclosures than comply or explain. It is difficult to answer this question unless there are two sets of sustainability reporting requirements, the contents of which are identical, except that the first set is comply or explain and the second mandatory. But no such data are available. Even if the requirements are identical, the companies that are subject to them will be different because of variations in firm characteristics and governance structures as well as differences in the industries to which the firms belong, all of which have an impact on the quality of the sustainability report.

In any event, there are key differences in the contents of the sustainability reporting rules in the four common law Asian jurisdictions that render any comparison difficult. It is apposite at this juncture to evaluate the contents of the rules.

B Contents

Three features of the reporting requirements – materiality of ESG factors, indicators and India's BRRs – deserve scrutiny.

1 Materiality of ESG Factors

Under the listing rules of Bursa Malaysia, the sustainability report must contain, among other things, material economic, environmental and social (EES) risks and opportunities.[41] Similarly, the SEHK[42] and the Singapore Exchange[43] require issuers to disclose material ESG factors. Bursa Malaysia defines 'materiality' as matters that 'reflect the listed issuer's significant economic, environmental and social impact'[44] or

---

[41] Bursa Malaysia LR, Appendix 9C, Part A (supplemented by Practice Note 9) paras 9.45(2) and 29; Bursa Malaysian, Sustainability Reporting Guide (2015).
[42] HKEX LR, Appendix 27, Environmental, Social and Governance Reporting Guide.
[43] SGX Listing Rule 711A; SGX-ST Listing Rules, Practice Note 7.6, Sustainability Reporting Guide para 6.1.
[44] Bursa Malaysia LR, Practice Note 9 para 6.3.

that 'substantively influence the decisions of stakeholders'.[45] The SEHK listing rules define materiality as issues that are of sufficient importance to investors and other stakeholders.[46] However, there appears to be no definition of materiality in the Singapore Exchange listing rules, although general guidance is provided on how companies should identify material factors.[47]

Bursa Malaysia requires the company to disclose how the material EES factors are identified and why they are important to the company.[48] The practice note to the Singapore Exchange listing rules clarifies that companies should describe both the reason and the process of selection of the material ESG factors,[49] but it is not clear whether the note forms part of the listing rules. If not, it is not compulsory and listed companies in Singapore will still be in compliance with the listing rules even if they do not disclose why and how they selected the material ESG factors. If that is the case, it will be difficult for stakeholders to evaluate the extent to which the ESG factors identified by companies have any material bearing on their present or future business operations and the risks and challenges faced by these companies. However, unlike Singapore, the SEHK does not mention that companies have to disclose the reasons and process for selecting the ESG factors.

Under the listing rules in Malaysia and especially in Singapore, substantial discretion is given to the company to decide which material factors to disclose. It may be argued that a listed company in Singapore is not in breach of the listing rules even if it omits environmental factors as long as it discloses social and governance factors – and, even then, only selectively discloses certain aspects within the social and governance category, while omitting information that it regards as unfavourable. This is because, in Singapore, the comply or explain requirement applies to the component of 'material ESG factors',[50] thus it may be argued that only if the company decides to omit the component entirely does it have to give an explanation. But once the company includes that component in its report, there seems to be no rule stipulating that the company has to explain why it has omitted one of the three ESG categories. In other

---

[45] Ibid.
[46] HKEX LR, Appendix 27, Environmental, Social and Governance Reporting Guide para 11(1).
[47] SGX-ST LR, Practice Note 7.6, Sustainability Reporting Guide paras 4.7–4.10.
[48] Bursa Malaysia LR, Practice Note 9 para 6.2(c).
[49] SGX-ST LR, Practice Note 7.6, Sustainability Reporting Guide para 4.2.
[50] Ibid para 3.2.

words, under the Singapore Exchange listing rules, the comply or explain mechanism applies only to five primary components: (1) material ESG factors; (2) policies, practices and performance; (3) targets; (4) the sustainability reporting framework; and (5) the board statement. Only if the company omits any of the five components does it have the obligation to furnish an explanation. But once it includes the component, then it is up to the company to decide what, how and to what extent it wants to report on.

For example, a property development company listed in Singapore omitted information on the environment from its sustainability report, although it disclosed information related to the social and governance categories, albeit only superficially.[51] It is surprising that the company did not regard resource consumption and emission of waste/greenhouse gas emissions as well as measures to reduce consumption as material environmental factors. But under the listing rules, it may not be required to explain this omission. In any event, while the company provided reasons for its selection of material social and governance factors, the explanation was cursory and uninformative.

Another problem is that even if an issuer in Singapore discloses ESG information, it can selectively disclose certain aspects within each category while omitting information that it regards as unfavourable. For example, the same property development company disclosed information on employees (which would fall under the category of 'social'), but it reported only on employee safety,[52] saying nothing about employee training and retention.

To improve the reporting requirements in Singapore, two aspects of the Bursa Malaysia listing rules should be considered. First, the Singapore Exchange listing rules should state explicitly that companies are required to state the reasons and process for selection of each of the material ESG factors. Currently, this regulation is found only in the practice note, which may not be binding. However, the requirement to specify why and how the factors are selected is mandatory in Malaysia.[53]

Second, clear and detailed guidelines and examples for all the five primary components should be provided. For example, regarding

---

[51] Yanlord Land Group, 2017 Sustainability Report. For example, the report disclosed the reasons for and the process of selecting the material ESG factors. But the process of selecting material ESG factors was poorly explained. Moreover, of the ESG factors identified, only the section 'Caring for our customers' (para 13) had targets.
[52] Ibid at 14.
[53] Bursa Malaysia LR, Practice Note 9 para 6.2; Sustainability Reporting Guide (2015) at 30.

the second primary component that companies have to disclose – policies, practices and performance – the practice note, which may or may not be binding, merely states that companies have to provide 'descriptive and quantitative information on each of the identified material ESG factors ... and performance should be described in the context of previously disclosed targets'.[54] In Malaysia, the listing rules state that companies must disclose policies and measures to manage sustainability matters as well as indicators showing how the issuers have performed in managing those sustainability matters.[55] Importantly, the Bursa Malaysia Sustainability Guide, which is non-binding, provides clear and detailed examples for the policies and measures[56] and a comprehensive list of indicators is also provided.[57] While these examples and guidelines, which are best practices, are illustrative, they are far better than the brief guidance provided in Singapore's practice note.

In Hong Kong, significant discretion is also given to issuers, but it is more circumscribed than that provided under the listing rules in Singapore and Malaysia. The SEHK reporting guide, which is part of the listing rules, stipulates two major factors of disclosure, namely, environmental and social.[58] The environmental factor is subdivided into three aspects: (1) emissions; (2) use of resources; and (3) environmental and natural resources. Under the social factor, there are eight aspects: (1) employment; (2) health and safety; (3) development and training; (4) labour standards; (5) supply chain management; (6) product responsibility; (7) anti-corruption; and (8) community investment.

The company is required to disclose information on the policies and compliance with relevant laws and regulations related to each of these aspects under the environmental and social factors. By contrast, neither Malaysia nor Singapore has broken down the environmental and social factors into subcategories. As a result, companies in Malaysia and Singapore are given discretion to decide the contents of the disclosures under these two factors.

---

[54] SGX-ST LR, Practice Note 7.6 para 4.1(ii).
[55] Bursa Malaysia LR, Practice Note 9 para 6.2(c).
[56] Sustainability Reporting Guide (2015) at 40–7.
[57] Ibid, Appendix A.
[58] HKEX, Appendix 27, Environmental, Social and Governance Reporting Guide at 1, 4–13. The governance factor is addressed separately in Hong Kong's Corporate Governance Code.

I STRUCTURE & CONTENTS OF REPORTING REQUIREMENTS 73

2 Indicators

The Singapore Exchange listing rules require companies to disclose their targets for the coming year for each material ESG factor that they have identified.[59] Bursa Malaysia requires companies to disclose indicators that show how they have performed and will perform in managing the EES risks and opportunities.[60] In short, they are past and forward-looking indicators. Hong Kong, too, has adopted indicators (termed 'key performance indicators' (KPIs))[61] and they are an improvement over those stated in the Singapore and Malaysian listing rules in two ways. First, for each of the environmental and social factors, the SEHK listing rules set out granulated KPIs that specify what must be evaluated and the measures that have to be taken. By contrast, although Malaysia has granulated indicators, they are used merely as illustrations that companies can choose to ignore. Singapore seems to have no list of indicators.

Second, for each of the granulated KPIs under the environmental and social factors, the Hong Kong listing rules specify whether it is subject to comply or explain, or whether it is a recommended disclosure. Thus, for example, under the category of environmental factors, the listing rules divide it into three aspects: emissions; use of resources; and environment and natural resources.[62] And within each of these aspects, there are one to six KPIs.[63] For each of the KPIs, the Hong Kong listing rules stipulate whether it is subject to comply or explain or whether it is a recommended disclosure.[64] Malaysia has not adopted this approach, let alone Singapore, which in the first place provides no examples or case studies of indicators.

Nevertheless, there are two major problems with the indicators: one that is specific to Hong Kong and a second that applies to all three jurisdictions. Regarding the specific problem, it is surprising that, while a majority of the KPIs for the environmental factor are classified as comply or explain, all twenty KPIs for the social factor (which is subdivided into eight aspects, namely, employment, health and safety, development and training, labour standards, supply chain management, product responsibility, anti-corruption, and community investment) are classified as recommended disclosures. There is not a single KPI

---

[59] SGX-ST LR, Practice Note 7.6, Sustainability Reporting Guide at 4.1(iii).
[60] Bursa Malaysia LR, Practice Note 9 para 6.2(c).
[61] HKEX, Appendix 27, Environmental, Social and Governance Reporting Guide para 5.
[62] Ibid at 4–6.
[63] Ibid.
[64] Ibid.

under the social factor that is subject to comply or explain. This is puzzling and unfortunate and it calls into question the effectiveness and even the legitimacy of the KPIs.

For example, under 'product responsibility' (one of the eight aspects under the social factor) it is surprising that even for a basic and important KPI such as that which merely asks the company to state the 'percentage of total products sold or shipped subject to recalls for safety and health reasons', it is classified as a recommended disclosure.[65] Another example is that under 'labour standards' (another of the eight aspects under the social factor) it is unacceptable that an elementary yet important KPI such as 'description of measures to review employment practices to avoid child and forced labour' has been relegated to a recommended disclosure.[66]

The SEHK decided not to upgrade the social factor to comply or explain because it took the view that it would be 'setting the bar too high prematurely',[67] which may lead to unintended consequences such as inexperienced companies adopting a box-ticking attitude when they seek to comply. Further, if a sizeable number of companies fail to comply (because the bar is too high), then other companies may think it is acceptable to do so.

BlackRock has convincingly shown that the SEHK's concerns are unfounded in its responses to the SEHK's Consultation Paper. First, BlackRock observed that many of the KPIs are designed as 'fill-the-blank' rather than 'tick-the-box'.[68] For example, one of the social KPIs asks for the 'total workforce by gender, employment type, age group and geographical group'.[69] Under comply or explain, the company needs to disclose only the figures, but if it fails to do so, it has to provide an

---

[65] Ibid at 11. In view of the food scandals coming from Chinese companies ('China Food Safety', *South China Morning Post* www.scmp.com/topics/china-food-safety), it is unacceptable that this KPI is merely a recommended disclosure.

[66] Ibid at 10. It is unacceptable that 'labour standards' is classified as a recommended disclosure given that modern slavery is a serious contemporary issue. The Asia and the Pacific region has a high incidence of forced labour. China and Hong Kong are ranked twenty-one and twenty-four, respectively, out of twenty-eight countries in Asia and the Pacific in terms of prevalence of modern slavery (with North Korea being the most notorious case as it is ranked first): 2018 Global Slavery Index www.globalslaveryindex.org/2018/findings/regional-analysis/asia-and-the-pacific/.

[67] Hong Kong Exchanges and Clearing Limited, Consultation Paper: Review of the Environmental, Social and Governance Reporting Guide (July 2015) para 7.

[68] BlackRock response to the Consultation Paper (ibid) (15 September 2015) at 4.

[69] HKEX, Appendix 27, Environmental, Social and Governance Reporting Guide at 7.

I STRUCTURE & CONTENTS OF REPORTING REQUIREMENTS 75

explanation; it involves no box-ticking here.[70] Second, BlackRock rebutted the assertion that upgrading the social KPIs to comply or explain will result in a perverse consequence, ie non-compliance.[71] After all, the point of comply or explain is to give companies the power to decide whether they can comply but if not to explain the lack of non-compliance. Further, because only material ESG issues have to be disclosed, companies are given discretion and flexibility. This will not be unduly onerous on companies. Further, if it were true that elevating the social KPIs to comply or explain would set the bar too high, then the SEHK would not impose comply or explain for a majority of the environmental KPIs, many of which are more onerous than the social KPIs. Moreover, as another institutional shareholder has pointed out, elevating social KPIs to comply or explain will benefit companies as this will allow them to identify at an early stage the social risks they are facing that will be considered important and relevant to investors, and then to consider the measures that they should take to address the risks.[72] But if the social KPIs are merely recommended disclosures, companies are unlikely to be incentivised to conduct a risk assessment in that area. Finally, BlackRock also said that by restricting comply or explain only to the environmental factor, the SEHK is implying that the social factor is less important or relevant than the environmental factor, but this is not true as the social factor is particularly important for technological companies.[73] This point was reiterated by another institutional investor that implied that, because social KPIs are relegated as recommended disclosures, there is a risk that companies will pay less attention to issues that may be material to them such as supply chain management, product responsibility and anti-corruption.[74]

It may be argued that the SEHK may want to take a gradual approach by first subjecting the indicators for the environmental factor to comply and explain and, depending on the quality of disclosures provided by companies, incrementally applying the comply or explain mechanism to certain KPIs for the social factor. But this seems excessively cautious, given that compliance with these indicators is not mandatory. After all, if

---

[70] BlackRock response to the Consultation Paper (15 September 2015) at 4.
[71] Ibid.
[72] Local Authority Pension Fund Forum, Response to Hong Kong Exchange Consultation on the Environmental, Social and Governance Guide (September 2015) at 3.
[73] BlackRock response to the Consultation Paper (15 September 2015) at 2.
[74] BMO Global Asset Management response to the Consultation Paper on Review of the ESG Reporting Guide (26 August 2015).

companies are not willing or able to comply, they merely have to give an explanation, which is not even subject to any verification or audit.

However, there might be two reasons for relegating the social factor to recommended disclosures. First, it has been said that it is more difficult to quantify the impact of social actions on share price (or return on assets or return on equity) than the impact of environmental actions.[75] For example, there are studies showing that environmental initiatives result in cost-savings, because of the income generated from energy conservation or recycling.[76] The cost-savings in turn increase the company's market value. But the benefits of social initiatives are less easily quantifiable. For instance, a company's pursuit of philanthropic activities to enhance its reputation among its employees and consumers will lead to financial benefits if the firm is more highly regarded than other companies, but if other companies also start to engage in philanthropy, then this may not yield financial gains.[77] The problem with this argument is that it can also be said of environmental initiatives. More importantly, there is research suggesting that corporate philanthropy has improved firm value.[78]

The second reason that may be used to support the claim that the social factor should be recommended disclosure is that corporate financial performance correlates with 55 per cent of social KPIs whereas it correlates with 65 per cent of environmental indicators.[79] But the lower percentage may be the result of the choice of indicators, rather than demonstrating a lower correlation between social initiatives and corporate financial performance.

In sum, none of the above explanations justifies the wholesale exclusion of social KPIs from comply or explain. Worse still, by exempting the social KPIs from comply or explain, the SEHK is sending a message to companies and their stakeholders that disclosure of the social factor is far less important than that of the environmental factor.

---

[75] John Peloza, 'The Challenge of Measuring Financial Impacts from Investments in Corporate Social Performance' (2009) 35 *Journal of Management* 1518 at 1525.

[76] Peloza, ibid at 1525–6.

[77] John Peloza, 'Using Corporate Social Responsibility as Insurance for Financial Performance' (2006) 48 *California Management Review* 52.

[78] Hao Liang and Luc Renneboog, 'Corporate Donations and Shareholder Value' (2017) 33 *Oxford Review of Economic Policy* 278; Michael E Porter and Mark R Kramer, 'The Competitive Advantage of Corporate Philanthropy' (2002) *Harvard Business Review*. Cf Ronald Masulis and Syed Reza, 'Agency Problems of Corporate Philanthropy' (2015) 28 *Review of Financial Studies* 592.

[79] John Peloza, 'The Challenge of Measuring Financial Impacts from Investments in Corporate Social Performance' (2009) 35 *Journal of Management* 1518 at 1521–2.

I STRUCTURE & CONTENTS OF REPORTING REQUIREMENTS 77

Tellingly, the SEHK has acknowledged that 'by keeping the reporting obligation of Social KPIs as voluntary, the level of disclosure for Social KPIs has been relatively low. This may give the wrong impression that they are less important than Environmental KPIs, resulting in less attention being paid by the issuers.'[80] Thus, the SEHK has launched a consultation exercise, one of the purposes of which is to solicit views on its proposal to upgrade the disclosure of the social KPIs to comply or explain. Subject to the responses received, the SEHK has stated that it intends to implement the revised listing rule for the financial year commencing on or after 1 January 2020. This is a step in the right direction.

Regarding the general problem that is common to all three jurisdictions, while companies are urged to disclose the targets (which are part of the indicators) that they have set for each material ESG factor for the forthcoming year, there appears to be no requirement to disclose the basis of, or the process through which they have come up with, the targets. Without disclosing the basis or process, there is no way to challenge or evaluate the appropriateness of the targets.

3 India: BRRs and the CSR 2 Per Cent Spending Requirement

a BRRs   The contents of the reporting requirements in India are very different from those of the other three Asian jurisdictions. The top 100 companies by market capitalisation must include a BRR in their annual reports under the rules issued by SEBI.[81] SEBI has come up with nine sustainability principles,[82] wholly non-binding, to guide companies in their BRRs. However, there is a fundamental problem with BRRs. Unlike the listing rules in Singapore, Malaysia and Hong Kong, which require companies to produce narrative statements, SEBI has produced

---

[80] HKEX, Consultation Paper on Review of the ESG Reporting Guide and Related Listing Rules (May 2019) para 108.
[81] SEBI circular CIR/CFD/CMD/10/2015 (4 November 2015) www.sebi.gov.in/legal/circulars/nov-2015/format-for-business-responsibility-report-brr-_30954.html.
[82] 'P1: Businesses should conduct and govern themselves with Ethics, Transparency and Accountability; P2: Businesses should provide goods and services that are safe and contribute to sustainability throughout their life cycle; P3: Businesses should promote the wellbeing of all employees; P4: Businesses should respect the interests of, and be responsive towards all stakeholders, especially those who are disadvantaged, vulnerable and marginalized; P5: Businesses should respect and promote human rights; P6: Businesses should respect, protect, and make efforts to restore the environment; P7: Businesses, when engaged in influencing public and regulatory policy, should do so in a responsible manner; P8: Businesses should support inclusive growth and equitable development; and P9: Businesses should engage with and provide value to their customers and consumers in a responsible manner.'

a framework that requires companies to disclose their sustainability practices only in binary terms, namely, companies are merely required to answer either yes or no to nine superficial questions. For example, the first question requires companies to disclose whether or not they have a policy related to the nine sustainability principles. There is no requirement whatsoever to describe the contents of the policy. Should the company answer no, it is not required to provide any narrative explanation or clarification. The second question requires companies to disclose whether the policy has been formulated in consultation with the relevant stakeholders. The third question, which requires companies to disclose whether the policy conforms to any national/international standards, is the only one out of the nine questions that states that companies have to 'specify' regardless of whether they answer yes or no. The other six questions simply require the companies to answer yes or no. These nine questions are worded extremely broadly, allowing companies to answer yes regardless of the degree of compliance. Take, for example, the second question: 'Has the policy been formulated in consultation with the relevant stakeholders?' Or the seventh question: 'Does the company have in-house structure to implement the policy/policies?' Given that SEBI has not provided any guidelines on how these questions should be interpreted, and because these questions are framed so broadly and vaguely, it is entirely up to the company to answer no or, more likely than not, yes. For an illustration, consider the disclosure by Tata Consultancy Ltd, which is the largest company by market capitalisation, in Table 2.1.

Thus, one serious objection to the BRR is that it provides no meaningful or adequate information to enable the relevant stakeholders to have a clear understanding of the sustainability policies of the company, let alone how the policies are related to the business and operations of the company and their impacts on societies. It is impossible to evaluate the merits of the policies given the binary yes/no answer. Should a company provide a negative answer, there is no requirement for it to provide any explanation. This effectively allows companies to get away with not complying. Even if the company provides a positive answer, SEBI provides no verification mechanisms.

But it may be argued that this is not entirely true because should companies answer no to the first question ('Do you have a policy for each of the nine principles?') in relation to any of the nine principles, SEBI has provided a checkbox for them to fill in. For each of the nine principles for which the company has no policy, SEBI has provided a mechanical list of five reasons which the company can check against.

I STRUCTURE & CONTENTS OF REPORTING REQUIREMENTS

Table 2.1 *Extract from the BRR of Tata Consultancy Ltd*

S.N.	Questions	P1	P2	P3	P4	P5	P6	P7	P8	P9
1	Do you have a policy/polices for …	Y	Y	Y	Y	Y	Y	Y	Y	Y
2	Has the policy been formulated in consultation with the relevant stakeholders?	Y	Y	Y	Y	Y	Y	Y	Y	Y
3	Does the policy conform to any national/international standards?	Y	Y	Y	Y	Y	Y	Y	Y	Y
4	Has the policy been approved by the Board? If yes, has it been signed by the MD/owner/CEO/appropriate Board Director?	Y	Y	Y	Y	Y	Y	Y	Y	Y
5	Does the company have a specified committee of the Board/Director/Official to oversee the implementation of the policy? Indicate the link for the policy to be viewed online.	Y*	Y*	Y*	Y**	Y*	Y***	Y*	Y*	Y*
6	Has the policy been formally communicated to all relevant internal and external stakeholders?	Y	Y	Y	Y	Y	Y	Y	Y	Y
7	Does the company have in-house structure to implement the policy/policies?	Y	Y	Y	Y	Y	Y	Y	Y	Y
8	Does the company have a grievance redressal mechanism related to the policy/policies to address stakeholders' grievances related to the policy/policies?	Y	Y	Y	Y	Y	Y	Y	Y	Y
9	Has the company carried out independent audit/evaluation of the working of this policy by an internal or external agency?	Y	N	Y	N	N	Y	N	N	Y

* Tata Code of Conduct (https://on.tcs.com/2HSIMQU)
** CSR Policy (https://on.tcs.com/2riPUyl)
*** Environment Policy (https://on.tcs.com/2wbkkl7)

They are: 'the company has not understood the Principles'; the company is not at a stage where it finds itself in a position to formulate and implement the policies on specified principles; the company does not have financial or manpower resources available for the task; it is planned to be done within the next 6 months; it is planned to be done within the next 1 year'. These check boxes provide hardly any qualitative information. At best, they perpetuate a box-ticking culture, and at worst, they exacerbate the lack of accountability.

Further, although there are companies that have voluntarily complied with international reporting standards such as the GRI-G4,[83] which are far more demanding, the point is that companies can still opt to disclose under the disclosure requirements in BRR and can thus get away with poor disclosure because of the poorly drafted requirements.

b   CSR 2 Per Cent Expenditure Requirement   Under s 135 of the Indian Companies Act 2013, the boards of companies of certain net worth or turnover[84] are required, with effect from 2015, to form a CSR committee. This committee needs to have at least three directors, of which at least one must be an independent director. The CSR committee is required to (a) formulate and recommend to the board a CSR policy that has to indicate the activities to be undertaken by the company as specified in the statute;[85] (b) recommend the amount of expenditure to be incurred on the activities referred to in clause (a); and (c) monitor the CSR policy of the company from time to time. The board has to approve the CSR policy for the company, to disclose the policy in its annual report and on its website and to ensure that the activities included in the CSR policy are undertaken by the company. Remarkably, the board is required to ensure that the company spends, in every financial year, at least 2 per cent of the average net profits of the company made during the three immediately preceding financial years, in pursuance of its CSR

---

[83] Global Reporting Initiative (GRI), G4 Sustainability Reporting Guidelines www2.globalreporting.org/standards/g4/Pages/default.aspx.

[84] The Act applies to every company having net worth of rupees five hundred crore or more, or turnover of rupees one thousand crore or more, or a net profit of rupees five crore or more during any financial year.

[85] Schedule VII of the Companies Act lists out the activities that the CSR policy may include, namely, 'eradicating extreme hunger and poverty; promotion of education; promoting gender equality and empowering women; reducing child mortality and improving maternal health; combating human immunodeficiency virus, acquired immune deficiency syndrome, malaria and other diseases; ensuring environmental sustainability; employment enhancing vocational skills; social business projects; contribution to the Prime Minister's National Relief Fund or any other fund set-up by the central government or the state governments for socio-economic development and relief, and funds for the welfare of the scheduled castes and Tribes, other backward classes, minorities and women; and any other matters prescribed by the legislation'.

policy, and should the company fail to spend such amount, the board is required to give reasons for not spending the amount in its annual report. In short, the 2 per cent spending requirement is subject to the comply or explain mechanism. Importantly, under s 450 of the Companies Act 2013, the company and every officer can be fined up to 10,000 rupees for failing to comply with s 135.

Trenchant criticisms have been made of s 135.[86] First, it has been said that it does not promote sustainability that is integrated into the company's key decision-making process or linked to the board's risk assessment of its key business operations, but, rather, it seems like a corporate philanthropic activity. For example, a petroleum company will have complied with s 135 if it has a policy and practice of donating cash amounting to 2 per cent of its net profits to a charitable organisation that seeks to reduce child mortality and improve maternal health (provided that this donation is not on a one-off basis, as one-off events are not counted). This is despite the fact that the most pressing sustainability issue facing the company is environmental pollution. Unsurprisingly, a study of forty-five Indian companies from 2016–7 found that their CSR disclosures are rhetorical and standard descriptions that are not linked to their specific business operations.[87] This is unfortunate given that different businesses have different social, environmental and economic impacts on societies. The CSR policies of companies were also found to contain boilerplate language related to the positive impact of their CSR actions and 'shared values', although the needs of the communities within which the companies operate are different.[88]

But it may be argued that the purpose of s 135 is not to promote sustainability. Rather, to promote sustainability, one has to turn to the BRRs. However, I have shown that the BRR provides wholly inadequate information for any meaningful evaluation to be carried out.

---

[86] Arjya Majumbar, 'India's Journey with Corporate Social Responsibility: What Next?' (2015) 33 *Law and Commerce* 165; Sandeep Gopalan and Akshaya Kamalnath, 'Mandatory Corporate Social Responsibility as a Vehicle for Reducing Equality: An Indian Solution for Piketty and the Millennials' (2015) 10 *Northwestern Journal of International Law and Business* 34; Afra Afsharipour and Shruti Rana, 'The Emergence of New Corporate Social Responsibility Regimes in China and India' (2014) 14 *UC Davis Business Law Journal* 175; Afra Afsharipour, 'Corporate Social Responsibility and the Corporate Board: Assessing the Indian Experiment' in Jean J du Plessis, Umakanth Varottil and Jeroen Veldman (eds), *Globalisation of Corporate Social Responsibility and Its Impact on Corporate Governance* (Springer 2018) at 109–15.

[87] Shyam Singh, Nathalie Holvoet and Vivek Pandey, 'Bridging Sustainability and Corporate Social Responsibility: Culture of Monitoring and Evaluation of CSR Initiatives in India' (2018) 10 *Sustainability* 1 at 13–14.

[88] Ibid.

A valid criticism would be that there is no clear connection between, on the one hand, the CSR policy and the 2 per cent spending requirement and, on the other hand, the BRR. No consideration is given to the question of whether the CSR policy and expenditure requirement under s 135 are consistent, conflict or overlap with the policy stated in the BRRs; nor is consideration given to the goals of s 135 and the BRRs.

The second criticism is that, although Indian companies have business activities abroad, and even if the most serious challenge to sustainability faced by the companies stems from their overseas operations (including but not limited to supply chain abuses), the 2 per cent requirement applies only to expenses incurred in India and not overseas.[89] The consequence is that companies will focus on CSR pertaining to only domestic activities and are likely to interpret s 135 to refer to only philanthropic initiatives.

Third, it has also been said that s 135 may give rise to fraudulent activities as companies can channel money to fraudulent charitable organisations which in turn can transfer most of the money back to them.

Fourth, a study that focused only on central public sector undertakings (PSUs) found that 47 out of 110 of them could not comply with the 2 per cent expenditure guideline issued by the Department of Public Enterprises in 2010, from which the 2 per cent requirement in the Companies Act was derived.[90]

Fifth, s 135 merely requires the CSR policies to have connections with the philanthropic activities listed in Schedule VII but does not require companies to set forth any strategies for implementing them. As a result, most of the CSR policies rarely exceed six pages, the majority consisting of two to three pages.[91] A recent study of the sustainability disclosures of the central PSUs found that there was a low level of disclosure.

---

[89] Ministry of Corporate Affairs, FAQ on CSR Cell www.mca.gov.in/MinistryV2/faq+on+csr+cell.html.

[90] Monika Kansal, Mahesh Joshi, Shekar Babu and Sharad Sharma, 'Reporting of Corporate Social Responsibility in Central Public Social Enterprises: A Study of Post Mandatory Regime in India' (2018) 151 *Journal of Business Ethics* 813 at 827.

[91] Shyam Singh, Nathalie Holvoet and Vivek Pandey, 'Bridging Sustainability and Corporate Social Responsibility: Culture of Monitoring and Evaluation of CSR Initiatives in India' (2018) 10 *Sustainability* 1 at 15.

Finally, there are no criteria for evaluating the adequacy or appropriateness of the explanation given for not complying with the 2 per cent spending requirement, let alone any third-party verification or audit.

Despite these criticisms, a positive aspect of s 135 is that enforcement measures have been taken against companies by the MCA, which asserted that '[i]n 221 number of cases, prosecutions have been sanctioned against companies and its officer in default for the financial year 2014–15 for violation relating to CSR. Further, penal action is taken wherever misuse of CSR funds stands confirmed against any company.'[92] The problem with this statement is that the government fails to specify the violations that have been committed by the companies; for example, it is not clear if the violation relates to the failure to comply with the 2 per cent spending requirement, to the failure to form a CSR committee or to the failure to disclose a CSR policy.

II Qualitative Evaluation of Sustainability Reports

There are two principal types of research that have been conducted with respect to the sustainability disclosures in the four Asian jurisdictions. The first type examines the effect of corporate characteristics (such as firm size, industry sector, size of board, percentage of independent directors and level of government ownership) on sustainability disclosures, and the second investigates the extent and quality of disclosures. Note that both types of research were carried out prior to the listing rules regulating sustainability reporting in Singapore, Hong Kong and Malaysia came into effect. After summarising the findings in these two types of research, I will provide a qualitative assessment of the sustainability disclosures of the top fifty listed companies in Singapore, Hong Kong, Malaysia and India.

A Effect of Corporate Characteristics

1 Singapore

Regarding the first type of research, a 2018 empirical study of 462 companies listed on the Singapore Exchange as of 30 June 2016 found that there was a correlation between the likelihood and quality of sustainability disclosures and the number of directors, the number of board

---

[92] Government of India, Ministry of Corporate Affairs, Lok Sabha, Unstarred Question No. 4791 (23 March 2018) http://mca.gov.in/Ministry/pdf/lu4791_26032018.pdf.

meetings and the proportion of independent directors.[93] It concluded that if companies wish to improve their sustainability, they should increase the number of directors and board meetings and the proportion of independent directors.[94] However, a 2003 study of 158 companies in Singapore found that an increase in the number of outside directors led to a reduction in sustainability disclosures; the authors suggested that this is because these directors were appointed by the controlling shareholders to represent their interests and were able to acquire the necessary information from the controllers.[95] By contrast, a 2000 study showed that more outside directors correlated with higher disclosures because these directors are less aligned with management and encouraged companies to disclose more information to outside investors.[96]

The 2003 study found that government ownership of companies correlates with more sustainability disclosures.[97] The authors gave three reasons for this. First, the directors who are appointed by the controlling shareholder, ie the government, have to act consistently with the wishes of the controller. Second, GLCs are subject to more pressure from stakeholders. And tied to the second reason is the final one: the government uses the sustainability disclosures to maintain and defend its legitimacy.

2 Malaysia

A study of eighty-five listed companies in Malaysia from 2006 to 2009 suggested that there was likely to be a significant and positive association between the size of the board and the extent and quality of disclosures in 2009 after the revised Code of Corporate Governance came into effect in 2007.[98] However, this study showed no correlation between independent

---

[93] Meibo Hu and Lawrence Loh, 'Board Governance and Sustainability Disclosure: A Cross-Sectional Study of Singapore-Listed Companies' (2018) 10 *Sustainability* 1.

[94] Ibid at 11.

[95] LL Eng and YT Mak, 'Corporate Governance and Voluntary Disclosure' (2003) 22 *Journal of Accounting and Public Policy* 325 at 336.

[96] Ibid at 331; Charles JP Chen and Bikki Jaggi, 'Association between Independent Non-executive Directors, Family Control and Financial Disclosures in Hong Kong' (2000) 19 *Journal of Accounting and Public Policy* 285.

[97] LL Eng and YT Mak, 'Corporate Governance and Voluntary Disclosure' (2003) 22 Journal of Accounting and Public Policy 325 at 336; Shayuti Mohamed Adnan, Chris J van Staden and David Hay, 'The Legitimacy of Institutional Theory: The Case of CSR Reporting in Cross-Cultural Settings' (18 September 2014) https://papers.ssrn.com/sol3/papers.cfm?abstract_id=2498257.

[98] Abdifatah Ahmed Haji, 'Corporate Social Responsibility Disclosures Over Time: Evidence from Malaysia' (2013) 28 *Managerial Auditing Journal* 647.

directors and sustainability disclosure (unlike the 2018 study of the Singapore companies discussed earlier).[99] With respect to government ownership, the study found that there was a positive but marginally significant association between that factor and the extent and quality of sustainability disclosures in 2006 but that there was no correlation in 2009.[100] However, there are two other studies that showed clear evidence of government ownership affecting the level of sustainability disclosures, as GLCs produce more disclosures than non-GLCs.[101] Another study found that a higher number of independent directors in GLCs correlated with fewer disclosures in these companies because it was suggested that the independent directors were not primarily concerned with CSR activities and were more concerned with financial performance.[102] However, that same study found that there was a positive correlation between a larger board size and greater CSR disclosure as more directors might lead to more discussions on CSR and hence more disclosure.[103]

3 India

A study of the sustainability disclosures of 200 companies ranked among the top 500 companies in India based on revenue and profitability[104] found that SOEs demonstrated better quality of disclosures (based on compliance with Global Reporting Initiative (GRI-G4) guidelines) than non-SOEs.[105] The authors also found that companies with better financial performance (ie the top 100 companies among the 500) produced higher quality disclosures.[106] They explained this finding on the basis that such companies are subject to greater scrutiny from stakeholders and the media, and they are expected to contribute more to sustainability in view

---

[99] Ibid at 669.
[100] Ibid at 667.
[101] NA Mohamed Ghazali, 'Ownership Structure and Corporate Social Responsibility Disclosure: Some Malaysian Evidence' (2007) 7 *Corporate Governance* 251; A Amran and SS Devi, 'The Impact of Government and Foreign Affiliate Influence on Corporate Social Reporting: The Case of Malaysia' (2008) 23 *Managerial Auditing Journal* 386.
[102] Elinda Esa and Nazli Anum Mohd Ghazali, 'Corporate Social Responsibility and Corporate Governance in Malaysian Government-Linked Companies' (2012) 12 *Corporate Governance* 292 at 300.
[103] Ibid at 299–300.
[104] Rajul Jain and Lawrence H Winner, 'CSR and Sustainability Reporting Practices of Top Companies in India' (2016) 21 *Corporate Communications: An International Journal* 36.
[105] Ibid at 49.
[106] Ibid.

of their financial performance.[107] They also explained the better disclosure levels of SOEs (as compared to non-SOEs) on that basis.[108]

B Extent and Quality of Disclosures

1 Singapore and Malaysia

Regarding the second type of research, there is an empirical study of the level of sustainability disclosures of the top 100 listed companies in Indonesia, Malaysia, Thailand and Singapore as of March 2015.[109] The authors relied on the framework provided by the Global Report Initiative (GRI-G4) Guidelines, which provided twenty-three criteria (categorised under 'Governance', 'Economic', 'Environmental' and 'Social') for disclosing and evaluating sustainability information.[110] The extent of disclosure was determined by assigning scores ranging from one to five for each criterion. One point was awarded if no information was provided, whereas five points were awarded if qualitative and quantitative information was disclosed. For example, the lowest score possible would be four points (ie one point for 'Governance', one point for 'Economic', one point for 'Environmental' and one point for 'Social') and the highest twenty points (ie five points for each of the four categories). These scores were then converted to a scale of 100. It was found that the overall level of disclosure in the four countries was 56.8 (Thailand), 48.8 (Singapore), 48.4 (Indonesia) and 47.7 (Malaysia).[111] It was also found that there was a higher level of disclosures by SOEs in each of the four countries than non-SOEs. For example, in Malaysia, the score for SOEs was 49.8 as compared to 46.5 for non-SOEs, and in Singapore, the score was 59.4 for SOEs and 45.2 for non-SOEs.[112] Another interesting finding made by the report is that a low percentage of companies explained the process and basis for selecting the material ESG factors: 85 per cent and 67.6 per cent of companies in Malaysia and Singapore did not disclose, respectively.[113]

---

[107] Ibid at 51.
[108] Ibid.
[109] Lawrence Loh, Nguyen Thi Phuong, Isabel Sim, Thomas Thomas and Wang Yu, 'Sustainability Reporting in ASEAN: State of Progress in Indonesia, Malaysia, Singapore and Thailand' (2015).
[110] Ibid at 7–8.
[111] Ibid at 4.
[112] Ibid at 14.
[113] Ibid at 16.

Another empirical study investigated the extent and quality of sustainability disclosures of eighty-five listed companies in Malaysia from 2006 to 2009.[114] The authors constructed a checklist containing twenty-three items (related to employee training and welfare, product safety, environmental protection and other philanthropic activities).[115] These items were drawn from the existing literature and the annual reports of Malaysian companies that have won reporting awards. To assess the extent of disclosure, the authors awarded one if information was disclosed but zero if not. To evaluate the quality of disclosure, the authors gave a zero if the information was provided, one if qualitative or general information was provided, two if quantitative or monetary information was given and three if both qualitative and quantitative information was provided.[116] The authors found that there was a 'significant increase in both the extent and quality of CSR disclosures'[117] as a result of developments such as the issuance of new sustainability regulations, foreign direct investments, the government's introduction of the CSR award and, in particular, the global financial crisis. It was also found that there was a positive, albeit marginally significant, association between government ownership and the extent and quality of disclosure in 2007, but no association was found in 2009.[118] That said, the authors concluded that, overall, the extent and quality of disclosure were, on average, low.[119]

2   India

There is also a recent study of the level and quality of CSR disclosures by all the central public sector enterprises (CPSEs) in India as of 31 March 2012.[120] The authors constructed an index of 111 disclosure items (categorised into community development; human resources; product safety and innovation; environment; energy; and carbon/GHG emissions) based on previous indices and their understanding of items of social importance.[121] They used a five-point rating scale to measure the

---

[114] Abdifatah Ahmed Haji, 'Corporate Social Responsibility Disclosures Over Time: Evidence from Malaysia' (2013) 28 *Managerial Auditing Journal* 647.
[115] Ibid at 659–60.
[116] Ibid at 660–1.
[117] Ibid at 669.
[118] Ibid.
[119] Ibid.
[120] Monika Kansal, Mahesh Joshi, Shekar Babu and Sharad Sharma, 'Reporting of Corporate Social Responsibility in Central Public Sector Enterprises: A Study of Post Mandatory Regime in India' (2018) 151 *Journal of Business Ethics* 813.
[121] Ibid at 817–22.

quality (ie narrative, qualitative and monetary) of the disclosures for each of the 111 items.[122] They concluded that the level of disclosure was low, although companies produced disclosures for most of the 111 items.[123] In addition, the study found that more disclosure was made under the categories of community development and human resources than the environment.[124] Regarding the quality of disclosure, the authors expressed disappointment at the fact that, although CPSEs play a crucial role in India, 'the overall disclosures are low and mainly narrative'.[125]

3 Hong Kong

The SEHK conducted an analysis of the environment, social and governance disclosures of 400 randomly selected companies across different industries with financial year end dated 31 December 2016, 31 March 2017 and 30 June 2017.[126] The environmental factor consisted of three aspects[127] and the social factor consisted of eight aspects.[128] The analysis did not include the governance factor as it was classified under the corporate governance code and assessed separately. The report found that out of these eleven aspects, 38 per cent of companies complied with all of them, 80 per cent complied with at least nine of them and 94 per cent complied with at least seven of them.[129] By compliance, the report meant whether the company disclosed any statements under the eleven aspects; it did not refer to the quality of disclosure.[130] However, where the disclosure was vague or partial, the report stated that it classified the disclosure as non-compliant.[131] Regarding the quality of disclosure, the report did not provide any quantitative evaluation such as

---

[122] Ibid at 819–22.
[123] Ibid at 825.
[124] Ibid.
[125] Ibid at 826.
[126] HKEX, Analysis of Environment, Social and Governance Practice Disclosure in 2016/7 (May 2018).
[127] Ibid para 13: Aspect A1: Emissions; Aspect A2: Use of Resources; Aspect A3: The Environment and Natural Resources.
[128] Ibid: Aspect B1: Employment; Aspect B2: Health and Safety; Aspect B3: Development and Training; Aspect B4: Labour Standards; Aspect B5: Supply Chain Management; Aspect B6: Product Responsibility; Aspect B7: Anti-corruption; Aspect B8: Community Investment.
[129] Ibid at 5.
[130] An implicit distinction between level of compliance and quality of disclosure is drawn in para 5.
[131] Ibid para 56.

by ranking the companies or by providing examples of what the SEHK considered to be high- or low-quality disclosures. Nor did the report provide any criteria for assessing the quality of the disclosure. Rather, the report noted that, on one end of the spectrum, there was excellent reporting: considered explanations were given for the failure to comply; there was comprehensive description of policies; and there was materiality assessment.[132] But, on the other end of the spectrum, the report noted that a box-ticking approach was adopted, examples of which include disclosure of short and simple statements and lack of disclosure of the basis on which the material aspects of the factors were identified.[133]

C   Qualitative Evaluation of the Sustainability Reports in Common Law Asia

An evaluation of the quality of the sustainability reports of the top 50 listed companies in each of the four jurisdictions in Asia, ie Singapore, Malaysia, Hong Kong and India, a total of 200 reports, has to take into account at least four limitations. First, the reporting rules in each of the four jurisdictions are different. This makes it difficult to compare the quality of the sustainability reports in one jurisdiction with another.

Second, jurisdictions such as Malaysia[134] and Hong Kong[135] permit companies to opt out of the stock exchange reporting rules if they choose to comply with other internationally recognised reporting standards such as those set out by the Global Reporting Initiative. This makes it difficult to compare the quality of the disclosures of companies even within the same jurisdiction, given that some companies have chosen to comply with the GRI-G4 Guidelines[136] whereas others have chosen to adhere to the reporting requirements set out by the stock exchange. Further, while the SEHK states that the issuer may adopt international ESG reporting guidance provided that it includes comparable disclosure provisions to the comply or explain provisions stated in the listing rules, the SEHK does not provide any guidelines as to what a comparable disclosure is.

---

[132] Ibid para 5.
[133] Ibid para 6.
[134] Bursa Malaysia LR, Practice Note 9 para 6.4.
[135] HKEX LR, Appendix 27, Environmental, Social and Governance Reporting Guide para 7.
[136] Note that the GRI-G4 Guidelines have been recently superseded by the GRI Sustainability Reporting Standards (GRI Standards) www2.globalreporting.org/standards/g4/Pages/default.aspx.

Moreover, given that the GRI-G4 Guidelines do not have a comply or explain mechanism, unlike Hong Kong, should companies decide to report according to the GRI-G4 Guidelines, they can cherry-pick which of the indicators under which of the ESG factors to disclose.

Third, because the top fifty companies in each of the four jurisdictions span many different industries, the differences in the business strategies and practices will result in different emphasis in the reports. This makes it difficult to conduct a meaningful comparison of companies of different industries because investors will give greater weight to certain disclosures in certain companies. For example, investors will arguably pay more attention to the environmental disclosures of an oil and gas company. But in a manufacturing company, investors are likely to put more emphasis on product safety.

The final limitation concerns the methodology. Different methodologies have been deployed by researchers in different countries to evaluate the extent and quality of sustainability disclosures. There is neither consistency nor uniformity. This is evident in the different methodologies used to assess the extent and quality of disclosures in the studies described earlier concerning Singapore, Malaysia and India.

More importantly, a significant difficulty with these methodologies is that they are not nuanced or granulated and hence fail to distinguish disclosures that are of good quality from those that are bad. For example, in one study (which includes companies in Malaysia and Singapore), zero points were awarded if no information was disclosed, one point if qualitative descriptions were provided, two if quantitative information was disclosed and three if there was both qualitative and quantitative information.[137] A slightly more fine-grained methodology is used in the Indian study mentioned above: zero points if the sustainability items were not disclosed; one point if one or less than one sentence was disclosed; two points if more than one sentence was disclosed; three points if one quantitative figure was provided; four points if the disclosure was 'non-monetary' and comprised more than one figure; and five points if the information was provided in monetary terms.[138] However, the methodology in these two studies does not provide any guidance or

---

[137] Lawrence Loh, Nguyen Thi Phuong, Isabel Sim, Thomas Thomas and Wang Yu, 'Sustainability Reporting in ASEAN: State of Progress in Indonesia, Malaysia, Singapore and Thailand' (2015) at 7.

[138] Monika Kansal, Mahesh Joshi, Shekar Babu and Sharad Sharma, 'Reporting of Corporate Social Responsibility in Central Public Social Enterprises: A Study of Post Mandatory Regime in India' (2018) 151 *Journal of Business Ethics* 813.

criteria as to what a good qualitative or quantitative disclosure is. This may be because the researchers wished to avoid injecting an element of subjectivity into the methodology. This may be defensible, but, as a result, their research is not able to provide any information beyond whether qualitative and/or quantitative information was provided. For example, with respect to the sustainability reports issued by the companies in Singapore and Malaysia, readers will not be able to know whether the company explained the basis and process in their selection of material ESG factors. Further, even if quantitative information was provided in terms of the targets that they have set for the material ESG factors, there is no assessment of how the targets were arrived at.

I have attempted to formulate a tentative, preliminary framework to analyse the quality of the sustainability reports for the financial year ending December 2017 of the top 50 listed companies in each of Singapore, Malaysia, Hong Kong and India (a total of 200 reports). These sustainability reports are published by the companies either as a standalone report, as part of their annual reports or on their website, for the purposes of complying with the stock exchange listing rules (as is the case of Singapore, Hong Kong and Malaysia) or the rules set out by SEBI (as is the case in India). This framework will not address all four limitations satisfactorily, but it does seek to minimise them. Instead of providing a numerical figure for the disclosure like the earlier mentioned studies, I have endeavoured to provide three suggested sets of guidelines that can facilitate the evaluation of the quality of the disclosures. The first two sets of guidelines should be applicable to all the companies in all four jurisdictions and the third set applies only to listed companies in Singapore and Malaysia. It is suggested that these guidelines are considerations that a reasonable investor or stakeholder would regard as material in assessing the quality of the sustainability disclosures.

First, a distinction is drawn between in-depth and shallow disclosure. Any assertions made in the report must be supported by clear evidence. It is necessary but insufficient that companies disclose the actions they have taken in the past or the actions they plan to carry out; they should also provide the justifications for those actions and clearly explain with sufficient detail how they intend to carry them out. Attention will be paid to how the disclosure is connected to the risks and challenges faced by the companies. This is important because a common criticism of the disclosures provided by the companies is that they do not demonstrate the relationship between the disclosures and the impacts of the company's business and operations on society. Further, in-depth disclosure goes beyond qualitative information to include concrete, quantitative information in the form of data that support the qualitative information.

Second, there should be a time frame for comparison. This means that companies should provide data from previous years, as well as roadmaps or future milestones that they have set for themselves. This allows stakeholders to hold the companies accountable and provides a basis for stakeholders to judge the progress made by the companies.

Third and finally, given that the listing rules provide considerable discretion to the companies to decide which ESG (in Singapore) or EES (in Malaysia) issues are material to the companies, it is important for stakeholders to know why and how they have been selected.

Before applying these three sets of guidelines to the companies, I placed the top fifty companies in each of the four jurisdictions into seven industries: telecommunication, information technology and internet services; natural resources, energy, oil and gas; industrial services and consumer services; investments and diversified conglomerates; manufacturing and consumer products; property development and management; and financial institutions. Understanding the industry to which the companies belong will tell us what sorts of disclosure are likely to be more important to those companies. This in turn will enable us to better understand what amounts to a deep or shallow disclosure for companies that belong to certain industries.

Appendix 2 lists out the top fifty companies in each of Hong Kong, Singapore, Malaysia and India by market capitalisation. Appendix 3 categorises them under seven industries, ranks them based on the quality of their sustainability disclosures and provides brief reasons for the ranking.

1 Hong Kong

The key findings for each of the four jurisdictions are as follows. Regarding Hong Kong, there are thirteen SOEs and thirty-seven non-SOEs. All thirteen SOEs issued sustainability reports. As for the thirty-seven non-SOEs, only one has not issued a report and one has issued a report but in Chinese. Thus, only the reports of forty-eight listed companies have been reviewed. Applying the guidelines described earlier, five out of the thirteen SOEs (38 per cent) have fallen short of quality disclosures in the following ways. First, no quantitative information with regard to the environment is provided. For example, because two of these

11 QUALITATIVE EVALUATION OF SUSTAINABILITY REPORTS 93

SOEs belong to the oil and gas companies, careful attention is paid to their environmental disclosures, specifically their compliance with the KPIs under the environmental factor.[139] With regard to the KPI to disclose total hazardous and non-hazardous wastes and the KPI to disclose greenhouse gas production, these SOEs disclosed no data; instead, terse and vague statements to the effect that they are attempting to implement the applicable environmental regulations are made. Second, either no, little or uninformative quantitative information is provided with regard to labour and employment.[140] Third, the disclosures do not demonstrate how they are connected to the risks and challenges to the company. For example, one SOE[141] has extensive reports on its charitable endeavours, but it does not show how these initiatives address the impacts that its business and operations have on society. Finally, there is no comparison of the future data with the past data (ie no time frame for comparison), thus making it difficult for investors to evaluate the progress that the company has made. For example, although one SOE[142] disclosed both qualitative and quantitative information with regard to the environment and social KPIs, no yearly comparisons of the data are made.

With regard to the thirty-five non-SOEs (that produced English language sustainability reports), thirteen have poor-quality disclosures (37 per cent). Among those thirteen non-SOEs, one belongs to the telecommunications/internet service industry; three are energy, oil and gas companies; one is an investment company; three are manufacturing/consumer product companies; two are real estate companies; one is a pharmaceutical company; and two are financial institutions. The main problems with their disclosures are these. First, either no or inadequate qualitative or quantitative explanations are provided with regard to the environment, as well as employment and labour. For example, regarding the three oil and gas companies, a common problem is that environmental data are absent from the report. In one real estate company, no data are provided for the environment and social factors.[143] The second key problem is that there is often disclosure of the policies and compliance with applicable regulations, but there is no or little disclosure of the reasons for these policies and practices; nor is there

---

[139] Sinopec Corp and Petrochina: Appendix 3.
[140] See for example the disclosures in CITIC and ICBC in Appendix 3.
[141] Bank of China: Appendix 3.
[142] BOC Hong Kong: Appendix 3.
[143] Wharf REIC: Appendix 3.

explanation of the process according to which these policies and practices were developed or of how these policies are implemented. Examples include the three manufacturing/consumer product companies as well as one of the financial institutions.[144]

Three important points emerge from the analysis of the sustainability reports. First, applying the guidelines described earlier, given that 38 per cent of the SOEs have poor disclosures as compared to 37 per cent of non-SOEs, there is a slightly greater proportion of SOEs that have poor-quality disclosures. Second, a serious and common problem with the disclosures of both SOEs and non-SOEs is the lack of quantitative information in terms of no data being provided. Finally, and this is important, seventeen out of the forty-eight companies (35.4 per cent) do not even provide any explanations for failing to comply with the two or more environmental indicators. This is despite the fact that the listing rules apply the comply or explain mechanism only to the environmental factor (and its KPIs) but not to the social factor (or its KPIs). Out of the seventeen companies that provided no explanation, four are SOEs (23.5 per cent). And as for those companies that did provide explanations, they are of a boilerplate kind that is uninformative. For example, one company[145] explained its failure to disclose any information on hazardous wastes production by stating that it is a massive entity that has businesses covering a large geographic region. Another company[146] stated that it is presently working on identifying and assessing solid waste and could not calculate data on hazardous and non-hazardous waste production.

2 Singapore

Only forty-four out of the fifty listed companies in Singapore have issued sustainability reports. Further, one company has not issued a sustainability report in accordance with the Singapore Exchange listing rules but has instead issued a report according to the SEHK listing rules.[147] Thus, only the reports of forty-three companies will be analysed. Out of these forty-three companies, twenty-four are non-SOEs and nineteen are SOEs. Applying the suggested guidelines, one remarkable feature of the sustainability reports of the nineteen SOEs is that all the reports save for three produced in-depth disclosure in the sense that the reasons

---

[144] Standard Chartered: Appendix 3.
[145] China Unicom: Appendix 3.
[146] Sinopec Corp: Appendix 3.
[147] Fortune REIT.

and process for selecting the material ESG factors were disclosed and backed up with clear quantitative information. Further, time frames for comparison were also included that set out the targets to be achieved. In short, 84.2 per cent of the SOEs published high-quality sustainability reports. However, one SOE failed to disclose the reasons and process for selecting the material ESG factors and failed to provide any explanation.[148] The environmental data of one SOE[149] were sparse, although it disclosed the reasons and process for selecting its material ESG factors in a comprehensive and detailed manner. As for the third SOE,[150] the environmental data were not comprehensive, no time frame for comparison was disclosed, and the data on employee turnover and training were missing.

Regarding the twenty-four non-SOEs, eight (33.3 per cent) produced reports that fell short of the guidelines in the proposed framework and the listing rules. The three most common problems were that there were no time frames for comparison,[151] quantifiable targets for the purpose of achieving the objectives were missing[152] and the disclosures related to the environment and social factors were very sparse.[153]

Two important points emerge from the analysis. First, the sustainability reports of the SOEs in Singapore are of a higher quality than those of the non-SOEs because only 15.8 per cent of the reports of SOEs are of poor quality as compared to 33.3 per cent of the reports of non-SOEs. Second, thirty-five out of forty-three companies did not comply with one or more of the components stipulated by the listing rules and thirty-four of these companies provided no explanation whatsoever. The most common component not complied with was the requirement to select a sustainability reporting framework and to disclose the reasons for choosing this framework. All thirty-four of the companies that did not comply with this component did not provide any explanation. Of these thirty-four companies, sixteen are SOEs (47 per cent).

---

[148] Singapore Technologies Engineering: Appendix 3.
[149] SIA Engineering Company: Appendix 3.
[150] Mapletree Commercial Trust: Appendix 3.
[151] See for example the disclosure by Hutchinson Port Holding Trust, and Jardine Cycle and Carriage in Appendix 3.
[152] See for example the disclosure by Hutchinson Port Holding Trust, Jardine Cycle and Carriage, Haw Par Corporation, Venture Corporation, Yanlord Land Group, and United Overseas Bank in Appendix 3.
[153] See for example the disclosure by Haw Par Corporation, Venture Corporation and Yanlord Land Group in Appendix 3.

3 Malaysia

Out of the top fifty listed companies, thirty-one published sustainability reports based on the GRI-G4 standards. As a result, evaluation was carried out only in respect of the nineteen companies that published their reports based on the Bursa Malaysia listing rules. Out of these nineteen companies, six are SOEs and thirteen non-SOEs. The main problem with the sustainability reports of the SOEs was insufficient depth, specifically, inadequate disclosure on how the material sustainability matters were identified.[154] The other problem was that key issues were not disclosed or were disclosed inadequately. For example, one SOE[155] that specialises in real estate did not disclose data on occupational safety (namely, fatality and injury rates), although that would be of concern to a reasonable investor; moreover, disclosure on the environmental impact was sparse.

As for the non-SOEs, the most widespread problem was insufficient depth in the disclosure, specifically, inadequate disclosure on how the material sustainability matters were identified.[156] Another issue was the failure to explain how the sustainability materials that were identified by the company were connected to the impact of the company's business operations.[157]

4 India

Recall that SEBI has created a framework that requires companies to disclose their sustainability practices only in binary terms. Companies merely need to answer yes/no to a list of superficial queries relating to nine sustainability principles. As such, it is difficult to evaluate the quality of disclosures. Nevertheless, companies are given the opportunity to elaborate their answers under Annex 1 to Section E, 'Principle-wise performance'. I have focused on the elaborations given by the top fifty companies in response to Principle 2,[158] Principle 3[159] and Principle 6[160] because most of the elaborations are given in response to these principles,

---

[154] See for example the disclosure by Dialog Group and Sime Darby Property in Appendix 3.
[155] SP Setia: Appendix 3.
[156] See for example the reports by Inari Amertron, Top Glove Corporation, Hartalega Holdings, QL Resources and Press Metal Aluminium Holdings in Appendix 3.
[157] See for example Public Bank: Appendix 3.
[158] Businesses should provide goods and services that are safe and contribute to sustainability throughout their life cycle.
[159] Businesses should promote the well-being of all employees.
[160] Business should respect, protect, and make efforts to restore the environment.

thus, comparing the responses of the top fifty companies allows us to evaluate the quality of disclosures provided by the companies. Among the fifty companies, eight are SOEs and the rest non-SOEs. Of these eight SOEs, one did not use the BRR reporting format but instead the GRI-G4. Out of the seven SOEs that reported using BRR, one provided barebones answers to Principles 2, 3 and 6,[161] and another provided no additional data or qualitative disclosure under Principles 3 and 6.[162] The other five SOEs did provide additional data or qualitative disclosure with respect to at least two principles. As for the forty-two non-SOEs, five relied on GRI-G4. Regarding the other thirty-seven non-SOEs that used the BRR format, eighteen did not provide any additional data or qualitative disclosure with respect to at least two principles. Thus, close to half of the disclosures by non-SOEs are unsatisfactory.

III Suggested Reforms

A Oversight Mechanism

The sustainability reporting rules in Singapore, Hong Kong, Malaysia and India suffer from two common afflictions: the rules do not provide for any oversight, verification or assessment of the disclosures made by the companies; nor do the rules impose sanctions for failure to adhere to them (whether they are in the form of comply or explain or mandatory), with the exception of s 135 of the Indian Companies Act whereby the company and every officer in default may be fined. The reporting rules are designed in such a way that the onus is placed primarily on the company's stakeholders, principally the shareholders, to hold the companies accountable should they fail to comply with the rules.

As a result, commentators have proposed oversight mechanisms such as having a regulatory body to evaluate the explanations provided by companies (where the rules are of comply or explain) and to assess whether companies have complied with the rules (where they are mandatory). For example, the securities commission or stock exchange could assume the role of monitoring disclosures and imposing sanctions for violations. Other commentators have suggested that private, independent bodies should monitor instead. For example, companies should be required to seek assurance for their disclosures from audit firms.

---

[161] Oil and Natural Gas Corporation: Appendix 3.
[162] SEI Life Insurance Company: Appendix 3.

However, there is a key problem with these proposals that has been overlooked by the commentators, namely conflicts of interest. Where the regulator is the government (for example, the securities commission) there will be a conflict of interest because the SOEs' controlling shareholder is also the government. Although the government is not a unitary entity and it consists of different departments with different objectives and strategies, it is open to doubt whether the government as the regulator will apply the same standards to both SOEs and non-SOEs. To address this concern, it may be argued that the stock exchange, which is a non-governmental body, should assess whether companies have complied with the listing rules. However, the risk of conflicts of interest remains. This is because the SOEs hold significant shares in the stock exchanges of India[163] and Malaysia.[164] As a result, the government as the controller of the SOEs may exert pressure on the stock exchange. Regarding the SEHK, there is still the risk of conflicts of interest because the government has the right to appoint eight directors in the SEHK,[165] and these directors can exert influence over SEHK's policies and practices of monitoring companies for their disclosures. In any event, even if the SOEs do not own shares in the stock exchange and even if the government does not have the right to appoint the exchange's directors, the government is still responsible for regulating the stock exchange. Thus, there is still the risk that the stock exchange may be subject to influence by the government, which may affect how it monitors the SOEs.

It may be said that the solution is to have a private body, especially an auditing firm, to provide assurance for the reports issued by the company. But based on my research of the top fifty listed companies in each of the four Asian jurisdictions, only a minority of companies have obtained assurance, and the scope of the work conducted by auditing firms is narrow and limited: it does not cover all the disclosures provided by companies such as aspirational or predictive statements; the scope covers

---

[163] The Life Insurance Corporation of India and the State Bank of India own 12.5 per cent and 5.2 per cent of the shares in the National Stock Exchange of India, respectively: National Stock Exchange of India, 26th Annual Report 2017–18 at 71 www.nseindia.com/global/content/about_us/nseannualreport26agm.pdf.

[164] Capital Market Development Fund and Kumpulan Wang Persaraan own 18.6 per cent and 13.6 per cent of the shares in Bursa Malaysia, respectively: Bursa Malaysia, Annual Report 2017 at 202 http://disclosure.bursamalaysia.com/FileAccess/apbursaweb/download?id=184701&name=EA_DS_ATTACHMENTS.

[165] Securities and Futures Ordinance (Cap 571), ss 77(1), 77(5).

only certain parts of the disclosure.[166] And the opinion issued by the auditing firm does not provide assurances on the reliability of the past data that the company disclosed. Apart from this issue, there is the risk of conflicts of interest. For example, the auditing firm engaged by the company to provide assurance for its sustainability report is also the company's auditor with respect to its financial statements. Or the auditing firm provides other services to the company (such as those related to compliance with anti-money laundering regulations, M&A, etc) or to the controlling shareholder. Given that the auditor wishes to maintain its existing business relationship with the company (or the controlling shareholder), there is the concern that the former may not issue an adverse opinion against the company. To ameliorate this concern, the regulator may require the auditing firm or the third-party vendor to be independent. There are at least three difficulties with this. First, how narrow or broad should the definition of independence be? And should there be preclusive bright line rules or standards that are subject to discretionary interpretation by the company? Second, should the entity be independent of the company, the directors and officers, and/or the controlling shareholder? Third, should the regulator disqualify any entity that is not independent from being engaged by the company or would it suffice if, although the entity did not meet the definition of independence, it had policies to show how it could manage the conflicts? These are difficult issues and do not lend themselves to easy resolution. But provided that they are carefully addressed, having an independent, third-party entity verify and assess companies' sustainability reports seems preferable to having the stock exchange, let alone a government body, monitor the disclosures.

B Sanctions

However, there is still the issue of sanctions. Even if the independent third party delivers an opinion that the company has not complied with the sustainability rules, there should be follow-up actions on the part of the stock exchange. Currently, a key problem with the sustainability reporting rules in the four common law jurisdictions is that no sanctions are imposed on companies where there is non-compliance. It is suggested that the stock exchange should adopt a wide range of disciplinary tools such as private warnings/criticisms, public reprimand, fines and, in the

---

[166] Appendix 1.

case of persistent egregious offenders, delisting. However, there is still the concern discussed earlier with regard to conflicts of interest involving the stock exchange: the stock exchange may not impose sanctions against SOEs, particularly if these SOEs are substantial shareholders of the exchange. And if the SOEs are not shareholders of the stock exchange, there is the risk that the government as the regulator of the stock exchange may exercise influence over the decision-making process of the stock exchange as to whether sanctions should be imposed, and, if so, the nature and extent. While this risk remains, it should not be overstated. This risk may be outweighed by the benefit of strict rules and robust monitoring because the stock exchange, as a profit-making entity, may wish to attract more listings.[167] After all, stringent regulatory requirements and effective enforcement by stock exchanges have been positively associated with higher share price.[168] Further, the stock exchange runs the risk of harming its reputation should it give preferential treatment to SOEs. It is plausible that on a cost–benefit analysis, the stock exchange may take the decision that the cost of not enforcing sanctions against the SOEs or positively discriminating in favour of the SOEs is not worth bearing. In sum, it is suggested that, provided the concerns and issues discussed above are satisfactorily addressed, it is advisable to have an independent non-governmental body monitor and assess the sustainability reports backed up by sanctions from the stock exchange.

However, should the regulator decide not to impose any sanctions, the question is whether directors may be held liable for breaching their duty to exercise reasonable care, skill and diligence if they fail to comply with the sustainability reporting requirements. To begin with, the board of directors has a duty to ensure that the company has put in

---

[167] See for example the stricter regulatory strategy adopted by Shenzhen Stock Exchange in order to attract more listings as compared to its rival the Shanghai Stock Exchange: Benjamin L Liebman and Curtis J Milhaupt, 'Reputational Sanctions in China's Securities Market' (2008) 108 *Columbia Law Review* 929 at 958, 978.

[168] Khaled Amira and Mark L Muzere, 'Competition among Stock Exchanges for Equity' (2011) 35 *Journal of Banking and Finance* 2355 at 2363, 2369; Andrei Shleifer and Daniel Wolfenzon, 'Investor Protection and Equity Markets' (2002) 66 *Journal of Financial Economics* 3; John C Coffee, 'Racing towards the Top: The Impact of Cross-Listing and Stock Market Competition on International Corporate Governance' (2002) 102 *Columbia Law Review* 1757; Yan-Leung Cheung, J Thomas Connelly, Piman Limpaphayom and Lynda Zhou, 'Do Investors Really Value Corporate Governance? Evidence from the Hong Kong Market' (2007) 18 *Journal of International Financial Management & Accounting* 86.

place appropriate risk management and internal control systems. And the board is also legally responsible for evaluating and determining the nature and extent of risks faced by the company. Given that sustainability reporting has a material bearing on the company's risks and challenges, the SEHK has made it clear that the board is responsible for the company's ESG risk and strategies. Bursa Malaysia has also said that evaluation and determination of material sustainability matters should be undertaken and approved by the board. In short, the board should be ultimately responsible for the company's compliance with the reporting requirements.

If that is the case, the question is whether directors may be in breach of their duty to exercise reasonable care, skill and diligence should the company breach the listing rules by failing to provide an explanation or by providing a wholly inadequate explanation insofar as it falls short of the standard of care that is expected of a reasonable director, in relation to a comply or explain regime as is the case in Hong Kong and Singapore. For example, there are three companies among the top fifty listed companies in Hong Kong that did not provide any explanation for failing to disclose information on the types of emissions and emissions data. And in the case of Malaysia, where the reporting rules are mandatory, the question is whether directors may be held liable for breaching the duty of care should they fail to comply with the rules, such as by failing to disclose one or more of the requirements stipulated in the listing rules. For example, as discussed earlier, a number of companies have failed to disclose how the material sustainability matters are identified, which is one of the requirements prescribed by the listing rules. Further, a connected issue is whether, even if companies have complied with the comply or explain or mandatory regime, they can be held liable for breaching the duty to exercise reasonable care, skill and diligence should they be found to have made false statements of fact in their sustainability reports.

It is suggested that directors should be held liable for breaching the duty of care if companies fail to provide any explanation for not complying with the rules (in Hong Kong and Singapore) or if they fail to comply with the mandatory requirements (in Malaysia and India). They should also be liable if the report contains false statements of fact. But with respect to comply or explain, the difficulty is whether the directors can be held liable if, although the company has provided explanation for its non-compliance, the explanation is inadequate or of a boilerplate nature.

The other difficulty that applies to both comply or explain and the mandatory regime is determining who is likely to bring the lawsuit against the delinquent directors. It is unlikely that the controlling shareholder, particularly in an SOE, will sue the board for breach of the duty of care. This is because, in the Chinese, Indian and Malaysian SOEs, the government is interventionist and wields significant influence over the board and it is likely that the board has sought the acquiescence of the controller prior to publishing the report. Even if there is no acquiescence, if the failure to comply or the failure to provide an explanation is attributable to wrongdoing on the part of the controller, the controller is unlikely to take action against the board because the controller's wrongdoing may be exposed. If this is the case, the onus will be on the non-controlling shareholder to bring a derivative action against the directors for breach of the duty of care. Given that any award the court may give will go to the company and not to the affected shareholders and in view of the procedural restrictions in bringing a statutory derivative action, it is questionable whether a non-controlling shareholder would bring the action. However, one cannot rule out the possibility of lawsuits or non-litigious actions taken by a non-controlling institutional shareholder if it, or it together with other institutional shareholders, owns a significant percentage of shares in the company, has the resources, intends to hold on to the shares in the company for the long term and views ESG considerations as important to its investment strategies and portfolio.

3

Board Gender Diversity

I Rationales for Female Directors   104
   A Enhances Corporate Governance   105
   B Improves Firm Value   106
   C Equality Justifications   108
      1 Equality of Outcome   110
      2 Equality of Resources and Opportunity   111
II Mechanisms to Promote Female Directors   115
   A Quota Requirement   115
   B Apply or Explain an Alternative   120
   C A Combined Approach: Monitoring Disclosure and 'Name and Shame'   124
   D Setting Targets   130
III State-Owned Enterprises   133
   A Malaysia   134
   B Singapore   135
   C India   136
   D Hong Kong   136
   E SOEs with No Female Directors   137
   F Connected to the Government   137
   G Repeat Players   139
IV Conclusion   140

It has been observed that 'between 2008 and 2015 32 countries implemented 42 boardroom diversity policies in the form of legal quotas for listed or state-owned firms (8 and 5 countries respectively), governance code amendments (26 countries) and disclosure requirements (4 countries)'.[1] India and Malaysia are classified among the countries that have quotas for listed firms. While this is true for India,[2] it is not

---

[1] Renée B Adams, 'Women on Boards: The Superheroes of Tomorrow' (2016) 27 *Leadership Quarterly* 371 at 372.

[2] Companies Act 2013, s 149(1).

technically accurate for Malaysia. Malaysia, as will be elaborated in Section II(B), requires listed companies to have a certain percentage of directors on an 'apply or explain an alternative'[3] basis. Thus, companies need not comply with this requirement if they can come up with an alternative practice. Singapore is listed under the category of countries with corporate governance codes that state that nominating committees have to consider gender diversity. As for Hong Kong, with effect from 2019, companies will be required on a comply or explain basis to disclose their diversity policies.[4] This chapter has three principal aims. First, it critically analyses the reasons for having female directors. Second, it evaluates the corporate mechanisms that have been used in these four common law Asian jurisdictions to promote board diversity. Finally, it assesses the key findings of the empirical research on the state of female directors in the four jurisdictions.

I Rationales for Female Directors

The rationales articulated by policy makers and scholars for promoting board gender diversity commonly include improvement of good corporate governance and increase in firm value. For example, the Singapore Diversity Action Committee (now known as the Council for Board Diversity), a task force set up by the government but led and managed by representatives from the public and private sector to promote board gender diversity, set out five justifications: (1) given that women bring new perspectives to the board, the board will be equipped to handle complex challenges; (2) the board decision-making process will be strengthened; (3) the board will have a better understanding of the needs of female employees, female customers and female stakeholders; (4) business outcomes will be improved (as a result of enhanced decision-making processes); and (5) investments will be increased because board gender diversity is one of the factors that investors take into account in their investment decisions.[5] The first to third reasons can be considered part of the improvement of corporate governance and the fourth and fifth the increase in firm value. Likewise, similar reasons also motivated the SEHK to require boards to disclose their diversity policies (including

---

[3] 2017 Malaysian Code on Corporate Governance para 5.2.
[4] HKEX LR, Appendix 14, Corporate Governance Code and Corporate Governance Report para L(d)(ii).
[5] Singapore's Diversity Action Committee, Women on Boards: Tackling the Issue (September 2016) at 6.

gender diversity) with effect from 2019. The SEHK said that board gender diversity is 'positively associated with the issuer's financial performance, more effective board and risk management'.[6]

A Enhances Corporate Governance

There is evidence to support the claim that female directors promote corporate governance in the sense that they improve board decision-making processes by counteracting groupthink, bringing diverse perspectives,[7] encouraging more questions to be raised,[8] improving the attendance and level of participation of male directors,[9] enhancing collegiality,[10] collaboration and engagement,[11] spending more time on preparing for board meetings,[12] raising difficult issues that may be avoided by male colleagues[13] and increasing the level of monitoring of management.[14] For example, one study found a correlation between boards with female directors and higher CEO turnover, which suggests that there is a higher level of monitoring in boards by female directors.[15]

---

[6] HKEX, Guidance for Boards and Directors (2018) para 4.6.
[7] Vicki W Kramer, Alison M Konrad and Sumru Erkut, 'Critical Mass on Corporate Boards: Why Three or More Women Enhance Governance', Wellesley Center Report (2006) at 74.
[8] Ibid.
[9] Morten Huse and Anne G Solberg, 'Gender-Related Boardroom Dynamics: How Scandinavian Women Make and Can Make Contributions on Corporate Boards' (2006) 21 *Women Management Review* 113.
[10] Diana Bilimoria, 'Building the Business Case for Women Corporate Directors' in Ronald J Burke and Mary C Mattis (eds), *Women on Corporate Boards of Directors: International Challenges and Opportunities* (Kluwer Academic Publishers 2000) at 31.
[11] Ibid.
[12] Morten Huse and Anne G Solberg, 'Gender-Related Boardroom Dynamics: How Scandinavian Women Make and Can Make Contributions on Corporate Boards' (2006) 21 *Women Management Review* 113.
[13] Nancy McIrnerney-Lacombe, Diana Bilimoria and Paul F Salipante, 'Championing the Discussion of Tough Issues: How Women Corporate Directors Contribute to Board Deliberations' in Susan Vinnicombe, Val Singh, Ronald J Burke, Diana Bilimoria and Morten Huse (eds), *Women on Corporate Boards of Directors: International Research and Practice* (Edward Elgar Publishing 2008) at 12.
[14] Amy J Hillman and Thomas Dalziel, 'Board of Directors and Firm Performance: Integrating Agency and Resource Dependence Perspectives' (2003) 28 *Academy Management Review* 383; Amy J Hillman, Albert A Cannella, Jr and Ira C Harris, 'Women and Racial Minorities in the Boardroom: How Do Directors Differ?' (2002) 28 *Journal of Management* 747.
[15] Renée B Adams and Daniel Ferreira, 'Women in the Boardroom and Their Impact on Governance and Performance' (2009) 94 *Journal of Financial Economics* 291; Miriam Schwartz-Ziv, 'Does the Gender of Directors Matter?' (2 May 2013), https://papers.ssrn.com/sol3/papers.cfm?abstract_id=2257467.

There are also studies that found that women are more risk-averse than men and hence tend to make less risky decisions.[16] This explains why commenters have hypothesised that the Lehman crisis would not have happened if it had been Lehman sisters instead of Lehman brothers.[17] However, there is also a study holding a contrary view: banks with more female directors do not pursue fewer risk-taking activities and do not have lower risks than other banks.[18] Another study concerning Norwegian boards found that female directors are better at critically questioning and providing strategic guidance to management without disrupting board dynamics.[19] Nevertheless, it has also been found that female directors may hesitate in challenging board members for fear of disrupting board cohesiveness.[20]

B   Improves Firm Value

Although there are studies that show that female directors are positively correlated with corporate performance,[21] there are more studies that are far more equivocal. For example, one study found that female directors correlate with an increase in share price because they are less overconfident than male directors and hence they overestimate merger gains less, and hence

---

[16] James P Byrnes, David C Miller and William D Schafer, 'Gender Differences in Risk Taking: A Meta-Analysis' (1999) 125 *Psychological Bulletin* 367; Rachel Croson and Uri Gneezy, 'Gender Differences in Preferences' (2009) 47 *Journal of Economic Literature* 1; Binay K Adhikari, Anup Agrawal and James Malm, 'Do Women Managers Keep Firms Out of Trouble? Evidence from Corporate Litigation and Policies' (2019) 67 *Journal of Accounting and Economics* 202.

[17] Neelie Kroes, 'Good for Women and Good for Ireland', speech at the 'Women for Europe' event, Dublin (16 July 2009) https://europa.eu/rapid/press-release_SPEECH-09-344_en.htm?locale=en. But there is one study that finds that female directors are less risk-averse than male directors, and thus more prone to make over-risky decisions: Renée B Adams and Patricia Funk, 'Beyond the Glass Ceiling: Does Gender Matter?' (2012) 58 *Management Science* 219.

[18] Renée B Adams and Vanitha Ragunathan, 'Lehman Sisters' (1 August 2015), FIRN Research Paper, https://ssrn.com/abstract=2380036.

[19] Sabina Nielsen and Morten Huse, 'The Contribution of Women on Boards of Directors: Going beyond the Surface' (2010) 18 *Corporate Governance* 136.

[20] Ibid.

[21] Paul Gompers and Silpa Kovvali, 'The Other Diversity Dividend' (July–August 2018) *Harvard Business Review*; Meggin Thwing Eastman, Damion Rallis and Gaia Mazzucchelli, 'MSCI, The Tipping Point: Women on Boards and Financial Performance', Women on Boards Report (2016); Catalyst, 'The Bottom Line: Corporate Performance and Women's Representation on Boards' (2007); McKinsey, 'Women Matter: Gender Diversity, a Corporate Performance Driver' (2007).

pursue fewer acquisitions and, if they do, pay lower bid premia.[22] However, the study also recognised that more diverse boards may result in companies taking more time to make decisions and, thus, they may make fewer acquisitions which may in turn adversely affect their financing needs.

Further, there are studies analysing the effect of the Norwegian quota of 40 per cent on firm value: one study found that firm value decreased (as companies with more female directors had fewer employees being made redundant, which resulted in an increase in labour cost).[23] Another study also showed that the 40 per cent quota requirement decreased the value of firms (particularly in small firms) because the quota resulted in a significant increase in the percentage of independent directors (from 46 per cent to 67 per cent) as a result of the appointment of more female independent directors; but these companies need advice from inside directors the most and monitoring by outside (ie independent) directors the least.[24] Moreover, there are studies that show that companies with female directors did not outperform Standard & Poor's 500 (although they outperformed NASDAQ 100).[25] Finally, another study found that German banks with more female directors have a higher portfolio risk.[26] Accordingly, the overall evidence shows that the link between board gender diversity and firm performance is equivocal and tenuous.

Finally, a recent analysis highlights three persistent problems with studies that tout the benefits of board gender diversity, namely, data limitations, selection and causal inference.[27] One example of the problem related to selection and data limitation relates to the difficulties of measuring board diversity. All studies measure diversity by calculating the average percentage of women on boards.[28] But this will not be accurate if the same women assume more board seats than men as the former are directors in different companies. This is because the data will

---

[22] Maurice Levi, Kai Li and Feng Zhang, 'Director Gender and Mergers and Acquisitions' (2014) 28 *Journal of Corporate Finance* 185.
[23] David A Matsa and Amalia R Miller, 'A Female Style in Corporate Leadership? Evidence from Quotas' (2013) 5 *American Economic Journal: Applied Economics* 136.
[24] Øyvind Bøhren and Siv Staubo, 'Mandatory Gender Balance and Board Independence' (2016) 22 *European Financial Management* 3.
[25] Virtcom Consulting, 'Board Diversification Strategy: Realizing Competitive Advantage and Shareholder Value' (2009).
[26] Allen N Berger, Thomas Kick and Klaus Schaeck, 'Executive Board Composition and Bank Risk Taking' (2014) 28 *Journal of Corporate Finance* 48.
[27] Renée B Adams, 'Women on Boards: The Superheroes of Tomorrow' (2016) 27 *Leadership Quarterly* 371 at 372.
[28] Ibid at 375.

give the misleading impression that there are more female directors when the reality is that it is the same women holding board directorships with no new female directors. Regarding causal inference, while the studies suggest that board gender diversity leads to corporate outcomes (such as increase in firm value), corporate outcomes can also result in more female directors.[29] This is because female directors are attracted to companies with good reputation and strong financial performance. This is what has been termed 'reverse causality'.[30]

In light of the problems with the instrumentalist justifications of board gender diversity (ie the business case for female directors), it is important to engage with the intrinsic (ie moral) justifications. In other words, the business case for board gender diversity, which has been relied upon by the common law jurisdictions in Asia, is necessary but insufficient. It is striking and interesting that regulators, policy makers and companies in the four Asian jurisdictions did not resort to moral reasons when they advocated for more female directors. This might be because moral justifications for having more female directors that are based on equality reasoning may pose a challenge to the political, cultural and social order in these Asian jurisdictions in which patriarchal norms seem to be prevalent. Another plausible reason is that instrumentalist reasons are likely to gain more traction among companies than those based on equality; after all, it is easier for companies to buy into arguments of improved firm value or enhanced decision-making process. One other reason is that equality remains a controversial and contested concept and hence regulators are wary of utilising it to justify board gender diversity.

C Equality Justifications

However, given that sustainability is concerned with the responsibilities of companies for the impacts that they have on societies, having women on boards cannot be justified solely in terms of the benefits that they bring to companies, however crucial such reasoning is. To properly understand board gender diversity in the context of sustainability, one has to also analyse the issue in terms of the role of boards in perpetuating unfairness and inequality,[31] or, conversely put, the role of the boards in promoting fairness and equality in society. Justifying having more female

---

[29] Ibid at 373–4.
[30] Ibid.
[31] Barnali Choudhury, 'New Rationales for Women on Boards' (2014) 34 *Oxford Journal of Legal Studies* 511.

directors solely in terms of instrumentalist reasoning is problematic for three reasons. First, it occludes the debates on corporate law and the role of boards in promoting distributive justice: whether there should be equality of outcome (whether measures should be taken to ensure that women are appropriately represented on boards), equality of opportunity (whether the nomination criteria for directors are biased in favour of male candidates and the measures that have to be taken to ensure a level playing field) and equality of resources (whether the difficulty in having female directors is because of structural, systemic disadvantages faced by women, and thus boards need to provide more resources to advance the welfare of women in their companies). Second, if a company is profitable, it might not see the pressing need to appoint women on boards. Even if a company is not profitable and therefore subscribes to the business case for gender diversity on boards, should the company not see any subsequent improvement in its decision-making process or share price after having women on boards, its support for having women on boards may diminish. Finally, given that a key reason for having women on boards is to have diversity of perspectives, companies can use other qualities and attributes such as varied expertise, experience, background, ethnicity or nationality as proxies for gender. For example, under the 2017 MCCG, should companies not have a gender diversity policy, or have one but not have targets or measures to attain the targets, they need to disclose only an alternative approach that will promote diverse perspectives on their boards.[32] Companies can assert that, despite the lack of female directors, their boards are sufficiently diverse because they consist of different backgrounds and ethnicities and possess different types of relevant expertise. Similarly, under the Singapore Code of Corporate Governance, companies are required on a comply or explain basis only to have boards that 'provide the appropriate balance and mix of skills, knowledge, experience, and other aspects of diversity such as gender and age'.[33] Hence, gender is merely one of the many elements that constitute diversity. Technically, the company need not hire female directors to show that it has a diverse board. As long as the company can show that it has a diverse board despite lacking female directors, or that it is sufficiently diverse (although it has only one female director), this will be sufficient to comply with the code.

---

[32] 2017 Malaysian Code on Corporate Governance paras 5.2–5.4.
[33] 2018 Singapore Code of Corporate Governance para 2.4.

So what are the intrinsic (ie moral) justifications that ought to be relied on to make the case for board gender diversity? It is suggested that equality forms the moral basis for board gender diversity. To say that women and men are equal is to say that they deserve to be treated with the same respect and the same dignity. But what does it mean to interpret and apply the concept of equal treatment in the context of board gender diversity? There are three conceptions of equality that are relevant here: equality of outcome, equality of resources and equality of opportunity.[34]

1   Equality of Outcome[35]

Equality of outcome means that men and women deserve the same level of goods, services and/or positions. Translating this to the context of board gender diversity would mean that the number of female directors should be as close to the number of male directors as is practicable. For example, the MCCG requires boards of large companies to have at least 30 per cent women directors (on an apply or explain an alternative basis).[36] Norway has a quota requirement of 40 per cent.[37] And thirteen jurisdictions also impose a quota requirement on either SOEs or listed companies.[38]

But there are four objections to equality of outcome. First, it is inefficient because resources have to be allocated to ensure that there is a sufficient number of female directors to meet the quota requirement even if the female directors do not have the necessary skills or expertise; in short, equality of outcome may result in a misallocation of scarce resources. Second, it may reduce the incentives for achievement in the sense that having a quota requirement means that a certain number of board seats are automatically reserved for women, the consequence being that women may be less incentivised to work hard to acquire the requisite skills and abilities to be appointed to the board. Third, equality of outcome in the form of quota requirement imposes an onerous compliance

---

[34] Stefan Gosepath, 'Equality', *Stanford Encyclopedia of Philosophy* (2001) https://plato.stanford.edu/entries/equality/.

[35] See eg Anne Phillips, 'Defending Equality of Outcome' (2004) 12 *Journal of Political Philosophy* 1; Kota Saito, 'Social Preferences under Risk: Equality of Opportunity versus Equality of Outcome' (2013) 103 *American Economic Review* 3084.

[36] 2017 Malaysian Code on Corporate Governance para 4.5.

[37] Mari Teigen, 'Gender Quotas on Corporate Boards' in Frederik Engelstad and Mari Teigen (eds), *Firms, Boards and Gender Quotas: Comparative Perspectives* (Emerald Group Publishing Ltd 2012) at ch 4.

[38] Renée B Adams, 'Women on Boards: The Superheroes of Tomorrow' (2016) 27 *Leadership Quarterly* 371 at 372.

burden on companies. If the purpose of equality of outcome is to promote a level playing field for women and to change cultural and social attitudes towards women, it is suggested that regulators should restrict the quota to a certain period of time once a level playing field has been attained. In short, there should be a sunset clause to the quota requirement. Finally, by focusing exclusively on results, equality of outcome fails to consider the moral validity of the circumstances that produced an unequal result. The fact that, on average, listed companies have no or very few female directors reflects inequality, but a proper moral assessment will consider not only the result (how many female directors there are) but also the causes and circumstances that led to the inequality. For example, has the company taken measures to incentivise its female employees to apply, required its head hunters to produce a suitable slate of female candidates, and interviewed them but found them to be unsuitable? Or the lack of female directors may not be the fault of the company; the problem may lie with systemic, structural policies that are disadvantageous to women (such as insufficient childcare support, inadequate maternity leave and/or pay discrepancies between men and women) as well as with cultural attitudes that are patriarchal in nature.

2 Equality of Resources and Opportunity[39]

Given the problems with equality of outcome, it is apposite to consider the other conceptions of equality, namely, equality of resources and equality of opportunity. Regarding the former, Rawls argues that human beings should be accorded primary goods (which include basic rights and liberties, income and wealth, positions of responsibility and powers of office, and the social bases of self-respect).[40] Once human beings are accorded these basic goods, inequalities are justifiable only if, first, the positions and offices are open to all according to the criterion of fair equality of opportunity and, second, the greatest possible advantage is provided to the least

---

[39] See eg Ronald Dworkin, *Sovereign Virtue: The Theory and Practice of Equality* (Harvard University Press 2000); Shlomi Segall, *Equality and Opportunity* (Oxford University Press 2013); John E Roemer, *Equality of Opportunity* (Harvard University Press 1998).

[40] John Rawls, *Political Liberalism* (Columbia University Press 1993) at 5, 356-63; John Rawls, *A Theory of Justice* (revised edn, Harvard University Press 1999). See Barnali Choudhury, 'New Rationales for Women on Boards' (2014) 34 *Oxford Journal of Legal Studies* 511 at 519-20; Choudhury also relies on Rawls to support her equality rationale for female directors.

advantaged members.[41] The difference principle is the cornerstone of a just society and that principle should be chosen by members of society under a veil of ignorance concerning their personal circumstances (such as their sex, race, sexual orientation, wealth, social status and intelligence).[42]

The lesson that Rawls's theory holds for board gender diversity is this. A crucial issue is whether women are provided with sufficient level of primary goods such that they are in an effective position to be able to be considered for directorship. The next question is whether there is fair equality of opportunity. Regarding primary goods, for instance, if there is either no or inadequate legal protection for women against discrimination, then it is arguable that women do not have sufficient levels of the basic rights and liberties that are important aspects of primary goods. It is important to consider primary goods in the context of board gender diversity as these goods (if they are lacking or inadequate) may affect the conditions and circumstances under which women are willing or able to put themselves forward as board candidates. For instance, if there is actual or perceived discrimination against women in the workplace or in society in general and if women have little effective recourse for addressing such discrimination, then it will be much harder to convince women to run for board positions; likewise, if cultural attitudes towards women are unfavourable.[43] For example, women are often perceived as less experienced than men[44] and as tending to avoid competitive situations;[45] such perceptions could result in discrimination.

Regarding fair equality of opportunity, the issue is whether there are social and institutional obstacles to women becoming directors. One

---

[41] John Rawls, *Political Liberalism* (Columbia University Press 1993) at 5; John Rawls, *A Theory of Justice* (revised edn, Harvard University Press 1999) at 13.

[42] John Rawls, *A Theory of Justice* (revised edn Harvard University Press 1999) at 11.

[43] Rohini Pande and Deanna Ford, 'Gender Quotas and Female Leadership: A Review', Background paper for World Development Report on Gender Equality and Development (2012) https://openknowledge.worldbank.org/handle/10986/9120.

[44] Alice H Eagly and Steven J Karau, 'Role Congruity Theory of Prejudice toward Female Leaders' (2002) 109 *Psychological Review* 573; Elena Doldor, Susan Vinnicombe, Mary Gaughan and Ruth Sealy, 'Gender Diversity on Boards: The Appointment Process and the Role of Executive Search Firms', Equality and Human Rights Commission Research Report (2012) at 85.

[45] Rachel Croson and Uri Gneezy, 'Gender Differences in Preferences' (2009) 47 *Journal of Economic Literature* 448; Marianne Bertrand, 'New Perspectives on Gender' in Orley Ashenfelter and David Card (eds), *Handbook of Labor Economics*, vol 4B (Elsevier 2011) at 1543; Muriel Niederle, 'Gender' in John Kagel and Alvin E. Roth (eds), *Handbook of Experimental Economics*, vol 2 (Princeton University Press 2016) at ch 8.

I RATIONALES FOR FEMALE DIRECTORS

major obstacle that women have to overcome is the dual challenge of being the primary caregiver (particularly for children)[46] and having to do well at work. For instance, if a country has insufficient childcare support, then fewer women will have the opportunities to work full-time and for an extended period of time. As a result, they have fewer opportunities to gain the necessary experience even to be considered as viable board candidates, let alone get appointed. One study finds that there is a correlation between labour force participation and board membership, suggesting that 'promot[ing] full-time employment by women may be important for generating a pipeline of women who eventually end up in top corporate positions'.[47] The same study finds that the barriers to having more female directors include disparity in wages, discrimination, motherhood and the lack of policies that promote full-time employment for women.[48]

Interestingly, out of 149 countries, Singapore, Malaysia and India are ranked 67, 101 and 108, respectively, in the World Economic Forum's Global Gender Gap Report.[49] There is no separate ranking for Hong Kong, which is subsumed under China, which is ranked 103. The ranking covers four areas: economic participation and opportunity; educational attainment; health and survival; and political empowerment. In terms of economic participation and opportunity, Singapore, Malaysia, India and China are ranked 24, 84, 142 and 86, respectively.[50]

Thus, it is necessary but insufficient that the support for female directors is based on instrumental justifications, namely, they improve both corporate governance and firm value. Moral or intrinsic justifications are necessary. Such justifications bring to light the background conditions that pose an impediment to women being directors. An equality justification for female directors is more compelling than instrumentalist justifications because the former requires the state to ask itself whether women are given sufficient rights and liberties and it requires the state to address systemic, structural disadvantages that women face at work and in society. Hence, passing a law that imposes a quota

---

[46] Marianne Bertrand, Claudia Goldin and Lawrence F Katz, 'Dynamics of the Gender Gap for Young Professionals in the Financial and Corporate Sectors' (2010) 2 *American Economic Journal: Applied Economics* 228.
[47] Renée B Adams and Tom Kirchmaier, 'Barriers to Boardrooms', ECGI Finance Working Paper No. 347/2013 at 5 https://papers.ssrn.com/sol3/papers.cfm?abstract_id=2192918.
[48] Ibid.
[49] World Economic Forum, Global Gender Gap Report (2018) www3.weforum.org/docs/WEF_GGGR_2018.pdf.
[50] Ibid.

requirement or applying pressure on companies to hire more female directors are superficial and inadequate solutions to a persistent, long-term problem of female under-representation in boards and key management positions.

In addition to the Rawlsian theory of equality, a different version of equality of resources was put forward by Dworkin that also has implications for board diversity. An important starting point for Dworkin is that people should not be held responsible for the choices that they made based on their unchosen circumstances, the latter of which include not only gender and race but also endowments that predispose them to be beautiful (or ugly), strong (or weak), intelligent (or stupid) or talented (or untalented).[51] Thus, it is important to ensure that there is a fair initial endowment and distribution of resources to make sure that people are not disadvantaged by their unchosen circumstances. The lesson for board gender diversity is that women have to be provided with fair resources such that they can compete effectively with male candidates for board positions. One suggested implication is that boards should put in place measures to ensure that there is a 'level playing field' for women. Thus, merely requiring boards to disclose their diversity policy (such as the case in Singapore and Hong Kong) is necessary but grossly insufficient. It is suggested that equality of resources should require companies to devote appropriate resources to (1) identifying and grooming potential internal female candidates for board positions; (2) promoting the welfare of women such as flexible work arrangements and enhanced maternal benefits; and (3) ensuring that there is a sufficient number of female candidates in the nomination and interview process. The government must do its part by addressing the systemic, structural disadvantages that women face and by incentivising women to return to the workforce after giving birth through measures such as improving childcare support, tax breaks, reducing pay discrepancies, enacting or enforcing antidiscrimination laws, etc.

In short, justifications for board gender diversity that are based on equality of resources and opportunity rightly draw our attention to the deep-seated and widespread problems faced by women in society and the need for the state and companies to come up with effective measures to address them. Merely tinkering with board composition by mandating or pressuring companies to have female directors is inadequate.

---

[51] Ronald Dworkin, *Sovereign Virtue. The Theory and Practice of Equality* (Harvard University Press 2000) at 65–119.

II Mechanisms to Promote Female Directors

The four common law Asian jurisdictions have deployed a variety of mechanisms to promote board gender diversity. Four principal mechanisms have been utilised, namely, a quota requirement; an 'apply or explain an alternative' requirement; a combination of disclosure of diversity policy and a 'name and shame' approach; and setting targets.

A Quota Requirement

India is the only jurisdiction among the four common law Asian jurisdictions that has implemented a quota requirement. Under Indian law, every listed company and every other public company having (i) paid-up share capital of 100 crore rupees or more or (ii) turnover of 300 crore rupees or more is required to have one female director.[52] The quota requirement in India can be criticised on seven grounds.

First, India's quota requirement can be criticised for being mere tokenism. Unlike countries such as Norway, which require a certain percentage of the board to consist of female directors, Indian law merely requires companies to have at least one female director, without regard for the actual, total number of directors. For example, out of the top fifty listed companies in India, only twenty-four have one female director, although seventeen of these twenty-four companies have a total of ten or more directors.

As a result, there is a real risk that companies will merely comply with the quota requirement for its own sake, without appreciating the importance of having female directors. For example, companies such as Reliance Industries,[53] HDFC Bank[54] and Oil and Natural Gas Corporation,[55] which have one female director each, do not appear to have any diversity policy. It is necessary but insufficient that companies comply with the quota requirement. They must also demonstrate why they regard board gender diversity as important to their business and operations and the concrete actions that they have taken or will take to remove the barriers in relation to the nomination and appointment of female directors.

---

[52] Indian Companies Act 2013, s 149.
[53] Reliance Industries Limited Integrated, Annual Report 2017–8 at 10.
[54] HDFC Bank, Annual Report 2017–8 at 4.
[55] Oil and Natural Gas Corporation, Annual Report 2017–8 at 17.

Second, India's quota requirement can also result in appointments based on nepotism and cronyism.[56] For example, Reliance Industries, which is one of India's largest private sector conglomerates by market capitalisation, appointed a female director to comply with the law.[57] She is, however, the wife of the board chairman. It is doubtful whether having a female director in this situation would bring about any material improvement in the board decision-making process, given that she is unlikely to openly question, let alone criticise her husband, particularly in a country such as India where patriarchal norms are prevalent.

Third, there seem to be no sanctions imposed for the violation of the quota requirement in India. By contrast, countries that have imposed quotas such as France, Norway and Italy have imposed sanctions including fines, removal of board members and even delisting.[58] These countries have achieved significant progress in having female directors.[59]

Fourth, an analysis of the annual reports for the financial year 2017–18 of the top fifty listed companies by market capitalisation in each of India, Singapore, Malaysia and Hong Kong shows that India is ranked only third in terms of the percentage of female directors, despite being the only jurisdiction to impose a quota requirement. The percentage of female directors in the top fifty listed companies in Malaysia, Hong Kong, India and Singapore is 21.82 per cent, 15.41 per cent, 14.29 per cent and 13.64 per cent, respectively.

By contrast, although Malaysia and Hong Kong do not have a quota system, they have a higher percentage of female directors than India. This suggests that mechanisms other than quotas such as Malaysia's 'apply or explain an alternative approach' backed by government pressure may be more effective for promoting board gender diversity. Further, although Hong Kong has no legal mechanism to promote board gender diversity

---

[56] According to the Economist Crony-Capitalism index, Malaysia and Singapore have been ranked among the top five countries, and India among the top ten, in its 2014 and 2016 index. There is no separate ranking for Hong Kong, which is classified under China, which was ranked eleven in both 2014 and 2016. See http://infographics.economist.com/2016/Cronyism_index/.

[57] Diksha Madhok, 'India's Effort for More Women on Boards Is Backfiring in the Worst Way', *Quartz India* (19 June 2014).

[58] Hampton-Alexander Review, 'FTSE Women Leaders: Improving Gender Balance in FTSE Leadership' (2017) at 30.

[59] Ibid, 31; 39.8 per cent, 37.2 per cent and 32.2 per cent of the boards of the listed companies in France, Norway and Italy, respectively, consist of female directors.

11 MECHANISMS TO PROMOTE FEMALE DIRECTORS

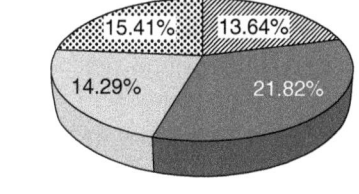

Figure 3.1 Proportion of female directors in Singapore, Malaysia, India and Hong Kong (in %) (in the top fifty companies by market capitalisation)

(until recently, in which companies are required by the listing rules to disclose their diversity policies on a comply or explain basis with effect from 2019[60]), it has the second highest percentage of female directors. This suggests that there are other factors such as pressure from institutional shareholders and the degree of internationalisation of companies that can promote board gender diversity, which will be elaborated subsequently.

Fifth, while there appears to be no empirical study on the impact of the quota requirement on the firm value of Indian companies, three out of four studies of the Norwegian quota system (under which boards of public companies are required to consist of 40 per cent female directors) showed that the quota system reduced share price. The other study found neither a positive nor a negative effect on the share price.[61] To elaborate, a 2012 study found that there was a reduction in share price of 3.5 per cent after Norway imposed the 40 per cent quota requirement (but the authors acknowledge that the reduction in firm value may also have been due to the reduction of the age and experience of directors as a whole due to the presence of female directors who are relatively younger).[62] A 2013 study found that a drop in share price was not

---

[60] HKEX LR, Appendix 14 Corporate Governance Code and Corporate Governance Report at 28.

[61] B Espen Eckbo, Knut Nygaard and Karin S Thorburn, 'Does Gender-Balancing the Board Reduce Firm Value?' (March 2016) CEPR Discussion Paper No. DP11176 https://ssrn.com/abstract=2766471.

[62] Kenneth R Ahern and Amy K Dittmar, 'The Changing of the Boards: The Impact on Firm Valuation of Mandated Female Board Representation' (2012) 127 *Quarterly Journal of Economics* 137–97.

because of younger and less experienced boards, but because boards with female directors laid off fewer employees, which led to a reduction in short-term profits.[63] A 2015 study found that female directors significantly increased the number of independent directors, which led to a reduction in firm value.[64] This is because more independent directors resulted in greater monitoring of the company at the expense of the advice needed from and provided by inside (ie non-independent) directors. In other words, there is a trade-off between monitoring and advice; and the large number of female directors (due to the 40 per cent quota requirement) resulted in more independent directors than is optimal in companies that require more advice than monitoring.

However, it may be argued that the adverse effects on firm performance documented in these studies on the Norwegian quota system either are not relevant to the situation in India or, even if relevant, are not severe. After all, Indian law merely requires one female director as opposed to 40 per cent of the board. However, after California passed a law in 2018 requiring all publicly traded companies headquartered in California to have at least one female director by the end of 2019,[65] one study found a significant abnormal reduction of share price of 1.4 per cent in some companies.[66] The reason is that these companies have difficulty attracting female directors due to the fact that there is a limited pool of qualified female directors and, more importantly, these companies already suffer from low profitability and weak corporate governance. By contrast, high-performing companies have little difficulty in appointing female directors and, thus, did not have a reduction in share price. This suggests that imposing a quota requirement, even if it merely requires one female director, may not improve the corporate performance of companies that are already under-performing, and may instead exacerbate their performance. As for companies that are already profitable and have strong corporate governance, the quota requirement has a negligible effect on corporate performance. This calls into question

---

[63] David A Matsa and Amalia R Miller, 'A Female Style in Corporate Leadership? Evidence from Quotas' (2013) 5 *American Economic Journal: Applied Economics* 136.

[64] Øyvind Bøhren and Siv Staubo, 'Mandatory Gender Balance and Board Independence' (2016) 22 *European Financial Management* 3.

[65] In addition, the law requires that by the end of 2021 all companies must have at least one female director if the board has four or fewer directors, two female directors if the board has five directors and three female directors if the board has six directors or more.

[66] Sunwoo Hwang, Anil Shivdasani, Ele Anil and Elena Simintzi, 'Mandating Women on Boards: Evidence from the United States' (13 October 2018) Kenan Institute of Private Enterprise Research Paper No. 18-34, https://ssrn.com/abstract=3265783.

the effectiveness of the quota as a mechanism for improving corporate performance.

Sixth, if having female directors improves corporate governance because women possess certain character and personality traits that are different from men such as being more risk-averse, more other-regarding, less over-confident and more collaborative, then it is doubtful whether having one female director will make any material difference to the board decision-making process and board dynamics. This is particularly the case where the board has ten or more directors. For example, my survey of the top fifty listed companies in India shows that there are seventeen companies in which the total number of directors in each of these companies is ten or more and, yet, each of them has only one female director.[67]

Finally, improving board gender diversity through quotas is not effective unless reforms are made to address persistent female subordination in the political, social and economic realms. It may be instructive to compare Norway and India in this regard. Norway did not impose the board quota requirement out of nowhere. Rather, the board quota requirement imposed in Norway was part of its long-standing political and social commitment to gender equality as evidenced in the fact that political parties and public committees in Norway have relied on quotas to achieve gender equality.[68] Norway is ranked second overall by the World Economic Forum's Global Gender Gap Report and ranked third, eleventh and forty-first in areas such as political empowerment, economic opportunity and participation, and education, respectively.[69] By contrast, in India, patriarchy and female subordination are the norm. The board gender quota requirement is an anomaly in India as it imposes no gender quotas in the political or social realm. India's female infant mortality rate is one of the highest in the world, the majority of women do not have tertiary qualifications, and discrimination of women in the

---

[67] See the 2017–8 annual reports of Tata Consultancy Services Ltd, Reliance Industries Ltd, HDFC Bank Ltd, Hindustan Unilever Ltd, Housing Development Finance Corp Ltd, State Bank of India, Kotak Mahindra Bank Ltd, Oil and Natural Gas Corporation Ltd, Bajaj Finance Ltd, Sun Pharmaceutical Industries Ltd, Wipro Ltd, JSW Steel Ltd, Bajaj Auto Ltd, Dabur India Ltd, SBI Life Insurance Co Ltd, Tech Mahindra Ltd and Motherson Sumi Systems Ltd.

[68] Vibeke Heidenreichat, 'Why Gender Quotas in Company Boards in Norway – and Not in Sweden?' in Frederik Engelstad and Mari Teigen (eds), *Firms, Boards and Gender Quotas: Comparative Perspectives* (Emerald Group Publishing Ltd 2012) at 154–5; Drude Dahlerup, *Women, Quotas and Politics* (Routledge 2006).

[69] World Economic Forum, The Global Gender Gap Report (2018) at 10.

workforce and in society remains pervasive.[70] Unsurprisingly, India is ranked 108th overall. Given the systemic and structural impediments faced by women in society, it would be difficult for them to gain the requisite qualifications and experience to be appointed directors, to say the least.

Given the deficiencies of the quota requirement in India, the next mechanism that should be considered is Malaysia's 'apply or explain an alternative' approach.

B   Apply or Explain an Alternative

The 2017 MCCG requires every listed company to disclose its 'policies on gender diversity, its targets and measures to meet those targets. For Large Companies,[71] the board must have at least 30% women directors.'[72] The code adopts the 'apply or explain an alternative' approach to all its provisions. Under this approach, should a listed company fail to disclose a gender diversity policy or fail to provide any targets or measures to address gender diversity, it is required to give an explanation for the departure and, crucially, to disclose the alternative practice that it has adopted and how the alternative practice achieves the intended outcome stipulated in the code, which, in the case of board composition, relates to board decisions that are in the company's best interests taking into account diverse perspectives.[73]

There are two suggested notable effects of the MCCG apply or explain an alternative approach. First, among the top fifty listed companies in each of the four Asian countries, Malaysia is ranked first at 21.82 per cent in terms of having the highest percentage of female directors (see Figure 3.1). Second, companies that have fallen short of the requirement of 30 per cent have generally provided thoughtful explanation detailing the diversity measures that they have taken or will take. Consider, for example, Petronas Chemical, the fourth largest listed company (also a GLC), which states in its annual report that female employees make

---

[70] See eg Renu Batra and Thomas G Reio, Jr, 'Gender Inequality Issues in India' (2016) 18 *Advances in Developing Human Resources* 1; D Amutha, 'The Roots of Gender Inequality in India' (27 January 2017) https://ssrn.com/abstract=2906950.

[71] 2017 Malaysian Code on Corporate Governance para 2.6: Large companies are: 'Companies on the FTSE Bursa Malaysia Top 100 Index; or Companies with market capitalisation of RM2 billion and above, at the start of the companies' financial year.'

[72] Ibid para 4.4.

[73] Ibid para 4.0.

up 18.5 per cent of its total workforce and that its board consists of 25 per cent female directors.[74] It states that it has taken concrete actions to promote the career progression of women, which will in turn further gender diversity; the actions include having flexible work options to suit women's schedules, providing access to nursing facilities in the offices and hosting professional networking events to forge ties with successful women.[75] These measures address some of the root problems of low numbers of female directors, namely, women dropping out of the workforce to take care of children, the double burden of family and career responsibilities, insufficient number of or insufficient access to female role models. Thus, these measures are as important as measures that seek to improve board gender diversity through reforming the procedures related to the nomination of female directors. Another example is IHH Healthcare, the fifth largest listed company in Malaysia and also a GLC. Women comprise 'approximately 27%' of its board.[76] IHH Healthcare provides thoughtful and concrete explanation of its disagreement with the MCCG that the board must achieve a target of 30 per cent female directors. It states that board appointment should be based on 'objective criteria and merit and with due regard for diversity'.[77] It further states that it already has a board with diverse backgrounds, expertise, experience and ethnicity who contribute diverse viewpoints and improve board decision-making processes.[78] The company clarifies that it is committed to board gender diversity if the right candidates are available.[79] One may criticise IHH Healthcare for using 'objective criteria' or 'merit' as an excuse for not adhering to the 30 per cent target set by MCCG. But this criticism is misplaced. First, hiring female directors for the sake of meeting the target without considering whether the female directors have the requisite experience and expertise will ultimately undermine the reputation of female directors because their appointments will be regarded by the rest of the board members as tokenism. Second, it does not seem that IHH Healthcare is paying lip service to board gender diversity because it states that (1) it has put in place nomination criteria and procedures that

---

[74] Petronas Chemicals Group Berhad, Annual Report 2017 at 115.
[75] Ibid at 93.
[76] IHH Healthcare Berhad, Annual Report 2018 at 113.
[77] Ibid.
[78] Ibid.
[79] Ibid. ('Nevertheless, the Board remains committed in its efforts to source for and increase women representation on the Board by 2021 depending on the availability of the right candidates.')

promote diversity as candidates are identified not only by its existing board and internal employees but also by independent third-party referrals;[80] and (2) it has adopted diversity strategies related to recruitment at all levels, succession planning,[81] as well as training and mentoring programmes.[82]

The apply or explain an alternative approach in the MCCG is more rigorous and effective than the comply or explain approach adopted in Singapore, Hong Kong and the UK. The comply or explain approach merely requires the company to provide an explanation with no requirement whatsoever to state an alternative. Importantly, the explanation does not require companies to propose concrete remedial measures to address the issue of board gender diversity.

For example, the SEHK listing rules merely require companies, with effect from January 2019, on a comply or explain basis to 'disclose the policy on diversity or a summary of the policy'.[83] The note to the rule states that '[b]oard diversity will differ according to the circumstances of each issuer. Diversity of board members can be achieved through consideration of a number of factors, including but not limited to gender, age, cultural and educational background, or professional experience. Each issuer should take into account its own business model and specific needs.'[84] Thus, even if a company has no female directors or merely one, it can justify this situation on the basis that it has a diverse board because its male directors consist of different backgrounds, ethnicities or nationalities, and have diverse work experiences. For example, Sun Hung Kai Properties Limited, which has only one female director out of a total of twenty-one directors,[85] stated in its diversity disclosure: 'The Company sees diversity as a wide concept and believes that diversity of board members can be achieved through consideration of a number of factors, including but not limited to background, age, gender, culture, industry experience, skills and knowledge, educational background and other qualities. The Company takes into account these factors based on its own business model and specific needs from time to time.'[86] Further, an

---

[80] Ibid at 116.
[81] Ibid at 39; see also ibid at 118 (the Nomination Committee is 'responsible for ensuring that the boardroom diversity objectives are adopted in board recruitment, board performance evaluation and succession planning processes').
[82] Ibid at 65 and 117–18.
[83] HKEX LR 13.92.
[84] Ibid.
[85] Sun Hung Kai Properties Limited, Annual Report 2017/18 at 143–53.
[86] Ibid at 102.

oil and gas company can explain away its lack of female directors by stating that, in light of its business model and specific needs, it requires directors who have a specific experience and skills set in a particular industry and there are no female directors who fit this requirement. In these two situations, under the SEHK listing rules, a company with no female directors does not need to disclose the concrete alternative measures that it will put in place to promote board gender diversity. This is in contrast to the MCCG apply or explain an alternative approach. However, the SEHK states that the diversity policy or its summary has to include measurable objectives that the issuer has set for implementing the policy and the progress for achieving those objectives.[87] Although there are no data on the diversity policies of companies under the SEHK listing rules as the rules took effect only from January 2019 (meaning that the majority of annual reports will not be published until 2020), it remains to be seen whether companies will comply with the rules. After all, if companies choose not to do so, they merely have to give an explanation.

The 2018 Singapore Code of Corporate Governance (which applies to annual reports covering the financial year commencing January 2019) states that boards are required to have an 'appropriate balance and mix of skills, knowledge, experience, and other aspects of diversity such as gender and age'.[88] So, for example, should a company not have female directors, it merely has to explain how this deviation or variation is 'consistent with the aim and philosophy of the Principle in question', namely, the board has to have 'an appropriate level of independence and diversity of thought and background in its composition to enable it to make decisions in the best interests of the company'.[89] The board can explain that, despite the lack of female directors, it has diversity of thought and background as the male directors come from different backgrounds and are equipped with different skills, and thus it is able to make decisions in the company's best interests. In other words, as compared to the apply or explain an alternative approach in the MCCG, the Singapore code (similar to the SEHK listing rules) is less effective because nothing in the Singapore code requires the company to provide an alternative measure so that it has an appropriate level of diversity to enable the board to make decisions that are in the company's best

---

[87] HKEX, Appendix 14 Corporate Governance Code and Corporate Governance Report at 28.
[88] 2018 Singapore Code of Corporate Governance para 2.4.
[89] Ibid para 2.

interests. The predecessor to the 2018 code, which is the 2012 code, merely states that the board is required to have directors who 'provide an appropriate balance and diversity of skills, experience, gender and knowledge of the company'.[90]

A survey of the top fifty listed companies in Singapore in the financial year 2017–18 reveals that there are twelve companies that do not have a single female director. And among these twelve, while some pay lip service to diversity in their diversity policies, others such as Singapore Airlines, Jardine Cycle and Carriage, and Haw Par Corporation do not even have board diversity policies or explanations in their annual reports as to how their boards have complied with the 2012 code. Given that no sanctions are attached to the failure to comply with the 2018 code, it is questionable whether those companies that have no female directors will actually change their existing practices.

C A Combined Approach: Monitoring Disclosure and 'Name and Shame'

Absent measures to penalise companies for failure to comply, the comply or explain mechanism in Singapore and Hong Kong, in itself, is inadequate to promote board gender diversity. While the MCCG's apply or explain an alternative approach is an improvement over the comply or explain mechanism, it is also insufficient. The Malaysian government seems to be cognisant of the inadequacies. As a result, the Malaysia Securities Commission (MSC) stated that it would monitor and review the disclosures that companies are required to provide under the code and publish its findings.[91] The MSC has also publicly named those companies with all-male boards, noting that as at 17 January 2018 there were only seven companies with all-male boards, a 65 per cent improvement from twenty companies as at 31 December 2016.[92] The other example is the Council for Board Diversity in Singapore, formerly known as the Diversity Action Committee (DAC). In 2016, after finding out that 38 of Singapore's top 100 listed companies consist only of male directors, the DAC started to publish a ranking of gender diversity in companies twice a year. As a result, the number of listed companies with

---

[90] 2012 Singapore Code of Corporate Governance para 2.6.
[91] Securities Commission Malaysia, Corporate Governance Strategic Priorities 2017–2020 (2018) at 26.
[92] Securities Commission Malaysia, 'Positive Progress Made on Gender Diversity', *News & Media* (21 January 2018).

only male directors was reduced to twenty-seven in 2018, which is a 28.9 per cent improvement.[93]

There are two significant differences between the approaches taken in Singapore and in Malaysia. First, the MSC will not only publicly disclose those companies that have no female directors, but will also monitor the quality of the companies' diversity policy disclosure. By contrast, the DAC does not seem to have undertaken a review of the quality of the disclosures but will instead publicise only those companies that have no female directors. Nevertheless, the MSC has not made clear the level of monitoring that it will undertake and the criteria that it will adopt to determine the adequacy and comparability of the disclosures. The second difference is that, in addition to monitoring companies' diversity disclosures and publicising those companies that have only male directors, the MCCG requires large companies to have at least 30 per cent female directors, on an apply or explain an alternative approach. By contrast, the Singapore Code of Corporate Governance does not set a target. However, the DAC has set an informal target of 30 per cent by 2030[94] and, under the leadership of the DAC and its successor the Council for Board Diversity, the percentage of women directors in Singapore's top 100 listed companies increased from 7.5 per cent to 15.2 per cent from 2014 to 2018.[95]

It is suggested that the regulators in Singapore and Hong Kong should follow Malaysia's example by monitoring the quality of diversity policies, in addition to identifying and publicising those companies with no female directors (as is the case in Singapore). Otherwise, companies can disregard the requirement of a diversity policy given that no consequences are attached for non-compliance. For example, in Singapore, as of 2018, not only did Singapore Airlines[96] and Haw Par Corporation[97] have no female directors, but they also had no diversity policies. Further, while companies such as Jardine Strategic Holdings, Hong Kong Land

---

[93] Livia Yap, 'Name-and-Shame Approach Puts More Women on Singapore Boards', *Business Times* (31 July 2018) www.bloomberg.com/news/articles/2018-07-31/name-and-shame-approach-puts-more-women-on-singapore-boards.

[94] 'Diversity Action Committee Targets 30% of Board Seats for Women by 2030', *Channel News Asia* (4 April 2017) www.channelnewsasia.com/news/singapore/diversity-action-committee-targets-30-of-board-seats-for-women-b-8710462.

[95] Council for Board Diversity, 'Our Story' www.diversityaction.sg/about/council-for-board-diversity/.

[96] Singapore Airlines, Annual Report 2017–8 at 16–7. Note that as of January 2019, it has added one female director.

[97] Haw Par Corporation Limited, Annual Report 2018 at 6–12.

Holdings and United Industrial Corporation have diversity policies, the contents of the policies are vaguely worded and of a boilerplate nature, which hardly reflect a commitment to gender diversity. For example, United Industrial Corporation merely states that it will '[take] into account'[98] the importance of gender diversity in the workplace. Unsurprisingly, none of these three companies has female directors.[99]

A company's diversity policy, provided that due care and thought have been put into it by the company, is a valuable source of information on the company's purpose, value and culture with respect to diversity. A good diversity policy should: include specific reasons why the company believes that diversity, particularly gender diversity, is good for the company's business and operations; articulate what it means specifically to have a diverse board for the company; disclose the percentage of women on its board, as well as in its management and total workforce; identify the impediments to having female directors; and state in concrete and measurable terms the actions that have been and will be taken by the company to promote board gender diversity.[100]

Examples of good diversity policy disclosure in each of the four Asian countries can be found in Appendix 4; they include Singapore Telecommunications,[101] CK Infrastructure Holdings,[102] UMW Holdings[103] and HCL Technologies.[104]

It may be said that substance is more important than form, that is, as long as the company has a certain percentage of female directors (in the case of Singapore and Hong Kong) or complies with the requirement of having at least 30 per cent female directors in Malaysia, or one female director in India, deficient diversity policy or the absence of such policy is of little importance. And, as a result, it may be said that the regulator should monitor only the diversity policies of companies that have no

---

[98] United Industrial Corporation Limited, Annual Report 2017 at 33; note, also, that the words 'women', 'woman' and 'female' never appear in the report, while 'gender' appears only once at 33.
[99] Jardine Strategic Holdings, Annual Report 2017 at 19; Hong Kong Land Holdings Limited, Annual Report 2017 at 18–19; United Industrial Corporation Limited, Annual Report 2017 at 4–10.
[100] PwC, 'Enhancing Board Diversity Disclosures in Singapore: Taking the Next Steps' (November 2018) www.pwc.com/sg/en/publications/assets/board-diversity-disclosures-enhance.pdf.
[101] Singtel, Annual Report 2017 at 67, 85–6 (see also Singtel, Annual Report 2018 at 69, 91)
[102] CK Infrastructure Holdings Limited, Annual Report 2017 at 167, 196.
[103] UMW Holdings Berhad, Annual Report 2017 at 73–4 (see also UMW Holdings Berhad, Annual Report 2018 at 74).
[104] HCL Technologies, Annual Report 2017–18 at 19–21, 41–2, 106.

female directors or those that have fallen short of the target imposed by the law.

Consider, for example, Manulife-S, an insurance company listed in Hong Kong. It has the highest percentage of female directors among the top fifty listed companies in Hong Kong. Out of a total of sixteen directors in the company, six are female, accounting for 38 per cent of the board.[105] But, remarkably, there is no diversity policy; nor is there a statement on board gender policy. Another example is United Overseas Bank Limited (UOB), one of the top ten largest listed companies in Singapore, which has one female director out of a total of twelve directors.[106] UOB provides no justifications as to why diversity, especially the presence of female directors, is important to the company, apart from a vaguely worded statement that it seeks to hire from 'diverse cultural backgrounds, age groups, gender ... to champion a more inclusive society'.[107] While UOB has a separate, short paragraph on gender diversity, it merely cites the percentage of women in its total workforce, as well as in its senior and middle management.[108]

But providing a clear explanation of why the company takes the view that having female directors is beneficial for the company and is in line with its corporate purpose is crucial if the company is not to be perceived as appointing female directors merely for the sake of complying with the law. Absent such an explanation, there is a risk that female directors in the company may not be accorded the same level of respect as their male counterparts and that their views may not be given the weight that ought to be given to them. This explanation is more important in jurisdictions such as Malaysia (which has set a numerical target for female directors) and India (which has imposed a quota requirement). For example, although Hindustan Unilever has complied with the statutory requirement to have at least one female director, it fails to articulate in its diversity policy why female directors are important to the company.[109] The impression given is that the company has appointed a female director merely to comply with the law.

---

[105] Manulife Financial Corporation, Annual Report 2017 at 185.
[106] United Overseas Bank, Annual Report 2017 at 12-18. (Note, however, that in the recent United Overseas Bank Annual Report 2018 at 11-16, there are only eleven directors inclusive of one female director, thus increasing the proportion of female directors in UOB.)
[107] Ibid at 32 (see also United Overseas Bank, Annual Report 2018 at 32).
[108] Ibid at 65 (see also United Overseas Bank, Annual Report 2018 at 70).
[109] Hindustan Unilever Limited, Annual Report 2017-18 at 64.

Improving board gender diversity is not only about increasing the number of female directors; it is also about changing the widespread and persistent mindset that women do not have the requisite skills and capabilities to be directors. Thus, a good diversity policy will provide clear justifications as to why diversity is important and valuable to the company. For example, Petronas Gas, whose board consists of 42.8 per cent female directors, states that 'diversity is a key driver to enhancing its effectiveness by allowing for a broader scope for debate within itself . . . . A diverse board is necessary to provide [the] unique perspective, experience and expertise required to achieve stewardship and management.'[110] Singapore Exchange, which remarkably has 30 per cent female directors, states that it has a diverse board 'to promote the inclusion of different perspectives and ideas and mitigate against groupthink'.[111]

It is worth clarifying that failure to comply with the 30 per cent requirement in the MCCG or the failure to have a single female director (in the case of Singapore) does not entail poor diversity policy provided that proper justifications are given. Consider the example of IHH Healthcare, the sixth largest listed company in Malaysia. Female directors account for 'approximately 27%' of its board,[112] and hence it falls short of the 30 per cent requirement in the MCCG. And women consist of 30 per cent of the senior management.[113] Its diversity disclosure states that it does not set any fixed targets based on age, gender or ethnic diversity but that it has come up with strategies to promote diversity in areas including, but not limited to, recruitment and selection as well as succession plans.[114] Importantly, the company reiterates that it 'does not specify a target for board diversity as the appointment of Board members should be based on objective criteria, merit and with due regard for diversity'.[115] Emphasising that appointment should be based on objective criteria and merit is crucial for dispelling any lingering doubt that female directors are appointed despite not meeting the requisite standard of experience and expertise.

---

[110] Petronas Gas Berhad, Twenty Seventeen Annual Report at 159. (See also the recent Petronas Gas Berhad Annual Report 2018 at 114, which contains the same quote.)
[111] Singapore Exchange, Annual Report 2018 at 59.
[112] IHH Healthcare Berhad, Annual Report 2018 at 113.
[113] Ibid at 98–102.
[114] Ibid at 113.
[115] Ibid.

However, merit should not be used as a pretext for not appointing female directors or as an excuse for not increasing the number of female directors. For example, the reason given by Wilmar International Limited when it did not have female directors among its thirteen-member[116] board was this: 'While the Board is supportive of gender diversity, the Board's collective view is that it should not be the main selection criteria and that board appointments, based on the right blend of skills, ability to contribute effectively and experience relevant to the Group's business, should remain a priority.'[117] There is nothing objectionable about prioritising merits, ie skills and ability. But when the statement is placed in context, namely, the failure of the company to appoint a female director and the omission of concrete measures that the board has taken or will take to promote board gender diversity, the quoted statement seems self-serving and an ex post rationalisation. By contrast, the emphasis on merits by another company in a different context may not appear self-serving but will instead reflect a thoughtful and careful approach towards diversity. Consider Godrej Consumer Products, a listed company in India. Female directors account for 36 per cent of its board as it has five female directors out of a total of fourteen directors.[118] The diversity policy states that 'board appointments will be made on a merit basis, and candidates will be considered on the basis of objective criteria, with due regard for the benefits of diversity. The Board believes that such merit-based appointments will best enable the company to serve its stakeholders.'[119] Further and importantly, the company articulates the concrete measures it has taken to increase gender representation such as requiring a certain percentage of female candidates for every position at general manager and above.[120] Moreover, the company has policies and programmes in place to promote the careers of women such as having flexible and part-time work arrangements as well as a caregiver policy in which the company will

---

[116] Wilmar International Limited, Annual Report 2017 at 16–21. (Note, however, that in the recent Wilmar International Limited Annual Report 2018 at 44–9, it is reflected that there is one female director out of thirteen directors. She was appointed on 21 February 2019, thus 'fulfilling the gender diversity requirement': ibid at 60.)

[117] Wilmar International Limited, Annual Report 2017 at 57. (Note, however, that this statement cannot be found in Wilmar International Limited's Annual Report 2018. This might be due to the fact that a female director was appointed in 2019, thus fulfilling the gender diversity requirement.)

[118] Godrej Consumer Products, Annual Report 2017–18 at 8–9.

[119] Ibid at 104.

[120] Ibid at 14.

sponsor travel for the child and caregiver if a woman has to travel for work and has a child below one year old.[121]

The above analysis of the nature and quality of diversity policy seeks to underscore the importance of good diversity policy to promote gender diversity. If diversity policies are crucial, then they should be subject to scrutiny. Regulators should set aside resources to monitor the quality of the policies. In other words, to promote board gender diversity, regulators should not only put pressure on companies with no female directors by publicising them; they should also monitor the quality of diversity policies by providing clear guidelines to companies on what they regard as acceptable disclosure and making companies accountable if they fall short of the criteria. For instance, where companies fail to disclose any diversity policy or disclose deficient policies, regulators may privately admonish them and, for serious or repeat cases, publicly criticise them. It is hoped that such criticisms by the regulators, which are likely to have an impact on the reputation of the company, will result in the company taking remedial actions.

D Setting Targets

In addition to adopting a name and shame approach combined with monitoring of diversity policies, the Malaysian regulator requires large companies, on an apply or explain an alternative basis, to have at least 30 per cent female directors for large companies.[122] It is perhaps not surprising that among the four common law jurisdictions in Asia, Malaysia has the highest percentage of female directors in the top fifty listed companies. As seen in Appendix 5, female directors in the top fifty listed companies in Malaysia, Hong Kong, India and Singapore account for 27.9 per cent, 18.2 per cent, 16.7 per cent and 15.8 per cent, respectively.

However, it does not follow that the failure either to adopt a name and shame approach or to set a target is fatal to the promotion of board gender diversity. After all, Hong Kong has adopted neither mechanisms and yet it is ranked second, after Malaysia, in terms of having the highest percentage of female directors. Nor has Hong Kong imposed a quota requirement, unlike India. This suggests that there are other explanations as to why Hong Kong is ranked second, although it has arguably the least

---

[121] Ibid.
[122] 2017 Malaysian Code on Corporate Governance para 4.5.

developed mechanism to promote board gender diversity as compared to the other three jurisdictions. This is because, as discussed earlier, the SEHK requires only listed companies to disclose their diversity policies with effect from 2019 on a comply or explain basis. This suggests that while Malaysia's combined approach of target setting, monitoring, and name and shame has been effective in Malaysia and should be considered for adoption by other jurisdictions, the absence of such a combined mechanism does not necessarily lead to a low number of female directors, provided that there are other mechanisms in place to promote board gender diversity.

There is one possible explanation as to why Hong Kong does not have the worst record but, on the contrary, is ranked second after Malaysia, namely, certain institutional shareholders may have played a role in the appointment of female directors. BlackRock is one of the top five largest shareholders in twenty-one of the thirty largest companies by market capitalisation in Hong Kong.[123] It has been reported that BlackRock has been privately urging its portfolio companies to appoint at least two female directors and recently made public this request.[124] BlackRock has asserted that the lack of board diversity has impeded the board from making effective decisions. Vanguard is also one of the top five largest shareholders in twenty-nine of the thirty largest companies by market capitalisation in Hong Kong.[125] Vanguard has taken the view that gender diversity will improve corporate performance and has stated that it has been working to increase female board representation in its investee companies.[126] Although there appears to be no concrete evidence that BlackRock and Vanguard have been exercising their formal power (ie voting) or informal power (ie private engagement) to cause the boards of the Hong Kong listed companies to appoint female directors, one cannot rule out the effect of these institutional investors on board gender diversity especially if these investors own a not insignificant percentage

---

[123] Ernest Lim, *A Case for Shareholders' Fiduciary Duties in Common Law Asia* (Cambridge University Press 2019) at Appendix 5.
[124] Sarah Krouse, 'BlackRock: Companies Should Have at Least Two Female Directors', *Wall Street Journal* (2 February 2018) www.wsj.com/articles/blackrock-companies-should-have-at-least-two-female-directors-1517598407.
[125] Ernest Lim, *A Case for Shareholders' Fiduciary Duties in Common Law Asia* (Cambridge University Press 2019) at Appendix 5.
[126] Laura Colby, 'Why Wall Street's Finally Pushing to Add Women on Boards', *Bloomberg* (6 December 2017) www.bloomberg.com/news/articles/2017-12-06/why-wall-streets-finally-pushing-to-add-women-on-boards.

of shares in the company.[127] Admittedly, BlackRock and Vanguard are also among the top five shareholders in several listed companies in Hong Kong and Singapore, and to a lesser extent India. However, the fact that these two institutional shareholders are shareholders of more listed companies in Hong Kong than Singapore, India and Malaysia and the fact that they own a higher percentage of shares in the companies in Hong Kong as compared to the other three jurisdictions[128] suggest that they might have played a bigger role in the board's decision of a number of listed companies in Hong Kong to appoint female directors. In sum, despite the lack of rules requiring diversity policy until very recently and notwithstanding the absence of any law prescribing the level of gender representation in Hong Kong, the fact that Hong Kong is ranked second may be partly attributable to the actions of SRIs. This is consistent with studies showing that there is a positive correlation between institutional shareholder ownership and environmental and social performance.[129]

Another possible explanation is that there may be a correlation between board gender diversity and the extent of the company's internationalisation. The idea is that there is a positive association between companies with high internationalisation (ie they export or supply their products or services to countries outside their home jurisdiction) and strong CSR performance.[130] This is because the companies' overseas stakeholders (including but not limited to the foreign customers, importers, outsourcers, suppliers and NGOs) will pressurise the companies to

---

[127] One study of the top three listed companies found that BlackRock and Vanguard own approximately 7 per cent and 3 per cent of shares, respectively: Ernest Lim, *A Case for Shareholders' Fiduciary Duties in Common Law Asia* (Cambridge University Press 2019) at 306.

[128] Ernest Lim, *A Case for Shareholders' Fiduciary Duties in Common Law Asia* (Cambridge University Press 2019) at Appendix 5.

[129] Alexander Dyck, Karl V Lins, Lukas Roth and Hannes F Wagner, 'Do Institutional Investors Drive Corporate Social Responsibility? International evidence' (2019) 131 *Journal of Financial Economics* 693.

[130] Najah Attig, Narjess Boubakri and Sadok El Ghoul, 'Firm Internationalization and Corporate Social Responsibility' (2016) 134 *Journal of Business Ethics* 171; J Kang, 'The Relationship Between Corporate Diversification and Corporate Social Performance' (2013) 34 *Strategic Management Journal* 94; Stephen J Brammer, Stephen Pavelin and Lynda A Porter, 'Corporate Social Performance and Geographical Diversification' (2006) 59 *Journal of Business Research* 1025; cf Roy L Simerly, 'Corporate Social Performance and Multinationality: An Empirical Examination' (1997) 14 *International Journal of Management* 699; Roy L Simerly and Minfang Li, 'Corporate Social performance and Multinationality: A Longitudinal Study' (2000) www.westga.edu/~bquest/2000/corporate.html.

adhere to good CSR practices. Further, companies will seek to protect and promote their reputation by engaging in more CSR activities due to greater scrutiny by the press and a variety of stakeholders A study of 1,330 listed companies in China corroborates this hypothesis.[131] But this study also noted that SOEs are less susceptible to pressure by foreign stakeholders, given that the SOEs enjoy benefits and protection from the state, their controlling shareholder. Applying this insight to the case of Hong Kong, it is suggested that one possible reason why Hong Kong is ranked second (among the four Asian jurisdictions) in terms of the percentage of female directors in the top fifty listed companies and also ranked second when the analysis is focused only on non-SOEs, but is ranked third when only SOEs are accounted for, is the internationalisation of the non-SOEs. A majority of the non-SOEs among the top fifty listed companies whose principal base of business is Hong Kong have international operations. But in order to establish a correlation, much more work has to be done. After all, a number of domestic non-SOEs listed in Singapore and to a lesser extent in India have international businesses too. Yet, India and Singapore are ranked third and fourth, respectively, in terms of the percentage of female directors in non-SOEs.

III State-Owned Enterprises

As mentioned earlier, my empirical study of the annual reports of the financial year 2017–18 of the top fifty listed companies, comprising both SOEs and non-SOEs, shows that Malaysia is ranked first in terms of having the highest percentage of female directors, followed by Hong Kong, India and Singapore. The rankings remain the same when we focus only on the non-SOEs in the four jurisdictions. However, an interesting and revealing finding is that when we look at the percentage of female directors in SOEs only, while Malaysia retains the highest percentage of female directors (26.18 per cent), it is followed by Singapore (17.59 per cent), Hong Kong (12.15 per cent) and India (9.16 per cent), as shown in Figure 3.2. A breakdown by non-SOEs is also shown in Figure 3.3. Several inferences can be drawn from the figures.

---

[131] Yan-Leung Cheung, Dongmin Kong, Weiqiang Tan and Wenming Wang, 'Being Good When Being International in an Emerging Economy: The Case of China' (2015) 130 *Journal of Business Ethics* 805.

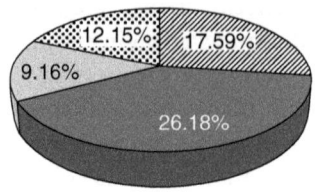

▨ Singapore ■ Malaysia ▩ India ⁖ Hong Kong

Figure 3.2 Proportion of female directors in Singapore, Malaysia, India and Hong Kong (in %) (among GLCs/SOEs in the top fifty companies by market capitalisation)

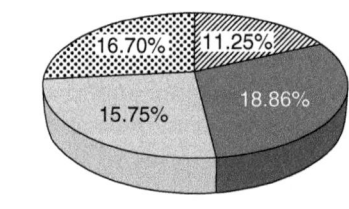

▨ Singapore ■ Malaysia ▩ India ⁖ Hong Kong

Figure 3.3 Proportion of female directors in Singapore, Malaysia, India and Hong Kong (in %) (among non-GLCs/SOEs in the top fifty companies by market capitalisation)

A Malaysia

The fact that Malaysia has emerged as the top-ranking country in all three categories (overall, non-SOEs and SOEs) suggests that the approaches taken by Malaysia – apply or explain an alternative, target setting, monitoring disclosure, and name and shame – have been more effective than those taken by the other three jurisdictions. It is also telling that in the category of the percentage of female directors in SOEs, Malaysia ranks first among the four Asian jurisdictions. Nineteen of the top fifty listed companies are SOEs. The percentage of female directors in these nineteen SOEs ranges from 10 per cent to 42.86 per cent. Four of the nineteen SOEs have at least 33 per cent female directors. While the remaining fifteen SOEs have fallen short of the 30 per cent requirement, nine of them have at least 25 per cent female directors.

III STATE-OWNED ENTERPRISES 135

Moreover, it is important to note that the percentage of female directors in the SOEs versus non-SOEs in Malaysia is 26.18 per cent and 18.86 per cent, respectively. The strong performance of the SOEs suggests that the government as the controlling shareholder has played a role in promoting board gender diversity. This suggests that not only is a multi-pronged approach comprising target setting, monitoring disclosure and name and shame necessary, but so is the function played by the government as the controlling shareholder. One possible reason why SOEs have outperformed the non-SOEs in terms of female directors is because the government's reputation is at stake. Given that the code states that large companies (which are likely to include most of the SOEs) must have at least 30 per cent female directors (on an apply or explain an alternative basis), the SOEs have to lead by example.

B Singapore

The fact that Singapore is ranked second in terms of the percentage of female directors in SOEs but last in terms of the percentage of female directors in (a) the top fifty listed companies and (b) the non-SOEs suggests that the controlling shareholder of SOEs, the government, has played a crucial role in the promotion of board gender diversity. Moreover, the fact that the percentage of female directors in SOEs versus non-SOEs is 17.59 per cent versus 11.25 per cent, respectively, supports the point that the government as the controller plays an important role. After all, nearly all the SOEs have at least one female director. Not only has the government generally led by example by putting pressure on the companies of which it is a controlling shareholder to appoint female directors, but it has also worked closely with companies, NGOs and industry organisations to promote board gender diversity. With the strong support of the government, the Council for Board Diversity (CBD), previously known as the Diversity Action Committee, was formed in 2014 to raise awareness of the importance of board gender diversity and to increase the number of female directors in listed companies by engaging with companies.[132] The CBD consists of members drawn from the listed companies, government departments, regulatory bodies, NGOs and industry organisations. The CBD combines public advocacy with behind-the-scenes engagement. The results are promising.

---

[132] Council for Board Diversity www.diversityaction.sg/about/council-for-board-diversity/.

The CBD claims that, after it was established, female directors in the top 100 listed companies increased from 7.5 per cent to 15.2 per cent from 2014 to 2018.[133] While the reasons for the increase in the female board representation are multi-faceted and difficult to trace to one single source, the CBD, given its strong government and industry backing, no doubt played an important role.

C India

India is ranked last among the four Asian jurisdictions in terms of the percentage of female directors in SOEs. There are nine SOEs among the top fifty listed companies in India. Out of these nine, two do not have a single female director, thereby violating the Companies Act. This raises the concern that when the government is both a corporate governance regulator and a controlling shareholder, there is the risk that it may not be willing to subject itself to the rules that it has imposed. As no sanctions appear to have been imposed for failing to appoint a female director, it is questionable whether the two recalcitrant SOEs will comply with the law. They might eventually if it results in adverse impact on their reputation to the extent that it negatively affects their share price.

Further, it is telling that female representation on the boards of non-SOEs and SOEs is 15.75 per cent and 9.16 per cent, respectively. This is in contrast to the situation in Malaysia and Singapore where the SOEs have a significantly higher percentage of female directors than non-SOEs. This is attributable in part to the vigorous action comprising a multi-pronged approach undertaken by the government and involving the industry bodies in Malaysia and Singapore to promote board gender diversity. By contrast, once India has legally imposed on companies the need to have at least one female director in the companies statute, there seems to be no follow-up action on the part of the government to monitor whether companies have complied and to name and shame those that have not.

D Hong Kong

As for Hong Kong, there are fifteen Chinese SOEs among the top fifty listed companies, four of which consist of all male boards (26.67 per cent). Nine SOEs (60 per cent) have at least one female

---

[133] Ibid.

director. Given that the SEHK imposes no requirement to appoint any female director, there is no incentive for these four SOEs with all male boards to do so, except that failure to do so will affect their reputation vis-à-vis other companies that have female directors. Further, the SEHK merely requires disclosure of diversity policy or a summary thereof, but even then, only on a comply or explain basis. There is thus the risk that SOEs that have no or deficient diversity policy may continue this practice. Unlike the situation in Malaysia and Singapore, where there is a strong advocacy on the part of the government to promote female directors coupled with, in the case of Malaysia, a requirement to have certain percentage of female directors, there is no such concerted action by the Hong Kong government (including its regulatory authorities) nor is there such a legal requirement.

E SOEs with No Female Directors

Among the four Asian jurisdictions, Malaysia is the only country in which all the SOEs among the top fifty companies have female directors. But in India, Hong Kong and Singapore, there are SOEs that have no female directors. The issue concerns the conflicts of interest between the government as the regulator and the government as the controlling shareholder of the SOEs: the regulator (or the applicable government body) has an interest in ensuring that SOEs have at least one female director. But it may be argued that because the government as the controlling shareholder of the SOEs wields the power to appoint female directors, it may not see the need to exercise the power.

By not having a single female director, the two SOEs in India are in breach of their obligations under the Companies Act. It remains uncertain whether and, if so, the extent to which the regulator (such as the MCA or SEBI) will censure these SOEs. While Singapore and Hong Kong impose no legal obligation on companies to have any female director, the question is whether conflicts of interest would undermine the ability or willingness of the government as the regulator to pressurise those SOEs with no female directors to appoint at least one.

F Connected to the Government

An important issue is whether female directors in the SOEs in the four Asian countries are connected to the government, that is, there is a risk that they may be appointed on the basis not of merit but rather of political connections. By connected, it means that the female directors either are currently working or used to work for the government or the controlling shareholder of the SOE. It is possible that the female directors are connected to the government and yet are appointed on the basis of merit because they have the requisite experience and expertise. Nevertheless, because of evidence of political interference in the appointment of directors and managers in the SOEs in Malaysia, India and Hong Kong,[134] the concern that female directors are appointed to the boards of SOEs on a basis other than merit remains; there is also the concern that they may do the bidding of the government who is the controlling shareholder. If these concerns are legitimate, then the presence of female directors may not necessarily be a positive thing.

In Malaysia, among the top fifty listed companies, there are nineteen SOEs, all of which have female directors. There are a total of fifty female directors, of whom twenty are connected to the government, which accounts for 40 per cent. In India, among the top fifty listed companies, there are seven SOEs with female directors. In these seven SOEs, there are a total of twelve female directors, of whom six are connected to the government, which accounts for 50 per cent. In Hong Kong, there are a total of fifteen SOEs out of the top fifty listed companies. Eleven of these SOEs have at least one female director. There are a total of twenty-two female directors in these SOEs, of whom thirteen are connected to the government (59 per cent). In Singapore, among the top fifty listed companies, there are eighteen SOEs with female directors. There are altogether thirty-five female directors in these eighteen SOEs. Out of these thirty-five, twenty-one of them are connected to the government, ie 60 per cent. Three of these twenty-one female directors used to work for or are currently working for the controlling shareholder of the SOEs (ie Temasek) or its affiliated companies or its ultimate controlling shareholder (ie Ministry of Finance). In summary, the percentage of female directors that have connections with the government in Malaysia, India, Hong Kong and Singapore is 40 per cent, 50 per cent, 59 per cent and 60 per cent, respectively.

However, it may be argued that even if a female director is connected to the government, she can still be classified as an independent director. The key question is not whether female directors are politically

---

[134] Ernest Lim, *A Case for Shareholders' Fiduciary Duties in Common Law Asia* (Cambridge University Press 2019) at 47–60.

connected but whether they are independent of the controlling shareholder. After all, there are female directors in the SOEs who are connected to the government and yet are classified as independent.[135] The counterargument is that a study of the rules on independent directors in India, Malaysia, Hong Kong and Singapore shows that a director is not necessarily disqualified from being an independent director even if (1) she is not independent of the controlling shareholder; or (2) she is employed by the controlling shareholder.[136] Thus, the fact that a female director is classified as independent does not assuage the concern that she may be appointed on the basis of political connections rather than merit.

Another possible argument is that a female director's connection to the government does not necessarily give rise to concerns. The government is a huge machinery consisting of different departments with different responsibilities. The point is that even if a female director is employed by the government, the latter might be a different entity from that which is the controlling shareholder of the SOE. If that is the case, her connection to the government as the controlling shareholder is highly tenuous. Put differently, in order to sustain the claim that the female director's connection to the government calls into question whether her appointment was merit-based, the connection has to be related to the controlling shareholder and not merely to any governmental entity. This is a fair point. But it depends on whether the governmental entity to which the female director is connected is closely related to the controlling shareholder (whether through a business, political or other types of relationship).

G   Repeat Players

The empirical analysis here, as well as in other studies, measures diversity based on the percentage of women on the boards of individual companies. Such a measure does not take into account the issue of repeat players, namely, female (or male) directors who hold multiple directorships. Given that there is a limited pool of female directors who have the requisite expertise and experience, the issue of repeat players for female

---

[135] For example, in the Singapore GLCs of CapitaLand Ltd and SATS Ltd, the female director Euleen Goh is classified as an independent director, but she is a member of the Board of Trustees of Temasek Trust, which is affiliated with Temasek Holdings Pte Ltd, the controlling shareholder of CapitaLand Ltd and SATs Ltd.

[136] Ernest Lim, *A Case for Shareholders' Fiduciary Duties in Common Law Asia* (Cambridge University Press 2019) at 224–9.

directors will be more salient than that of male directors. If a handful of female directors hold a number of directorships, this does not advance the goal of attracting more women to become female directors because the board positions are occupied by the same female directors. Further, it will result in an entrenchment of a small handful of female directors because they are more likely to be appointed as directors if companies decide they need more female directors. Holding multiple directorships also raises the secondary concern as to whether these female directors will have the time and resources to discharge their duties properly to all the companies of which they are directors. For example, consider the case of SOEs. In the Malaysian SOEs, there are seven female directors holding two directorships. In the Singapore SOEs, there are four female directors each of whom holds two or more directorships. However, among the PRC SOEs listed in Hong Kong, there is only one woman who holds more than one directorship. And in the Indian SOEs, there is no issue of repeat players at all. The numbers suggest that the higher the percentage of female directors, the higher the incidence of female directors holding more than one directorship.

In advancing the goal of board gender diversity, regulators should pay attention not only to the issue of the number of female directors in each company but also to the question of repeat players. Promoting female directors requires both a deep pool of female directors (ie women with the requisite experience and expertise) and a broad pool (to minimise the occurrence of the same women holding multiple positions).

IV Conclusion

Promoting board gender diversity is without a doubt important. But what is more vital is to critically analyse the justifications and measures behind it. The four Asian jurisdictions studied here (Singapore, Hong Kong, Malaysia and India) have relied on instrumental reasons – female directors improve corporate governance and firm value – to make the case for female directors. But a closer look at the empirical studies paints a mixed and equivocal view of the effectiveness of female directors in improving corporate performance. What is necessary is to supplement these instrumental justifications with intrinsic or moral ones based on equality of resources and opportunity. These equality-based justifications underscore the critical importance of addressing the systemic and entrenched social, economic and cultural impediments that women face in attaining board positions. For policy makers to focus only on the instrumental rationales and to neglect or downplay intrinsic ones is myopic and misguided. One cannot divorce the issue of increasing female directors from the broader issue of female empowerment and emancipation.

Having examined the justifications for female directors, I critically evaluated the different measures deployed by the four Asian jurisdictions to promote board gender diversity. I argued that the quota requirement in India suffers from many serious weaknesses and, as it stands, is a deeply unsatisfactory solution in promoting board gender diversity. I argued that the Malaysian multi-pronged approach consisting of apply or explain an alternative, target setting, monitoring of disclosures, and name and shame is the most effective in promoting board gender diversity. This multi-pronged approach has been largely initiated and delivered by the government. Unsurprisingly, among the four Asian jurisdictions, Malaysia has the highest percentage of female directors in the top fifty listed companies and it also remains the highest when the data are broken down into SOEs and non-SOEs. Nevertheless, while government actions are important, the case of Hong Kong suggests that factors such as pressure from influential institutional shareholders and the internationalisation of companies are also relevant and maybe significant.

Finally, given that SOEs play a crucial role in the economic and social development in the four jurisdictions and in light of the fact that they account for a significant percentage of the market capitalisation of the top fifty listed companies in the four jurisdictions, it is important to know the proportion of female directors in the SOEs and the issues arising from them. Three matters may be a cause of concern and deserve further study. First, where the SOEs have no female directors, the government as the regulator may not monitor or discipline these SOEs in light of the conflict of interest between the government as the regulator and the government as the controlling shareholder of the SOEs. Second, the female directors of the SOEs may be appointed on the basis not of merit but of political connection. The final matter concerns the correlation between increased female directors and increased incidence of repeat players, ie the same women holding more than one directorship.

4

Constituency Directors

I German Co-determination   143
   A Costs and Benefits   145
      1 Costs   145
      2 Benefits   149
   B Adoption by Other Jurisdictions   152
      1 Singapore   153
      2 Malaysia   156
      3 Hong Kong   159
      4 India   161
II Indian CSR Board Committee   162
III Conclusion   168

This chapter critically assesses two models of constituency directors – the more well-known German model of co-determination and the Indian version – with a view to determining whether the common law Asian jurisdictions should adopt constituency directors as a mechanism to promote sustainability. The term 'constituency directors' is understood here to mean either that the directors are appointed by (or are representatives of) certain stakeholders to advance their interests or that the directors, while appointed by shareholders, are specifically required under the law to promote the interests of stakeholders. The prime example of the first version of constituency directors is the German co-determination board, and the second version is the Indian CSR board. While Germany's co-determination model is the most prominent and well-established one, it is by no means the only country that has required employee representation on boards. There are nineteen states in the EU that provide for employee representation on boards once companies reach a certain size.[1] Further, two different bills have been introduced in the United States, one that

---

[1] European Trade Union Institute, 'Board level representation in Europe: Overview in 2017' www.worker-participation.eu/National-Industrial-Relations/Across-Europe/Board-level-Representation2.

requires 40 per cent of boards in companies worth $1billion to be elected by employees,[2] and another that requires all listed companies to have one-third of their boards elected by employees.[3] Thus, a timely and salient issue is whether the structure and composition of the board should be reformed such that the board will be responsive to the interests of constituencies other than those of shareholders. The key question for our consideration is whether the German co-determination model or the Indian CSR board committee is a suitable mechanism for promoting sustainability and whether jurisdictions such as Singapore, Hong Kong and Malaysia, which have not adopted either of these two models, should consider doing so.

I German Co-determination

Two caveats are in place. First, I recognise that the purpose of the German co-determination model is not to promote sustainability, but to promote the interests of employees by giving them governance rights. Advancing employee welfare is clearly one of the central social considerations within the ESG framework that listed companies are required to apply to their business decisions. The question then is whether this model can be adapted with appropriate modifications to promote sustainability more generally. Second, the German co-determination model consists of representation at the supervisory level of the board by employee representatives as well as a works council that allows workers to participate in decisions that affect their employment.[4] In addition to these two components, it has also been said that the German co-determination model consists of collective bargaining, which takes place outside the company with an employers' association.[5] The analysis here concerns only representation at the board level. This is to enable comparison with the Indian model of constituency directors.

Under German law, a two-tier board, comprising the supervisory and management board, is compulsory.[6] The importance of the supervisory

---

[2] Accountable Capitalism Act (2018), s 3348 www.congress.gov/bill/115th-congress/senate-bill/3348/text.
[3] Reward Work Act (2018), s 2605 www.congress.gov/bill/115th-congress/senate-bill/2605/text.
[4] Paul Davies, 'Efficiency Arguments for the Collective Representation of Workers' in Alan Bogg, Cathryn Costello, ACL Davies and Jeremias Prassl (eds), *The Autonomy of Labour Law* (Hart Publishing 2015) at 382–4.
[5] Ibid.
[6] Markus Roth, 'Corporate Boards in Germany' in Paul Davies, Klaus Hopt, Richard Nowak and Gerard van Solinge (eds), *Corporate Boards in Law and Practice* (Oxford University Press 2013); Ewan McGaughey, 'The Codetermination Bargains: The History of German Corporate and Labour Law' (2016) 23 *Columbia Journal of European Law* 135.

board lies in the fact that it appoints and monitors members of the management board who are responsible for the business and operations of the company. Companies with more than 2,000 employees (except for the iron, steel and coal industries) are required to have 50 per cent of the supervisory board consisting of employee representatives and the other 50 per cent shareholder representatives.[7] If there is a deadlock because the employee bench and the shareholder bench disagree on the appointment of candidates, the law gives the shareholder bench the right to elect a chairman who has the casting vote, and the chair is usually a representative of the shareholders.[8] Two-thirds of the supervisory board's vote is required for appointment of the members of the management board.[9] In other words, because the election of the members of the management board requires support from the employee representatives (and not merely the shareholder representatives), the management board will consult, and take into account the interests of, the employees. Further, the power of the supervisory board is not restricted to the appointment of the management board. While the supervisory board is not permitted to interfere with the operations of the management board, the company's constitution can provide that the decisions taken by the management board are required to be approved by the supervisory board.[10]

Unsurprisingly, co-determination has been concisely described as 'giving economic power to those who control the means of production and [using] employee participation as a tool to counter the interests of capital'.[11] In short, co-determination provides 'social governance, whereas corporate governance provides firm-level governance'.[12] An important impetus underlying the development of the co-determination model was to combat fascism post–World War II.[13]

---

[7] Mitbestimmungsgesetz 1976 (4 May 1976) (Codetermination Act 1976) BGBl I S 1153, §9; Wolfgang Streeck, 'Codetermination: The Fourth Decade' in Bernhard Wilpert and Arndt Sorge (eds), *International Perspectives on Organizational Democracy* (John Wiley 1984).

[8] Mitbestimmungsgesetz 1976 §§27, 29, 31 and 33.

[9] Ibid.

[10] Katharina Pistor, 'Codetermination: A Sociopolitical Model with Governance Externalities' in Margaret Blair and Mark J Roe (eds), *Employees and Corporate Governance* (Brookings Institution Press 1999) at 184.

[11] Ibid at 163.

[12] Ibid.

[13] Hans G Nutzinger, 'Codetermination in West Germany: Institutions and Experiences' in Hans G Nutzinger and Jürgen Backhaus (eds), *Codetermination: A Discussion of Different Approaches* (Springer 2000); Friedrich Kubler, Walter Schmidt and Spiros Simitis, *Mitbestimmungsproblem als Gesetzgebungspolitische Aufgabe* (Nomos Verlagsgesellschaft 1978).

A significant source of fascist power was the alliance between the government and private capital, particularly the steel and coal industries, both of which were accused of exploiting their power to the detriment of the German workers. As a result, social measures were taken to curtail the power of private capital, one manifestation of which was co-determination. Unsurprisingly, co-determination in the form of giving workers the right to be represented on the supervisory board was first applied to mining, coal and steel companies. The law was later amended and extended to companies outside these industries with more than 2,000 employees. Understanding the historical and political context in which co-determination came about is relevant to analysing the question of whether and if so how the co-determination model could be transplanted to the three Asian jurisdictions (Singapore, Malaysia and Hong Kong), each of which has differing political, social and economic contexts, and none of which has (yet) the mechanism of constituency directors. I will elaborate on this point in Section I(B).

A   Costs and Benefits

1   Costs

Putting aside for now the historical rationale for co-determination, in order to understand whether the German co-determination model could be modified to promote sustainability and whether it could be adapted by other jurisdictions, we have to first analyse the costs of this model and whether they are outweighed by the benefits. There are three costs.

a   Render the Decision-Making Process Inefficient   The first cost is that it may render the decision-making process of the supervisory board inefficient.[14] This is partly due to the fact that the interests of employees are likely to conflict with those of shareholders. And among the employees themselves, their interests could diverge because, under the law, the employee bench on the supervisory board has to consist of white- and blue-collar workers as well as labour union representatives.[15] In practice, in addition to the workers and labour union representatives, there is

---

[14] Katharina Pistor, 'Codetermination: A Sociopolitical Model with Governance Externalities' in Margaret Blair and Mark J Roe (eds), *Employees and Corporate Governance* (Brookings Institution Press 1999) at 177–9.
[15] Ibid at 169.

a third group that consists of the members of the works councils of subsidiaries.[16]

Not only might the interests of blue- and white-collar workers diverge, but the interests of these two groups of workers may conflict with those of the labour union.[17] This is because the labour union will be concerned with broader considerations involving itself, different industry sectors and the economy in general, as opposed to specific considerations related to the particular company and its employees. As a result of the divergence of interests, the employee representatives will have separate meetings to sort things out among themselves before the actual supervisory board meeting with the shareholder representatives. Otherwise, if the employee representatives split their votes, it is likely that the outcome of the votes will be in favour of the shareholder representatives.[18]

If the co-determination model were to be modified, for the purpose of promoting sustainability, to include not only employee representatives but also, for example, representatives from customers or the community, the cost of the decision-making process would increase. There would be greater heterogeneity of interests and hence increased inefficiency in the management of the company. However, a recent analysis of the empirical evidence concluded that 'the impact of the [German] system on the production costs of German companies is not negative and may be positive'.[19]

b Render the Decision-Making Process Uncertain and Unpredictable The second cost of the co-determination model is that, in general, it will render the overall decision-making process in the company uncertain and unpredictable and, specifically, that it will render the monitoring and disciplining of management much more difficult. The management board could form a coalition with the shareholder representatives or with the employee representatives in order to out-manoeuvre either one of

---

[16] Walther Muller-Jentsch, 'Germany: From Collective Voice to Co-management' in Joel Rogers and Wolfgang Streek (eds), *Works Councils* (University of Chicago Press 1995) at ch 3.

[17] Katharina Pistor, 'Codetermination: A Sociopolitical Model with Governance Externalities' in Margaret Blair and Mark J Roe (eds), *Employees and Corporate Governance* (Brookings Institution Press 1999) at 182–3.

[18] Ibid at 183.

[19] Paul Davies, 'Efficiency Arguments for the Collective Representation of Workers' in Alan Bogg, Cathryn Costello, ACL Davies and Jeremias Prassl (eds), *The Autonomy of Labour Law* (Hart Publishing 2015) at 390.

these two groups.[20] This is not an unlikely scenario because the management board has access to and is in control of material information on the business strategies, business operations and finances, and is able to selectively disclose the information to the employee and shareholder benches of the supervisory board for different purposes and to achieve different goals. For example, before the employee bench of the supervisory board attends the board meeting with the shareholder bench, it is likely to have considered how it should vote on a particular matter. And prior to arriving at its decision, it will seek information from and discuss with the chair of the management board. The shareholder bench of the supervisory board is also likely to do the same prior to voting at the supervisory board. Thus, the chair of the management board will have three meetings, one with the employee bench, a second with the shareholder bench and a third with the full supervisory board.[21]

Given that the management board is in control of certain material information and, depending on the circumstances, can enter into (and exit from) coalitions with the employee bench or the shareholder bench, it would be much more difficult for the supervisory board to monitor the management board. But one may argue that the employee bench and the shareholder bench could also form a coalition to restrain the management board. This is theoretically possible, but, given that the interests of both benches are generally not aligned, particularly for transactions related to takeover or reorganisation, it is doubtful whether an effective coalition could be formed to effectively monitor the management board.

Similar to the first cost, if co-determination were modified to include more representatives on the supervisory board (such as consumers or members of the community) so as to promote sustainability, then opportunities for the management board to form opportunistic coalitions would also arise. Not only would it be difficult to monitor the management board but there would also be the risk that, instead of acting in good faith and independently to promote sustainability, the management board would play off the interests and demands of one constituency against another to secure the best possible deal for itself.

However, one study that involved interviews with employees, labour unions and the government found that the benefits of co-determination

---

[20] Peter A Gourevitch and James Shinn, *Political Power and Corporate Control: The New Global Politics of Corporate Governance* (Princeton University Press 2005) at 59–62.
[21] Katharina Pistor, 'Codetermination: A Sociopolitical Model with Governance Externalities' in Margaret Blair and Mark J Roe (eds), *Employees and Corporate Governance* (Brookings Institution Press 1999) at 190.

outweigh the costs.[22] The study found that employees' involvement in the company's decision-making process at an early stage, while resulting in more time and expenses, is good for the company as it reduces the incidence of conflict with respect to certain decisions that adversely affect the interests of employees, such as restructuring and takeovers. It is telling that the study clarified that employees' participation in the decision-making process did not result in the abandonment of these decisions; rather, the company went ahead with them, but the adverse impact on employees was ameliorated. Further, the study acknowledged that employees have not been successful in the development of the long-term strategies of the company, which is the other objective of co-determination. This is because employee representatives do not have the requisite expertise, particularly if it pertains to finance and accounting.

c **Reduced Responsiveness by Management Board to the Controller's Interests** The third and final cost of the co-determination model is that the management board will be less responsive to the interests of shareholders, particularly if the shareholders are controllers and, thus, object to this co-determination model. Given that the majority of the listed companies in the four Asian jurisdictions consist of controlling shareholders, a significant proportion of which comprises the government (or the companies it controls), it is doubtful that the controllers will be willing to give up part of their power, specifically the right to appoint and dismiss directors (the equivalent of which will be the members of the management board).

However, there are ways to mitigate dilution of the controller's power. For example, shareholders could alter the company's constitution to insert a provision that the chairman of the supervisory board has to be elected from among the shareholder representatives.[23] Under German law, if there is a deadlock, a chairman with the casting vote is elected by the shareholder bench. Thus, while the law requires the chair to be elected by the shareholder representatives, it does not state whether the chair has to be someone from the shareholder bench or the employee bench. Another example is that shareholders do not seem to be precluded from including a provision in the company's constitution stipulating that the slate of nominees for the management board is required to be

---

[22] Ibid at 188–9.
[23] Ibid at 185.

approved by the shareholders before the nominees are presented to the supervisory board for approval.

In sum, with respect to the first cost, limited empirical evidence suggests that it is outweighed by the benefit of involving employees in the decision-making process. Regarding the second cost, there is a study suggesting that the benefits of co-determination outweigh the costs. As for the third cost, it can be mitigated with appropriate alterations in the company's constitution.

2 Benefits

These costs have to be weighed against the benefits. Ensuring that employees' interests are considered and protected by the management board is important not only to reduce conflicts between the shareholders and employees with regard to certain business decisions that could have an adverse impact on employees but also to effectively promote long-term firm-specific investments by employees that are crucial for the company's long-term success. Employees acquire specialised skills that are unique or specific to the company and that are not easily transferrable to another company.[24] As these employees' investments are 'locked' into the company, there is a risk that employers may exploit workers by reducing their salaries or denying them bonuses, laying them off once the company has reaped the benefits of their investments or reneging on implicit expectations as to the benefits that should be given to employees. Importantly, employees are not able to factor in these risks in the employment contracts.[25] Their contracts are necessarily incomplete.[26] One reason is the inequality of bargaining power between employees and employers. Another reason relates to uncertainties and contingencies: whether employees will be awarded bonuses, get promoted or continue to

---

[24] See eg James M Malcolmson, 'Individual Employment Contracts' in Orley Aschenfelter and David Card (eds), *Handbook of Labor Economics*, vol 3B (Elsevier 1999) at 2330–3; Larry Fauver and Michael E Fuerst, 'Does Good Corporate Governance Include Employee Representation? Evidence from German Corporate Boards' (2006) 82 *Journal of Financial Economics* 673 at 679; Gavin Kelly and John Parkinson, 'The Conceptual Foundations of the Company: A Pluralist Approach' in John Parkinson, Gavin Kelly and Andrew Gamble (eds), *The Political Economy of the Company* (Hart Publishing 2001) at 123–9.

[25] See eg Thomas Eger, 'Opportunistic Termination of Employment Contracts and Legal Protection against Dismissal in Germany and the USA' (2004) 23 *International Review of Law and Economics* 381 at 383–4.

[26] Paul Davies, 'Efficiency Arguments for the Collective Representation of Workers' in Alan Bogg, Cathryn Costello, ACL Davies and Jeremias Prassl (eds), *The Autonomy of Labour Law* (Hart Publishing 2015) at 374–9.

remain employed depends on the business and financial conditions as well as the organisational dynamics of the company, which are difficult to stipulate in advance in the contract. A similar logic applies to suppliers who may have invested in resources to produce and supply certain products that are unique to the company. It may be argued that suppliers can take into account these expenses in the negotiation of their contract with the company. But there could be inequality of bargaining power and incomplete contracts.

Further and importantly, it has been argued that, in concentrated ownership companies, controlling shareholders have incentives to extract private benefits of control at the expense of not only minority shareholders but also other stakeholders including employees.[27] If their control rights exceed their cash flow rights (such as in a company with a pyramid structure or a dual class share structure), controlling shareholders can cause the board to pay them special dividends, cut employees' salaries, forgo the production of environmentally sustainable products or reduce investments in R&D that could eventually lead to better and cheaper products for consumers. Moreover, the controlling shareholder may put pressure on the company to pursue highly risky investments as he will gain the benefit if the investment succeeds but the creditors will bear the brunt should the investment fail. Or the controlling shareholder could cause the company to restructure and downsize to increase profits, resulting in adverse impact on employees. In short, a co-determined board is an important mechanism for constraining controlling shareholders from acting to the detriment of stakeholders.

However, it is not always or necessarily the case that controlling shareholders will engage in such actions. For example, the government in certain SOEs has social objectives such as promoting employment, income redistribution and provision of subsidies.[28] In addition to social objectives, the government in SOEs could have political objectives such as gaining political support in exchange for provision of benefits to stakeholders.[29] This partially constrains the controller's temptation to

---

[27] Martin Gelter, 'The Dark Side of Shareholder Influence: Managerial Autonomy and Stakeholder Orientation in Comparative Governance' (2009) 50 *Harvard International Law Journal* 129 at 154–67; Andrei Shleifer and Robert W Vishny, 'A Survey of Corporate Governance' (1997) 52 *Journal of Finance* 737 at 760; Mike Burkart, Denis Gromb and Fausto Panunzi, 'Large Shareholders, Monitoring, and Fiduciary Duty' (1997) 112 *Quarterly Journal of Economics* 112.

[28] See Chapter 1, Section III(A).

[29] Ibid.

pursue their own interests to the detriment of stakeholders. That said, political and social objectives may not be sufficient constraints where the gains from extractions of private benefits of control exceed the cost. In any event, even if controllers do not engage in expropriation, they could sell their stakes to other investors who are willing to offer a higher price than the current share value because they know that they could maximise share price by acting opportunistically at the expense of the interests of stakeholders.

It is thus suggested that co-determination will help to reduce the incidence of opportunistic behaviour by controlling shareholders and to promote long-term firm-specific investments by stakeholders. There is evidence suggesting that co-determined boards constrain extractions of private benefits of control and facilitate long-term investments by stakeholders because of enhanced job security. The study found a correlation between companies with partially co-determined boards and employees' job security and wage levels.[30] It was found that employees in such companies have higher percentage of employment (about 15 per cent) but lower percentage of salary (about 3 per cent) than companies without co-determined boards, as higher salary was traded for job security.

Another benefit, as studies suggest, is that co-determined boards are not detrimental to firm value. One study showed neither positive nor negative correlation between firm value and co-determined boards;[31] although another study showed a connection between co-determined boards (in which the employee bench consists of 50 per cent) and 31 per cent reduction in firm value,[32] and a later study found that moderately co-determined boards (in which the supervisory board consists of 30 per cent employee bench) have increased firm value.[33] An earlier study showed that the introduction of co-determination resulted

---

[30] E Han Kim, Ernst Maug and Christoph Schneider, 'Labor Representation in Governance as an Insurance Mechanism' (2018) 22 *Review of Finance* 1251.

[31] Bernd Frick and Erik Lehman, 'Corporate Governance in Germany: Ownership, Codetermination and Firm Performance in a Stakeholder Economy' in Howard Gospel and Andrew Pendleton (eds), *Corporate Governance and Labour Management* (Oxford University Press 2006) at ch 5.

[32] Gary Gorton and Frank A Schmid, 'Capital, Labor and the Firm: A Study of German Codetermination' (2004) 2 *Journal of the European Economic Association* 863.

[33] Larry Fauver and Michael E Fuerst, 'Does Good Corporate Governance Include Employee Representation? Evidence from German Corporate Boards' (2006) 82 *Journal of Financial Economics* 673 at 679.

in firm productivity.[34] It has been recently concluded that 'the empirical evidence about the German system suggests, overall, that it is a system in which the employees' governance rights over the corporation facilitate long-term implicit contracts between employees and managers and that the impact of the system on the production costs of German companies is not negative and may well be positive'.[35]

B Adoption by Other Jurisdictions

Nevertheless, it is one thing to evaluate the costs and benefits of co-determination. It is another thing to assess whether the German co-determination model should be adopted by the other three Asian jurisdictions (Singapore, Malaysia and Hong Kong). The German co-determination model was initially developed and subsequently maintained in a historical, political and social context that is different from that in the other three Asian jurisdictions. This consideration alone does not determine the answer to the question of whether a transplant is justified. But the analysis is important as it shows us that the institutional factors that resulted in the initial implementation and subsequent sustenance of the German co-determination model may not be present or easily replicated in the three Asian jurisdictions. If that is the case, it would be more difficult for these jurisdictions to adopt the model.

As mentioned earlier, a key historical rationale underlying German co-determination was to address the exploitation of workers by the coal and steel industries, which were in collusion with the political regime, by empowering the workers with governance rights. Further, the German co-determination model comprises not only co-determined boards but also works councils and collective bargaining. While these three mechanisms were not implemented at the same time, they complemented and sustained each other. If a key function of the co-determined board is to provide strategic direction, set up internal controls and reporting systems, and ensure oversight of the management board, the role of the works council is to provide specific rights to the workers within the

---

[34] Felix FitzRoy and Kornelius Kraft, 'Co-determination, Efficiency and Productivity' (2005) 43 *British Journal of Industrial Relations* 233.

[35] Paul Davies, 'Efficiency Arguments for the Collective Representation of Workers' in Alan Bogg, Cathryn Costello, ACL Davies and Jeremias Prassl (eds), *The Autonomy of Labour Law* (Hart Publishing 2015) at 390.

company.³⁶ They include the right to information on the company, the right to be consulted on matters such as pay, job allocation, working hours, and the right to veto termination of employment. Collective bargaining takes place outside the company and with an employers' association, pertaining to specific industries.³⁷ The point of mentioning these two aspects of the co-determination system (ie the works council and collective bargaining) is not that without them the co-determined board is not sustainable and cannot be transplanted to other jurisdictions. Rather it is to point out that the viability or effectiveness of the co-determined board operates within a specific setting where there are other mechanisms that could facilitate or undermine it.

The historical rationale of the German co-determined board and its surrounding supporting mechanisms have a bearing on the question not only of whether companies should voluntarily choose to have co-determined boards but also of whether co-determined boards should be made mandatory by the state. Analysis of the latter issue is more complex as it requires us to understand the labour policies and mechanisms in the three Asian jurisdictions (Singapore, Malaysia and Hong Kong).

1 Singapore

Singapore's labour policies and practices are heavily regulated by the state (through the Ministry of Manpower, the Singapore National Employers Federation and the National Trade Union Congress), a central objective of which is to ensure a compliant workforce and stable employment relations such that Singapore continues to remain an attractive venue for multinational business and foreign investments.³⁸ After all, the lynchpin of Singapore's economic policy is reliance on foreign capital. In short, labour policies are highly pro-business. About 7,000 MNCs operate out of Singapore and they collectively constitute more than three-quarters of the manufacturing output.³⁹

---

[36] See eg Michael Oberfichtner, 'Works Council Introductions in Germany: Do They Reflect Workers' Voice?' (2019) 40 *Economic and Industrial Democracy* 301.

[37] See eg John T Addison, Paulino Teixeira, Katalin Evers and Lutz Bellmann, 'Collective Bargaining and Innovation in Germany: A Case of Cooperative Industrial Relations?' (2017) 56 *Industrial Relations* 73.

[38] Richard W Carney, 'Singapore: Open State-Led Capitalism' in Michael A Witt and Gordon Redding (eds), *The Oxford Handbook of Asian Business Systems* (Oxford University Press 2014) at 193–4, 202–3.

[39] 'Singapore Can Be Asia Hub for MNCs as HK Turns to China', *Business Times* (30 March 2018); Kalim Siddiqui, 'The Political Economy of Development in Singapore' (2010) 2 *Research in Applied Economics* 1 at 9–14.

An important implication is that, in general, the rights of labour are subordinated to those of capital. Employment at will remains a cornerstone of employment law, strikes are illegal, and collective bargaining is severely curtailed.[40] While Singapore has unions and employers' associations, they are co-opted into and regulated by the government. For example, trade unions are under the control of the National Trade Union Congress (NTUC) which is under the control of the government.[41] A key purpose of the NTUC is to communicate the government's policy to the unions and to mobilise support for government initiatives.

Thus, if co-determined boards were to become mandatory, one concern is that the power balance between employers and employees would be tilted in favour of the latter, and it would be more difficult for companies, particularly MNCs, to prioritise the interests of shareholders or profit maximisation over the interests of employees. For example, companies would encounter greater difficulty in laying off workers should the circumstances warrant doing so. In other words, Singapore may become a less attractive venue for MNCs to set up businesses. The response to this concern is twofold. First, the German experience suggests that co-determination has not prevented companies from taking difficult but necessary business decisions that have resulted in employees being let go (as a result of, say, corporate restructuring or reorganisation).[42] Rather, co-determination has broadened the decision-making process because employees' voices are heard and their interests taken into account, the result of which is that conflicts are reduced. Second, whether Singapore will remain an attractive venue for MNCs depends on a variety of considerations, including, but not limited to, tax benefits, quality of infrastructure, protection of contractual and property rights, rule of law, macroeconomic conditions and political stability.[43] Labour policies and practices are just one of the many factors. Thus, the concern that co-determination will discourage investments by MNCs seems exaggerated.

---

[40] Richard W Carney, 'Singapore: Open State-Led Capitalism' in Michael A Witt and Gordon Redding (eds), *The Oxford Handbook of Asian Business Systems* (Oxford University Press 2014) at 202–3.

[41] Ibid.

[42] Katharina Pistor, 'Codetermination: A Sociopolitical Model with Governance Externalities' in Margaret Blair and Mark J Roe (eds), *Employees and Corporate Governance* (Brookings Institution Press 1999) at 188–9.

[43] See World Bank, *Doing Business 2019* (16th edn, 2018) www.worldbank.org/content/dam/doingBusiness/media/Annual-Reports/English/DB2019-report_web-version.pdf.

Another concern is that by giving employees governance rights through the co-determined boards, it will reduce the power of the government as the controlling shareholder in SOEs. Although the controller of the Singapore GLCs, Temasek Holdings, generally avoids an interventionist approach towards the business and operations of its GLCs (unlike the Chinese SOEs, Indian PSUs and Malaysian GLCs), it still retains and exercises the critical power of appointing and dismissing the directors in the GLCs. A co-determined board in effect removes partial power from Temasek and transfers it to the employee bench. This dilution of power is likely to be met with objection from the government as the controller, unless it can be demonstrated that co-determined boards will promote long-term shareholder value, the latter of which remains an important goal of Singapore GLCs. This concern can be addressed in three ways. First, instead of having an equal division of power, namely, the shareholder bench and the stakeholder bench each constituting 50 per cent of the supervisory board, it is suggested that there could be partial co-determination: for example, 65 per cent and 35 per cent of the supervisory board could consist of the shareholder bench and the stakeholder bench, respectively, but the appointment and removal of the members of the management board require a special resolution comprising a majority of at least 75 per cent of the supervisory board. Second, the general meeting (which is under the control of the controlling shareholder) could alter the company's constitution such that certain transactions, which would otherwise remain within the scope of authority of the management board, would require approval by ordinary resolution by the supervisory board. And approval would be easily obtained because the shareholder bench would account for more than 50 per cent of the supervisory board. Finally, the general meeting could alter the constitution to stipulate that the slate of nominees for the management board has to be approved by the shareholders before being voted on by the supervisory board.

A further concern is that even if co-determined boards are implemented in Singapore, there is nothing in Singapore that is comparable to the rights and powers wielded by workers through the works council or collective bargaining in Germany. After all, the largest trade union in Singapore, the NTUC, is a de facto organ and a mouthpiece of the state.[44] Further, while collective bargaining is possible, it does not extend to

---

[44] Cho-Oon Khong, 'Singapore: Political Legitimacy Through Managing Conformity' in Muthiah Alagappa (ed), *Political Legitimacy in Southeast Asia: The Quest for Moral Authority* (Stanford University Press 1995) at ch 5; Alex Kwee Yeow Teck, 'The Role of the NTUC in Singapore' (2001), Dissertation, National University of Singapore.

termination of an employee's contract or dismissal of employees.⁴⁵ Further, as compared to Germany, employment law and practice in Singapore are generally pro-business insofar as there is no minimum wage requirement, employers are free to terminate their employees, employers do not need to consult with unions regarding retrenchment, and employees are not entitled to retrenchment benefits as a result of reorganisation or redundancy (unless they have been in continuous employment for at least two years).⁴⁶ It is more challenging to address this concern than the first two concerns because the effectiveness of co-determined boards depends on other supporting conditions (such as the works council, collective bargaining, or pro-employee employment law) which are absent in Singapore.

2 Malaysia

With regard to Malaysia, its labour policies are characterised by the dual objective of attracting MNCs and affirmative action for the Malays.⁴⁷ But these objectives are in tension. On the one hand, the government seeks to create a stable, compliant and capable workforce to attract foreign businesses to Malaysia. Measures taken by the government include, but are not limited to, curtailing legal strikes, imposing restrictions on collective bargaining, importing low-cost labour and suppressing the wages of workers. On the other hand, the government or its affiliated companies that are the controlling shareholders of GLCs have social and political objectives, and thus seek to promote and protect the interests of the Malays by generating jobs, subsidising the prices of goods and redistributing income through the GLCs. As a result, there is likely to be a risk of over-hire; workers may be retained in the company not based on merit or efficiency justifications but on the grounds of social welfare and political expediency; and wages may be inflated to promote political allegiance to the government.⁴⁸ However, it may be argued that these problems affect only GLCs, not non-GLCs. Nevertheless, where the government or its affiliated company is a minority shareholder in non-GLCs, it could also exert influence (either alone or together with other minority investors)

---

[45] Industrial Relations Act (Cap 136), s 17(3)(b).
[46] Employment Act (Cap 91), ss 9–11, s 45.
[47] Michael Carney and Edo Andriesse, 'Malaysia: Personal Capitalism' in Michael A Witt and Gordon Redding (eds), *The Oxford Handbook of Asian Business Systems* (Oxford University Press 2014) at 144–6, 149–50, 155–6.
[48] See eg Edmund Terence Gomez and KS Jomo, *Malaysia's Political Economy: Politics, Patronage and Profits* (2nd edn, Cambridge University Press 1999).

on non-GLCs such as by applying pressuring on these companies to reduce retrenchments in exchange for the provision of capital by the government.[49]

Thus, it seems that it is not necessary for co-determined boards to be made compulsory in Malaysia, at least with respect to the Malaysian GLCs, because, in light of the social goals of GLCs, the interests of stakeholders, particularly employees, will be well taken care of. But a number of problems arise from GLCs' pursuit of social and political objectives that suggests that co-determined boards may have a useful role to play in promoting the interests of employees and other stakeholders.

First, the government (or its affiliated company) as the controlling shareholder in the GLCs may not effectively monitor the management tasked with implementing the social objectives of the GLCs. Given that social objectives encompass not only employees' welfare but also considerations related to consumers, community, economy and environment, different departments and ministries within the government could be involved.[50] The management may not know with whom they should consult or to whom they should be accountable. In a co-determined board, the supervisory board can consist of representatives not only of employees and shareholders but also of consumers and other relevant constituencies. These different benches within the supervisory board have to work together to come up with strategic policies and directions for the management board to act on, and the supervisory board has to develop accountability, oversight and internal control mechanisms for the company. A co-determined board arguably provides more well-defined monitoring measures. But, as discussed earlier, the downside to having multiple benches on the supervisory board is that multiple alliances and coalitions among the benches and between the benches and the management board could be formed, which makes the decision-making process cumbersome.

The second problem is that the government as the controlling shareholder of the GLCs can use its power of appointment and dismissal to appoint its favoured board directors to bring political benefits to the ruling party, and hire managers who will heed the wishes of the board.[51]

---

[49] See eg Aldo Musacchio and Sérgio G Lazzarini, *Reinventing State Capitalism: Leviathan in Business, Brazil and Beyond* (Harvard University Press 2014) at 62–4, 197–201.

[50] Terry M Moe, 'The New Economics of Organization' (1984) 28 *American Journal of Political Science* 739; Avinash Dixit, 'Incentives and Organizations in the Public Sector: An Interpretative Review' (2002) 37 *Journal of Human Resources* 696.

[51] Ernest Lim, *A Case for Shareholders' Fiduciary Duties in Common Law Asia* (Cambridge University Press 2019) at 54–5.

In other words, there is a risk that, in GLCs, the pursuit of political objectives will be at the expense of giving effect to social welfare. While it may be said that there is no contradiction between the pursuit of both political and social goals by the GLCs as promoting the interests of employees and other stakeholders can enhance the political legitimacy of the ruling coalition, the government is likely to prioritise the interests of employees or other stakeholders who have political connections to it.[52] This will disadvantage other constituencies who have no such connections.

A co-determined board may address the problem of controlling shareholders extracting private benefits of control (through the exercise of the controllers' powers to appoint and dismiss directors). This is because the appointment of the management board requires the support of the employee (and other applicable stakeholder) bench of the supervisory board. These employee (and stakeholder) representatives are nominated and elected by the employees (and stakeholders). Co-determination may also address the issue of cronyism involving the controlling shareholder and certain employees (and stakeholders), if there are proper mechanisms in place to ensure, first, that the nomination and election procedures for the employee (and stakeholder) representatives are fair and transparent and, second, that any conflicts of interest between the controller, on the one hand, and the employees and stakeholders, on the other, are disclosed and avoided. The controlling shareholder may object to its dilution of power of appointment and dismissal, but, as discussed above (in relation to Singapore), there are ways to ameliorate this concern.

If the two problems above suggest that co-determined boards have a valuable role to play in SOEs, then what about non-GLCs in Malaysia, especially MNCs? On one view, co-determined boards may be an important mechanism for promoting employees' interests and sustainability. And sustainability has been shown to correlate positively and significantly with corporate performance.[53] On another view, co-determined boards

---

[52] There is extensive literature on cronyism in Malaysia, see eg Jeff Tan, 'Rent-Seeking and Money Politics in Malaysia' in Meredith L Weiss (ed), *Routledge Handbook of Contemporary Malaysia* (Routledge 2014); Vighneswaran Vithiatharan and Edmund Terence Gomez, 'Politics, Economic Crises and Corporate Governance Reforms: Regulatory Capture in Malaysia' (2014) 44 *Journal of Contemporary Asia* 599; Ferdinand A Gul, 'Auditors' Response to Political Connections and Cronyism in Malaysia' (2006) 44 *Journal of Accounting Research* 931.

[53] Chapter 1 (n 21, 31–6).

may reduce economic competitiveness in Malaysia because they may disincentivise MNCs from setting up businesses in Malaysia because it may be much more difficult to implement cost-cutting measures (such as redundancy or restructuring which involves laying off workers or reducing their salaries) to boost profits. This may possibly undercut a central labour policy in Malaysia which is to attract foreign businesses. However, this concern should not be overstated. As discussed in Section I(B.1) in relation to Singapore, factors such as tax benefits, macroeconomic conditions, political stability, enforcement of contractual and property rights and tax benefits are as important, if not more so.

3 Hong Kong

Whether Hong Kong should adopt co-determined boards depends on an understanding of the employment relations, labour policies and practices of Hong Kong, situating them within the general non-interventionist policy approach of the HKSAR government through which the state generally takes a laissez-faire approach towards industrial policy.[54] This means that the HKSAR government provides an environment that facilitates economic development but generally eschews top-down regulatory interference (except, for example, in relation to the property market and during times of economic crisis such as the Asian Financial Crisis).[55] In other words, unlike Singapore which has deliberately designed its policies and laws to attract MNCs and foreign investments, Hong Kong provides an open regulatory framework for business to flourish. Accordingly, political and economic setup costs are generally low and there are no considerable barriers to entry for businesses to operate.[56]

This positive non-interventionist approach also translates to labour laws and practices. Although Hong Kong has a minimum wage legislation,[57] its employment law is pro-business as there are minimal restrictions on employers' ability to terminate the employment of

---

[54] See eg Gordon Redding, Gilbert YY Wong and William KW Leung, 'Hong Kong: Hybrid Capitalism as Catalyst' in Michael A Witt and Gordon Redding (eds), *Oxford Handbook of Asian Business Systems* (Oxford University Press 2014) at 37, 42–3; Donald C Donald, Jiangyu Wang and Jefferson P VanderWolk, *A Financial Center for Two Empires: Hong Kong's Corporate, Securities and Tax Laws in Its Transition from Britain to China* (Cambridge University Press 2014) at 44–9.
[55] Ibid.
[56] World Bank, *Doing Business 2019* (16th edn, 2018), www.worldbank.org/content/dam/doingBusiness/media/Annual-Reports/English/DB2019-report_web-version.pdf.
[57] Minimum Wage Ordinance (Cap 608).

employees.[58] While trade unions are permitted in Hong Kong, membership generally remains low and members' participation remains sporadic (with the exception of large companies such as airlines and utilities).[59] Further, the growth of trade unions has been frustrated by business elites with whom the government has a strong relationship.[60] Moreover, there is no statutory recognition of collective bargaining or works councils. Industrial actions including strikes are rare.

It is suggested that the above brief description of the labour laws and practices and the context in which they operate have at least two implications for the question of whether Hong Kong should adopt co-determined boards. First, given the positive non-interventionist approach of the Hong Kong government, it is unlikely to initiate co-determined boards unless there is a strong external impetus. Further and importantly, implementation of co-determined boards is likely to be opposed by businesses, unless it can be shown that co-determined boards will have positive effects, or at least no negative effect, on firm value. This opposition would be heightened in the case of PRC SOEs. PRC SOEs listed on the SEHK are subject to the listing rules and certain provisions of the Hong Kong company law.[61] In other words, should the SEHK amend its listing rules to require companies to have co-determined boards, PRC SOEs would be subject to this requirement, unless they are specifically exempted. The PRC government as the controlling shareholder of the SOEs would be likely to object to the dilution of power in a co-determined board under which employees are given a real say in the appointment of the management board.

This dilution of power objection is also likely to be raised by the government as the controller in a Singapore GLC or Malaysian GLC. This objection can be addressed in three ways as mentioned in Section I(B.1) regarding Singapore. Another way of addressing this concern is to have a dual listing regime. So, the SEHK can come up with two-tier listing

---

[58] Hong Kong Employment Ordinance (Cap 57), ss 6–7.
[59] See eg Nigel Francis and Winnie Wong, 'The Legal Essentials of Trade Unions in Hong Kong' (2010) 16 *China Staff; Hong Kong* 35; Ed Snape and Andy W Chan, 'Whither Hong Kong's Unions: Autonomous Trade Unionism or Classic Dualism?' (1997) 35 *British Journal of Industrial Relations* 39.
[60] Ibid.
[61] HKEX LR 19.01; HK CO, s 2 'non-Hong Kong company'.

standards,[62] where the first tier imposes the co-determined board requirement and the second tier does not. Existing listed companies (including SOEs) can choose to either voluntarily migrate to the first tier or remain in the second tier. Newly listed companies (including SOEs) can choose to be listed on either the first or the second tier.

The second implication is that even if companies in Hong Kong adopt co-determined boards, Hong Kong does not have the sort of works councils or collective bargaining by unions in Germany in which significant powers are given to workers. This is identical to the third concern raised in relation to Singapore. In Germany, while the supervisory board in a co-determined model plays a critical role in setting the strategic direction and providing key oversight of the management board, important matters such as the right to financial information on the company, the right to be consulted on matters regarding job scope and allocation as well as salaries, and veto rights over termination of employment are within the remit of the works council. In other words, the German co-determined board is supported by two other mechanisms that facilitate and enhance the comprehensive and long-term rights and welfare of employees. Thus, in Hong Kong, co-determined boards alone may not be sufficient to promote employees' interests, unless reforms are made to employment law to augment the rights of employees.

4 India

Among the four Asian jurisdictions, it may be argued that India is least likely to resist having co-determined boards in order to promote employees' interests and sustainability. Section 166(2) of the Indian Companies Act states that directors are required to 'act in good faith in order to promote the objects of the company for the benefit of its members as a whole, and in the best interests of the company, its employees, the shareholders, the community and for the protection of environment'. Requiring companies to have co-determined boards can be seen as giving effect to the statutory provision. However, it may be said that it is neither necessary nor desirable to have co-determined boards in India because

---

[62] An example is Brazil's Sao Paulo Stock Exchange, which has four levels of listing, the highest of which is Novo Mercado. See Ronald J Gilson, Henry Hansmann and Mariana Pargendler, 'Regulatory Dualism as a Development Strategy: Corporate Reform in Brazil, the United States, and the European Union' (2011) 63 *Stanford Law Review* 475 at 482–501; Marina Pargendler, 'State Ownership and Corporate Governance' (2012) 80 *Fordham Law Review* 2917 at 2962–8.

boards are required under s 135 of the Companies Act 2013 to constitute a CSR committee for the purpose of formulating CSR policy, and this, it may be said, is likely to include the protection of employees' interests and promotion of sustainability. Boards are required to disclose and give effect to the CSR policy. But it will be argued below that the protection of employees' interests, let alone the promotion of sustainability, is not covered by s 135, as it is currently interpreted and applied.

II Indian CSR Board Committee

The enactment of s 135 has to be situated within the context of India's corporate reforms. The authorities including the MCA and SEBI initiated several actions related to CSR as part of the overall corporate governance reforms. The CSR actions include the issuance by the MCA of the Voluntary Guidelines for Corporate Social Responsibility[63] in 2009 and the National Voluntary Guidelines on Social, Environmental and Economic Responsibilities of Business in 2011[64] as well as the 2012 circular by SEBI requiring the top 100 listed companies based on market capitalisation to publish BRRs disclosing their sustainability initiatives.[65] Other significant reforms include the amendment of the Companies Act. The Companies Bill initially imposed a mandatory requirement on large companies to spend at least 2 per cent of their profits on CSR activities, but, in light of criticisms, this mandatory requirement was changed to comply or explain.[66]

As it stands, under s 135 of the Indian Companies Act 2013, the boards of companies of certain net worth or turnover are required, with effect from 2015, to form a CSR committee. This committee needs to have at least three directors, of which at least one must be an independent director. The CSR committee is required to (a) formulate and recommend to the board a CSR policy that has to indicate the activities to be undertaken by the company as specified in the statute; (b) recommend

---

[63] Ministry of Corporate Affairs, Corporate Social Responsibility Voluntary Guidelines (2009) www.mca.gov.in/Ministry/latestnews/CSR_Voluntary_Guidelines_24dec2009.pdf.
[64] Ministry of Corporate Affairs, National Voluntary Guidelines on Social, Environmental and Economic Responsibilities of Business (2011) www.mca.gov.in/Ministry/latestnews/National_Voluntary_Guidelines_2011_12jul2011.pdf.
[65] SEBI, Business Responsibility Reports, CIR/CFD/DIL/8/2012 (13 August 2012).
[66] Afra Afsharipour and Shruti Rana, 'The Emergence of New Corporate Social Responsibility Regimes in China and India' (2014) 14 *UC Davis Business Law Journal* 175 at 215–16.

the amount of expenditure to be incurred for the activities referred to in clause (a); and (c) monitor the CSR policy of the company from time to time. The board has to: approve the CSR policy for the company; disclose the policy in its annual report and on its website; and ensure that the activities included in the CSR policy are undertaken by the company. Schedule VII of the Companies Act lists out the activities that the CSR policy may include.

Remarkably, under s 135(5), the board is required to ensure that the company spends, in every financial year, at least 2 per cent of the average net profits of the company made during the three immediately preceding financial years, in pursuance of its CSR policy, and should the company fail to spend such amount, the board is required to give reasons for not spending the amount in its annual report. Note, however, that s 135 operates on a comply or explain basis, which means that companies that decide to spend less than the 2 per cent stipulation merely have to provide an explanation. In other words, companies are not legally obligated to spend at least 2 per cent, but they must give reasons if they do not meet the 2 per cent threshold.

There are consequences attached to the failure to comply with s 135. Under s 450, the defaulting company and every defaulting officer may be fined up to Rs 10,000. And if the contravention persists, the fine may be increased to Rs 1,000 every day.

There have been empirical studies carried out before and after s 135 took effect. Of the former, after the authorities announced that the CSR spending requirement might be mandatory (but before it subsequently took the shape of s 135 in which it became comply or explain rather than mandatory), one study found that the announcement had a negative effect on firm value.[67] Of the latter, one study by the MCA found that, as of 2016, only 70 per cent of companies reported on CSR, and out of the 70 per cent, about 30 per cent spent on CSR.[68] There is another study of Nifty 100 companies for the financial year 2014–16.[69] For FY 2014–15, it

---

[67] Dhammika Dharmapala and Vikramaditya Khanna, 'The Impact of Mandated Corporate Social Responsibility: Evidence from India's Companies Act of 2013' (8 September 2018) University of Chicago, Public Law Working Paper No. 601 https://ssrn.com/abstract=2862714.

[68] Ministry of Corporate Affairs, 'A Snapshot of CSR Spent for 2014–15' (2016) www.mca.gov.in/MinistryV2/csrdatasummary.html.

[69] Umakanth Varottil, 'Analysing the CSR Spending Requirements under Indian Company Law' in Jean J du Plessis, Umakanth Varottil and Jeroen Veldman (eds), *Globalisation of Corporate Social Responsibility and Its Impact on Corporate Governance* (Springer 2018) at 243–8.

was found that only 40.65 per cent of companies complied with the 2 per cent CSR spending requirement.[70] For FY 2015–16, 55 per cent complied with the requirement.[71]

Companies that have failed to comply with the 2 per cent spending requirement have had enforcement measures taken against them by the MCA, which asserted that '[i]n 221 number of cases, prosecutions have been sanctioned against companies and their officers in default for the financial year 2014–15 for violation relating to CSR. Further, penal action is taken wherever misuse of CSR funds stands confirmed against any company.'[72] The problem with this statement is that the government failed to specify the violations that were committed by the companies. For example, it is not clear if the violations relate to failure to disclose the CSR policy or failure to provide explanation for not meeting the 2 per cent spending requirement.

Having provided a brief explanation of s 135 and a summary of the studies conducted on this provision, the key issue, for our purposes, is whether s 135 can be an effective mechanism for promoting sustainability. There are at least three reasons to be doubtful.

First, s 135 does not promote sustainability that is integrated into the company's key decision-making process or linked to the board's risk assessment of its key business operations, but, rather, seems like a corporate philanthropic activity. For example, an oil and gas company would be seen as complying with s 135 if it has a policy and practice of donating cash amounting to 2 per cent of its net profits to a charitable organisation that seeks to promote education or that aims to reduce child mortality (provided that this donation is not on a one-off basis, as one-off events are not counted[73]). This is despite the fact that the most pressing sustainability issue facing the company is environmental pollution. But it may be argued that the purpose of s 135 is not to promote sustainability. Rather, to promote sustainability, one has to turn to the BRRs, the problems of which have been critically analysed in Chapter 2.

Second, the CSR rules issued by the MCA, the purpose of which is to interpret and clarify s 135, state that activities undertaken by the company in the normal course of business will not be considered as CSR; nor

---

[70] Ibid at 243.
[71] Ibid at 244.
[72] Ministry of Corporate Affairs, Lok Sabha, Unstarred Question No. 4791 (23 March 2018) http://mca.gov.in/Ministry/pdf/lu4791_26032018.pdf.
[73] Ministry of Corporate Affairs, FAQ on CSR Cell, FAQ 9, 'Which Activities Would Not Qualify as CSR Expenditure?' www.mca.gov.in/MinistryV2/faq+on+csr+cell.html.

are projects or programmes undertaken to promote employees' interests.[74] This is because the MCA draws a distinction between CSR expenditure (of which the 2 per cent spending is a part) and business expenditure (of which the company's ordinary business policies and activities are a part). This implies that, for example, if a company spends money to: increase the employment benefits of employees or to monitor its suppliers and contractors in its supply chain to ensure that there are no labour law violations, such conduct will not be regarded as fulfilling the spending requirement under s 135, because it will be treated as business expenditure. As a result, s 135 may have the perverse side effect of inducing companies to engage in corporate philanthropy instead of considering and attending to the interests of their stakeholders including employees, consumers and suppliers. Moreover, it is unclear what constitutes 'normal course of business'. For example, if a company decides to spend money to make its products environmentally friendly, it is not clear if that would be considered activities undertaken in the normal course of business and hence not constitute CSR, or if it would fall within the fourth activity enumerated in Schedule VII, namely, 'ensuring environmental sustainability', and is thus part of CSR.

Third, even if the court takes a liberal and inclusive approach towards what constitutes CSR expenditure, the 2 per cent requirement applies only to expenses incurred in India and not overseas.[75] Thus, even if Indian companies have business activities abroad, and even if the most serious challenge to sustainability facing the company stems from their overseas operations, the 2 per cent requirement applies only to expenses incurred in India and not overseas. The consequence is that companies are likely to focus on CSR in relation to domestic activities, neglecting or downplaying the impacts of their foreign operations or foreign subsidiaries.

In addition to the three concerns above, which cast doubt on whether s 135 can effectively promote sustainability, there are criticisms of its specific mechanism, namely, disclosure. For example, given that the 2 per cent spending requirement is subject to comply or explain, one study of the top 100 listed companies found that the majority of companies that did not comply with this requirement (which accounted for 59 per cent for the fiscal year 2014–15 and 45 per cent for 2015–16) gave

---

[74] Ministry of Corporate Affairs, Companies (Corporate Social Responsibility Policy) Rules (2014), s 4(1), 4(5), www.mca.gov.in/Ministry/pdf/CompaniesActNotification2_2014.pdf.
[75] Ibid at s 4(4).

poor disclosure consisting of generic and boilerplate statements.[76] Some did not even provide any explanation at all.[77] Further, there are no criteria for evaluating the adequacy or appropriateness of disclosure of non-spending, let alone any third-party verification or audit. A more serious concern is that s 135 can give rise to fraudulent activities because companies can channel money to fraudulent charitable organisations which, in turn, can transfer most of the money back to them.[78]

To address the first three concerns regarding s 135 so that this provision can be used to promote sustainability, it is suggested that s 135 ought to be amended. Section 135 and the BRR (discussed in Chapter 2) should be explicitly linked. Currently, they operate in silos. The regulations on BRRs require companies to disclose in their annual reports the initiatives taken by them from an ESG perspective based on the nine principles stated in the format for BRR. There is a close connection between BRR and CSR. After all, '[c]orporate social responsibility encompasses not only what companies do with their profits, but also how they make them. It goes beyond philanthropy and compliance and addresses how companies manage their economic, social, and environmental impacts, as well as their relationships in all key spheres of influence: the workplace, the marketplace, the supply chain, the community, and the public policy realm.'[79]

To ensure that s 135 can be used to promote sustainability, it is suggested that it should be amended to (i) clarify that the CSR policy which the CSR committee is required to formulate encompasses the company's disclosure in the BRR; and (ii) state that the activities listed in Schedule VII are intended to give effect to the nine principles stated in the BRR. Further, the MCA should repudiate the distinction between business expenditure and CSR expenditure and clarify that business expenditure does fall within s 135 (ie is part of CSR expenditure)

---

[76] Umakanth Varottil, 'Analysing the CSR Spending Requirements under Indian Company Law' in Jean J du Plessis, Umakanth Varottil and Jeroen Veldman (eds), *Globalisation of Corporate Social Responsibility and Its Impact on Corporate Governance* (Springer 2018) at 245–6.

[77] Ibid.

[78] Dhammika Dharmapala and Vikramaditya Khanna, 'The Impact of Mandated Corporate Social Responsibility: Evidence from India's Companies Act of 2013' (8 September 2018) University of Chicago, Public Law Working Paper No. 601 at 21 https://ssrn.com/abstract=2862714; Dinesh Narayanan, 'How Indian Companies Are Misusing Public Trusts to Launder Their CSR Spending', *The Economic Times* (21 October 2015).

[79] Beth Kytle and John Ruggie, 'Corporate Social Responsibility as Risk Management: A Model For Multinationals' Corporate Social Responsibility Initiative', Working Paper No. 10 (2005) Harvard University, Cambridge at 9.

provided that it relates to the company's BRR. Moreover, the MCA should not restrict the activities carried out pursuant to s 135 to only domestic activities; it should extend the definition to include overseas activities provided that they are carried out to give effect to the principles stated in the BRR.

Regarding the problem of the quality of disclosure by companies that do not comply with the 2 per cent requirement, it is suggested that the MCA should provide clear guidelines on what it considers adequate, meaningful and comparable disclosure. Currently, companies are given extensive leeway to determine the adequacy and appropriateness of disclosure, the result of which is that most of the disclosures are boilerplate in nature at best. In addition to providing guidelines, it is suggested that regulators (such as the MCA or SEBI) should monitor the quality of companies' disclosures and publicise the names of companies that flout those guidelines. But one concern is that the regulator may not have the resources to do so. Another concern relates to conflicts of interest between the government as the regulator and the government as the controlling shareholder of the SOEs: the regulator may apply a different approach towards the disclosure of the SOEs as compared to that of the non-SOEs. Thus, another suggestion that has been put forward is that companies should engage an external auditor that is paid for by the company but accredited by the authorities for the purpose of certifying that (i) the company has complied with the disclosure requirements in s 135; and that (ii) the company's profits have indeed been used for the intended purposes.[80] For the external auditor suggestion to work, it is imperative that there should be no conflicts of interest. For example, the company (or its controlling shareholder) could have engaged the auditor for other transactions that are not related to s 135. If an external auditor were engaged to provide the certification for s 135, there is a risk that it would provide the certification as it would not want to jeopardise its existing business relationship with the company (or the controller). To address the problem of conflicts of interest, another suggestion is to have an independent agency review the disclosures;[81] this is feasible provided that the rules governing independence are strict and enforceable.

---

[80] Umakanth Varottil, 'Analysing the CSR Spending Requirements under Indian Company Law' in Jean J du Plessis, Umakanth Varottil and Jeroen Veldman (eds), *Globalisation of Corporate Social Responsibility and Its Impact on Corporate Governance* (Springer 2018) at 250.

[81] Arjya B Majumdar, 'India's Journey with Corporate Social Responsibility: What Next?' (2015) 33 *Journal of Law and Commerce* 165 at 196.

III Conclusion

Assuming that the concerns related to s 135 can be addressed, and provided that reforms can be made to s 135, the question is whether Singapore, Malaysia and Hong Kong should adopt co-determined boards or a reformed version of s 135 to promote sustainability. I have analysed the issue of whether Singapore, Hong Kong and Malaysia should adopt co-determined boards, placing the analysis within the institutional, social and economic contexts of each jurisdiction. The main advantage of having a reformed s 135 over the co-determined boards is that it does not a pose a threat to the power of the controlling shareholders, particularly the government in SOEs. This is because the controllers still wield the power to appoint and dismiss the directors. From a political standpoint, a reformed s 135 would be much more palatable to the three concentrated ownership jurisdictions than co-determined boards.

In terms of which mechanism would be more effective in delivering sustainability, it is suggested that studies have shown that co-determined boards have resulted in the protection of employees' interests (although the extent of which is disputed) and obviously increased engagement between the board and employees. But given that co-determined boards have yet to be extended to include other constituencies such as consumers, suppliers or members of the community, it is premature to even come to a tentative conclusion as to whether or not co-determined boards are effective in promoting sustainability. However, provided that the problems with s 135 are effectively addressed, it could be an effective tool for delivering sustainability.

Another possible solution is to look at the 2018 UK Corporate Governance Code under which listed companies are required on a comply or explain basis to engage with employees using one of the following methods: (i) a director appointed from the workforce; (ii) a formal workforce advisory panel; or (iii) a designated non-executive director.[82] The UK code goes on to state that if the board has not chosen one or more of these methods, it should explain what alternative arrangements are in place and why it considers that they are effective. Note that the UK code merely requires boards to engage with employees and, even then, only on a comply or explain basis. They are not required to act on employees' interests.

---

[82] Provision 5 to Principle 1, 2018 UK Corporate Governance Code www.frc.org.uk/getattachment/88bd8c45-50ea-4841-95b0-d2f4f48069a2/2018-UK-Corporate-Governance-Code-FINAL.pdf.

So, on the one hand, the UK code can be criticised for not going far enough in protecting employees' interests as compared to co-determined boards. On the other hand, this provision is not an insignificant step in ensuring that boards in a shareholder primacy jurisdiction such as the UK publicly disclose how they have considered the interests of constituencies beyond those of shareholders. Importantly, although the UK provision (even if reformed to require boards to engage with stakeholders other than employees) is the weakest mechanism for promoting sustainability as compared to co-determined boards and India's CSR board committee, it is likely to be far more acceptable to the SOEs and non-SOEs in Singapore, Malaysia and Hong Kong, as compared to the other two mechanisms, and hence more likely to be adopted. It is likely to be considered an acceptable compromise between having a 'full-blown' mechanism such as co-determined boards or s 135 and maintaining the status quo. For the purpose of utilising this mechanism to facilitate sustainability, it is suggested that it can be extended to require boards to engage with stakeholders (in addition to employees) that are relevant to the company.

5

Stewardship Codes

I   Emergence of Stewardship Codes   172
II Stewardship Codes and Sustainability   175
   A Rationales   175
      1 Singapore   175
      2 Malaysia   176
      3 Hong Kong   180
   B Contents   180
   C Compliance Structure   183
   D Scope   185
III Controlling Shareholders   188
   A How the Code Reinforces the Power of Controlling Shareholders   188
   B How Controlling Shareholders' Presence and Power Are Likely to Disincentivise Institutional Shareholders from Actively Engaging with the Company   189
      1 Formal Power   189
      2 Informal Power   193
   C Conflicts of Interest between the Controlling Shareholder (or Its Company) and the Institutional Shareholders   194
IV Fiduciary Duties of Institutional Shareholders   196
   A First Interpretation   196
   B Second Interpretation   199
      1 The First View   199
      2 The Second View   202
   C Third Interpretation   202
V   Conclusion   204

There has been a proliferation of stewardship codes around the world. There are eighteen jurisdictions in different parts of the world that have adopted stewardship codes in one form or another.[1] The four common

---

[1] Ernst & Young, Q&A on Stewardship Codes (August 2017) www.ey.com/Publication/vwLUAssets/ey-stewardship-codes-august-2017/$FILE/ey-stewardship-codes-august-

law jurisdictions in Asia are no exceptions. The Malaysian Code for Institutional Investors (MCII) was issued in 2014, the Hong Kong Principles of Responsible Ownership (HKPRO) in 2016 and the Singapore Stewardship Principles for Responsible Investors (SSP) in 2016. While India has no general stewardship code, it has issued industry-specific codes that apply only to institutional shareholders that are insurance companies,[2] mutual funds[3] and pension funds,[4] and has been considering having a general code that applies to all institutional shareholders.[5] While there is an emerging body of literature on stewardship codes,[6] and although fifteen codes in a variety of jurisdictions make references to sustainability,[7] there is little critical evaluation of whether stewardship codes are an effective mechanism for promoting sustainability and what reforms are needed. Tellingly, no consideration seems to be given to the role of controlling shareholders, particularly the government, in SOEs in promoting or inhibiting sustainability under the stewardship codes. After all, the form and substance of the UK Stewardship Code was essentially transplanted to Hong Kong, Singapore and Malaysia with little consideration given to how the code should be modified in light of the different ownership structures in these Asian jurisdictions.

I begin by explaining how stewardship codes came about and why they have been adopted. After that, I critically appraise the specific features of the codes – the rationales, contents, compliance structure and scope – in

---

2017.pdf; Kerrie Waring, 'Investor Stewardship and Future Priorities' *Ethical Boardroom* (Spring 2017) https://ethicalboardroom.com/investor-stewardship-and-future-priorities/.

[2] See Insurance Regulatory and Development Authority, Guidelines on Stewardship Code for Insurers in India, 22 March 2017.

[3] Securities and Exchange Board of India, Master Circular for Mutual Funds (31 December 2010) paras 6.15–6.18, www.sebi.gov.in/sebi_data/attachdocs/1295932761762.pdf.

[4] Pension Fund Regulatory and Development Authority, Common Stewardship Code (PFRDA/2018/01/PF/01, 4 May 2018) www.pfrda.org.in/writereaddata/links/circular-%20common%20stewardship%20code%2004-05-186ec9a3b4-566b-4881-b879-c5bf0b9e448a.pdf.

[5] 'Sebi to Finalise Common Stewardship Code Soon' *Outlook* (21 June 2018) www.outlookindia.com/newsscroll/sebi-to-finalise-common-stewardship-code-soon/1334891.

[6] For a good overview, see Jennifer Hill, 'Good Activist/Bad Activist: The Rise of International Stewardship Codes' (2018) 41 *Seattle University Law Review* 497.

[7] See the stewardship codes from Australia, Canada, Denmark, the Netherlands, Hong Kong, Italy, Japan, Kenya, Malaysia, Singapore, South Africa, Korea, Switzerland, Taiwan and the UK. See Dionysia Katelouzou, 'Shareholder Stewardship: A Case of (Re)-Embedding the Institutional Investors and the Corporation?' in Beate Sjåfjell and Christopher M Bruner (eds), *Cambridge Handbook of Corporate Law, Corporate Governance and Sustainability* (Cambridge University Press 2019).

Singapore, Hong Kong and Malaysia with a view to determining their effectiveness as a tool to promote sustainability. I then examine the effect of controlling shareholders on the stewardship codes. Next, I show that the different interpretations of fiduciary duties by institutional shareholders to their clients/beneficiaries will have an important bearing on the promotion of sustainability. Finally, I conclude by suggesting reforms to the codes.

I Emergence of Stewardship Codes

There are three main reasons why countries have adopted stewardship codes. First, shareholder engagement improves corporate governance and thus the long-term success of companies. In other words, a central and common feature of the codes – both formal and informal shareholder engagement – will address the problems of shareholder passivity and short-termism. The stewardship code, which originated in the UK, was developed and issued in response to the global financial crisis, given that one of its key causes lay in poor corporate governance. Institutional shareholders in financial institutions have been said to be absentee landlords who have failed to monitor and discipline directors.[8] Conversely, institutional investors have been accused not so much of being apathetic but of pressuring companies to pursue short-term gains at the expense of fundamental, long-term value creation.[9] The 2012 UK Stewardship Code, which urges institutional shareholders to undertake stewardship activities (including monitoring and engagement) to promote the company's long-term success, is seen as a panacea to these two sets of problems.[10] Under the UK Stewardship Code[11] and MCII,[12] engagement means 'purposeful dialogue' with the investee companies. But the HKPRO has a broader definition which includes private communication with the companies (such as dialogue or writing letters), public communication (using the media or proposing

---

[8] Speech by Lord Myners, Financial Services Secretary to the Treasury, NAPF Annual Investment Conference, 12 March 2009.
[9] National Association of Pension Funds Limited, *Institutional Investment in the UK: Six Years On* (November 2007), 25; European Commission Green Paper, *Corporate Governance in Financial Institutions and Remuneration Policies* COM (2010) 284 final at 8; European Commission Green Paper, *The EU Corporate Governance Framework* COM (2011) 164 final at 11.
[10] UK Stewardship Code (September 2012) (a revised version is expected to be issued in the summer of 2019). For a compelling critique, see Arad Reisberg, 'The UK Stewardship Code: On the Road to Nowhere?' (2015) 15 *Journal of Corporate Law Studies* 217.
[11] Ibid Principle 1.
[12] MCII Principle 3.

shareholder resolutions), voting and speaking at general meetings, selling shares and litigation.[13] Similarly, concerns about short-termism and inadequate monitoring by shareholders also motivated in part the adoption of stewardship codes in Hong Kong,[14] Malaysia[15] and Singapore[16] and the industry-specific codes in India.

Connected to the first reason is the second, namely, the recognition that institutional shareholders play and should play an important role in the corporate governance of listed companies in view of the percentage of shares they hold and the volume of assets they manage. In the UK, institutional shareholders own about 90 per cent of the shares of listed companies.[17] In the United States, the shares held by institutional shareholders have increased from 10 per cent in the 1950s to over 70 per cent currently.[18] In India, the amount of shares held by institutional shareholders constitutes about 17 per cent of all listed companies and 25 per cent of the top 200 listed companies.[19] Institutional shareholders are also among the top five shareholders in the top thirty listed companies by market capitalisation in Singapore, Hong Kong, Malaysia and India.[20] For example, some of the world's largest shareholders, BlackRock and Vanguard, own as much as 7 per cent shares in the top thirty listed companies in the four countries in Asia.[21] The importance of institutional shareholders is reflected not only in the percentage of shares held by them but also in the volume of assets they

---

[13] HKPRO Principle 2 para 19.
[14] Securities Futures Commission, *Consultation Conclusions on the Principles of Responsible Ownership* (7 March 2016) paras 9–11 www.sfc.hk/edistributionWeb/gateway/EN/consultation/conclusion?refNo=15CP2.
[15] This is implied in the emphasis on monitoring and engagement as well as the delivery of long-term sustainable value: see MCII at 2–3.
[16] SSP, Preamble.
[17] Paul Davies, 'Shareholders in the United Kingdom' in Jennifer G Hill and Randall S Thomas (eds), *Research Handbook on Shareholder Power* (Edward Elgar 2015) at 358, 360; Suneela Jain, Barbara Blackford, Donna Dabney and James Small, 'What Is the Optimal Balance in the Relative Roles of Management, Directors, and Investors in the Governance of Public Corporations?' (11 March 2014) https://ssrn.com/abstract=2407716.
[18] Robert B Thompson, 'The Power of Shareholders in the United States' in Jennifer G Hill and Randall S Thomas (eds), *Research Handbook on Shareholder Power* (Edward Elgar 2015) at 441, 447; Suneela Jain, Barbara Blackford, Donna Dabney and James Small, 'What Is the Optimal Balance in the Relative Roles of Management, Directors, and Investors in the Governance of Public Corporations?' (11 March 2014) https://ssrn.com/abstract=2407716.
[19] OECD, *The Role of Institutional Investors in Promoting Good Corporate Governance* (OECD Publishing 2011) at 30.
[20] See Ernest Lim, *A Case for Shareholder's Fiduciary Duties in Common Law Asia* (Cambridge University Press 2019) at Appendix 5.
[21] Ibid.

manage. For example, between 2007 and 2017, the AUM in Hong Kong and Singapore increased from US $19 billion and US $10 billion, to US $92.4 billion and US $30 billion, respectively.[22] Crucially, in Hong Kong, out of the different pools of AUM by mutual funds (such as fixed income, equity, money market and multi-asset), equities account for the majority of assets in the past ten years.[23] In Malaysia, pension and insurance funds have also increased their investments in equities. For example, the largest institutional shareholder in Malaysia, the Employees Provident Fund, increased its investments in equity from 10 per cent in the late 1980s to 43.8 per cent in 2015.[24]

The final reason why countries, particularly those that seek to attract foreign investments or listings from overseas companies (such as Singapore, Hong Kong and Malaysia), have imitated the UK is because the adoption of such codes, which are essentially best practices, will act as an important signal to global capital markets that corporate governance is taken seriously.[25] The failure of a country to come up with a stewardship code, especially if a number of leading jurisdictions have done so, may send the wrong message that it does not place a premium on shareholder engagement. Unsurprisingly, the stewardship codes are not purely a private initiative launched by institutional shareholders. Rather, the government (or an entity owned by it) and regulators, together with leading institutional shareholders, have been involved in the development and implementation of the codes. In short, adoption of stewardship codes is a signalling mechanism of good corporate governance.

If these are the motivations underlying the adoption of stewardship codes, the next question for our purposes is whether the stewardship codes can be and should be used as a mechanism for promoting sustainability. To answer this, we have to begin by critically analysing the rationales, contents, compliance structure and scope of the codes.

---

[22] Piotr Zembrowski, 'Hong Kong Domiciled Funds Growth Outpaces Singapore' *International Adviser* (8 August 2017) https://international-adviser.com/hk-domiciled-funds-outpace-singapore-counterparts.

[23] Ibid.

[24] Institutional Investor Council, Malaysia, *Investor Stewardship and Future Key Priorities* (2016) at 4.

[25] On signalling in corporate governance, see eg Amal Hamrouni, Anthony Miloudi and Ramzi Benkraiem, 'Signaling Firm Performance through Corporate Voluntary Disclosure' (2015) 31 *Journal of Applied Business Research* 609.

II Stewardship Codes and Sustainability

There are several differences pertaining to the rationales, contents, compliance requirement and scope in the stewardship codes in Singapore, Hong Kong and Malaysia that have an important bearing on the question of whether the stewardship codes should and could be used to promote sustainability.

A Rationales

1 Singapore

Among the three Asian countries, the SSP make it clear and explicit that the aim of the code is to promote sustainability. The MCII underscores the need to promote sustainability but in a different way from the SSP. As compared to those two codes, there is less focus on sustainability in the rationales in the HKPRO.

The SSP preamble begins by stating that 'stewardship is about building and growing sustainable businesses to produce long-term benefits for all stakeholders, and in the process contributing to the community and economy as a whole'.[26] There are seven principles in the SSP, the aim of which is to foster 'good stewardship in discharging their responsibilities'[27] and create 'sustainable long-term value for all stakeholders'.[28] The SSP are 'intended'[29] to 'help shape positive corporate behaviour and to benefit all stakeholders in the long term',[30] and the way to do so is 'by encouraging investors to be responsible and active stewards who contribute positively to the welfare of the economy, community and society at large'.[31] In short, the SSP define stewardship in terms of building 'sustainable business' and a crucial goal of the SSP is to engender 'sustainable long-term value'. But what is the meaning of these terms?

There is little guidance on what 'sustainable business' means. To say that growing sustainable business is to be a good steward seems tautological and circular because the SSP define stewardship in terms of growing sustainability. Further, whose 'sustainable business' do the SSP refer to – that of the investee company or that of the asset managers or their clients,

---

[26] SSP, Preamble at 3.
[27] Ibid at 5.
[28] Ibid.
[29] Ibid at 4.
[30] Ibid.
[31] Ibid.

the asset owners? One slender piece of guidance can be found in para 2.3 which states: 'Investors may engage with their investee companies on a full spectrum of topics, including strategy, long-term performance, risk, financials, culture and remuneration, social and environmental considerations, and corporate governance.'[32] Thus, one understanding of 'growing sustainability business' is that it refers to that of the investee company, and thus institutional shareholders should engage and monitor their investee companies with regard to ESG issues including but not limited to assessing their sustainability reports and taking further actions where appropriate. But apart from this guidance, the rest of the SSP do not shed any light.

Similarly, the SSP also do not specify what is meant by 'sustainable long-term value for all stakeholders'. Despite the ambiguity in this statement, one thing that is relatively clear is that the term 'all stakeholders' refers not only to the shareholders (including controlling shareholders, institutional and retail investors) of the investee companies but also to the employees, creditors, suppliers and the wider needs of the environment, community and society. It is the antithesis of short-termism under which the sole or primary pursuit is the maximisation of share price. It is concerned with the impacts of the business and the operations of the company on the society and community. But how should this goal be implemented? The idea is that stewardship will deliver this goal. But, as I will explain in Sections II(B), II(C), II(D), III and IV, it is doubtful whether this is feasible for several reasons including the non-binding nature of SSP; the weak contents (ie principles); conflicts of interest between the controlling shareholder (and the company), on the one hand, and the institutional shareholders, on the other; and the fact that the asset owners and asset managers can interpret the fiduciary duties that they owe to their beneficiaries to exclude or reduce the consideration of sustainability considerations.

2 Malaysia

There are two issues. The first is that the goal of stewardship – whose interests it seeks to protect and promote – is not clear. The second issue concerns the lack of clarity of the term 'sustainable value'.

Regarding the first issue, three categories of interest are discernible from the MCII: the ultimate beneficiaries and clients of the institutional shareholders; the investee companies; and all stakeholders.

---

[32] Ibid at 6.

Regarding the first category, paragraph 4 of the Background to the MCII states: 'The Code is intended to give institutional investors guidance on effective exercise of stewardship responsibilities *to ensure delivery of sustainable long-term value to their ultimate beneficiaries or clients.*'[33] This is also reiterated in the main body of the MCII, which states that institutional investors should have regard to both the corporate governance and the sustainability of the company as this is expected to be in the interests of the ultimate beneficiaries.[34]

As for the second category, in the foreword to the code, the Minority Shareholders Watch Group (MSWG), which has played a key role in the development of the MCII, states that 'a good take-up and application of the Code by institutional investors encourages good governance and *long-term sustainability of their investee companies* which spurs further development of the capital market'.[35]

Concerning the third category, in the prelude to the code, the Securities Commission Malaysia emphasises the need 'to ensure the delivery of *sustainable long-term value for all stakeholders*'.[36]

Thus, a critical goal of stewardship in the MCII is to achieve sustainability, but three different categories of beneficiaries are contemplated.

The first category is the ultimate beneficiaries or clients of the institutional shareholders. As an asset manager, its client is the asset owner. As an asset owner, its ultimate beneficiaries are likely to be pensioners (in the case of a pension fund), employees and financial institutions (in the case of mutual funds) and policy holders (in the case of insurance funds), etc. The second category, as stated by the MSWG, is the investee company. The third and final category, stated by the Securities Commission, is all stakeholders. While this term is not defined in the text, it presumably includes the beneficiaries in the first and second categories as well as employees, suppliers, the environment, society and the economy. The last category – all stakeholders – is consistent with the beneficiaries of sustainability articulated in Chapter 1, namely, those who are affected by the business and operations of companies.

The lack of clarity as to whose interests are sought to be advanced by stewardship will hamper the promotion of sustainability. After all, at a most basic level, institutional shareholders should know the ends that are sought to be achieved by stewardship so that they can come up with

[33] MCII at 2 (emphasis added).
[34] MCII para 3, p. 4.
[35] Ibid at ii (emphasis added).
[36] Ibid at iii (emphasis added).

measures to further them. So, to whom should institutional shareholders deliver sustainable value – their beneficiaries/clients, investee companies or the society at large?

Thus, for example, if the intended beneficiaries of stewardship under the MCII are merely the beneficiaries/clients of the institutional shareholders (first category), then they may invest in companies only insofar as the products and services of those companies are consistent with the sustainability values of their beneficiaries/clients (insofar as they are ascertainable). And they will engage with the investee companies to ensure that the latter's outputs and the production processes are aligned with the values of their clients/beneficiaries. However, if the intended beneficiaries are the stakeholders in general (third category), then the institutional shareholders will engage with the company so that it can produce socially valuable outputs for society and thus deliver sustainable value to all. In other words, there is a difference between value alignment (first category) and social value creation (third category) and there are distinct issues associated with each.[37]

The other problem is that, in addition to the ambiguity surrounding whose interests are sought to be advanced by the stewardship codes, there is also ambiguity in the term 'sustainable value'. For example, under the first category, institutional shareholders may take the approach that delivering long-term sustainable value means promoting long-term financial interests of their present and future clients or beneficiaries, which precludes the consideration of ESG matters, unless doing so will increase the financial value of the assets that they manage.[38] Alternatively, institutional shareholders may take the approach that delivering sustainable value to their clients/beneficiaries necessitates giving effect to ESG considerations in their investment decision-making process, even if it does not increase the financial returns of their beneficiaries.[39] The fact that Principle 5 of the MCII states that institutional investors should incorporate sustainability considerations – referred to as the ESG factors – into their investment decision-making process does not tell us which approach the institutional shareholders will take under the first category. Moreover, because the MCII is purely voluntary, institutional shareholders can refuse

---

[37] Paul Brest, Ronald J Gilson and Mark A Wolfson, 'How Investors Can (and Can't) Create Social Value' (March 2018) http://ssrn.com/abstract_id=3150347.

[38] See eg Anna Tilba and Arad Reisberg, 'Fiduciary Duty under the Microscope: Stewardship and the Spectrum of Pension Fund Engagement' (2019) 82 *Modern Law Review* 456 at 470–80.

[39] Ibid.

II STEWARDSHIP CODES AND SUSTAINABILITY

to sign up; or should they decide to sign up, they can pick and choose whichever principles they want to subscribe to, and, having chosen the principles, they can interpret them as they see fit.

Under the second category, institutional shareholders may take the view that delivering long-term sustainable value to their investee companies requires them to engage with these companies so that the latter can increase long-term share price (as opposed to short-term share price which is manifestly unsustainable). In other words, sustainability of companies refers to long-term financial sustainability. Thus, institutional shareholders will monitor and engage with the board so that it will pursue an enlightened shareholder value, namely, the board's overriding duty is to benefit the shareholders as a whole and directors should have regard to sustainability considerations only if it increases share price in the long term.[40] Alternatively, the institutional shareholders may take the view that sustainability requires companies to reject a shareholder primacy approach (including the enlightened shareholder value approach) and instead adopt a stakeholder value approach and, as such, they will engage with the directors to pursue that approach in relation to the directors' duty to act in the company's best interests.

The approach taken in the first category may conflict with that in the second and third. Under the first category, it is possible for institutional shareholders to take the approach that they will not take into account sustainability considerations in their investment decision-making process; nor will they engage with the company on ESG issues. This is because they take the view that it will not maximise the economic interests of their beneficiaries. However, this may conflict with the approach under the second category if institutional shareholders take the view that to increase the long-term sustainability of their investee companies, they should urge the board to adopt a stakeholder value approach which certainly requires giving effect to ESG considerations. And the approach taken in the first category will conflict with that taken in the third category. This is because, under the first category, institutional shareholders may take the approach that they will only exclusively promote the interests of their beneficiaries/clients, whereas under the third category, institutional shareholders have to promote the interests of all stakeholders, which of course extend beyond those of their beneficiaries/clients.

In short, there are two key problems with the rationales in the MCII. The first concerns to whom institutional shareholders should deliver

---

[40] UK Companies 2006 s 172.

sustainable value and the second relates to the meaning of sustainable value. Resolving these two ambiguities is important to the issue of whether and how the stewardship codes can be used to promote sustainability.

3 Hong Kong

As compared to Singapore and Malaysia, the HKPRO does not make any reference to sustainability in its rationale. The HKPRO state that 'to discharge their ownership responsibilities, investors should engage with the companies in which they invest to promote the long-term success of these companies',[41] but the latter phrase is nowhere explained in the HKPRO. The closest, albeit indirect, reference to sustainability is para 17 to Principle 2, which states that 'investors should encourage their investee companies to have policies on environmental, social and governance (ESG) issues and engage with investee companies on significant ESG issues that have the potential to impact on the companies' goodwill, reputation and performance'. Note that Principle 2 does not tell us the rationale of stewardship; rather, it tells us how the investors should engage with their investee companies. As a result, the HKPRO is the weakest among the three codes in terms of articulation of sustainability in its rationale. But because of the ambiguity of 'long-term success' of investee companies, considerable discretion is given to shareholders to interpret this phrase. They may interpret it as referring to the sustainability of companies. Or, at the very least, they may interpret it as not excluding sustainability considerations.

B Contents

The contents of the code refer to the principles and their guidelines. The question here is whether the principles and their guidelines contain any meaningful references to or explanations of sustainability. The MCII has the most references to sustainability, followed by the HKPRO and the SSP.

To begin with, the MCII states that 'while corporate governance matters should be the issue of main consideration in the investment decision-making process, the issue of sustainability must equally be considered'[42] as 'such an approach is expected to be in the interest of the ultimate beneficiaries'.[43] The MCII has devoted an entire principle to sustainability. Principle 5 is entitled 'Incorporating sustainability considerations'.

---

[41] HKPRO para 6.
[42] MCII para 3, p 4.
[43] Ibid.

The principle is stated: 'Institutional investors should incorporate corporate governance and sustainability considerations into the investment decision-making process.'[44] It then lists out detailed guidelines on this principle. Sustainability considerations include ESG factors[45] and the latter are explained as including 'corporate governance and business ethics; employee benefits and corporate culture; products, customers and supply chain; and environmental and social impact'.[46] The guidelines state that institutional investors should develop a policy on how they incorporate sustainability considerations into their investment analysis and activities, and the policy should include matters such as assessment of (i) the quality of the company's sustainability report and (ii) disclosure and adherence to responsible investment codes.[47]

There are several shortcomings to the guidelines to Principle 5. First, they are process oriented and do not state any targets or outcomes that should be aimed at. Second, they merely state that the policy should include assessment of the quality of the sustainability report and not whether the institutional shareholder has in fact assessed. Nevertheless, it is important for these guidelines to be included in the MCII. This is because one main problem with sustainability reports, as examined in Chapter 2, is that there is no mechanism to effectively monitor and verify the quality of disclosures in those reports. It is entirely up to the shareholder to monitor and to take any follow-up actions if they wish to. Thus, it is noteworthy and important that the MCII states that monitoring the quality of sustainability reports is part of the incorporation of sustainability considerations in the policies that should be developed by institutional shareholders.

As compared to Principle 5 and the guidance set forth in the MCII, the principle and guidelines stated in the SSP are weak. The first problem is that there is no mention of sustainability in any of the principles in the SSP. Rather, explicit mention of sustainability is made only in one of the guidelines to Principle 2. Principle 2 states that 'responsible investors communicate regularly and effectively with their investee companies'.[48] The first guideline to this principle states that investors should communicate with their investee companies in order to attain the objective of 'long-term value creation, capital efficiency, and sustainable growth'.[49] This is the only

---

[44] Ibid at 13.
[45] Ibid, Guidance 5.1 at 13.
[46] Ibid, Guidance 5.4 at 14.
[47] Ibid, Guidance 5.3 at 13.
[48] SSP at 6.
[49] Ibid, Guidance 2.1 at 6.

reference to sustainability in the entire principles and guidelines. The third guideline is that investors should engage with their investee companies on a full spectrum of topics including strategy, risks, financials, culture, social and environmental considerations, etc.[50] The mention of social and environmental considerations may be construed as a reference to sustainability but it is not clear.

The first deficiency with the SSP is that no explanation is given to the term sustainability, unlike the MCII, which states that sustainability considerations include ESG. The second deficiency is that even if the contents contain a reference to sustainability, it is merely relegated to one of the numerous topics that investors may choose to engage with their investee companies on under the third guideline in the SSP. Finally, although the fourth guideline to the principle states that investors should have a policy, it is not related to the incorporation of sustainability considerations, but, rather, to managing disclosures of material information that could lead to breach of the listing rules.[51] Thus, despite the lofty proclamation of the importance of sustainability as a goal of the SSP, nothing in the contents (the principles and guidance) shows how this is to be translated into a measure, standard or procedure that can be adopted by the institutional shareholders. The contrast between the bold and lofty statements in the preamble and the vapid principles and guidelines could not be greater.

As for the HKPRO, nothing in the principles mentions sustainability. However, in its guidance to Principle 2 ('investors should monitor and engage with their investee companies'), it states that 'investors should encourage their investee companies to have policies on ESG issues and engage with investee companies on significant ESG issues that have the potential to impact on the companies' goodwill, reputation and performance'.[52] This guidance is more helpful than that of the SSP in two ways. First, it specifically states that investee companies should have an ESG policy, unlike the SSP which states that investee companies should have a policy on managing disclosures of information. Second, it specifically sets aside one guideline for ESG issues[53] and a separate guideline on the fact that investors should engage with their investee companies on strategy, performance, risk, etc.[54] In doing so, the guidance seeks to underscore the importance of investors engaging the company

---

[50] Ibid, Guidance 2.3 at 6.
[51] Ibid, Guidance 2.4 at 6.
[52] HKPRO para 17, p 3.
[53] Ibid.
[54] Ibid para 15, p 3.

on ESG issues. By contrast, the guidance to Principle 2 in the SSP lumps everything together.

C Compliance Structure

None of the stewardship codes is binding. They operate on a wholly voluntary basis. Failure to sign up, or to comply after signing up, attracts no legally enforceable consequences. No sanctions are attached whatsoever. Unlike the UK Stewardship Code which has a comply or explain mechanism – institutional investors are required to comply but if they choose not to do so, they are required to give an explanation – the codes in Singapore, Malaysia and Hong Kong do not have such a mechanism. It is entirely up to the institutional shareholders to choose whether to sign up to the code, and, if so, which (if any) principles they wish to apply. Tellingly, the Securities and Futures Commission changed the word 'comply' in the proposed version of the HKPRO to 'apply' in the final version to make it clear that the HKPRO is voluntary and that failure to sign up or apply it (after signing up) attracts no legal consequences.[55] The SSP deliberately emphasise the entirely voluntary and unenforceable nature of the codes by clarifying that the principles are 'not intended to be rigid rules to be enforced or prescriptive measures to be adhered to, nor are they intended to constitute a code'.[56] In doing so, the SSP make it plain that the 'principles' are not best practices but merely suggestions. Unsurprisingly, given that the stewardship codes are wholly voluntary and unenforceable, Hong Kong and Singapore do not seem to have implemented a mechanism to monitor whether institutional shareholders have implemented the codes. In Malaysia, while the Institutional Investors Council Malaysia, an umbrella body for institutional shareholders, was formed to discuss stewardship matters and to monitor the take-up of the code, it is not apparent that it has assessed whether the signatories have actually implemented the code.[57]

To be clear, despite the weaknesses of the soft law nature of the stewardship codes, I am not implying that hard law is necessarily superior to soft law and should be adopted. After all, there are pros

---

[55] Securities Futures Commission, *Consultation Conclusions on the Principles of Responsible Ownership* (7 March 2016) para 3(a) www.sfc.hk/edistributionWeb/gateway/EN/consultation/conclusion?refNo=15CP2.
[56] SSP, Preamble at 3.
[57] www.iicm.org.my/list-of-signatories/.

and cons to each of them and different circumstances may warrant the adoption of different regimes. But what I am suggesting is that should regulators decide to retain the soft law nature of the codes, reforms have to be made to them; otherwise the codes remain at best a pious aspiration. The first suggested reform is that there should be a comply or explain mechanism along the lines of the UK Stewardship Code. Institutional shareholders should be legally required to comply with the code and should they decide not to do so, they should be required to give an explanation. And where investors have claimed that they have complied with the code, they should disclose how they have done so. There are obviously shortcomings with the comply or explain mechanism (as examined in relation in Chapter 2 on 'Sustainability Reporting'). However, not adopting it and instead retaining the codes as they stand in the three jurisdictions will not improve the situation. Second, the regulators should consider monitoring the disclosures and explanations provided by the investors. For example, the UK has introduced a tiering system to rank the quality of disclosures provided by the investors.[58] Asset managers are subject to three tiers: under the first tier, the signatories have complied or, if not, given proper explanations; under the second tier, signatories have complied with most aspects of the code but fallen short on some aspects or not provided explanations when they have not followed the code; and under the third tier, significant reporting improvements have to be made because the signatories' statements are generic or provide no or poor explanations for their departures from the code. There is a bite to this tiering system because asset managers who are not classified under the second tier after six months will be removed from the list of signatories. Asset managers will be incentivised to be on the first tier in order to attract business from asset owners. Alternatively, the regulators should require the investors to subject their disclosures to assurance by auditing firms. However, if these two suggestions are rejected by the regulators, it is suggested that, at the minimum, the regulators should put pressure on institutional shareholders who have not signed up to the code by 'naming and shaming them' on an annual basis, that is, by publicising the names of those investors that have not signed up and strongly urging them to do so.

---

[58] Financial Reporting Council, Tiering of Stewardship Code Signatories www.frc.org.uk/investors/uk-stewardship-code/uk-stewardship-code-statements.

D Scope

The issue of scope refers to the shareholders who are subject to the stewardship codes. As mentioned earlier, in India, the stewardship codes cover only selected institutional shareholders, ie mutual funds, pension funds and insurance companies. Under the SSP[59] and the MCII,[60] only institutional shareholders, ie asset owners and asset managers (although service providers are encouraged to be signatories) are subject to the code. Although the HKPRO use the term 'investors' without defining it, the issuing body has stated that it does not cover retail and individual shareholders.[61]

The SSP define asset owners as providers of capital to investee companies and they are in effect stewards of assets entrusted to them by their own clients who are the ultimate beneficiaries.[62] Asset managers are not the owners of the assets because they act on the asset owners' behalf by managing their assets. The MCII has a similar definition but provides more specificity by stating that asset owners are collective investment vehicles such as pension funds, private investment scheme providers, insurance companies and investment trusts.[63]

Given that the majority of listed companies are owned by controlling shareholders, namely families and the government, an important question is whether the SSP, the MCII and the HKPRO cover controllers. It will be anomalous that these codes deliberately omit controlling shareholders given that they wield more power and influence than the minority institutional shareholders, and thus their actions could have a greater adverse impact on the companies and society. In other words, controllers play a far more significant role in promoting or undermining sustainability than the minority institutional investors. Further, given the critical importance that the SSP ascribe to the promotion and protection of sustainability so as to produce long-term benefits for all stakeholders, and in view of the MCII's statement that application of the code will spur long-term sustainability of the investee companies, it would be odd that only asset owners and managers – who are the minority shareholders – are urged to be stewards, ie to be active and responsible shareholders –

---

[59] SSP at 3–4.
[60] MCII at 2.
[61] Hong Kong Securities and Futures Commission, *Consultation Conclusions on the Principles of Responsible Ownership* (7 March 2016) paras 54–55.
[62] SSP at 3–4.
[63] MCII at 2.

but not controlling shareholders. After all, in view of the persistent and pervasive problem of extractions of private benefits of control by controlling shareholders, it is more crucial for controlling shareholders to act responsibly.

However, the intention of the SSP is to regulate institutional investors; they are the minority shareholders of the investee companies because the majority of listed companies are dominated by controlling shareholders who are either the government or families. Institutional investors, not controlling shareholders, are subject to the code because the SSP state that stewardship is important in light of the complex investment chain, fragmented ownership and short-term horizons of investors; these problems are peculiar to asset owners and asset managers and not controlling shareholders.[64] It also seems that the purpose of the MCII is not to regulate controlling shareholders because MCII states that the code is intended to provide guidance on effective stewardship to institutional shareholders to 'ensure delivery of sustainable long-term value to their ultimate beneficiaries or clients',[65] which applies to asset owners and asset managers. As for the HKPRO, controlling shareholders (ie the families and the PRC government) are not subject to the code because the issuing body has stated that 'those who are accountable only to themselves for their investments (or are accountable only to family members pursuant to a personal relationship, with no intention to create a client or business relationship)'[66] should not fall within the scope of the HKPRO. Further, it may be said that the principles in the codes are formulated specifically to target the conduct of asset owners and asset managers, in order to urge them to engage with and to monitor the investee companies – in view of the problem of shareholder passivity, which was one of the underlying motivations for the issuance of the code. By contrast, the problem with controlling shareholders is not that they are passive but that they are interventionist (in order to achieve political or social objectives or to extract private benefits of control).[67]

The question then is whether the stewardship codes should be reformed so that the scope is extended to cover controlling shareholders with corresponding amendments to the principles; or whether there is a need to have a separate stewardship code specifically for controlling

---

[64] SSP, Preamble at 3.
[65] MCII para 4, p 2.
[66] Hong Kong Securities and Futures Commission, *Consultation Conclusions on the Principles of Responsible Ownership* (7 March 2016) para 54.
[67] See Chapter 1, Section IV.

shareholders in view of the important role that they play in the promotion of sustainability and in light of the problem of extractions of private benefits of control.

Singapore has recently issued a stewardship code for family owned companies but not for SOEs called Stewardship Principles for Family Businesses (SPFB).[68] Unfortunately, this code, like the SSP, is purely voluntary and non-binding; no sanctions or disincentives are imposed. The SPFB make it clear that they are not intended to be prescriptive. Rather, they are merely guidelines or 'signposts'.[69]

Next, while achieving sustainability is one of the rationales for the SPFB, it is not defined. Rather, its meaning has to be gleaned from the code. The primary meaning of the term refers to the long-term viability or functioning of the family business. This is evident in the 'central question'[70] that the SPFB seek to address: 'How does Family Business thrive and sustain growth while enhancing the wealth of its stakeholders and the well-being of the societies in which it operates over the long term?'[71] Further, a number of principles in the SPFB are geared towards the promotion of the long-term functioning of the company. The secondary meaning refers to the economic, social and environmental impact that family companies have on society. Principle 6 states: 'Do well, do good, do right; contributing to community.'[72] One of the guidelines to the principle states that quality products have to be delivered with environmental sustainability in mind.[73] Another guideline states that family business should integrate social responsibility into its corporate philosophy.[74] Other than this principle, the other six principles mention nothing about sustainability.

Moreover, unlike the stewardship codes, one glaring omission in the SPFB is that they do not state who are subjected to the code: the directors, management, shareholders (which ones?) or employees. This failure to articulate who should be responsible and for what means that it is impossible to hold any constituency within family-owned companies accountable. In sum, the SPFB is not an effective mechanism for promoting sustainability.

---

[68] Stewardship Principles for Family Businesses: Fostering Success, Significance and Sustainability (2018).
[69] SPFB at 2.
[70] Ibid at 8.
[71] Ibid.
[72] Ibid at 6.
[73] Ibid.
[74] Ibid.

III Controlling Shareholders

If the rationales, contents, compliance structure and scope of the stewardship codes call into question the effectiveness of the code as a mechanism to promote sustainability, the other problem concerns the controlling shareholder, particularly where it is the government (or a company owned by it). This problem is manifested in three ways. First, controlling shareholders have the incentive to support the code because it does not disrupt or undermine their power and influence; on the contrary, it further reinforces them. Second, the presence and power of controlling shareholders will disincentivise minority institutional shareholders from monitoring and engaging with investee companies. Finally, the conflicts of interest between the controlling shareholder and the company, on the one hand, and the institutional shareholders, on the other, mean that institutional shareholders are likely to defer to the controller and the management.

A How the Code Reinforces the Power of Controlling Shareholders

Controlling shareholders will have incentive to support these codes because these codes as they stand not only do not impose any additional regulatory burden on them but also, crucially, preserve and even entrench their incentives and powers. As examined earlier, these codes are purely voluntary and non-enforceable, and apply only to institutional shareholders (ie asset owners and asset managers) but not to controlling shareholders (ie the families and government or companies controlled by it). Further, the controlling shareholders are well aware that, given their voting rights, engagement by institutional shareholders does not pose any real challenge to their powers and is unlikely to make any material difference to the outcome of the votes. Thus, stewardship codes preserve the status quo by not threatening or disrupting the incentives and legal powers of the controlling shareholders or the companies they control. Yet, by expressing support for these codes, controllers gain the benefit of being perceived as good corporate citizens.

For example, the SSP were issued by the Stewardship Asia Center, which is part of the Temasek Management Services Group, a wholly owned subsidiary of Temasek Holdings Pte Ltd, the controlling shareholder of the GLCs in Singapore.[75] But, ironically, Temasek as the controller is exempted from the SSP. The MCII was developed and issued by a steering committee and working group comprising different parties including five companies who are the controlling shareholders of the GLCs.[76] To the extent that four[77] of them are also asset owners (they are the government-linked investment companies) and, thus, are subject to the code, it is wholly voluntary and non-binding. Thus, these four asset owners can signal their commitment to good corporate governance by playing an important role in developing and issuing the code, as well as signing up to it. However, they can choose not to apply any of the principles in the MCII with no sanctions attached whatsoever, or they may cherry-pick those principles that suit them and disregard those that do not.

B   How Controlling Shareholders' Presence and Power Are Likely to Disincentivise Institutional Shareholders from Actively Engaging with the Company

1   Formal Power

Controlling shareholders, by virtue of their voting powers, are able to effectively control the company, given that most of the transactions or actions that the companies statute or the companies legislation authorises the shareholders to take require only an ordinary resolution; seldom is a special resolution[78] or disinterested shareholders' approval[79] required. Arguably, the most potent power that controllers have is the power to appoint and dismiss directors with no cause, despite anything contrary in the company's constitution or any agreement between the director and

---

[75] Temasek Management Services, 'A Fresh Perspective: SAC and IMD Partner to Publish "Inspiring Stewardship"' www.temasekmanagementservices.com.sg/tms/newsletter_6.html.
[76] MCII at 18–19. The five shareholders who are controlling shareholders are Permodalan Nasional Bhd (PNB), Lembaga Tabung Angkatan Tentera (LTAT), Lembaga Tabung Haji (LTH), Employees Provident Fund (EPF) and Kumpulan Wang Persaraan. CG Work Team for the Government Linked Companies Transformation Program, FAQs, What Are GLC and GLIC? www.pcg.gov.my/faqs#.
[77] Ibid: PNB, LTAT, LTH and EPF.
[78] Alteration of the company's constitution (HK CO, s 88(2); SG CA, s 26(1); IN CA, s 13(1); MY CA, s 36(2)); approving schemes of arrangement (HK CO, s 674(2); SG CA, s 210 (3AB); IN CA, s 230; MY CA, s 366(2)); alteration of company's status from public to private (HK CO, ss 88(2), 95; SG CA, s 31(1); IN CA, ss 13, 14; MY CA, s 41(1)) and reduction of share capital (HK CO, s 217; SG CA, s 78C(1); IN CA, s 66; MY CA, s 117(1)).
[79] Approval of related party transactions under the stock exchange listing rules (HKEX LR14A; SGX LR 906; Bursa Malaysia LR 10.08).

the company.[80] Thus, although Guidance 3.4 to Principle 3 of the MCII states that institutional shareholders can engage with the investee companies by requisitioning a general meeting in order to remove poorly performing directors,[81] it would be virtually impossible for institutional shareholders to remove incompetent directors as they are the minority shareholders.

But it may be argued that, while an institutional investor holding an insubstantial percentage of shares will not be able to make any material difference to the outcome of the votes, it can lobby and coordinate with other investors. As a result, even though it still cannot outvote the controller (and thus it fails to dismiss the directors), the controller or the board will not disregard the concerns expressed by a coalition of institutional investors. The counterargument is that coordination is costly as it will incur time and resources. There is also the free rider problem: the benefit that improved governance will bring about (such as increased share price) will be enjoyed by all the minority institutional shareholders, whereas the resource cost will be borne solely by those institutional investors who have undertaken stewardship activities. Thus, it is questionable how likely institutional investors will collaborate and coordinate among themselves, particularly if their investment strategies are passive and their portfolios are highly diversified.

For example, a study of the top thirty listed companies in Singapore, Hong Kong, Malaysia and India found that, although BlackRock and Vanguard, which are among the world's largest institutional shareholders, constitute the top five shareholders in many of the top thirty listed companies, the percentage of shares owned by them ranges only from about 1 per cent to 7 per cent (in the case of BlackRock) and 1 per cent to 3 per cent (in the case of Vanguard).[82] Because of their insubstantial ownership of shares, they may not be incentivised to engage with the controllers or the directors (over whom the controllers exercise the power of appointment and removal), given that it is unlikely to make any material difference to the outcome and in view of their passive investment strategy. For example, a recent and comprehensive study of the incentives and behaviour of the top three US index funds, BlackRock, Vanguard and State Street, found that the index fund managers have little incentive to

---

[80] HK CO, s 462; SG CA, s 152; MY CA, s 206; IN CA, s 169. An ordinary resolution means a resolution that is passed by a simple majority.
[81] MCII at 11.
[82] Ernest Lim, *A Case for Shareholders' Fiduciary Duties in Common Law Asia* (Cambridge University Press 2019) at Appendix 5.

undertake stewardship activities in relation to the company; the evidence shows that they persistently under-invest in stewardship.[83] There are two important reasons.[84] The first is that the fee revenue they will receive amounts to a small percentage of the gains (in terms of the increase in the value of assets they manage) from stewardship activities. In other words, the cost (ie time and resources) they will incur from stewardship exceeds the benefit (ie the fee revenue) they will receive. The second reason is that if an index fund manager incurs cost by undertaking stewardship activities in a portfolio company and as a result increases the share price of that company in the index, the other index funds that are its competitors will also benefit from the rise in share price.

If these three index funds together manage more than US $5 trillion assets and have voting rights over 20 per cent of the shares in S&P 500 companies,[85] which are predominantly dispersed ownership companies, and yet they have little incentive to pursue stewardship and the evidence shows that they have indeed done little,[86] then they have even less incentive to do so in companies dominated by controlling shareholders, particularly the government (or companies owned by it), such as those in the four common law jurisdictions in Asia.

But it may be argued that a study of the voting records of US institutional shareholders (the vast majority of whom are mutual funds) in 8,160 non-US companies in 43 countries which include Singapore, Malaysia and India (3 of the common law Asian jurisdictions examined in this book) shows that US institutional shareholders have a higher rate of voting against resolutions proposed or supported by management with respect to director elections and M&A when they expect more expropriation by controlling shareholders.[87] In other words, the study asserts that there is higher dissent voting when there is a higher incidence of extractions of private benefits of control by controllers. Thus, US institutional shareholders have not only actively exercised their voting rights, but their voting

---

[83] Lucian Bebchuk and Scott Hirst, 'Index Funds and the Future of Corporate Governance: Theory, Evidence, and Policy' (2019) 119 *Columbia Law Review* (forthcoming). But see institutional investors' role in promoting board gender diversity: Chapter 3 at 131–2.
[84] Ibid.
[85] William McNabb, 'The Ultimate Long-Term Investors', Vanguard Blog for Advisers (6 July 2017).
[86] Lucian Bebchuk and Scott Hirst, 'Index Funds and the Future of Corporate Governance: Theory, Evidence, and Policy' (2019) 119 *Columbia Law Review* (forthcoming).
[87] Peter Lliev, Karl V Lins, Darius P Miller and Lukas Roth 'Shareholder Voting and Corporate Governance around the World' (2015) 28 *Review of Financial Studies* 2167 at 2168–71.

Table 5.1 *Country distribution and summary statistics*

	Voting for (%)	
Country	Directors	M&A
India	95.2	70.8
Malaysia	91.8	97.0
Singapore	90.7	97.3
UK	93.5	93.4

also performs an important corporate governance function. However, the evidence at least in relation to Singapore, Malaysia and India does not support the study's conclusion.[88] This is because, as Table 5.1 (extracted from the study) shows, with respect to director elections, there is actually a lower rate of dissent voting by US institutional shareholders in companies in India as compared to those in the UK. In other words, there is a higher percentage of shareholders voting in favour of the management slate of directors in India than in the UK. Regarding M&A elections, there is a lower rate of dissent voting in Malaysia and Singapore than in the UK. In other words, there is a higher percentage of US institutional shareholders who voted for the M&A in Singapore and Malaysia than in the UK. If the data have supported the claim made by the study – greater dissent voting when there is expectation of greater expropriation by controlling shareholders – one would have expected there to be a lower percentage of 'voting for' in India, Singapore and Malaysia.

In any event, even if there is greater dissent voting where there is an expectation of greater expropriation by controllers, voting is only one aspect of stewardship as it also consists of monitoring, private engagement (such as dialogue and meetings), public engagement (including, but not limited to, proposing shareholder resolutions and actively participating in corporate reforms such as submitting written comments in response to consultations on proposed corporate reforms initiated by the regulators). A comprehensive study of the US index funds found that they: devoted only a small percentage of their fee revenue to stewardship; privately engaged with only a small percentage of companies consisting of not more than one conversation; failed to engage with the company regarding dismissing or appointing directors; failed to submit any shareholder

---

[88] Ernest Lim, *A Case for Shareholders' Fiduciary Duties in Common Law Asia* (Cambridge University Press 2019) at 68–9.

proposals; hardly contributed comments on corporate reforms; and did not take lead plaintiff positions in securities class action lawsuits.[89]

That said, even if the evidence overall shows that index funds and mutual funds do not actively engage with the company, this is not necessarily the case for hedge funds. There has been an increase in hedge fund activism, particularly in Hong Kong.[90] The reason is not because of the stewardship code. Rather, it is because, unlike other institutional investors, hedge funds are given incentive payments amounting to about 20 per cent of the increase in the value of the shares that they hold in their investee companies, and hedge funds have concentrated shareholdings in ten or fewer companies.[91] Thus, hedge funds will engage with the company despite the presence of controlling shareholders. But the question is whether their engagement (whether through voting or influence) is motivated by and will result in the long-term success of companies, which is a key rationale underlying the HKPRO, the SSP and the MCII. There is evidence to suggest that that has not been the case in Hong Kong; the activism has resulted in short-termism and value transfer rather than long-term value creation.[92]

2 Informal Power

In addition to the formal powers wielded by controlling shareholders which will disincentivise minority institutional shareholders from actively engaging, they also wield informal powers, namely influence. A controlling shareholder can put pressure on the directors to take or refrain from taking different kinds of actions.[93] After all, intervention by controlling shareholders in the SOEs in Malaysia, India and Hong Kong is relatively common.[94] Even if the controller does not exert influence, the directors are likely to consult with it before pursuing any major

---

[89] Lucian Bebchuk and Scott Hirst, 'Index Funds and the Future of Corporate Governance: Theory, Evidence, and Policy' (2019) 119 *Columbia Law Review* (forthcoming); see also Dorothy Shapiro Lund, 'The Case against Passive Shareholder Voting' (2018) 43 *Journal of Corporation Law* 101.

[90] Frank Wong, 'Shareholder Engagement and Activism under the Radar: Empirical Evidence from Hong Kong (2003–15): Rethinking Disclosure of Interests Regime' (23 June 2017), https://papers.ssrn.com/sol3/papers.cfm?abstract_id=2725318.

[91] Kenneth R French, 'Presidential Address: The Cost of Active Investing' (2008) 63 *Journal of Finance* 1537; Lucian A Bebchuk, Alma Cohen and Scott Hirst, 'The Agency Problems of Institutional Investors' (2017) 31 *Journal of Economic Perspectives* 89.

[92] Ernest Lim, *A Case for Shareholders' Fiduciary Duties in Common Law Asia* (Cambridge University Press 2019) at 70–7.

[93] Ibid at 263–5.

[94] Chapter 1, Section IV(B).

transaction,[95] given that the power to appoint and dismiss directors lies with the controlling shareholder. If that is the case, it is highly questionable whether institutional shareholders will be effective in making any changes when they seek to put pressure on the directors through private dialogue, which is one of the means of engagement. It may be said that institutional shareholders can publicly criticise the controlling shareholder or they can threaten to sell their shares. But public criticisms if sufficiently serious may cause a drop in share price, which will also hurt the institutional shareholders. And unless they own a significant amount of shares, the threat to exit from the company is unlikely to be effective.

C *Conflicts of Interest between the Controlling Shareholder (or Its Company) and the Institutional Shareholders*

Where the institutional shareholders have (or intend to have) business relationships with the controlling shareholder or the company, they are less likely to challenge the controller or the directors (over whom the controller exercises the power of appointment and dismissal); in other words, they are more likely to defer to the controller and the directors.[96] Of course, it is not always beneficial to challenge the controller but only if doing so will bring about an improvement in the corporate governance and share price of the company and thus increase the financial returns of the beneficiaries/clients of the institutional shareholders. But where the institutional shareholders have business ties with the controlling shareholder or the company, they are likely to support them at the expense of increased financial returns for their beneficiaries. Unsurprisingly, it has been found that institutional shareholders voted in favour of board resolutions when they have business ties with the company. It has also been said that the company has

---

[95] Lucian A Bebchuk and Assaf Hamdani, 'Independent Directors and Controlling Shareholders' (2016) 165 *University of Pennsylvania Law Review* 1271 at 1286–7.

[96] Dragana Cvijanović, Amil Dasgupta and Konstantinos E Zachariadis, 'Ties that Bind: How Business Connections Affect Mutual Fund Activism' (2016) 71 *Journal of Finance* 2933; Gerald F Davis and E Han Kim, 'Business Ties and Proxy Voting by Mutual Funds' (2007) 85 *Journal of Financial Economics* 552; Rasha Ashraf, Narayanan Jayaraman and Harley E Ryan, 'Do Pension-Related Business Ties Influence Mutual Fund Proxy Voting? Evidence from Shareholder Proposals on Executive Compensation' (2012) 47 *Journal of Financial and Quantitative Analysis* 567; Assaf Hamdani and Yishay Yafeh, 'Institutional Investors as Minority Shareholders' (2013) 17 *Review of Finance* 691.

pressured institutional shareholders to vote in favour of management proposals.[97]

Further and arguably more important, it has been argued that in order to be in the good books of the controlling shareholder or the directors, the institutional shareholders can design their policies and practices in such a way as to favour the controller (or the directors).[98] Thus, instead of evaluating the particular resolution proposed by management and deciding whether to vote in favour of it, the institutional shareholders will design a general voting policy that is pro-controller. Such a policy undermines stewardship. This is because institutional shareholders will not monitor and engage with the company by devoting time and resources to investigate the proposed resolutions. They will instead rely on the pre-determined voting policy that is pro-controller (or pro-investee company) to make their voting decision. As a result, institutional shareholders no longer serve the critical function envisaged by the stewardship codes, which is to monitor and where appropriate challenge the controlling shareholders and directors.

The above two types of conflicts of interest (business relationships and being in the good books) are exacerbated in SOEs where the controlling shareholder is the government (or an entity that it owns). This is particularly the case when the government is a highly interventionist controlling shareholder, as is the case in the PRC SOEs, the Malaysian GLCs and the Indian PSUs.[99] When the government is the controller, the institutional investors may be even less inclined to engage with the investee companies for the purpose of expressing concerns or objections; or even if they do engage by voting, they may be disinclined to vote against proposals that are supported by the controller. An important reason is that the government who is the controller is also a regulator, and thus the institutional investors may depend on the government for approvals or assistance with respect to other matters. Another reason is that even if institutional shareholders do not expect any assistance or favours from the government as the regulator, they may be worried that the government may retaliate against them should they vote against resolutions that are proposed by the state or its management. A third is that the government can use the SOEs as a conduit to give preferential treatment to the

---

[97] James E Heard and Howard D Sherman, *Conflicts of Interest in the Proxy Voting System* (Investor Responsibility Research Center 1987) at 99.
[98] Lucian Bebchuk and Scott Hirst, 'Index Funds and the Future of Corporate Governance: Theory, Evidence, and Policy' (2019) 119 *Columbia Law Review* (forthcoming).
[99] See Chapter 1, Section IV(B).

institutional investors in return for the latter supporting its business decision or supporting its political parties during elections.[100]

IV Fiduciary Duties of Institutional Shareholders

Institutional shareholders' different interpretations of their fiduciary duties[101] to their clients/beneficiaries have an important bearing on how they engage with their investee companies under the stewardship codes, which in turn have an impact on sustainability. This is because, under the stewardship codes, institutional shareholders are urged to incorporate sustainability considerations in their decision-making processes,[102] as well as to monitor and engage with the company on sustainability matters.[103]

Institutional shareholders can adopt three different interpretations of the fiduciary duties that they owe to their clients/beneficiaries. First, institutional shareholders may interpret their fiduciary duties as precluding them from considering sustainability considerations (consisting usually of ESG factors). Second, they may interpret the duties as permitting them to take into account sustainability considerations provided that certain conditions are satisfied. Third and finally, institutional shareholders may take the view that discharging their fiduciary obligations requires (rather than merely permits) them to take into account and give effect to sustainability considerations. I argue that the first and third interpretations are incorrect and that the second one is correct, but the contention lies in the circumstances under which institutional shareholders can pursue sustainability investments.

A First Interpretation

Under this interpretation, institutional shareholders, such as pension fund trustees, take the view that their fiduciary duties prohibit the consideration of any sustainability matters (defined to mean ESG factors).[104] They are of the opinion that fiduciary obligations require them only to

---

[100] Aldo Musacchio and Sergio G Lazzarini, *Reinventing State Capitalism: Leviathan in Business, Brazil and Beyond* (Harvard University Press 2014) at 63–4, 75.
[101] Fiduciary duties here refer to (1) the duty to act in good faith in the best interests of the principals; (2) the duty to avoid unauthorised conflicts of interest; and (3) the duty to avoid unauthorised receipt of profits.
[102] MCII, Guidance 5.1, 5.3 at 13.
[103] HKPRO para 17, Principle 2; SSP, Guidance 2.3 at 6.
[104] Anna Tilba and Arad Reisberg, 'Fiduciary Duty under the Microscope: Stewardship and the Spectrum of Pension Fund Engagement' (2019) 82 *Modern Law Review* 456 at 471–3.

maximise the financial returns of their clients/beneficiaries.[105] In other words, they interpret the fiduciary duty to act in good faith in the best interests of their clients/beneficiaries as requiring the maximisation of their financial/economic interests, ie their risk-adjusted returns. Thus, they will neither incorporate ESG considerations into their investment decision-making process nor engage with their investee companies on ESG matters, contrary to the statements in the MCII, the HKPRO and the SSP.

The problem with this interpretation is that it wrongly assumes that maximising the economic interests of their clients/beneficiaries necessarily precludes taking into account sustainability considerations.[106] To begin with, if nothing in the purposes and terms of the agreement or instrument[107] precludes consideration of sustainability factors, institutional shareholders should not be prohibited from considering sustainability matters in their decision-making process if they honestly believe that they are acting in the best interests of their clients/beneficiaries.

Thus, a key question is what is meant by acting in the best interests. This depends on the purposes and terms of the contract and instrument that confer the powers on the institutional shareholders, in addition to any applicable statutory law. For example, in a typical pension fund, the primary purpose is to increase the risk-adjusted returns for the beneficiaries.[108] Thus, if institutional investors equate best interests

---

[105] *Cowan v Scargill* [1985] Ch 270 at 286–7.
[106] For criticisms of *Cowan v Scargill* [1985] Ch 270, see Paul Watchman, Jane Anstee-Wedderburn and Lucas Shipway, 'Fiduciary Duties in the 21st Century: A UK Perspective' (2005) 19 *Trust Law International* 127 at 127 where it was stated that the view that profit maximisation is the fundamental fiduciary duty is 'based on a fundamental misunderstanding of the law' and should not be followed. See also SEK Hulme, 'The Basic Duty of Trustees of Superannuation Trusts: Fair to One, Fair to All?' (2000) 14 *Trust Law International* 130; Xenia Frostick, 'Is There a Duty to Act in the Best Interests of the Beneficiaries?' (2000) 83 *Pension Lawyer* 2. Freshfields Bruckhaus Deringer, *A Legal Framework for the Integration of Environmental, Social and Governance Issues Into Institutional Investment* (2005) concluded that *Cowan v Scargill* was 'not a reliable legal authority' (at 89) and that it should be limited to its facts; further, the case should stand for the proposition that fiduciary powers must be exercised 'fully and fairly for the purposes for which they are given and not to accomplish any ulterior purpose'. This view was also confirmed by the judge in that case, Sir Robert Megarry VC, and by Lord Nicholls: see Lord Nicholls, 'Trustees and Their Broader Community: Where Duty, Morality and Ethics Converge' (1996) 70 *Australian Law Journal* 205 at 211.
[107] *Hospital Products Ltd v United States Surgical Corporation* (1984) 156 CLR 41 at 97; *Kelly v Cooper* [1993] AC 205 at 215 (PC).
[108] UK Law Commission, *Fiduciary Duties of Investment Intermediaries* (Law Commission No 350) (1 July 2014) para 6.6.

with only financial returns, then it can be argued that, because there is evidence that taking into account ESG factors has improved financial returns (or at the very least, there is a correlation between socially responsible investments and firm value),[109] then complying with the fiduciary duty requires them to consider these factors in their decision-making process. Indeed, one can go further and say that because the law requires fiduciaries to take into account all relevant considerations[110] that have a bearing on the risk-adjusted returns of their beneficiaries, failure to do so is a breach of the fiduciary obligation. Putting it differently, because the law prohibits fiduciaries from fettering their discretion,[111] institutional shareholders will violate their duties if they exclude consideration of sustainability matters based on a pre-existing policy without a reasonable basis. Conversely, if the investors genuinely believe that taking into account ESG factors in a particular investment decision does not improve the financial returns for that portfolio of assets, then they will not be in breach of fiduciary duties if they do not incorporate these factors. That said, there are dicta to the effect that pension fund trustees should take into account sustainability considerations, even if doing so will adversely affect the financial interests of their beneficiaries, provided that it is in accord with the views of their beneficiaries.[112]

Although the case law and literature do not subscribe to this rigid interpretation of fiduciary duties, ie consideration of sustainability matters is barred,[113] there is research showing that certain institutional investors do hold this view.[114] Thus, insofar as there is a disconnect between the law and social practices, it is an impediment to stewardship.

---

[109] See eg Lucian Bebchuk, Alma Cohen and Charles CY Wang, 'Learning and the Disappearing Association between Governance and Returns' (2013) 108 *Journal of Financial Economics* 323; Allen Ferrell, Hao Liang and Luc Renneboog, 'Socially Responsible Firms' (2016) 122 *Journal of Financial Economics* 585.

[110] *Snell's Equity* (33rd edn, 2018) para 10-013.

[111] Ibid para 10-016.

[112] *Cowan v Scargill* [1985] Ch 270 at 288 (Sir Robert Megarry VC gave the example of the beneficiaries with 'very strict views on moral and social matters, condemning all forms of alcohol, tobacco and popular entertainment, as well as armaments' and, in that situation, 'the beneficiaries might well consider that it was far better to receive less than to receive more money from what they consider to be evil and tainted sources').

[113] UK Law Commission, *Fiduciary Duties of Investment Intermediaries* (Law Commission No 350) (1 July 2014) paras 4.42–4.45, 7.8; UK Law Commission, *Pension Funds and Social Investment* (Law Com No 374) (12 June 2017) at ch 5.

[114] Anna Tilba and Arad Reisberg, 'Fiduciary Duty under the Microscope: Stewardship and the Spectrum of Pension Fund Engagement' (2019) 82 *Modern Law Review* 456 at 471–3.

B Second Interpretation

Under this interpretation, institutional shareholders are permitted to take into account sustainability considerations in their investment decision-making process and they are permitted to monitor and engage with the board and controller with respect to sustainability matters. The contention lies in the circumstances or conditions under which they are allowed to do so. At a fundamental level, if the terms or purposes of the contract or instrument permit (or require) institutional shareholders to consider sustainability considerations, then they are permitted to do so because compliance with the written terms (expressed or implied) of the documents by which they are legally bound is the most basic requirement of fiduciary obligations[115] because the contract will shape the scope of fiduciary obligations.[116] The question is what if the terms or purposes of the document are silent as to whether institutional shareholders can take into account sustainability considerations? There are two views. The first view is that institutional shareholders are permitted to consider sustainability matters even if it does not increase the risk-adjusted returns for their beneficiaries provided that (1) they have a valid basis for thinking that their beneficiaries prefer them to take into account these matters; and (2) the decision does not result in any significant financial detriment to the beneficiaries.[117] The second view is that institutional shareholders can take into account ESG matters only if (1) they have a reasonable basis for concluding that it will benefit the beneficiaries by increasing the risk-adjusted returns; and (2) the institutional shareholders are motivated only to increase the financial returns.[118] There are difficulties with both views, particularly the first.

1 The First View

The first view comprises a two-part test.[119] The first part of the test is that as long as the institutional shareholders have good reason to think that the beneficiaries would share the concern for non-financial factors such

---

[115] Lord Nicholls, 'Trustees and Their Broader Community: Where Duty, Morality and Ethics Converge' (1996) 70 *Australian Law Journal* 205.

[116] *Hospital Products Ltd v United States Surgical Corporation* (1984) 156 CLR 41 at 97; *Kelly v Cooper* [1993] AC 205 at 215 (PC).

[117] UK Law Commission, *Fiduciary Duties of Investment Intermediaries* (Law Commission No 350) (1 July 2014) para 6.34.

[118] Max M Schanzenbach and Robert H Sitkoff, 'Reconciling Fiduciary Duty and Social Conscience: The Law and Economics of ESG Investing by a Trustee' (2020) 72 *Stanford Law Review* (forthcoming).

[119] UK Law Commission, *Fiduciary Duties of Investment Intermediaries* (Law Commission No 350) (1 July 2014) para 6.36 stated that these two tests can be departed from if the

as improving the members' quality of life or showing disapproval of certain industries, they can consider these factors.[120] This raises the issue of how institutional shareholders can ascertain the preferences or concerns of their beneficiaries. It has been said that formal consultation is not always necessary and that institutional shareholders can make assumption in some cases such as when certain activities violate international law (one example given being the manufacture of cluster bombs).[121] Where consultation is necessary, it has been said that there need not be unanimous agreement among the beneficiaries such that it would suffice if the majority opposed an investment while the minority was neutral.[122]

To begin with, it is not easy to ascertain the preferences of their clients/beneficiaries. For example, where an asset owner is responsible for the pension funds of thousands of corporate employees, it is virtually impossible to know what their preferences are. Even if it were possible to know the majority preferences, fiduciary law does not permit asset owners to give effect to only these preferences because the law requires the fiduciary to promote the interests of the beneficiaries as a whole; in other words, the fiduciary is not permitted to discriminate in favour of one group of beneficiaries (even if it were the dominant one);[123] it has to act fairly among different classes of beneficiaries.[124] However, it does not follow that institutional shareholders cannot incorporate ESG considerations into their investment decision-making process if they do not or cannot know their beneficiaries' preferences. They can and should do so if they believe that it will benefit the beneficiaries by increasing the risk-adjusted returns. This is because the fiduciary duty (as reflected in the obligation to act for the purposes stated in the contract or instrument) generally requires them to promote the beneficiaries' financial interests.

This brings us to the second part of the test: incorporating sustainability considerations must not result in 'significant financial detriment'. This is highly problematic. For example, assume that an institutional shareholder is faced with two investment options,

decisions have been authorised by the trust deed; or, if in defined contribution schemes, the beneficiary has chosen to invest in a specific fund.

[120] UK Law Commission, *Fiduciary Duties of Investment Intermediaries* (Law Commission No 350) (1 July 2014) paras 6.40–6.49.
[121] UK Law Commission, *Pension Funds and Social Investment Summary* (Law Com No 374 (Summary)) (12 June 2017) para 1.47.
[122] Ibid para 1.48.
[123] *Re Tempest (1886)* 1 Ch App 485 at 487–8.
[124] *Nestle v National Westminster Bank (1996)* 10 *Trust Law International* 112 at 115.

both of which provide identical risks and returns.¹²⁵ Let us suppose that the institutional shareholder decides to pursue one but not the other because the former is an SRI. Suppose also that the pursuit of this chosen investment not only does not pose a significant financial detriment, but it also does not diminish the risk-adjusted returns of the portfolio. However, it is not clear that institutional shareholders are permitted to do so under fiduciary law. This is because the fiduciary 'may not act for his own benefit or the benefit of a third person without the informed consent of his principal'.¹²⁶ But, by incorporating sustainability considerations if it does not increase the risk-adjusted returns for its beneficiaries, the institutional shareholder, who is a fiduciary, may have acted for the benefit of third parties. Further, the fiduciary may be in breach of the no-conflict rule which forbids fiduciaries from putting themselves in a position in which their interests (which include both financial and non-financial ones) conflict with those of their beneficiaries. There need not be actual conflict because a real sensible possibility of conflict¹²⁷ will suffice. In the example I have just given, by selecting the investment on the basis of sustainability considerations, one cannot rule out the possibility that the institutional shareholder's decision may be challenged on the basis that it has acted in its own interests, ie its personal ethical beliefs that the interests of third parties, such as employees, community or society should be protected. But it may be rebutted that the institutional shareholders' interests do not conflict with the beneficiaries' interests if institutional investors can point to surveys they have conducted which show that the majority of beneficiaries would like them to take into account sustainability considerations. The objection is that where the survey shows that the majority would like to have sustainability considerations incorporated but the minority are either lukewarm or do not want, it can be said that the institutional shareholders have acted on the basis of their own ethical beliefs if they prefer the views of the majority over those of the minority where taking into account these views does not increase the financial returns of the portfolio.

---

[125] Max M Schanzenbach and Robert H Sitkoff, 'Reconciling Fiduciary Duty and Social Conscience: The Law and Economics of ESG Investing by a Trustee' (2020) 72 *Stanford Law Review* (forthcoming).
[126] *Bristol & West Building Society v Mothew* [1998] Ch 1 at 18.
[127] *Boardman v Phipps* [1967] 2 AC 46 at 124.

2 The Second View

Under this view, institutional shareholders are permitted to take into account sustainability matters only if (1) it increases the risk-adjusted returns for their beneficiaries; and (2) they do so only to benefit the beneficiaries and not for any ulterior or extraneous motive.[128] There is an important advantage to this view: as compared to the first interpretation in Section IV(A), the first view of the second interpretation in Section IV(B.1) and the third interpretation in Section IV(C), it is the most consistent with fiduciary law and hence makes it unlikely that the institutional shareholders' investment decisions will be challenged. But there is a downside: it seems unduly harsh and inflexible. Is it possible for institutional shareholders to take into account sustainability matters and yet comply with fiduciary law in a situation where taking into account these considerations may not increase the risk-adjusted returns?

The short answer is that it is possible given that fiduciary law prohibits only unauthorised conflicts of interest. So, provided that the fiduciary has obtained the advance consent of the beneficiaries, it can take into account sustainability considerations, even if it does not increase the risk-adjusted returns. But the difficulty lies in whether unanimous consent is required or whether approval from a majority of the beneficiaries would suffice. Because institutional shareholders owe their fiduciary duties to each of the beneficiaries/principals, authorisation has to be obtained from each of them,[129] subject to any applicable statutory law, that is, unless there is any applicable statute that provides an exception. To address this problem, it is suggested that the contract or instrument can include a clause expressly permitting the institutional shareholders to incorporate sustainability considerations and to engage with the investee companies on sustainability matters.

C Third Interpretation

Under this interpretation, fiduciary duties require (and not merely permit) institutional shareholders to consider and give effect to

---

[128] Max M Schanzenbach and Robert H Sitkoff, 'Reconciling Fiduciary Duty and Social Conscience: The Law and Economics of ESG Investing by a Trustee' (2020) 72 *Stanford Law Review* (forthcoming).

[129] L Tucker, N Le Poidevin and J Brightwell, *Lewin on Trusts* (18th edn, 2012) para 45-03.

sustainability factors in their decision-making process.[130] Institutional shareholders may take this view because they are of the opinion that incorporating sustainability considerations will improve the financial returns of their beneficiaries and will benefit third parties such as the community, society and the environment. So they are motivated to enhance the risk-adjusted returns of their beneficiaries and to improve the welfare of others on ethical grounds. As a result, as compared to the first and second fiduciary interpretations, the third interpretation would best facilitate the stewardship objective of the codes because investors who subscribe to this interpretation will actively monitor and engage with their investee companies with respect to sustainability matters.

Assuming that the purposes or terms of the contract or instrument do not preclude institutional shareholders from adopting this interpretation of fiduciary duties which require (as opposed to permit) them to incorporate sustainability considerations, it is doubtful whether such a view is consistent with fiduciary law. Fiduciary law requires fiduciaries to avoid unauthorised conflicts of interest. Hence, it can be said that the interest of institutional shareholders, which is to benefit third parties, conflicts with their duty to their beneficiaries to increase risk-adjusted returns. This is because taking into account sustainability matters may not increase the risk-adjusted returns of their beneficiaries.[131] Further, fiduciary law requires the fiduciary not to fetter its discretion.[132] Thus, if institutional shareholders take the view that they must incorporate sustainability considerations into all of their investment decision-making process, regardless of whether it will enhance the financial returns of their beneficiaries in a particular investment, then this will amount to fettering their discretion. For these reasons, it is questionable whether this interpretation of fiduciary duty is consistent with fiduciary law.

---

[130] UNEP Finance Initiative, *A Legal Framework for the Integration of Environmental, Social and Governance Issues into Institutional Investment* (2005) at 13; UNEP Finance Initiative, *Fiduciary Duty in the 21st Century* (2015) at 9; Susan N Gary, 'Best Interests in the Long Term: Fiduciary Duties and ESG Integration' (2019) 90 *University of Colorado Law Review* 731; Susan N Gary, 'Values and Value: University Endowments, Fiduciary Duties, and ESG Investing' (2016) 42 *Journal of College and University Law* 247.

[131] Max M Schanzenbach and Robert H Sitkoff, 'Reconciling Fiduciary Duty and Social Conscience: The Law and Economics of ESG Investing by a Trustee' (2020) 72 *Stanford Law Review* (forthcoming).

[132] *Snell's Equity* (33rd edn, 2018) para 10-016.

V Conclusion

In view of the problems surrounding the rationales, contents, compliance structure and scope of the stewardship codes, the following reforms should be made so that the codes can be an effective mechanism for promoting sustainability. The rationales of the codes have to clearly articulate the meaning of sustainability, and the codes have to clearly identify who the intended beneficiaries are (ie the ultimate beneficiaries/ principals of the institutional investors; the investee companies; and/or the stakeholders broadly defined). The contents of the codes (ie the principles and guidelines) have to specify the requirements of sustainability. Assuming that the regulators wish to preserve the soft law nature of the codes instead of turning them into hard law, a comply or explain mechanism coupled with an effective and independent monitoring mechanism should be implemented. Further, consideration has to be given to the issue of whether the scope of the codes – the shareholders who are subject to the code – should be reformed to include controlling shareholders, or whether a separate code for controllers is preferable.

With regard to the potentially adverse effect of controlling shareholders on institutional shareholders' pursuit of stewardship, it is suggested that various solutions can be adopted. For a start, given that monitoring and engagement by asset managers are costly, the cost incurred can be partially borne by the asset owners and beneficiaries. Another solution is to impose a requirement on institutional shareholders to undertake stewardship activities in the company by setting aside a certain percentage of funds based on the assets that they manage. Regarding the problem of conflicts of interest, one solution is to prohibit institutional shareholders from doing business with the controlling shareholders. One difficulty with this solution is that it may not find favour with the government as a controlling shareholder that has business ties with the institutional shareholders, particularly if they know that it can use the existing (or potential) businesses as leverage to secure the allegiance of the institutional shareholders. Another difficulty is that, should the law prohibit such business relationships, the government or its SOE may lose an important source of revenue; but this is doubtful because, given the disparity in resources and bargaining power, it is the institutional shareholders rather than the government or its SOE who stand to lose (or to lose more). Another solution is to impose a requirement on institutional shareholders to disclose their business ties with the controller and the company, or any conflicts of interest. But

V CONCLUSION

it is questionable whether disclosure alone would reduce conflicts of interest and hence improve engagement and monitoring by the institutional investors. Another possible solution is that where there is inadequate disclosure of conflicts of interest policies or poor management of conflicts of interest, proxy advisors could criticise the institutional shareholders and/or the investee companies. But the problem is that these proxy advisors may also suffer from conflicts of interest because of their existing or potential business relationships with the institutional investors and/or investee companies.

Other than the problems concerning the codes and controlling shareholders, another factor that will have a bearing on whether institutional shareholders will monitor and engage with their investee companies in order to promote sustainability lies in the investors' different interpretations of their fiduciary duties. As I have argued, fiduciary law does not bar institutional shareholders from taking into account sustainability considerations; nor does it require them to do so under all circumstances. Rather, the question lies in the circumstances under which fiduciary law permits institutional shareholders to incorporate sustainability considerations into their decision-making process. It is suggested that these investors could and should take into account these considerations if they have a reasonable basis that it will increase the financial returns for their beneficiaries. But if it has an adverse impact on the financial interests of their beneficiaries, institutional shareholders should not do so. Given the lack of clarity in the law, it is necessary for the legislature or courts to specify the circumstances under which institutional shareholders can incorporate sustainability considerations and engage with the company on these matters.

6

Directors' Duty to Act in the Best Interests of the Company

I   Shareholder Primacy, Stakeholder Value, and Long-Term Value and Viability   208
    A Shareholder Primacy   208
    B Stakeholder Value   212
    C Long-Term Value and Viability   215
II Evaluation of the Law in the Four Asian Jurisdictions   217
    A India   217
    B Hong Kong   220
    C Singapore   223
    D Malaysia   225
    E Lessons   226
III Implications of Directors' Best Interest Duty for Corporate Governance Mechanisms   228
    A Sustainability Reporting   228
    B Stewardship Code   229
    C Constituency Directors   231
IV Conclusion   232

This chapter examines how the duty of directors to act in good faith in the best interests of the company could be used to promote sustainability in the four Asian jurisdictions. Forceful critiques have been put forward that shareholder primacy – often defined as the maximisation of share price – is a considerable impediment to promoting sustainability.[1] This is because maximising share price has been said to result in short-termism which is detrimental to long-term value creation that will benefit the company, society and the environment. It has also been argued that

---

[1] See eg Beate Sjåfjell, Andrew Johnston, Linn Anker-Sorensen and David Millon, 'Shareholder Primacy: The Main Barrier to Sustainable Companies' in Beate Sjåfjell and Benjamin J Richardson (eds), *Company Law and Sustainability* (Cambridge University Press 2015) at ch 3; Beate Sjåfjell, 'Dismantling the Legal Myth of Shareholder Primacy:

the laws of the two most famous shareholder primacy jurisdictions – the United States and the UK – do not support the claim that where there is a conflict between the short-term interests of shareholders and the long-term ones of the company, directors are legally required to act in the interests of the former and to disregard the latter.[2]

Nevertheless, the laws of shareholder primacy jurisdictions such as the United States and the UK do require directors to be solely accountable to shareholders.[3] This means that, in theory and in practice, stakeholders' interests are subordinated to those of shareholders in the United States and the UK. Generally speaking, even when the board takes into account or advances stakeholders' interests, it is a means to promote an end, namely, shareholders' interests.[4] This shareholder-centric view of directors' duties is supported by the fact that only shareholders and not stakeholders in the United States and the UK have governance rights including, but not limited to, the right to appoint and dismiss directors and to sue them for breach of duties in a derivative action.[5]

Thus, proponents of sustainability argue that shareholder primacy is an obstacle to advancing sustainability, and ought to be replaced by the stakeholder value theory which requires directors to balance and give

---

The Corporation as a Sustainable Market Actor' in Nina Boeger and Charlotte Villiers (eds), *Shaping the Corporate Landscape* (Hart 2018) at ch 4.

[2] On Delaware law, see Cynthia Williams, 'Corporate Social Responsibility and Corporate Governance' in Jeffrey N Gordon and Wolf-Georg Ringe (eds), *Oxford Handbook of Corporate Law and Governance* (Oxford University Press 2015) at 48–9; on UK law (s 172 of Companies Act 2006), see David Kershaw, *Company Law in Context: Text and Materials* (2nd edn, Oxford University Press 2012) at 382–3 (stating that success means long-term shareholder value and directors are required to consider the long-term implications of their decisions).

[3] On Delaware law, see E Norman Veasey and Christine T DiGuglielmo, 'What Happened in Delaware Corporate Law and Governance from 1992–2004? A Retrospective on Some Key Developments' (2005) 153 *University of Pennsylvania Law Review* 1399 at 1431; Leo E Strine, Jr., 'The Dangers of Denial: The Need for a Clear-Eyed Understanding of the Power and Accountability Structure Established by the Delaware General Corporation Law' (2015) University of Pennsylvania Law School Institute for Law and Economics Research Paper No 15-08 http://ssrn.com/abstract=2576389 at 143–4. On UK law, see s 172(1) of Companies Act 2006: directors are required to act for the benefit of the company's members as a whole.

[4] See eg s UK 172(1) Companies Act 2006 which requires directors to have regard to employees' interests, the impact of the company's operations on the community and environment and other considerations but only for the purpose of promoting the company's success for the benefit of its members.

[5] On Delaware law, see *Unocal Corp. v Mesa Petroleum Co.*, 493 A.2d 946 (Del. 1985); *North American Catholic Educ. Prog. Foundation, Inc. v Gheewalla*, 930 A.2d 92, 101 (Del. 2007). On UK law, see ss 168 and 260 of Companies Act 2006.

effect to the interests of different stakeholders.[6] However, in light of the problems with the stakeholder value theory, as I will explain, it is not clear that stakeholder value theory is the obvious solution to promote sustainability. Further, in jurisdictions in which directors are legally required to promote the interests of stakeholders, such as India, shareholders continue to wield the exclusive right to appoint and dismiss directors and the sole right to sue directors.

As I will show, the solution is not necessarily to choose either a shareholder primacy or a stakeholder value approach. Jurisdictions such as Singapore and Malaysia show that there is a third way. The laws in both jurisdictions are flexible enough to permit directors to take a nuanced approach as to what is meant by the company's interests. Directors are permitted to give effect to the interests of different constituencies depending on the specific circumstances. As for jurisdictions whose law is based on shareholder primacy, such as Hong Kong, it is possible to reconceptualise shareholder primacy such that it can be deployed to promote sustainability, although there are difficulties in doing so.

The structure of this chapter is as follows. This chapter critically analyses how the mechanism of the directors' duty to act in good faith in the best interests of the company could be used to promote corporate sustainability in the four Asian jurisdictions. First, I assess the three main theories of the best interest duty, namely, shareholder primacy, stakeholder value, and long-term value and viability of the company with a view to considering the advantages and drawbacks of each theory in promoting sustainability. Second, I show how the different theories are reflected in the laws in the four Asian jurisdictions and I examine whether and how the laws in these four jurisdictions can promote sustainability. Finally, I analyse the implications of directors' best interest duty for the other corporate mechanisms, namely, sustainability reporting, stewardship code and constituency directors.

I Shareholder Primacy, Stakeholder Value, and Long-Term Value and Viability

A Shareholder Primacy

The debate on shareholder primacy and stakeholder value is a well-trodden one and there is extensive literature on the arguments for and

---

[6] Beate Sjåfjell (n 1).

against both theories. This debate has implications for corporate sustainability. It has been argued that shareholder primacy is one of the greatest obstacles to corporate sustainability and, thus, stakeholder value theory should be adopted.[7] This is because shareholder primacy has been understood as requiring boards to exclusively or predominantly maximise share price, which has resulted in excessive risk-taking and short-termism (the latter of which has been defined as inordinate emphasis on quarterly earnings and neglecting long-term value creation).[8] This is detrimental to the promotion of sustainability as the interests of other constituencies such as those of the employees, customers, suppliers and environment have been subordinated or neglected. No wonder maximising shareholder value has been said to result in 'reckless, sociopathic and socially irresponsible behaviors'.[9] Even the enlightened shareholder value approach of s 172 of the UK Companies Act – under which directors are permitted to take into account the interests of different stakeholders only if it benefits shareholders – has been understood by boards to maximise (short-term) shareholder value.[10]

---

[7] Ibid.
[8] See eg Lynn Stout, *The Shareholder Value Myth: How Putting Shareholders First Harms Investors, Corporations, and the Public* (Berrett-Koehler Publishers 2012) at ch 4; European Commission Green Paper, *Corporate Governance in Financial Institutions and Remuneration Policies* (COM (2010) 284 final) at 8; European Commission Green Paper, *The EU Corporate Governance Framework* (COM (2011) 164 final) at 11; John Kay, *The Kay Review of UK Equity Markets and Long-term Decision-Making, Final Report* (Department of Business, Innovation and Skills 2012) para 1.1–1.29; William Lazonick, 'Profits Without Prosperity' (2014) *Harvard Business Review* https://hbr.org/2014/09/profits-without-prosperity; Conference Board, *Is Short-Term Behavior Jeopardizing the Future Prosperity of Business?* www.wlrk.com/docs/IsShortTermBehaviorJeopardizingTheFutureProsperityOfBusiness_CEOStrategicImplications.pdf; Cf Mark J Roe, 'Stock Market Short-Termism's Impact' (25 May 2018) https://ssrn.com/abstract=3171090. A key evidence cited by Roe to refute the point that short-termism has resulted in reduction of R&D is that R&D has overall increased, led by the top five tech companies in the United States (Apple, Amazon, Microsoft, Alphabet (Google) and Facebook), which are also the top five listed companies in the United States. But a review of the annual reports, mission statements and other publicly available documents shows that these top five tech companies do not adopt the maximisation of share price as the sole or predominant corporate purpose. Rather, they have defined their corporate purpose in terms of being the best customer-centric company in the world (Amazon) and delivering the best products and services to consumers and community in their respective domains (Apple, Google and Microsoft).
[9] Lynn A Stout, *The Shareholder Value Myth: How Putting Shareholders First Harms Investors, Corporations, and the Public* (Berrett-Koehler Publishers 2012) at vi; Lynn A Stout, 'New Thinking on "Shareholder Primacy"' (2012) 2 *Accounting, Economics and Law* 1.
[10] Eilis Ferran, 'Corporate Mobility and Company Law' (2016) 79 *Modern Law Review* 813 at 836.

However, it may be argued that shareholder primacy theory can accommodate sustainability practices, provided that they are consistent with the promotion of long-term shareholder value. After all, studies have shown that companies that have integrated ESG considerations into their decision-making process have achieved higher profitability and higher return on equity.[11] But the problem is that where it is not clear that the end result of the sustainability initiatives leads to material improvement in shareholder value, it is unlikely that shareholders would be willing to sacrifice short-term gains for long-term value that is difficult to predict and quantify. This is particularly the case if the investment strategies and portfolios of certain activist shareholders are not of a long-term nature, such as those of hedge funds. As I will explain, the tactics of hedge fund activists in Hong Kong have called into question the claim that such activism has resulted in long-term value creation. Further, where executive compensation is tied to share price such as stock option grants, it is doubtful that maximisation of shareholder value will not be prioritised.[12] Moreover, a shareholder primacy approach will exacerbate expropriation of stakeholders by controlling shareholders in concentrated ownership companies (such as those in the Asian jurisdictions analysed here).[13] Controlling shareholders, by virtue of their control rights (which may exceed their cash flow rights in companies with a pyramid or dual class share structure), will have the incentives and ability to pursue actions that will benefit them but at the expense of not only minority shareholders but also stakeholders, such as to cause the board to boost profits or to increase their dividends by causing the board to: let go of employees, increase the prices of goods and services to the detriment of consumers, reduce R&D investments which could lead to cheaper and better products for consumers or pursue highly risky investments.[14] Finally, in light of the courts' traditional reluctance to

---

[11] See Chapter 1 (n 31–6).

[12] Patrick Bolton, José Scheinkman and Wei Xiong, 'Executive Compensation and Short-Termist Behaviour in Speculative Markets' (2006) 73 *Review of Economic Studies* 577; Jonathan Pogach, 'Short-Termism of Executive Compensation' (2018) 148 *Journal of Economic Behavior and Organization* 150.

[13] Martin Gelter, 'The Dark Side of Shareholder Influence: Managerial Autonomy and Stakeholder Orientation in Comparative Governance' (2009) 50 *Harvard International Law Journal* 129 at 154–67; Andrei Shleifer and Robert W Vishny, 'A Survey of Corporate Governance' (1997) 52 *Journal of Finance* 737 at 760; Mike Burkart, Denis Gromb and Fausto Panunzi, 'Large Shareholders, Monitoring, and Fiduciary Duty' (1997) 112 *Quarterly Journal of Economics* 112.

[14] Ibid.

intervene in the business judgement of directors,[15] a decision taken that is harmful to the interests of stakeholders but beneficial to the short-term interests of shareholders will not be invalidated unless the minority shareholder (because non-shareholders cannot bring a derivative action or unfair prejudice claim) can show that the directors have been negligent or that they have breached their fiduciary duties.

Another way in which shareholder primacy theory can accommodate corporate sustainability is that shareholder primacy need not be understood in terms of maximisation of shareholder value. Shareholder primacy, it has been recently argued, could and should give effect to shareholders' preferences.[16] Thus, if shareholders have ethical and social preferences such as promoting sustainability, then the board should give effect to such preferences. And shareholders can convey their preferences formally through voting or informally through dialogue with the board. In short, boards should maximise shareholder welfare, not market value. But the risk is that whether corporate sustainability will be promoted depends on the happenstance of the identity and preferences of shareholders. So if the shareholders instruct the board to maximise share price, it should do so. The other concern is that where shareholders have conflicting preferences, directors are more likely to heed the voices of the controlling shareholders as they wield the power to dismiss them. Thus, if the controller happens to want the board to maximise short-term share price whereas the non-controlling shareholders take a contrary view, the board will listen to the former.

However, a narrow version of the shareholder preference/welfare claim is that where the company's maximisation of share price would result in externalities, and it would be more costly for shareholders than the company to fix these externalities, and the government is unwilling or unable to address these externalities, the company should do so. On this view, even if shareholders' preference is to maximise share price, boards should not do so. But the concern is that this view is restricted only to fixing or avoiding externalities, which is merely one aspect of sustainability. But sustainability

---

[15] Other than Malaysia, which has a statutory business judgment rule but which applies only to the duty to exercise reasonable care, skill and diligence (s 214 of the Companies Act 2016), the English common law position under which courts will generally not interfere in the business decisions of the board is applicable: *Howard Smith Ltd v Ampol Petroleum Ltd* [1974] 1 All ER 1126 at 1131. Delaware, by contrast, has a well-established business judgment rule: see eg *Aronson v Lewis*, 473 A 2d 805, 812 (Del 1984).

[16] Oliver Hart and Luigi Zingales, 'Companies Should Maximize Shareholder Welfare Not Market Value' (2017) 2 *Journal of Law, Finance, and Accounting* 247.

goes beyond that to include addressing the broader impacts that the companies will cause to society as well as integrating and giving effect to ESG considerations in the company's business operations and strategies.

B Stakeholder Value

The alternative to shareholder primacy theory is the stakeholder value theory under which the board can and should promote the interests of different stakeholders. Despite the problems with shareholder primacy theory, it provides a clear criterion to directors and managers on what to do and how their performance will be evaluated. By contrast, an unresolved problem with stakeholder value theory is that no clear guidance is provided to directors on how they can balance and give effect to the heterogeneous or conflicting interests of stakeholders.[17] As a result, there is a risk that boards and management may pursue their own interests under the guise of promoting stakeholders' interest. In addition, it would be difficult to appraise the performance of the board and management as there is no clear and determinate standard as to what is the correct way to balance the interests of different constituencies.

The response to these criticisms is as follows. To begin with, the claim that shareholder value can provide a clear and determinate criterion to hold the board accountable is incorrect. While short-term shareholder value can, it is not possible with long-term shareholder value because of the problem of uncertainty in relation to what the future outcomes might be and the probability of their occurrences.[18] It is difficult to know what long-term shareholder value means using the standard valuation techniques such as discounted cash flow, book value and earnings multiples.[19] Next, it has been argued that the board can and should enter into legally enforceable covenants with stakeholders, and that these covenants should specify who the stakeholders are as well as the standards and conduct expected of stakeholders and the procedural provisions that

---

[17] See eg Mark J Roe, 'The Shareholder Wealth Maximization Norm and Industrial Organization' (2011) 149 *University of Pennsylvania Law Review* 2063 at 2065; Stephen Bainbridge, 'The Siren Song of Corporate Social Responsibility' *TCS Daily* (14 November 2005); John Argenti, 'Stakeholders: The Case Against' (1997) 30 *Long Range Planning* 442; Elaine Sternberg, *Stakeholding: Betraying the Corporation's Objectives* (London Social Affairs Unit, Research Paper No 27, 1998).

[18] Tamara Belinfanti and Lynn Stout, 'Contested Visions: The Value of Systems Theory for Corporate Law' (2018) 166 *University of Pennsylvania Law Review* 579 at 597

[19] Ibid at 597–8.

guide decision-making.[20] Further, the objection that the adoption of stakeholder value theory will result in lack of accountability seems inflated. Having multiple metrics for measuring managerial performance that take into account the stock price, profitability, employee welfare, consumer satisfaction and environmental sustainability measures is not the same thing as having no or indeterminate metrics.[21] After all, companies have to produce goods and services that consumers want to have, they have to be places where employees want to work, they have to contribute meaningfully to the community in which they operate, and they have to be trustworthy and reliable partners with whom suppliers, bondholders and creditors would want to transact. And in light of the significant economic, social and increasingly political impact that their business and operations have on society, companies have to proactively address any negative consequences arising from their businesses and to augment positive ones. Moreover, the claim that maximisation of shareholder value is the sole or predominant purpose of the company which directors should promote fails to accord with reality: a study of the corporate purposes of 120 companies in the 4 Asian jurisdictions analysed here found that companies that subscribe to shareholder primacy are in the minority as they account for 20.83 per cent.[22] Tellingly, there is a higher percentage of companies that have non-shareholder primacy objectives such as stakeholder value (40 per cent) or the corporate entity (39.17 per cent).[23]

Another criticism is that the normative basis on which the board should pursue the interests of each stakeholder group is not clear. This criticism is unpersuasive because three principal normative justifications have been advanced. The first is fairness.[24] Stakeholders should be treated

---

[20] Iris Chiu, 'Operationalising a Stakeholder Conception in Company Law' (2016) 10 *Law and Financial Markets Review* 173.

[21] Joseph L Bower and Lynn S Paine, 'The Error at the Heart of the Corporate Leadership' (2017) *Harvard Business Review* https://hbr.org/2017/05/managing-for-the-long-term.

[22] Ernest Lim, *A Case for Shareholders' Fiduciary Duties in Common Law Asia* (Cambridge University Press 2019) at 510.

[23] Ibid.

[24] See eg R Edward Freeman, *Strategic Management: A Stakeholder Approach* (Pitman/Ballinger 1984); Thomas Donaldson and Lee E Preston, 'The Stakeholder Theory for the Corporation: Concepts, Evidence, Implications' (1995) 20 *Academy Management Review* 6; Ronald K Mitchell, Bradley R Agle and Donna J Wood, 'Toward a Theory of Stakeholder Identification and Salience: Defining the Principle of Who and What Really Counts' (1997) 22 *Academy Management Review* 853; Max BE Clarkson, 'A Stakeholder Framework for Analyzing and Evaluating Corporate Social Performance' (1995) 20 *Academy Management Review* 92 at 112.

as ends in themselves and not as means to promote the end of shareholder value. They make valuable contributions to the company and are as affected as the shareholders by the company's decisions or even more so. The problem with this view is that it provides no guidance to the board when it is confronted with competing and conflicting demands to be treated as ends by different groups of stakeholders such as consumers, employees and the community.[25] Ultimately, given that the company has finite resources, trade-offs and prioritisation of interests of these different groups are necessary.

The second justification is justice. Stakeholders, especially employees, are prone to exploitation because of inequality of bargaining power between them and the employers. The majority of employees cannot adequately protect themselves using contracts because they are necessarily incomplete. Further, the company's employees are not the only ones susceptible to exploitation; so are the workers in the complex supply chain of the parent company and its subsidiaries. This raises the difficult issue of the scope of the company's legal obligations towards these stakeholders.

The final justification is efficiency. On one view, failure to adequately protect the interests of stakeholders will reduce the willingness and ability of stakeholders, especially employees, to commit themselves to firm-specific investments; this will increase the firm's cost of capital.[26] One objection to the efficiency justification is that it seems to rest on the assumption that it is more efficient for the company to promote employees' interests than for the state to reform employment law to ensure that employees' interests are properly protected. Structural and systemic disadvantages faced by employees or other stakeholders may be more appropriately addressed through legislations.

A final criticism of the stakeholder value theory is that it does not pay sufficient attention to the ownership structure of companies. In jurisdictions such as the four common law Asian countries where the majority of listed companies have controlling shareholders, it is unlikely that

---

[25] Elaine Sternberg, 'The Defects of Stakeholder Theory' (1997) 5 *Corporate Governance* 3; Adolf A Berle, 'For Whom Corporate Managers Are Trustees: A Note' (1932) 45 *Harvard Law Review* 1365; E Merrick Dodd Jr, 'Is Effective Enforcement of the Fiduciary Duties of Corporate Managers Practicable?' (1934) 2 *University of Chicago Law Review* 194.

[26] See eg James M Malcolmson, 'Individual Employment Contracts' in Orley Aschenfelter and David Card (eds), *Handbook of Labor Economics*, vol 3B (Elsevier 1999) at 2330–3; Gavin Kelly and John Parkinson, 'The Conceptual Foundations of the Company: A Pluralist Approach' in John Parkinson, Gavin Kelly and Andrew Gamble (eds), *The Political Economy of the Company* (Hart Publishing 2001) at 123–9.

directors, whose appointment and dismissal rests with the controller, will prioritise the interests of stakeholders over those of the controllers if these interests conflict.

C   Long-Term Value and Viability[27]

Other than shareholder primacy and stakeholder value theory, there is another theory that arguably avoids the problems with those two theories and yet can be deployed to promote sustainability, namely, the long-term value and viability of the company. This theory argues that the interests of the company need not be equated with those of shareholders or stakeholders; rather, it should be understood as the long-term value and viability of the company. This theory takes the separate legal personality rule seriously and posits that a solvent company has interests that are separate and distinct from, but may overlap with, those of shareholders and stakeholders. The long-term value and viability of the company consists of protecting intellectual capital (R&D investments, intellectual property), human capital (employees and suppliers), social capital (customers and the community), natural capital (future generations and the environment) and financial capital (profits and share price).[28] Companies should have strong incentive to attend to non-financial capital because there are large-scale empirical studies demonstrating that high customer and employee satisfaction positively and significantly correlate with increased share price. The long-term value and viability of the company requires the board and management to eschew short-termism to ensure that the company not only survives but also flourishes in the long term. This theory recognises that while shareholders' interests (financial capital) have to be protected and promoted, they should not constitute a company's predominant purpose, let alone the sole purpose.

To be clear, under the long-term value and viability theory, financial capital is not relegated to a subordinate status and non-financial capital elevated to superordinate ones. It all depends on the purposes of the company and the particular circumstances facing the company in light of the economic and industry conditions. So, for example, one of the core businesses of a company has been unprofitable for some time. Failure to address this issue will have material and adverse effects on the company's

---

[27] The analysis here is drawn from Ernest Lim, *A Case for Shareholders' Fiduciary Duties in Common Law Asia* (Cambridge University Press 2019) at 166–75.
[28] Colin Mayer, 'Who's Responsible for an Irresponsible Business: An Assessment' (2017) 33 *Oxford Review of Economic Policy* 157 at 163.

cash flow and profitability. After carefully evaluating all available options, the board decides to shut down the business. Although employees in that business will be made redundant as a result, and existing contracts with the suppliers for that business will have to be terminated, it is justified on the basis that doing so is necessary to protect the long-term value and viability of the company. In other words, giving effect to the long-term value and viability of the company in that situation requires the board to give priority to financial capital rather than human capital. But in other situations, the long-term value and viability of the company may lead the board to make the reverse decision.

Finally, because companies have different corporate purposes and different types of business, this theory is flexible enough to allow directors and managers to give varying weight to intellectual, social, human, natural and financial capital, depending on the particular circumstances that the company is facing.

The differences between the long-term value and viability theory and stakeholder value theory are twofold.[29] First, while both theories attend to the interests of different constituencies, under the former, giving effect to these interests is not an end in itself unlike the latter theory; rather, it is a means to an end, ie to promote the interests of the company, an entity that is separate and distinct from the shareholders and stakeholders. So, for example, according to the long-term value and viability theory, where the company chooses to use its extra cash to increase employees' salaries or to invest in R&D to produce environmentally sustainable products, instead of using it to issue dividends to shareholders, the company is seeking to protect and promote the long-term interests of the corporate entity which in the particular circumstance requires the board to address the persistent problem of low retention rates of staff and to satisfy the demands of its consumers for environmentally sustainable products. The purpose is not to promote and prioritise the interests of the employees and consumers per se. In other words, under the stakeholder value theory, the company's decision is justified on the basis that, given the particular circumstances, the interests of employees and consumers should be preferred over those of shareholders. However, under the long-term value and viability theory, the decision is justified on the basis that it advances corporate interest, which may overlap with but is not equated with the interests of stakeholders and shareholders. Second, unlike under

---

[29] See also Andrew Keay, 'Ascertaining the Corporate Objective: An Entity Maximisation and Sustainability Theory' (2008) 71 *Modern Law Review* 663 at 696.

the stakeholder theory where the directors are the agents of the stakeholders, directors are the company's agents under the long-term value and viability theory. The latter theory is consistent with and gives effect to the separate legal personality rule under which the company, being a separate legal entity, can only act through agents who are required to promote and protect its interests and purposes, which are distinct from (but may overlap with) those of its agents.

Understanding and framing corporate interest in terms of the separate and distinct interests of the corporate entity as opposed to the interests of shareholders or stakeholders is consistent with how companies have articulated their purposes. An analysis of the publicly disclosed corporate documents of 120 companies in the 4 common law Asian jurisdictions found that a significant percentage (approximately 39 per cent) of these companies have articulated their purposes not in terms of shareholder primacy or stakeholder value but rather in terms of the protection and promotion of the corporate entity.[30]

Having explained the three theories of what constitutes the company's best interests in relation to the directors' best interest duty, the next issue is whether these three theories are reflected in the law of the four Asian common law jurisdictions, which will be addressed in Section II.

II Evaluation of the Law in the Four Asian Jurisdictions

The duty of directors to act in good faith in the best interests of the solvent company varies among the four Asian common law jurisdictions. India has a pluralist stakeholder model; Hong Kong adopts the shareholder primacy model; Singapore and Malaysia recognise that the interests of the solvent company vary with the context.

A India

Section 166 of the Indian Companies Act 2013 stipulates: 'A director of a company shall act in good faith in order to promote the objects of the company for the benefit of its members as a whole, and in the best interests of the company, its employees, the shareholders, the community and for the protection of environment.' There are two interpretations of this provision. On the first interpretation, a director has to promote the corporate object in order to benefit the members and all the

---

[30] Ibid at 190, 198, 200–4.

stakeholders.[31] On the second interpretation, a director has to promote the corporate object so as to benefit its members; in addition, the director has to act in the best interests of the company and stakeholders. The first interpretation is endorsed by the committee in charge of drafting, but the second interpretation is consistent with the natural and ordinary construction of the provision. There appears to be no case law yet on what the correct interpretation is. Nevertheless, regardless of the interpretation that one takes, s 166 is a repudiation of the shareholder primacy theory. Directors are no longer required to act solely or primarily in the interests of shareholders. On the contrary, the interests of other stakeholders have to be protected. It is also a rejection of the enlightened shareholder value model reflected in the UK's section 172 of the Companies Act under which directors are required to take into account the interests of stakeholders only as a means to further the end of benefitting shareholders. Thus, it would seem that s 166 is best poised to promote sustainability.

However, there may be three difficulties that cast doubt on the effectiveness of s 166 as a mechanism to advance sustainability. First, stakeholders are generally not given powers to enforce this provision; only shareholders do through derivative action. Thus, should directors decide not to promote the interests of stakeholders or to subordinate their interests to those of shareholders, stakeholders generally do not have any legal recourse. The response to this problem is that stakeholders can use this provision to apply pressure on the board if they regard the board's action as amounting to a breach of s 166. While stakeholders are not allowed to sue directors, they can publicly criticise directors for breaching their duty. The adverse publicity generated may affect the reputation of directors. This reputational effect may act as a possible deterrent. In addition, one cannot rule out the possibility that failure to act in the interests of stakeholders can amount to oppression and mismanagement in breach of s 241(2) of the Indian Companies Act 2013, which would entitle the government to bring an action against the delinquent directors if the government is of the opinion that the

---

[31] Ministry of Corporate Affairs, *Twenty-First Report, Standing Committee on Finance* (2009–2010) (Fifteenth Lok Sabha), The Companies Bill, 2009, Lok Sabha Secretariat, New Delhi (31 August 2010) para 11.80 www.prsindia.org/uploads/media/Companies%20Bill%202009.pdf; Mihir Naniwadekar and Umakanth Varottil, 'The Stakeholder Approach towards Directors' Duties under Indian Company Law: A Comparative Analysis' (11 August 2016) at 10 https://papers.ssrn.com/sol3/papers.cfm?abstract_id=2822109.

affairs of the company were being conducted in a manner prejudicial to the public interest.[32] But the counterargument is that because the oppression remedy is intended to remedy the wrongs done towards shareholders personally, it is unclear if this mechanism can be used where the interests of stakeholders are adversely affected. Further, a simple disregard for, or subordination of, stakeholders' interests may not be serious enough to rise to the level of the public interest being prejudiced.

Second, given that controlling shareholders wield the power to appoint and dismiss directors, directors are unlikely to prefer the interests of stakeholders to those of shareholders without at least first seeking the informal approval of shareholders. One way to address this problem is for directors to ensure that the promotion of stakeholders' interests is consistent with shareholders' interests. After all, studies have shown that promoting sustainability has the effect of improving share price.[33] Further, where shareholders have pro-social preferences, they will be aligned with the interests of the stakeholders. In such situations, directors need not promote the interests of stakeholders at the expense of those of shareholders. However, where the interests of the two groups conflict, directors are unlikely to defy the wishes of the controller.

Third, the statute does not provide any guidelines as to how directors should balance and weigh the interests of the different stakeholders and shareholders, particularly where there is a conflict among them. Thus, not only will directors be unsure as to how to effectively and appropriately balance the competing needs and demands of different constituencies, but directors may also use this provision to pursue their own interests. However, the former risk is exaggerated. Boards of listed companies routinely have to evaluate conflicting and competing demands arising from meeting the needs of employees (who must want to work for them), customers (who must want to buy the company's products), shareholders (who must want to invest in the company) and the community (who must want the company's presence) and then determine which trade-offs are necessary. After all, companies perform multiple functions and it is the job of the board to weigh and prioritise different interests. As for the latter risk, the controlling shareholder can monitor the board and this oversight will be effective as the controller wields the power of appointment and dismissal. The problem then is not so much that the

---

[32] Arvind P Datar and S Balasubramanian, *A Ramaiya Guide to the Companies Act* (18th edn, Lexis Nexis 2014) at 4020; *Bhalchandra Dharmajee v Alcock Ashdown and Co Ltd* 1972 (42) CC 190.
[33] See Chapter 1 (n 31–6).

board will pursue its own interests, but rather that the board will promote the interests of the controller at the expense of the minority shareholders because of the power wielded and the influence exerted by the controller. But this problem, which concerns conflict of interest involving controlling shareholders, is common to concentrated ownership jurisdictions and is not a valid criticism of s 166 per se.

In short, despite the problems with using s 166 to promote sustainability, they are not insurmountable. One suggestion is for India to seriously consider providing public and private enforcement mechanisms to protect the interests of stakeholders. This means that stakeholders (such as employees[34]) or their representatives should be given the right to bring derivative actions and that public authorities should be empowered to take action against the directors for failure to comply with s 166. Another suggestion is to impose fiduciary duties on controlling shareholders to the company as they will address the problem of conflicts of interest involving controllers.[35]

B Hong Kong

In contrast to India, the best interest duty in Hong Kong has been interpreted in terms of shareholder primacy. As Hong Kong does not have a statutory best interest duty, the English common law position applies. Where a company is solvent, its interests are equated with those of the current and future shareholders.[36] A leading textbook states that '[g]enerally, the interests of shareholders will be their financial interests flowing from maximisation of the company's profits'.[37] It may be said that Hong Kong's shareholder primacy notion of best interest duty is consistent with the promotion of sustainability. This is because the best interest duty not only does not prohibit directors from taking into account the interests of stakeholders, but, in order to promote the interests of future shareholders, the board has to also consider, if not protect, the interests of stakeholders. After all, if employees refuse to work for the company, or

---

[34] See eg Neshat Safari and Martin Gelter, 'British Home Stores Collapse: The Case for an Employee Derivative Claim' (2019) 19 *Journal of Corporate Law Studies* 43.
[35] Ernest Lim, *A Case for Shareholders' Fiduciary Duties in Common Law Asia* (Cambridge University Press 2019) at ch 3C.
[36] *Gaiman v National Association for Mental Health* [1970] 2 All ER 362.
[37] Hong Kong Companies Registry, *A Guide on Directors' Duties* (2009) at Principle 1; Stefan HC Lo and Charles Z Qu, *Law of Companies in Hong Kong* (2nd edn, Sweet & Maxwell 2015) para 8.030.

customers do not want to buy the company's products, or suppliers do not wish to transact with the company, then it is difficult to generate profits and the share price will drop. The problem with this argument is threefold. First, given that only current, not future, shareholders wield the power to appoint and dismiss directors, the latter will act in the interests of current shareholders.[38] In other words, while promoting sustainability is consistent with promoting shareholders' interests, should the present shareholders tell the board to pursue short-termism, which will result in the sacrifice of certain stakeholders' interests, the board is unlikely to defy the shareholders. Second, if the promotion of sustainability reduces in the short term the financial benefit to the current shareholders, or if the long-term benefits of sustainability cannot be clearly quantifiable, then it is unlikely for directors under Hong Kong law to pursue sustainability, or should they do so, only to a very limited extent.

The rebuttal is that shareholder primacy need not be equated with the maximisation of share price or profits as it could refer to the maximisation of shareholder welfare. But the problems with this alternative conception have been discussed in Section I(A). The fundamental premise underlying the shareholder welfare theory is that shareholders clearly communicate to the board their preferences and the board gives effect to them. Thus, it is important to ascertain the identity of these shareholders and their demands. In Hong Kong, for example, activists' hedge funds have increasingly played a prominent role and there is evidence that the boards of a number of listed companies in Hong Kong have succumbed to payout demands by minority hedge fund activists by issuing them special dividends or engaging in share buybacks. A study has been done to show that the activism by hedge funds has produced short-term increase in share price (8 per cent increase on average around the time the activists' investments were publicly disclosed) and, controversially, long-term increase (14 per cent rise on average 40 days before and 240 days after the investments were publicly disclosed).[39]

However, there are four key problems with this study. First, the correlation between activism and the long-term firm value is called into question because the study does not consider and exclude other factors or

---

[38] Leo Strine, Jr, 'Corporate Power Is Corporate Purpose II: An Encouragement for Future Consideration from Professors Johnson and Million' (2017) 74 *Washington & Lee Law Review* 1165 at 1171.

[39] Frank Wong, 'Shareholder Engagement and Activism under the Radar: Empirical Evidence from Hong Kong (2003–15): Rethinking Disclosure of Interests Regime' at 5 (23 June 2017) https://papers.ssrn.com/sol3/papers.cfm?abstract_id=2725318.

events that might have resulted in the increase in share price 240 days after the hedge fund investments were publicly announced. Second, a recent, comprehensive study found that long-term returns arising from hedge fund activism have been found to be 'insignificantly different from zero'.[40] Third, the payout outcomes desired and demanded by hedge fund activists have several undesirable consequences. To begin with, as a result of issuing payouts to shareholders, the company will be in need of cash, and thus it has to resort to equity finance and the shareholders will make further payout demands.[41] Further, as payouts result in companies becoming more highly leveraged, shareholders are likely to put more pressure on companies to undertake excessively risky investments.[42] Unsurprisingly, a key strategy of hedge fund activists is to cause the company to increase leverage and decrease investments, particularly R&D.[43] Fourth, studies have found that the abnormal returns to shareholders as a result of hedge fund activism have resulted in wealth transfer from stakeholders to shareholders.[44] One study found that employees' salaries stagnated three years after the hedge fund activism.[45] Another study showed that the interests of bondholders are adversely affected as the companies become more highly leveraged after issuing special dividends or share buybacks.[46] A further study argued that the share price increase has led to cutting down R&D investments, dismissing employees or reducing their benefits, or increasing the price of products to the detriment of consumers.[47]

---

[40] Ed deHaan, David Larcker and Charles McClure, 'Long-Term Economic Consequences of Hedge Fund Activist Interventions' (3 October 2018) at 7 https://papers.ssrn.com/sol3/papers.cfm?abstract_id=3260095.

[41] Frank Easterbrook, 'Two-Agency Cost Explanation of Dividends' (1984) 74 *American Economic Review* 650.

[42] Julian Franks, Colin Mayer and Luc Renneboog, 'Who Disciplines Management in Poorly Performing Companies?' (2001) 10 *Journal of Financial Intermediation* 209.

[43] John C Coffee Jr and Darius Palia, 'The Wolf at the Door: The Impact of Hedge Fund Activism on Corporate Governance' (2016) 1 *Annals of Corporate Governance* 1.

[44] Yvan Allaire and François Dauphin, *'Activist' Hedge Funds: Creators of Lasting Wealth? What Do the Empirical Studies Really Say?* (Institute for Governance and Public Organizations 2014).

[45] Alon Brav, Wei Jiang and Hyunseob Kim, 'The Real Effects of Hedge Fund Activism: Productivity, Asset Allocation, and Labor Outcomes' (2015) 28 *Review of Financial Studies* 2723.

[46] April Klein and Emanuel Zur, 'The Impact of Hedge Fund Activism on the Target Firm's Existing Bondholders' (2011) 24 *Review of Financial Studies* 1735.

[47] Martijn Cremers, Ankur Pareek and Zacharias Sautner, 'Short-Term Investors, Long-Term Investments, and Firm Value' (14 March 2017) https://papers.ssrn.com/sol3/papers.cfm?abstract_id=2720248.

As an illustration, consider the actions of the US hedge fund TCI Fund Management, one of the two activist funds in Hong Kong.[48] After TCI became the largest shareholder in the Hong Kong listed company Link REIT, TCI demanded that the board substantially increase the rent it charges to its tenants, as the principal source of revenue for Link REIT comes from leasing shopping centres and car parks. The previous chairman and CEO of the board rejected TCI's demands and was dismissed. He said he was concerned about CSR as the rent spike would result in adverse consequences including driving the small-medium enterprise tenants out of business. By contrast, TCI was concerned with maximisation of shareholder value. What happened to Link REIT was praised as 'the most successful intervention'[49] of all the shareholder activism in Hong Kong.

To be clear, I am not saying that hedge fund activism is bad. Activist shareholders can perform an important corporate governance function by monitoring and possibly disciplining the board and controlling shareholders.[50] But what I am arguing is that whether the best interest duty that is based on shareholder welfare maximisation (as opposed to shareholder value maximisation) can result in the successful promotion of sustainability depends on who the shareholders are, what their preferences are, and how they ensure that the board acts on their preferences. Hedge fund activism in Hong Kong, which appears to be on the rise, has called into question the notion that the best interest duty based on shareholder welfare maximisation theory can promote stakeholders' interests. Absent any legal requirement or incentive on the part of directors in Hong Kong to promote stakeholders' interests, it is unlikely for directors to do so.

C Singapore

Unlike India, Singapore does not have a statutory best interest duty. But, unlike Hong Kong, s 159(a) of the Singapore Companies Act states that in exercising their powers, directors are entitled to have regard for matters

---

[48] Frank Wong, 'Shareholder Engagement and Activism under the Radar: Empirical Evidence from Hong Kong (2003–15): Rethinking Disclosure of Interests Regime' (23 June 2017) https://papers.ssrn.com/sol3/papers.cfm?abstract_id=2725318.
[49] Ibid.
[50] Wolf-Georg Ringe, 'Shareholder Activism: A Renaissance' in Jeffrey N Gordon and Wolf-Georg Ringe (eds), *The Oxford Handbook of Corporate Law and Governance* (Oxford University Press 2018) at ch 15.

including 'the interests of the company's employees generally, as well as the interests of its members'. There is an important difference between this provision and the enlightened shareholder value model in s 172 of the UK Companies Act. Unlike s 172, the Singapore provision does not require directors to have regard to the interests of stakeholders in order to benefit shareholders. Thus, under Singapore law, directors are permitted, but not required, to have regard to the interests of employees, whether or not it benefits shareholders. Unlike under UK statutory law, the interests of employees and other stakeholders are not subordinated to those of shareholders under Singapore law. But it does not follow that Singapore adopts a stakeholder value model. This is because the legal position in Singapore is nuanced. It recognises that the interests of the solvent company are context dependent. While there is case law that states that the interests of the solvent company are equated with those of shareholders,[51] there is also case law that recognises not only that the interests of the solvent company are separate and distinct from those of the shareholders but also that corporate interest can be preferred over shareholders' interests under certain circumstances.[52] For example, the court has held that directors are not in breach of their duties if they prefer corporate interest to shareholders' interest by retaining profits instead of distributing them as dividends.[53] By recognising the separate and distinct interest of the company and that it can take precedence over the shareholders' interests, Singapore law implicitly rejects the shareholder primacy theory. It is inconsistent with the common law position under which the interests of the solvent company are equated with those of the present and future shareholders.

Recognising that the company has interests that are separate and distinct from those of its shareholders and stakeholders allows the directors to pursue and justify sustainability actions on the basis that it promotes corporate interest, which is understood as the long-term value and viability of the company, as discussed in Section I(C). Directors can promote social capital, human capital, natural capital, intellectual capital and financial capital on the basis that it advances corporate interest. Promoting these different kinds of capital is not an end in itself (as is the case in a stakeholder value model) but rather a means to an end, ie to sustain and advance the long-term value and

---

[51] See eg *Tong Tien See Construction Pte Ltd v Tong Tien See* (2002) MSCLC 97558 para 54.
[52] *Raffles Town Club Pte Ltd v Lim Eng Hock Peter* [2010] SGHC 163 para 162.
[53] Ibid.

viability of the company. And given that Temasek, as the controlling shareholder of the GLCs, does not interfere in the businesses and strategies of its GLCs (unlike the Chinese SOEs, the Malaysian GLCs and the Indian PSUs),[54] the best interest duty under Singapore law allows the board to pursue sustainability actions on the basis that they promote corporate interest. Not only that, but where there is a conflict between corporate interest and shareholders' interests, the board can prefer the former.

D Malaysia

Unlike Singapore and Hong Kong, Malaysia has a statutory best interest duty: s 213(1) of the Malaysian Companies Act 2016 states that '[a] director of a company shall at all times exercise his powers in accordance with this Act, for a proper purpose and in good faith in the best interests of the company'. However, the provision does not define what 'best interests' means. Nor does it stipulate for whose benefit directors have to exercise their powers. Case law in Malaysia states that 'the duty to act in the best interest of the company means different things, depending on the factual circumstances. Consequentially, depending on the type of dispute or issue, the directors must place a higher priority on the interest of the persons who are truly affected.'[55] In that decision, the court equated corporate interest with shareholders' interests. The court asked who were the persons truly affected by the directors' action. The court said that in view of the imminent delisting of the company, the directors were motivated to prevent the company from being delisted when it caused the subsidiary to enter into a joint development agreement with another company such that the revenue earned by the subsidiary from this agreement could be transferred to the parent company in the form of dividends. The court then held: 'Thus in this scenario, the shareholders are most affected, not so much the company. As such, the directors must act for the best interests of the shareholders . . . .'[56] The implication is that if, in the circumstances, the interests of constituencies other than those of shareholders are most affected, directors will not be in breach of their duty should they act on such interests.

---

[54] See Chapter 1, Section IV(C.1).
[55] *Pioneer Haven Sdn Bhd v Ho Hup Construction Company Berhad* [2012] 3 AMR 297 at 331.
[56] Ibid.

The court's reasoning is significant. It amounts to a repudiation of the shareholder primacy model under which corporate interest is necessarily equated with shareholders' interests. It recognises that what amounts to corporate interest is context-sensitive. While it is clear that the best interest duty under Malaysian law is not based on shareholder primacy, it cannot be categorised as stakeholder value.

The Malaysian case law has the following implication for the use of the best interest duty as a mechanism to promote sustainability. Directors are given the flexibility to determine whose interests should be given greater weight and what course of action should be taken in the particular circumstances of the case. Thus, directors will not be in breach of their duties should they decide to prioritise the interests of employees and customers over those of shareholders if the circumstances warrant doing so, and vice versa. But there are two drawbacks to this approach. First, Malaysian law seems to provide no guidance to the directors regarding which constituencies' interests should be equated with corporate interest and under what circumstances. Thus, courts will take a case-by-case approach in determining whether directors have breached their best interest duty. Second, given that the majority of listed companies in Malaysia are dominated by controlling shareholders who not only wield the power of appointment and dismissal over directors, particularly in the GLCs, but who are also highly interventionist, there is a risk that directors are more likely than not to equate the interests of the company with those of shareholders. In short, how a context-sensitive approach plays out is strongly influenced by the ownership structure of a company.

E Lessons

First, as the four common law Asian jurisdictions show, there is variation in the interpretation and implementation of the best interest duty. India clearly adopts a stakeholder value model, Hong Kong a shareholder primacy one, Singapore a real entity approach and Malaysia a context-sensitive approach. There is no single best model of the best interest duty to promote sustainability. There are costs and benefits to each.

Second, in contrast to the literature, which argues that the shareholder primacy model of the best interest duty is a threat to the promotion of sustainability and that the stakeholder model is preferred, the analysis of the best interest duty in the four Asian jurisdictions shows that the situation is nuanced. The shareholder primacy model of the best interest duty, if understood as maximisation of shareholder welfare as opposed to maximisation of share price, can facilitate sustainability provided that shareholders have pro-social preferences and that the board gives effect to them. But this is not necessarily the case, as shown in the demands of the hedge fund activists in Hong Kong. A stakeholder version of the best interest duty, as illustrated by the example of India, has its drawbacks, including the fact that stakeholders lack enforcement powers and, where the interests of the controlling shareholder conflict with the stakeholders', directors are unlikely to defy the controller as it can dismiss them. But these problems with the Indian stakeholder statutory law can be mitigated, as discussed in Section II(A).

Third, the best interest duty under Singapore law is an alternative to the shareholder primacy and stakeholder theory. Singapore law shows how this can be done. It is important to take the separate legal personality seriously by recognising that the company has interests that are separate and distinct from the shareholders' (and stakeholders'). Next, while corporate interest may and often does overlap with shareholders' interests, the former can be preferred to the latter where there are conflicts. The normative basis is that giving effect to corporate interest promotes the long-term value and viability of the company.

Finally, a critical factor that determines the success of the best interest duty in promoting sustainability relates to the concentrated ownership model and approach. As I have mentioned before, even if a jurisdiction adopts a stakeholder version of the best interest duty (as in India) or a context-sensitive approach that allows corporate interest to be equated with shareholders' or stakeholders' interests depending on the circumstances (as in Malaysia), it is unlikely for directors to defy the wishes of the controlling shareholders who have the power to dismiss and reappoint them. In other words, in order for the best interest duty to be utilised for promoting sustainability, we not only need to pay attention to the law on directors' duties; we also need to understand the political dynamics of the decision-making process in concentrated ownership jurisdictions in Asia where SOEs play a significant role. It is suggested that Singapore's legal environment is the most conducive for promoting sustainability as compared to the other three jurisdictions. This is not only because of its law on the best interest duty, but also because Temasek, as the controlling shareholder of the GLCs, takes the approach that GLCs should be run efficiently with a view towards long-term value creation and Temasek generally eschews intervention in the GLCs' business.[57] By contrast, there is evidence of extensive meddling in SOEs by the governments in the other three jurisdictions as well as tunnelling and corruption.[58] Thus, all factors being equal, there is a serious risk that the boards of the SOEs in the other three jurisdictions will promote the controller's interests at the expense of the stakeholders'.

III Implications of Directors' Best Interest Duty for Corporate Governance Mechanisms

The best interest duty is often analysed in an isolated fashion, without thinking through its implications for other corporate mechanisms. But it is important to understand how the best interest duty in the four Asian jurisdictions impacts the other corporate governance mechanisms – sustainability reporting, stewardship code and constituency directors – for promoting sustainability.

A *Sustainability Reporting*

Regarding sustainability reporting, the issue is whether it is supported or undermined by a shareholder primacy version of the best interest duty, which is endorsed in Hong Kong. The SEHK has stated that the board is responsible for the company's compliance with the ESG reporting listing rules.[59] Given that the ESG reporting rules adopt a comply or explain mechanism, the concern is that the best interest duty in Hong Kong may at best disincentivise the board from engaging in robust compliance with the ESG reporting; the board may take a minimalist approach towards compliance. At worst, the best interest duty may undermine compliance because, given that the overriding goal is to maximise share price, any sustainability actions that do not facilitate that goal will not be pursued. For example, between a choice of deciding to merely comply with the existing environmental regulation or taking additional steps to create, market and distribute environmentally sustainable products, the board of a listed company may opt for the former. This is because, first, in the short to medium term, the latter will result in lower net income and hence reduce share price. Second, because the long-term financial benefit of creating environmentally sustainable products may be difficult to

---

[57] Chapter 1, Section IV(C.1).
[58] Ibid.
[59] HKEX LR, Appendix 27, Environmental, Social and Governance Reporting Guide para 8.

quantify and predict,[60] a board that interprets its best interest duty in terms of maximising profits and share price, or that is under pressure to cater to the preferences of shareholders to maximise share price, will not expend additional resources to create those products. In short, the best interest duty that is founded on shareholder primacy will not facilitate sustainability initiatives that do not produce short-term (or even medium-term) financial gains for the shareholders.

By contrast, in a stakeholder version of the best interest duty (as in India), or where the best interest duty is interpreted in terms of the promotion of corporate interest (as in Singapore), or where the board takes a context-specific approach to the duty (as in Malaysia), it is suggested that the board is likely to be more inclined to pursue sustainability, even if doing so does not necessarily or always yield immediate or short-term financial gain for the shareholders. This implies that there may be greater compliance with sustainability reporting rules.

B Stewardship Code

The relationship between the directors' discharge of their best interest duty under company law and the institutional shareholders' discharge of their stewardship responsibilities under the stewardship code is rarely explored. But this relationship is important given that the best interest duty has an important bearing on what institutional shareholders have been told to do under the stewardship code. So, for instance, there will be inconsistency if directors interpret their best interest duty as requiring them to maximise shareholder value but the stewardship code urges institutional shareholders to engage with the board for the purpose of producing long-term gains for all stakeholders, or, although the code does not clearly make such stipulation, the institutional investors hold such a view. In short, given the critical importance of the role of directors and institutional investors in promoting sustainability, there should be an alignment of what is expected of them.

For example, consider Hong Kong. The HKPRO state that 'to discharge their ownership responsibilities investors should engage with the companies in which they invest to promote the long-term success of these companies'.[61] The term 'long-term success of these companies' is

---

[60] David Million, 'Corporate Social Responsibility and Environmental Sustainability' in Beate Sjåfjell and Benjamin J Richardson (eds), *Company Law and Sustainability* (Cambridge University Press 2015) at 72–3.
[61] Hong Kong Principles of Responsible Ownership para 6.

not defined in the code. And the other provisions in the code do not shed light on what this term means or should mean. Whether the best interest duty supports the central aim of this code would depend on whether the investors' interpretation of the long-term success of the company is in line with the interests of the company under the best interest duty, which, as examined in Section I(A), has been equated with the interests of shareholders. Thus, should investors have social and ethical preferences and engage with the board pursuant to the code in order to influence the board to promote sustainability, it is possible for the board to regard itself as being required by the best interest duty to maximise profits and hence reject the institutional investors' engagement.

However, consider Singapore. The SSP state that a key aim of stewardship is to build sustainable business 'to produce long-term benefits for all stakeholders .... It goes beyond short-term considerations and includes the sustainability of a company's long-term performance.'[62] Thus, institutional investors are urged to pursue formal and informal engagements with the board in order to produce long-term benefits for all stakeholders. While the best interest duty under Singapore law is not based on stakeholder value, promoting corporate interest, understood in terms of the long-term value and viability of the company, is in line with the central objective of the SSP, which is to produce long-term benefit for all stakeholders.

Next, consider Malaysia. It is stated in the MCII that it is 'intended to give institutional investors guidance on effective exercise of stewardship responsibilities to ensure delivery of sustainable long-term value to their ultimate beneficiaries or clients'.[63] At first blush, this seems in line with shareholder primacy theory because the central aim of the code is to produce long-term financial gains for the investors' beneficiaries. But the code then emphasises that institutional investors should incorporate sustainability and ESG considerations into their investment analysis and activities, the latter of which include, but are not limited to, assessing the company's sustainability disclosures and the company's adherence to responsible investment codes.[64] The ESG factors that the investors can evaluate include, but are not limited to, employee benefits, products, customers and supply chain, and environmental and social impact. This implies a stakeholder-oriented approach or at the very least shows

---

[62] Singapore's Stewardship Principles for Responsible Investors, Preamble at 3.
[63] 2014 Malaysian Code for Institutional Investors at 2.
[64] Ibid at 13–14.

a rejection of the shareholder value maximisation approach. The question then is whether the directors' best interest duty under Malaysian law is consistent with and facilitates such actions by the institutional investors under the code. In theory, the answer is in the affirmative because the context-sensitive approach of the best interest duty allows directors to prioritise different interests depending on the circumstances facing the company. Thus, the board can justify its pursuit of sustainability actions on the basis that, in the specific context or circumstance, giving effect to the interests of certain stakeholders is warranted.

In practice, however, the answer depends on the complex relationship between the controlling shareholders and the institutional shareholders. While it may be said that directors may pursue shareholder primacy because they are likely to yield to the demands of controlling shareholders who wield formal and informal powers over them, one cannot underestimate the formal and informal powers wielded by minority institutional shareholders, especially if the latter is the government or affiliated with the government.[65] For example, if the controller of a family-owned company favours maximisation of profit, but the government institutional shareholder who is a minority investor has strong pro-social preferences, it is not clear that directors will necessarily yield to the controller's wishes. It is possible that the controller will agree to prioritise sustainability in light of the pro-social preferences of the government institutional investors, in which case there will be an alignment of the best interest duty and the institutional investors' engagement under the stewardship code.

C Constituency Directors

Finally, the best interest duty has a bearing on the mechanism of constituency directors. An important reason why the mechanism of constituency directors was implemented in Germany and India is because the historical, political and social contexts enabled a pro-stakeholder oriented approach towards social and corporate governance to operate. Another manifestation of this approach lies in the directors' duties. As discussed in Chapter 4, co-determination under German law requires supervisory boards of certain types of company to have 50 per cent of

---

[65] On the influence exercised by the government as a minority investor over the company, see Aldo Musacchio and Sergio G Lazzarini, *Reinventing State Capitalism: Leviathan in Business, Brazil and Beyond* (Harvard University Press 2014) at 63, 197–9.

directors appointed by employees to represent and advance employees' interests. The purpose is to ensure that employees have a voice in the decision-making process in companies. Co-determination is complemented or reinforced by directors' duties. Under German law, the board has to take into account the interests of shareholders and stakeholders in order to ensure the company's sustainable value creation.[66] Under Indian law, a specially constituted board committee has to formulate and give effect to CSR policy, which may include sustainability considerations. This is enhanced by the best interest duty under which directors are required to promote the interests of employees, the community and the environment. Thus, the best interest duty complements and reinforces the mechanism of constituency directors.

The lesson for the other three Asian jurisdictions is that, in considering whether or not to adopt the mechanism of constituency directors, it is important to understand whether and, if so, how it is supported (or undermined) by the best interest duty. So, for example, should Hong Kong decide to have constituency directors (whether it is the Indian or German version or another version), consideration has to be given to the issue of whether doing so is consistent with the shareholder primacy version of its best interest duty. The same reasoning applies should Singapore or Malaysia decide to have constituency directors.

IV Conclusion

Regarding the question of whether the directors' duty to act in good faith in the best interests of the company can be used as an effective mechanism to promote sustainability in the four common law Asian jurisdictions, the short answer is that it depends on six factors. First, it depends on the normative basis of the company's best interests. As I have shown, the basis can be shareholder primacy, stakeholder value or the long-term value and viability of the company. In view of the deficiencies in the first and second models, the third is preferable.

Second, it depends on the purposes of companies: a company can define its objective in terms of shareholder primacy, stakeholder value or corporate entity. How a company defines its corporate purpose will have a critical bearing on the strategies and operations of the company's business, which in turn will affect how directors will discharge their best

---

[66] German Corporate Governance Code (2019), Foreword at 2.

interest duty. Given that SOEs have social and political objectives (in addition to commercial objectives), directors should, to the extent permitted by law, interpret their best interest duty to give effect to those corporate purposes that promote sustainability. For example, if the purpose of the SOE is to provide affordable and efficient public goods such as the provision of public utilities and infrastructure, then acting in that SOE's interests under the best interest duty should require directors to give effect to environmental considerations, because doing so will make the delivery of these public goods more cost-effective and efficient. If the main purpose of the SOE is to generate employment, then directors should, as part of their best interest duty, attend to labour practices (such as fair treatment of employees and promoting board diversity) and labour conditions (such as workplace safety and health). This is not only consistent with the corporate purpose, but it will also generate greater dedication, loyalty and efficiency among its workforce. If the purpose of the SOE is to provide certain goods and services to the public, then directors need to put in place systems to ensure that suppliers are carefully selected and monitored in order to ensure the quality and safety of the products and services, which is giving effect to social considerations.

Third, it depends on the identity and motivations of the controlling shareholders. While SOEs' social objectives can be linked to the promotion of sustainability, the interests of the government as the controlling shareholder may conflict with those of the stakeholders, and the government as the controller may extract private benefits of control at the expense of the stakeholders. As a result, the government as the controller who wields the power to appoint and dismiss the directors can cause the directors to take certain actions that benefit it but that are detrimental to stakeholders. To address the problem of conflicts of interest and expropriation, it is suggested that a combination of ex ante measures (such as active monitoring by minority institutional investors and NGOs) and ex post ones (such as subjecting controlling shareholders to fiduciary duties) should be considered.

Fourth, it depends on the existing law: whether the law reflects the shareholder primacy, stakeholder value or corporate entity approach. Insofar as the law requires directors to pursue a shareholder primacy approach when a company is solvent (such as the case of Hong Kong), it should be reformed to permit the directors to promote the interests of the corporate entity; this can and should refer to the company's long-term value and viability. The laws in Singapore and Malaysia provide good examples of how this can be done.

Fifth, it depends on the effectiveness of the corporate governance mechanisms. As argued in Section III, the efficacy of the mechanism of the best interest duty will be affected by (and will affect) the mechanisms of sustainability reporting, stewardship code and constituency directors. We must consider the mechanisms in an integrated and holistic fashion, for they have a bearing on the efficacy of each other.

Finally, it depends on the effectiveness of the public and private mechanisms for enforcing the directors' best interest duty. Even if this duty is successfully reformed to promote sustainability, it will not be effective if there are weak enforcement mechanisms. For example, under the laws of the four Asian jurisdictions, it is costly to bring a derivative action against the delinquent director not only because the claimant has to bear the costs (unless the court orders the company to pay cost to the claimant), but also because any compensation that the court will award will go to the company and not to the affected shareholder. It is worth considering whether the derivative action should be reformed such as to permit contingency fees or class action suits, as well as to allow employees to sue. Further, if private enforcement is ineffective, public enforcement will be necessary and desirable. These are formal enforcement measures. Consideration should also be given to informal enforcement measures such as public censure by the stock exchange or an independent and expert organisation.

7

Liability of Companies, Shareholders and Directors

I   Rationales for Limited Liability   237
II Existing Exceptions to Limited Liability   242
   A Distinguishing Limited Liability and Separate Legal Personality   243
   B Piercing the Corporate Veil   246
      1 Singapore and Hong Kong   247
      2 Malaysia   249
      3 India   250
   C Breach of Duty of Care by Parent Companies   252
III Proposed Exceptions to Limited Liability   261
   A Enterprise Liability   261
   B Liability on Shareholders of the Wrongdoing Company   264
IV My Proposal   267
   A Imposing Liability on the Controlling Shareholder   267
   B Liability in Networks   274
V   Breach of Public Interest Legislations   277
VI Conclusion   282

The business operations of companies can have serious and adverse impacts on the community and society including, but not limited to, physical injuries, environmental damage, destruction to livelihoods and infringements on human rights.[1] When companies impose externalities on societies, two major consequences arise. The first concerns whether and how the victims of the wrongdoing can bring a claim against the defendant, and the second relates to whether the delinquent company as

---

[1] Regarding the violations of human rights by companies, see the reports in the Business and Human Rights Center www.business-humanrights.org/en/corporate-legal-accountability; regarding environmental disasters caused by companies, the Union Carbide cyanide gas leak in Bhopal, India, the Exxon Valdez oil spill in Alaska, the British Petroleum oil spill in the Gulf of Mexico and the Jilin chemical plant explosions in China are the more notorious examples: see eg Robert Emmet Hernan, *This Borrowed Earth: Lessons from the Fifteen Worst Environmental Disasters around the World* (Macmillan Science 2010).

well as its directors and officers have breached their duties under public interest legislations. The focus of this chapter is on the first issue because of the critical need to ensure that effective redress and remedies are provided to the victims, and in light of the continual controversy and uncertainty surrounding this area.

To elaborate on the first issue, this chapter analyses one specific corporate mechanism for promoting sustainability by considering whether the involuntary creditors, ie the victims (such as employees, consumers or neighbours) of a wrongdoing committed by a subsidiary could and should seek redress from the parent company, other members of the corporate group, or shareholders of the parent company, assuming that the subsidiary is unable to compensate the victims because it is insolvent, undercapitalised or dissolved. The central concern raised in this issue is that imposing liability not only on the particular company that has committed the wrongdoing but also on other companies or shareholders will be contrary to the principle of limited liability. As I will show, the concern, properly understood, is not about disregarding the separate legal personality of the company, or, metaphorically put, piercing the corporate veil of the delinquent subsidiary. Rather, it relates to, first, why entities other than the delinquent subsidiary should not be afforded the protection of limited liability and, second, what the exceptions to limited liability ought to be. In analysing this issue, attention has to be paid to the ownership structure of the companies in the four Asian jurisdictions, which consists of controlling shareholders, particularly the government, given that the presence of controlling shareholders will have an important bearing on the exceptions to limited liability.

Regarding the second issue, this chapter analyses the structure of liability that is imposed on companies as well as their directors and officers for breach of the public interest statutes such as those related to the environment, health and safety, and operation of factories. In addition, the enforcement actions taken will be analysed. I make two main points. First, the burden of proof should be shifted from the authority to the defendant such that the authority should not bear the burden of proving that the directors and officers are guilty of the offences; rather, once the company has been proven to have committed the offence, the directors and officers should be presumed to be guilty unless they can successfully raise the due diligence defence. Second, while there is evidence of companies being prosecuted for violating the legislation, there seems to be no publicly disclosed successful formal and informal enforcement actions being taken against directors, which calls into question the effectiveness of the liability regime in general.

The structure of this chapter is as follows. Section I explains the rationales for limited liability. Section II analyses the judge made exceptions to limited liability, namely, the techniques of piercing the corporate veil and breach of duty of care by the parent company. Section III evaluates two main proposals that have been put forward by commentators to address the issue of uncompensated harms caused to innocent tort victims. The first is to deprive the entire corporate group of the protection of the limited liability, ie liability is imposed on all the companies within the group when one of the companies has committed a tortious act. And the second is to deprive only the shareholders of the wrongdoing subsidiary of the limited liability protection. In Section IV, I put forward my proposal, which is that, in light of the concentrated ownership structure of the listed companies in the Asian jurisdictions, a fault-based liability (subject to a reverse burden of proof) should be imposed on the controlling shareholder. I also address the issue of harms caused not by companies that fall within the traditional corporate group structure but, rather, by networks, that is, the tort is not committed by a company within the group but by a person (whether corporate or individual) that has a contractual relationship with the company. Section V analyses the public interest legislations that impose liability on companies as well as directors and officers. Section VI concludes.

I Rationales for Limited Liability

It is a central principle of company law that shareholders are given the protection of limited liability in a limited liability company; namely, shareholders are not liable for the debts of the company as they are liable only to the extent of any unpaid amount of their shares.[2] As a result, any exceptions to limited liability – such as imposing liability on a parent company (or its controlling shareholder) for the tortious wrongdoing committed by a subsidiary – have to be justified. To do so, it is important to first understand the rationales for limited liability and then to examine whether these rationales are applicable to the context of imposing liability on the parent company (or its controlling shareholder) for the uncompensated harms caused by the tortious acts of its subsidiary.

There are four common rationales for limited liability. First, limited liability promotes investment by members of the public.[3] Given that the

---

[2] HK CO, s 8; MY CA, s 10(2); SG CA, s 4(1); IN CA, s 2(22).
[3] Frank Easterbrook and Daniel Fischel, 'Limited Liability and the Corporation' (1985) 52 *University of Chicago Law Review* 89.

public in general are not likely to have the requisite expertise or experience in monitoring, let alone managing, companies, they will not be incentivised to invest if there is a risk of them not only losing their investments if the company performs badly but also being liable for the debts of the companies. Second, limited liability promotes the functioning of the securities market.[4] Because of limited liability, investors save time and expenses in monitoring the company. Equally important, they do not need to incur cost in monitoring the wealth of other shareholders.[5] This is because absent limited liability, shareholders will be liable for the debts of companies and hence the less wealthy the other shareholders are, the more the other shareholders have to shoulder the debts of the companies. Putting it differently, the value of an investor's share will increase if the other shareholders are wealthy. Third, limited liability enables shareholders to diversify their investments by incentivising them to invest in different companies in different industries and different jurisdictions.[6] Unlimited liability will discourage diversification as shareholders would have to incur cost in monitoring their investments. Finally, limited liability promotes monitoring by creditors.[7] This is because, given that limited liability reduces shareholders' incentives to monitor the company, and because creditors cannot assert claims against the shareholders' assets, they will be incentivised to monitor the company to ensure that it does not become insolvent. While these rationales for limited liability are derived from the context of individual shareholders and not the context of corporate groups, the protection of limited liability is extended to each individual company within the group, including the parent and its subsidiaries.[8]

The question then is whether these rationales still hold true in a corporate group structure; in other words, the issue is whether the advantages of limited liability are sufficiently compelling to justify its retention for a parent company (or its controlling shareholder or other companies within the corporate group) where the delinquent subsidiary is unable to compensate the victims for its tortious acts.

---

[4] Paul Halpern, Michael J Tebilcock and Stuart McLean Turnbull, 'An Economic Analysis of Limited Liability' (1980) 30 *University of Toronto Law Journal* 117.

[5] Larry E Ribstein, 'Limited Liability and Theories of the Corporation' (1991) 50 *Maryland Law Review* 80 at 102–3.

[6] Stephen M Bainbridge and M Todd Henderson, *Limited Liability: A Legal and Economic Analysis* (Edward Elgar 2016) at 59–60.

[7] Henry Hansmann and Reinier Kraakman, 'The Essential Role of Organization Law' (2005) 119 *Harvard Law Review* 1335.

[8] *Adams v Cape Industries Plc* [1990] Ch 433 at 544.

With respect to the first rationale, provided that the victims are not permitted to seek redress from the ordinary members of the public, ie the individual and retail investors, the latter will not be deterred from investing. In any event, it is unlikely that the tort victims will sue the individual and retail investors because the costs of the law suit (including court fees and lawyer fees) are likely to exceed the compensation that can be obtained from ordinary members of the public who are unlikely to have deep pockets.

As for the second rationale, depriving corporate entities such as the parent company of the protection of limited liability will not impede the functioning of the securities market where the subsidiary is wholly owned by the parent company; this is because there are no other shareholders (of the subsidiary) that have to monitor the wealth of the parent and vice versa. But where the delinquent subsidiary is not wholly owned by the parent company and there are minority (institutional) shareholders, it is unlikely that the latter would have to incur significant costs by monitoring the wealth of the parent company, if they are subject to pro rata liability, that is, if the liability imposed is proportionate to the amount of shares owned.[9] In other words, any monitoring undertaken by the minority shareholders will be minimal in view of the insignificant percentage of shares that they own; they are likely to be rationally apathetic.[10] Given that the parent company owns a majority of shares and has the expertise and resources to monitor, it is likely that minority shareholders will leave the monitoring to the hands of the parent company.[11]

Regarding the third rationale, which is about the benefits of diversification of investment, it is questionable whether it is applicable in a corporate group structure where there is usually integration of business operations in which the subsidiaries will handle the sales, marketing, manufacturing and other related businesses for the parent company.[12] The companies within the group are usually not independent in an

---

[9] Henry Hansmann and Reinier Kraakman, 'Towards Unlimited Shareholder Liability for Corporate Torts' (1991) 100 *Yale Law Journal* 1879.
[10] Stephen M Bainbridge and M Todd Henderson, *Limited Liability: A Legal and Economic Analysis* (Edward Elgar 2016) at 59–60.
[11] Ian Ramsay, 'Allocating Liability in Corporate Groups: An Australian Perspective' (1999) 13 *Connecticut Journal of International Law* 329 at 343.
[12] David W Leebron, 'Limited Liability, Tort Victims, and Creditors' (1991) 91 *Columbia Law Review* 1565 at 1616–17.

economic or commercial sense. The parent company benefits from this economic and operational integration, but that does not amount to a diversification of investment risk for the parent.

While depriving the parent company of limited liability for the torts committed by its subsidiaries will increase its monitoring costs, it is justified on the basis that failure to do so will externalise costs and impose serious and uncompensated harms (such as physical injuries and deaths) on innocent parties (including, but not limited to, employees and bystanders).[13] In other words, failure to impose unlimited liability on the parent company will have the perverse result of incentivising it to undercapitalise its subsidiaries and to pursue excessively risky businesses that are detrimental to the society and community.[14] Thus, the parent company can structure the companies within the group in such a way as to insulate the group's key assets from potential or future liability such as that arising from tort claims, a practice known as 'judgment-proofing'.[15] For example, the parent company can make sure that the valuable assets are owned by Subsidiary A but that all hazardous business operations are conducted by Subsidiary B which is deliberately undercapitalised such that should there be any lawsuits against it, it will not have any assets to compensate the victims. Further, in MNCs, a parent company can incorporate subsidiaries in jurisdictions that have lax regulations or weak enforcement mechanisms in order to minimise the chances of success of any claims against the foreign subsidiary. As will be examined in Section II, although such a group structure for the purposes of avoiding future liability is legally permissible, it does not mean that it is morally or socially justified, especially where the actions or omissions of the subsidiary result in physical injuries.

Moreover, unlike tort victims, creditors and shareholders do not have unlimited exposure as it is limited to the amount that they have invested in or lent to the company. Further, shareholders and creditors suffer financial losses; by contrast, tort victims suffer physical injuries, loss of future earnings and even deaths.

---

[13] Jamie Cassels, 'Outlaws: Multinational Corporations and Catastrophic Law' (2001) 31 *Cumberland Law Review* 311 at 323.

[14] TP Glynn, 'Beyond Unlimiting Shareholder Liability: Vicarious Tort Liability for Corporate Officers' (2004) 57 *Vanderbilt Law Review* 329 at 371.

[15] ML LoPucki, 'The Death of Liability' (1996) 106 *Yale Law Journal* 1; Christian Witting, *Liability of Corporate Groups and Networks* (Cambridge University Press 2018) at 80–4.

Equally important, tort victims are not able to bargain with the company to remove or modify the protection of limited liability for its shareholders.[16] And they are not able to contract around or out of the corporate or insolvency rules that disadvantage them. By contrast, creditors can insert covenants into their loan agreements with the company to protect themselves, such as cross-default and acceleration clauses. As for shareholders, they have significant and substantial governance rights which they can use to protect themselves and/or to exercise oversight of the company; these rights include, but are not limited to: altering the company's constitution (to insert provisions that favour shareholders); dictating to or overruling the directors (by altering the constitution); directing directors to take certain actions; exercising management powers (if provided for in the constitution); approving major transactions; and authorising and ratifying breaches of directors' duties.[17] These rights are further amplified in the case of concentrated ownership jurisdictions such as those in common law Asia covered in this book because of the presence of controlling shareholders which consist of the government and families.

Further and no less important, tort victims are not able to monitor the business operations of the subsidiary, unlike the parent company.[18] A parent company will have the incentive to monitor because it is the sole or majority shareholder of the subsidiary and its financial performance is impacted by the overall performance of the group, which includes the subsidiary. And it has the expertise and experience to monitor because it usually sets the strategic policies and provides supervision for the subsidiaries. Although being subject to unlimited liability may increase the monitoring cost for the parent company, it is likely to result in more effective and accurate risk assessment of the costs of doing business. Putting it differently, not only is the parent company in a better position to absorb the risks but it is fairer for it to do so.[19]

In relation to the fourth and final rationale, although imposing unlimited liability on the parent company may reduce the extent of monitoring by creditors, it is likely to increase the efficiency of monitoring by the

---

[16] David W Leebron, 'Limited Liability, Tort Victims, and Creditors' (1991) 91 *Columbia Law Review* 1565 at 1601–3.
[17] n 86–99.
[18] Ian Ramsay, 'Allocating Liability in Corporate Groups: An Australian Perspective' (1999) 13 *Connecticut Journal of International Law* 329 at 343.
[19] Henry Hansmann and Reinier Kraakman, 'Toward Unlimited Shareholder Liability for Corporate Torts' (1991) *Yale Law Journal* 1879 at 1916–19; Peter Muchlinski, 'Limited Liability and Multinational Enterprises: A Case for Reform?' (2010) 34 *Cambridge Journal of Economics* 915 at 923.

creditors.[20] This is because the parent company will exercise greater oversight of the relevant subsidiary and this could lead to more effective and efficient identification, assessment and prevention of potential tortious business operations. Consequently, the information obtained from the increased monitoring of potential tortious risks may be shared with the creditors of the subsidiary and this can allow them to focus their monitoring on other aspects of the subsidiary's business. Further, if creditors reduce their monitoring, their cost will be reduced and this may result in more favourable interest rates or terms for the subsidiary borrower.

For the reasons given above, the rationales for limited liability should not apply to a parent company (or its controlling shareholder) from which the tort victims of the subsidiary are seeking redress where the subsidiary is not able to compensate them, whether because it is undercapitalised, has become insolvent or has been dissolved.

Given that there are good justifications for not allowing parent companies (or their controlling shareholders) in this context to enjoy the privileges of limited liability, Section II examines the legal mechanisms for creating exceptions to limited liability.

II   Existing Exceptions to Limited Liability

I begin this section by arguing that it is important to distinguish limited liability and separate legal personality and I show that conceptually courts can create an exception to limited liability without piercing the corporate veil. The reason I draw this distinction is because the literature that considers the issue of whether claimants can seek redress from the parent company (or the shareholders of the delinquent subsidiary) for the harm caused by the delinquent subsidiary assumes that one chief obstacle in imposing liability on the parent company (or the shareholders of the delinquent subsidiary) is because that amounts to piercing the corporate veil. I argue that imposing liability on the parent company (or its controlling shareholder) amounts to creating an exception to the limited liability principle, but it does not amount to disregarding the separate legal personality rule. If my analysis is correct, then the cases concerning the circumstances under which the corporate veil can be pierced no longer pose an obstacle.

---

[20] David W Leebron, 'Limited Liability, Tort Victims, and Creditors' (1991) 91 *Columbia Law Review* 1565 at 1606.

II EXISTING EXCEPTIONS TO LIMITED LIABILITY

However, it may be argued that courts cannot simply create an exception to the limited liability principle, which is a protection conferred by the statute, unless there are authorities to support it. In other words, courts still have to rely on existing judicial techniques such as piercing the corporate veil to impose liability on the parent company (or its controlling shareholder). If that is the case, I examine two principal exceptions that have been created by the courts to hold companies liable for the tortious wrongdoing committed by their subsidiaries, the first of which is to pierce the veil of the subsidiary and the second of which is to impose a duty of care on the parent company. In this regard, I advance two key arguments. First, despite the oft-repeated criticisms of piercing the corporate veil, this judicial technique may still be useful in Singapore, Malaysia and India for the purposes of imposing liability on the parent company. Second, I argue that courts in the four Asian jurisdictions should consider following English law by imposing a duty of care on the parent company for the tortious acts of its subsidiaries.

A Distinguishing Limited Liability and Separate Legal Personality

Piercing the corporate veil means disregarding the separate legal personality of the company.[21] It does not necessarily entail that the shareholder will be responsible for the wrongdoing of the company. After all, shareholders have gained a benefit when courts have disregarded the separate legal personality.[22] When courts have imposed liability on a shareholder (whether corporate or personal) for the debts or wrongdoing of the company, they are, properly speaking, not piercing the corporate veil (ie disregarding the separate legal personality), even though that was what they claimed they were doing.[23] What they were in fact doing was disregarding the legal principle of limited liability. This is because to pierce the corporate veil, ie disregard the separate legal personality, is in effect to equate the company with its shareholders, the result of which is that the company can no longer, in its own name, own property,[24] enter into contracts,[25] or sue or be sued;[26] nor can the company delegate

---

[21] *Prest v Petrodel Resources Limited* [2013] UKSC 34 para 16.
[22] Paul Davies and Sarah Worthington, *Gower Principles of Modern Company Law* (10th edn, Sweet & Maxwell, 2016) para 8-8; *DHN Food Distributors Ltd v Tower Hamlets LBC* [1976] 1 WLR 852; *Trebanog Working Men's Club and Institute Ltd v MacDonald* [1940] KB 576; *Smith Stone & Knight Ltd v Birmingham Corp* [1939] 4 All ER 116.
[23] See eg *In re Darby* [1911] 1 KB 95.
[24] See eg *Macaura v Northern Assurance Co* [1925] AC 619 (HL).
[25] See eg *Lee v Lee's Air Farming Ltd* [1961] AC 12 (PC).
[26] See eg *Prest v Petrodel Resources Limited* [2013] UKSC 34.

authority to the directors to act on its behalf.[27] But when courts pierced the veil, they did not make any of these claims; nor have these consequences arisen.

Putting it differently, when courts refuse to pierce the corporate veil by upholding the separate legal personality of the company, they are in effect affirming that the company can enter into contracts in its own name even with its sole employee, shareholder and director. The courts are not affirming that the shareholder enjoys the protection of limited liability, which is a separate and distinct issue. Consider the case of *Lee v Lee's Air Farming Ltd*.[28] In that case, Lee was the sole shareholder, employee and director. As a director, he entered into an employment contract on the company's behalf with himself in his capacity as an employee. As a director, he caused the company to take up an insurance under a statute for the benefit of himself as an employee. His wife sought to claim compensation insurance after he died in an accident. At issue was whether he was a worker under the statute. The court answered in the affirmative. It affirmed the separate legal personality of the company and upheld the validity of the employment contract. It was not concerned with the limited liability principle.

In short, the court can hold shareholders liable without necessarily piercing the corporate veil.[29] Conversely, the court can disregard the separate legal personality rule without infringing the limited liability rule because liability was not imposed on the shareholder.[30] Thus, disregarding the separate legal personality rule is a separate and distinct issue from creating an exception to the limited liability principle.

Apart from doctrinal reasons, separate legal personality and limited liability are also distinguishable from an economic viewpoint.[31] Given that separate legal personality entails that the firm can own assets and they belong to it, this principle serves the crucial function of entity shielding,[32] namely, the assets are shielded from the shareholders' creditors. Entity

---

[27] See eg *Freeman and Lockyer v Buckhurst Park Properties (Mangal) Ltd* [1964] 2 QB 480.
[28] [1961] AC 12 (PC).
[29] See critique of *Jones v Lipman* [1962] 1 WLR 832 and *Gilford Motor Co Ltd v Horne* [1933] Ch 935 in Ernest Lim, 'Salomon Reigns' [2013] 129 *Law Quarterly Review* 480 at 483–4.
[30] n 22.
[31] Reinier Kraakman, John Armour, Paul Davies et al, *The Anatomy of Corporate Law: A Comparative and Functional Approach* (2nd edn, Oxford University Press 2009) at 6–11.
[32] Henry Hansmann, Reinier Kraakman and Richard Squire, 'Law and the Rise of the Firm' (2006) 119 *Harvard Law Review* 1333; Henry Hansmann and Reinier Kraakman, 'The Essential Role of Organization Law' (2005) 119 *Harvard Law Review* 1335.

shielding consists of two distinct rules: priority rule and a rule of liquidation protection. Under the priority rule, the firm's creditors' claim against the firm's assets is prior to the claim of the creditors of the firm's shareholders. Thus, the firm's creditors can enforce the assets of the firm against it. Under the liquidation protection rule, shareholders cannot demand the withdrawal of the money that they have invested in the company. The shareholders' creditors cannot assert a claim against the firm's assets.

By contrast, limited liability serves the function of owner shielding,[33] namely, the firm's creditors cannot assert a claim against the shareholders' assets. In short, the separate legal personality rule protects the firm's assets from the creditors of the firm's shareholders, and the limited liability rule protects the shareholders' assets from the firm's creditors. Both rules perform the function of asset partitioning in which the assets of the firm's shareholders belong to the shareholders' creditors, and the firm's assets belong to the firm's creditors. Accordingly, on the law and economics view, a distinction is and ought to be drawn between separate legal personality and limited liability.

Thus, whether courts ought to remove the protection of limited liability for shareholders should not depend on whether the separate legal personality should be disregarded because both are distinct and separate issues. Further, creating an exception to the limited liability principle does not violate the separate legal personality rule; nor does it frustrate the consequences of this rule. In other words, maintaining the separate legal personality of companies is not a legitimate basis for upholding the limited liability principle for shareholders. Thus, given that the separate legal personality rule is not disregarded because it is not in issue, the question then is whether courts should be allowed to create exceptions to the limited liability principle, which is a default and not a mandatory rule (given that incorporators can contract out of it by incorporating an unlimited liability company). Putting it differently, because the issue of piercing the corporate veil is not implicated if courts were to impose unlimited liability on the parent company (or its controlling shareholder) for the wrongdoing caused by its subsidiary, courts should not be precluded from doing so unless there are countervailing reasons. Further, as I have shown in Section I, there are compelling policy reasons to deprive the parent company of the protection of limited liability where its subsidiary has caused uncompensated harms to victims.

Accordingly, because the limited liability principle and the separate legal personality rule are separate and distinct and should not be

[33] Ibid.

conflated – and thus disregarding the limited liability rule (ie making shareholders liable for the debts or wrongdoing of the company) does not implicate, let alone infringe, the separate legal personality of the company – the cases on piercing the corporate veil do not and should not pose an obstacle to imposing liability on the parent company (or its controlling shareholder).

B   Piercing the Corporate Veil

However, it may be argued that courts cannot simply depart from the limited liability rule which is provided for in the statute, unless parties opt out of the rule (by incorporating an unlimited liability company) or the legislation specifically creates an exception to this rule. Alternatively, it may be said that courts can create judicial exceptions to the limited liability rule provided that they do so using existing legal techniques however problematic they are (such as piercing the corporate veil) or using established legal doctrines (such as agency, trust, tort or contract). As a result, even if the separate legal personality and limited liability rules are distinguishable, and although disregarding the limited liability rule does not infringe the separate legal personality rule, it seems inevitable that the cases on the piercing of the corporate veil have to be engaged with. If so, it is still possible for courts to impose liability on parent companies by piercing the corporate veil, but there are issues concerning the use of this mechanism that have to be addressed.

Consider the English Court of Appeal case of *Adams v Cape Industries plc* ('*Adams*').[34] A key issue in that case was whether the separate legal personality of the US subsidiary – which marketed asbestos in the United States resulting in physical injuries to employees and consumers – could be disregarded so as to impose liability on its parent company as well as on another UK subsidiary. The court answered in the negative. Four significant points emerged from the decision. First, the court will not pierce the corporate veil of the subsidiary in the corporate group which has committed the tort merely because the corporate structure has been used so as to ensure that the legal liability of any future activities of the group will fall on another member of the group rather than on the defendant company.[35] It is legally acceptable for companies to structure

---

[34] [1990] Ch 433.
[35] Ibid at 538.

their business operations to insulate the future liability of any member of the group as it does not involve the evasion of any pre-existing claims.[36]

Second, the court affirmed the separate legal personality of each member within the corporate group and would not pierce the corporate veil, even if justice demands otherwise,[37] and even if the parent company runs a single integrated business and provides critical oversight and coordination of the group's activities.[38] In short, the court rejected the characterisation of the relevant companies within the group as a single economic unit.[39] *Adams* held that the decision in *DHN Food Distributors Ltd v Tower Hamlets London Borough Council* ('*DHN*'),[40] in which the court stated there was complete identity of commercial interest and personality because the three companies had common directors and shareholders as well as common corporate objectives, does not stand for the proposition that the corporate veil can be pierced when group companies operate as a single economic entity. Instead, *Adams* confined *DHN* to its specific facts, namely, the piercing of the veil in the three companies in the group was to enable the parent company to claim compensation under the statute.

Third, although a subsidiary can act as an agent for the parent company (or another member of the group) if it has actual or apparent authority, the fact that the parent company wholly owns the subsidiary will not make the subsidiary the parent's agent; nor will the fact that the parent runs an integrated business and controls the appointment of the subsidiary's directors.[41]

Finally, the court held, but without providing any guidelines, that the corporate veil can be pierced if the corporate structure is a mere façade concealing the true facts.[42] However, the court held that the company in question in the United States did not amount to a mere façade.

1 Singapore and Hong Kong

The law in Singapore[43] and Hong Kong[44] is consistent with *Adams* in that the courts in both jurisdictions have held that the use of corporate structure is acceptable to avoid incurring potential future liability but not

---

[36] *Prest v Petrodel Resources Limited* [2013] UKSC 34 para 35.
[37] Ibid at 536.
[38] Ibid at 537.
[39] Ibid at 532.
[40] [1976] 1 WLR 852.
[41] *Adams*, n 8 at 537.
[42] Ibid at 539.
[43] *Public Prosecutor v Lew Syn Pau* [2006] 4 SLR(R) 210; *Cavenagh Investment Pte Ltd v Kaushik Rajiv* [2013] 2 SLR 543.
[44] *China Ocean Shipping Co v Mitrans Shipping Co* [1995] 3 HKC 123; *Winland Enterprises Group Inc v Wex Pharmaceuticals Inc* [2012] 2 HKLRD 757.

to evade existing legal obligations. Further, the courts in both Asian jurisdictions have also rejected the single economic unit argument.[45] As a result, it is unobjectionable if a parent company should deliberately undercapitalise a subsidiary that is engaged in hazardous business operations so as to ensure that it has no assets to satisfy any potential lawsuits brought against it by potential tort victims. Thus, under the laws in Singapore and Hong Kong, the courts will not pierce the corporate veil of the delinquent subsidiary to allow the tort victims to seek redress against the parent company or any members of the corporate group.

That said, given that Singapore[46] and Hong Kong[47] courts have also approved the use of mere façade as a basis for piercing the corporate veil, it is possible for courts to pierce the veil of the subsidiary in question if the facts so demonstrate. However, there is reason to doubt the effectiveness of this ground for disregarding the separate legal personality because courts that have relied on it require the controller to have used the company to perpetrate fraud or evade legal obligations or liabilities[48] – which are existing grounds for piercing the veil – and, thus, labelling the company a mere façade provides no additional or independent justification.[49]

Another possible basis for piercing the corporate veil that is recognised in Singapore and has been applied in the context of corporate groups is alter ego, namely, the person (whether the individual or company) has used the company as its alter ego, as an extension of itself.[50] In those cases where the court has disregarded the separate legal personality on this basis, the controller had used the company as though it were his own; the controller had misapplied the assets of the company for his own benefit or he had commingled his assets with those of the company; and there was a failure to comply with corporate formalities. But these cases predated *Prest v Petrodel* [2013] UKSC 34 and, in light of that decision, it is doubtful that the court would pierce the veil if the same facts were again to arise.[51] After all, in *Prest*, the defendant disregarded the separate legal personality of the company and misapplied the company's assets for his own benefit. Yet the

---

[45] n 43 and 44.
[46] *Dynasty Line Ltd v Sia Sukamto* [2013] 4 SLR 253; *Alwie Handoyo v Tjong Very Sumito* [2013] 4 SLR 308.
[47] *Winland Enterprises Group Inc v Wex Pharmaceuticals Inc* [2012] 2 HKLRD 757.
[48] Ibid.
[49] Hans Tjio, Pearlie Koh and Lee Pey Woan, *Corporate Law* (Academy Publishing 2016) paras 06.040–06.041.
[50] *Asteriod Maritime Co Ltd v Owners of the Ship or Vessel 'Saudi Al Jubail'* [1987] SGHC 71; *Tjong Very Sumito v Chan Sing En* [2012] 3 SLR 953.
[51] *Max Master Holdings Ltd v Taufik Surya Dharma* [2016] SGHC 147 paras 135–6.

court refused to pierce the corporate veil as the defendant's actions did not amount to an evasion of existing legal obligations. Further, it has also been argued that the alter ego is not an independent ground for piercing the veil; rather, it is best understood as implied agency where the court found that the subsidiary had acted as agent for the person (whether corporate or individual) who is the principal.[52] But if the basis is agency, then the corporate veil is not pierced, as the doctrine of agency presupposes and depends on the existence of two independent and separate legal personalities (ie the principal (parent) and the agent (subsidiary)).[53]

2 Malaysia

The situation in Malaysia is different and it is arguable that the corporate veil of the delinquent subsidiary can be pierced such that the parent company can be held liable for the wrongdoing of the subsidiary on the basis that the subsidiary and its parent company function as a single economic entity.[54] Thus, the position in Malaysia is inconsistent with *Adams* because the latter held that the fact that the group company in reality operates its business as a single economic unit does not warrant disregard for the separate legal personality of each company within the group.

The Malaysian court has pierced the corporate veil by making the parent liable for the debts of its subsidiary in a case where the companies operated as an integral whole, both companies had the same managing director who exercised oversight over the subsidiary, and both companies shared the same senior officers.[55] Thus, in Malaysia, it is possible for the court to pierce the corporate veil of the subsidiary and hold the parent company liable for the uncompensated torts of its subsidiary provided that the facts demonstrate that the companies operate as a single economic unit. However, it may be argued that companies can circumvent this by ensuring that there are different directors in the parent company and its subsidiary, different corporate objectives between the two companies, and the parent company does not exercise any substantive control over the subsidiary (other than the fact that it can appoint and dismiss the

---

[52] Hans Tjio, Pearlie Koh and Lee Pey Woan, *Corporate Law* (Academy Publishing 2016) para 06.054.
[53] *Garnac Grain Company Inc v H M F Faure & Fairclough Ltd* [1968] AC 1130; *Smith, Stone and Knight Ltd v Birmingham Corp* [1939] 4 All ER 116.
[54] *Hotel Jaya Puri Bhd v National Union of Hotel, Bar and Restaurant Workers* [1980] 1 MLJ 109; Aiman Nariman Mohd Sulaiman and Effendy Othman, *Malaysia Company Law: Principles and Practices* (Wolters Kluwer 2015) para 2.037.
[55] Ibid.

subsidiary's directors). Nevertheless, because there are efficiencies to the integration of business operations within the group that may outweigh the cost of the possibility of the parent being held liable, operating the companies as a single economic unit is still a viable option for companies.

Other than the single economic unit argument, it is difficult in Malaysia for courts to pierce the corporate veil on the basis of alter ego, unlike in Singapore. This is because the fact that the subsidiary in Malaysia is an alter ego of the parent company or the individual controller will not result in the piercing of the corporate veil unless it is accompanied by fraud.[56] Thus, it would be difficult to hold the parent company liable for the uncompensated torts of its subsidiary.

3 India

There are cases that seem to support the single economic entity argument.[57] The cases in which the corporate veil was pierced may be divided into two types, the first in which a benefit was conferred on the parent company, and the second in which either the parent company was restrained from doing an act or liability was imposed on the parent for the subsidiary's wrongdoing. Regarding the first type, in one case, a parent company and its subsidiary were treated as a single unit so that the parent company could claim a statutory benefit pertaining to utilities.[58] In another case, the corporate veil of the subsidiary was pierced so that the experience of the parent companies was treated as the experience of the subsidiary for the purposes of determining whether the latter had the requisite experience to supply telephone directories.[59] Further, a leading commentary on company law states: 'The modern tendency is where there is identity and community of interest between companies in the group, especially where they are related as holding company and wholly-owned subsidiary or subsidiaries, to ignore their separate legal entity and look instead at the economic entity . . . .'[60] The commentator then went on to qualify this broad statement by stating that the corporate

---

[56] *Golden Vale Golf Range & Country Club Sdn Bhd v Hong Huat Enterprises Sdn Bhd* [2005] 5 CLJ 289; *Tenaga Nasional Bhd v Irham Niaga Sdn Bhd* [2011] 1 MLJ 752.

[57] DHN has been endorsed in *Hackbridge-Hewittic and Easun Ltd v GEC Distribution Transformers Ltd* (1992) 74 Com Cases 543 at 555 (Mad). But a leading textbook has clarified that there is no general principle that all companies in the group are to be treated as a single economic entity: Arvind P Datar and S Balasubramanian, *A Ramaiya Guide to the Companies Act* (18th edn, Lexis Nexis 2014) at 494.

[58] *State of U.P. v Renusagar Power Co* (1991) 70 Comp Cas 127 (SC): AIR 1988 SC 1737.

[59] *New Horizons Ltd v Union of India* (1997) 89 Comp Cas 849 (SC).

[60] CR Datta on Company Law, vol 1 (7th edn, LexisNexis 2017) at 1585.

veil should be pierced 'when the subsidiary does not enjoy any real autonomy in the determination of its course of action on the market'. Alternatively, when the parent company has 'pervasive control over [the wholly-owned subsidiary] and the former acts as the hand and voice of the latter, the subsidiary in that event would be nothing but an instrumentality, rather a part, of the principal company'.[61] But this language suggests that the basis for piercing the veil is not the single economic entity unit but, rather, alter ego, or even agency. If that is the case, the concerns raised earlier in the section on Singapore would also apply, namely, the alter ego doctrine may be difficult to justify in light of *Prest*, and agency presupposes that the separate legal personality of the company is not disregarded.

The second type of case in which the corporate veil was pierced consists of either precluding the parent from taking an action or imposing liability on the parent. On the former, the parent and the subsidiary were treated as one entity in order to prevent the parent, an overseas company, from entering into a joint venture agreement with an Indian subsidiary.[62] Regarding the latter, the veil was pierced on the basis of the single economic unit in order to impose unlimited liability on the parent company. In the aftermath of the notorious and tragic Bhopal disaster in which the Indian subsidiary of a US parent company caused hundreds of thousands of injuries and deaths because of a gas leak arising from the negligent operations of the Indian subsidiary, the Indian Supreme Court held that the parent company and the other companies within the corporate group were liable to the tort victims for the wrongdoing of the delinquent subsidiary. The court held that where a company engages in hazardous or inherently dangerous business operations, the entire corporate group is liable for it and owes 'an absolute and non-delegable duty to the community that no harm results to any one'.[63] But the problem in this case is that the court confined liability only if the company is engaged in hazardous or inherently dangerous business.

In sum, regarding the question of whether the corporate veil of the delinquent subsidiary can be pierced so that the parent company (or other companies in the group) can be made liable to the tort victims for the wrongdoing of the subsidiary, the answer varies among the four Asian jurisdictions. In Hong Kong, the answer is most likely not. In

---

[61] Ibid.
[62] *UK Mehra v Union of India* (1997) 88 Comp Cas 213 (Deli) (DB).
[63] *MC Mehta v Shriram Food and Fertilizer Industries (Oleum Gas Leak)*, AIR 1987 SC 1965.

Singapore, the veil can be pierced if it can be shown that the subsidiary is an alter ego of the parent. In Malaysia, the answer is likely to be in the affirmative if the facts of the case demonstrate that the corporate group operates as a single economic unit. And as for India, the separate legal personality of the subsidiary can be disregarded and liability can be imposed on the entire group provided the subsidiary is engaging in hazardous or inherently dangerous business.

If the corporate veil cannot be pierced, agency is a possible basis for holding the parent company liable for the subsidiary's wrongdoing.[64] Another technique for depriving the parent company of the protection of limited liability that does not involve piercing the corporate veil is to impose a duty of care on the parent company to third parties (such as employees, consumers or bystanders) who have been injured by the tortious conduct of the subsidiaries. This will be examined in Section II(C).

C Breach of Duty of Care by Parent Companies

In the important decision in *Chandler v Cape plc* ('*Chandler*'),[65] the English Court of Appeal held that the parent company owed and breached its duty of care to the employees of its subsidiaries. In that case, an employee of the subsidiary contracted asbestosis as a result of being exposed to asbestos. He sued the parent company because the subsidiary had been dissolved. He alleged that the parent company had been derelict in its duty to provide a safe working environment for the subsidiary's employees. The court ruled in his favour, holding that the parent company had assumed responsibility for the health and safety of the subsidiary's employees. The court set out four factors for determining whether a duty of care has been established:

> (1) the business of the parent and subsidiary are in a relevant respect the same; (2) the parent has, or ought to have, superior knowledge on some relevant aspect of health and safety in the particular industry; (3) the subsidiary's system of work is unsafe as the parent company knew, or ought to have known; and (4) the parent knew or ought to have foreseen that the subsidiary or its employees would rely on its using that superior

---

[64] *The Asean Promoter [1981–1982]* SLR(R) 289 (cf *The Skaw Prince* [1994] 3 SLR(R) 146); *Yue Tai Plywood & Timber Co Ltd v Far East Wagner Construction Ltd* [2001] 2 HKLRD 446; Hans Tjio, Pearlie Koh and Lee Pey Woan, *Corporate Law* (Academy Publishing 2016) para 2.036; *Smith, Stone and Knight Ltd v Birmingham Corp* [1939] 4 All ER 116.
[65] [2012] 1 WLR 3111.

knowledge for the employees' protection. For the purposes of (4) it is not necessary to show that the parent is in the practice of intervening in the health and safety policies of the subsidiary. The court will look at the relationship between the companies more widely. The court may find that element (4) is established where the evidence shows that the parent has a practice of intervening in the trading operations of the subsidiary, for example production and funding issues.[66]

To begin with, the court found that the parent had control of parts of the subsidiary's business, including the formulation of the health and safety policies. With respect to the first factor, the court found that the parent and subsidiary belonged to an integrated business group and conducted operations in the same locality.[67] As for the second factor, the parent had superior knowledge about the risks and had conducted research on them.[68] Regarding the third factor, the parent was fully aware of systemic failures that resulted from the escape of asbestos dust from the factory, and thus it knew of the material risks to the health and safety of the subsidiary's employees, particularly the employees who worked in the brick-making business.[69] As for the last factor, the court found that the parent supervised the development of the products in a central laboratory; it made business decisions related to the expansion of the subsidiary's business; and it had superior knowledge of the asbestos business and provided technical expertise to the subsidiary.[70] Accordingly, the court imposed a duty of care on the parent, namely, 'either to advise Cape Products on what steps it had to take in the light of knowledge then available to provide those employees with a safe system of work or to ensure that those steps were taken'.[71] The court concluded that the parent had breached its duty of care to the subsidiary's employees and, thus, awarded compensation to the claimant. The court clarified that it was not piercing the corporate veil of the subsidiary so that the wrongdoing of the subsidiary was imputed to the parent so as to render the latter liable for the former's wrongdoing; the duty of care imposed on the parent was not derived from the subsidiary.[72] Instead, the claimant had to prove that the parent itself had breached the duty, although in establishing the duty of care, the acts of the parent in

---

[66] Ibid para 80.
[67] Ibid paras 8 and 10.
[68] Ibid para 75.
[69] Ibid para 77.
[70] Ibid paras 10, 14, 28 and 75.
[71] Ibid para 78.
[72] Ibid para 69.

relation to its subsidiary were relevant. In doing so, the court was actually upholding the separate legal personality of the companies. That said, whether the court had imposed the duty of care on the parent or had instead pierced the corporate veil of the subsidiary, the result would have been the same insofar as the parent company was deprived of the protection of limited liability.

One notable decision that has affirmed *Chandler* is the unanimous UK Supreme Court decision of *Vedanta Resources Plc v Lungowe* ('*Vedanta*').[73] There the claimants, who are citizens of Zambia, alleged that their health and livelihood had been harmed by the toxic emissions from a copper mine operated and owned by a Zambian company which is in turn owned by a parent company in the UK. The claimants sued the Zambian subsidiary and its UK parent company under the tort of negligence and for breach of statutory duty. The claimants alleged that the parent had exercised a high level of supervision and control over the activities of the subsidiary, which the court found to be a real triable issue.[74]

Although the only issue decided by the Supreme Court in this case was whether the courts of England and Wales have jurisdiction to determine those claims against both defendants (which it answered in the affirmative),[75] it made five important points.

First, in approving the decision in *Chandler*, the Supreme Court said that there is nothing novel or controversial about the issue of whether a parent owes a duty of care to a third party for the activity of its subsidiary given that it is to be determined by ordinary, general principles of tort law.[76] It clarified that *Chandler* did not lay down a separate test. Thus, the decision in *Chandler* follows well-established principles setting out the circumstances under which A owes a duty of care to C for the harmful activities of B. Given that *Chandler* is not a one-off, out of the ordinary decision, it is anticipated that the clarification by the Supreme Court in *Vedanta* will further enhance the significance and impact of the decision in *Chandler*, not only in the UK, but also in the four common law jurisdictions in Asia which have yet to cite the latter case.

Second, the Supreme Court said that although a duty of care may be owed to a third party where the parent company is involved in the management of the subsidiary's activity or where the parent has advised

---

[73] [2019] UKSC 20.
[74] Ibid para 61.
[75] Ibid para 4.
[76] Ibid paras 50 and 54.

the subsidiary on how it should manage a particular risk, one should not confine the parent's liability to these two situations as there could be others.[77] This clearly demonstrates that the court recognises that the categories of cases in which a parent company owes a duty of care to a third party for its subsidiary's wrongdoing are evolving. This seems to bode well for future cases that may not fit into the factual matrix of *Chandler* or the existing cases. That said, in *Thompson v The Renwick Group plc* ('*Thompson*')[78] (which was decided after *Chandler* but before *Vedanta*), the English Court of Appeal held that the parent company would not have assumed a duty of care to the subsidiary's employees for their health and safety on the basis that the parent had appointed the subsidiary's director with responsibility for health and safety matters. This is because the director of the subsidiary was acting on its behalf and not on the parent's behalf. Further and importantly, because the parent company was merely a holding company for the subsidiary's shares, the court found that the parent company did not have superior knowledge of some relevant aspect of health and safety such as to warrant the imposition of a duty of care to the subsidiary's employees. The court emphasised that what it was looking for in terms of allocation of responsibility were facts showing that the parent company was in a better position to protect the health and safety of the subsidiary's employees because of its superior knowledge or expertise.

Third, the Supreme Court rejected the defendants' argument that the parent could not owe a duty of care simply by laying down group-wide policies and guidelines; on the contrary, a duty of care will arise if the policies contain errors which when implemented cause harm to third parties, as shown in the facts in *Chandler*.[79] Further the court held that should a parent company hold itself out in its published materials as supervising its subsidiaries but it fails to do so in reality, this omission may amount to a breach of duty of care. Although the court's analysis is correct, the concern is that to avoid being subject to any duty of care going forward, a parent company will cease setting out any group guidelines or policies and will instead let each subsidiary formulate its own policies. And the parent company will also ensure that the subsidiary engaging in risky operations is deliberately undercapitalised such that it is unable to provide any compensation arising from potential lawsuits.

---

[77] Ibid para 51.
[78] [2015] 2 BCC 855.
[79] *Vedanta*, n 73 paras 52–3.

The net effect is arguably reduced operational efficiencies and diminished oversight of risk management in a group company; in addition, the parent company may escape liability altogether. The consequence is that no effective redress is available to the tort victims.

Fourth, the Supreme Court said that the '*Chandler* indicia are no more than particular examples of circumstances in which a duty of care may affect a parent'.[80] This implies that (a) the fact that a claimant cannot satisfy all of the *Chandler* indicia does not mean that a duty of care does not arise; and (b) there are other relevant factors that can give rise to a duty of care.

Finally, the Supreme Court stated that the reasoning in *Chandler* would also apply to foreign subsidiaries of UK parent companies.[81] The Court said that even if it concluded that the foreign jurisdiction (which was Zambia on the facts) was the proper place in which to try the case, it would still permit service of English proceedings on the foreign defendant if there was cogent evidence that substantial justice would be unobtainable in the foreign jurisdiction. And it was the case because the court said that it was impossible to fund group claims as the claimants were all extremely poor and there was a lack of experienced lawyers to handle such a complex litigation.

Other than the English decisions, there are cases from Australia which affirmed the proposition that the parent company owes a duty of care not only to the subsidiary's employees but also to the employees' children. In other words, a parent company owes a duty of care to third parties (if the tort law elements of proximity and foreseeability are satisfied) under certain circumstances. For example, in *CSR Ltd v Wren*,[82] the court found that the parent company was aware of the health risks arising from exposure of asbestos; the parent and the subsidiary shared the same management; and the parent exercised control and supervision of the business operations of the subsidiary. In a subsequent decision, *CSR Ltd v Young*,[83] the duty of care owned by the parent company was extended to the subsidiary's employee's child who died from asbestos exposure from the clothes of her father (who was the subsidiary's employee) and from the neighbouring factories which emitted the asbestos dust.

While it seems that *Chandler* and its progeny have not yet been cited by the courts in the four Asian jurisdictions being discussed here, it is

[80] Ibid para 56.
[81] Ibid para 88.
[82] (1997) 44 NSWLR 463.
[83] (1998) Aust Torts Reports 81-468.

submitted that the *Chandler* indicia should be considered for adoption by the courts in the four jurisdictions provided that they bear in mind that the indicia are examples and not a definitive test.

However, commentators have pointed out three weaknesses in *Chandler*.[84] First, there is uncertainty as to the nature and degree of control that the parent company needs to have over the subsidiary. In *Chandler*, the court found that the parent company had relevant control of the subsidiary as the former was involved in the operations of the latter. But the court did not lay down a test on what amounts to sufficient and relevant control. Second, it has been criticised that this notion of control is over-inclusive (because the subsidiaries are likely to be subject in certain aspects to a group policy that is set out by the parent) and under-inclusive (because the fact that a parent company does not intervene in its subsidiaries should not automatically exempt it from liability). Finally, to escape liability, the parent company will make sure that it does not exercise oversight of its subsidiaries, a prime example of which is a passive holding company as in the case of *Thompson*.[85]

However, these weaknesses are overstated. To begin with, although the court in *Chandler* recognised that the parent company had relevant control of the subsidiary, it did not include control in the *Chandler* indicia. This implies that while a parent company's control of its subsidiary is relevant, it is not crucial or decisive. More importantly, one should bear in mind that the second, third and fourth indicia in *Chandler* have both a factual and a normative component, that is, the parent company has *or ought to have* superior knowledge, knows *or ought to know* that the subsidiary's system of work is unsafe, and knows or *ought to have foreseen* that the employees would rely on its using that superior knowledge to protect them. Only the first indicium has no normative component, only a factual one, that is, the business of the parent and the subsidiary are in a relevant aspect the same. The implication of the normative component is significant. Even if the parent does not have superior knowledge, the question is whether it ought to have. Thus, it is not a conclusive answer to this question to assert that the parent company does not have superior knowledge on the basis that it is a passive holding company; nor is it a justifiable answer that the parent is not involved in the subsidiary's health and safety matters. The question is

---

[84] Barnali Choudhury and Martin Petrin, *Corporate Duties to the Public* (Cambridge University Press 2019) at 106–7.
[85] [2015] 2 BCC 855.

whether it ought to have superior knowledge, and, in this regard, it is submitted that, generally speaking, by virtue of the parent company's ability to control the subsidiaries, it should not be allowed to reap the benefits of limited liability and corporate group structure and yet be allowed to escape liability for the physical injuries, particularly the deaths of innocent, involuntary tort victims who remain uncompensated because the delinquent subsidiary is undercapitalised or insolvent.

A parent company, as the sole or controlling shareholder of the subsidiary, wields significant powers over the latter. These powers include, but are not limited to: appointing and dismissing the subsidiary's directors at any time without cause by an ordinary resolution despite anything contrary to the subsidiary's constitution;[86] unilaterally altering the subsidiary's articles by a special resolution;[87] dictating to or overruling the subsidiary's directors by altering the articles;[88] compelling the subsidiary's directors to call a general meeting at any time at the company's expense by members holding 5 per cent or 10 per cent of the voting capital or voting rights;[89] exercising management power if provided for in the statute or the subsidiary's constitution;[90] directing the subsidiary's directors to take or refrain from taking action by special resolution;[91] authorising transactions between the subsidiary and the latter's director by ordinary resolution that would otherwise amount to a breach of the director's duty;[92] ratifying breach of duties by the subsidiary's directors by ordinary resolution;[93] approving mergers and acquisitions;[94] approving loan transactions between the subsidiary and the latter's directors;[95] approving related party transactions;[96] approving significant

---

[86] HK CO, s 462; SG CA, s 152; MY CA, s 206; IN CA, s 169. An ordinary resolution means a resolution that is passed by a simple majority.

[87] HK CO, s 88; SG CA, s 26; MY CA, s 36; IN CA, ss 13, 14. A special resolution means a resolution that is passed by a majority of at least 75 per cent.

[88] *Bamford v Bamford* [1970] Ch 212 at 220 (Plowman J); *Automatic Self-Cleansing Filter Syndicate Co Ltd v Cuninghame* [1906] 2 Ch 34 at 38 (CA) (Collins MR).

[89] HK CO, ss 566, 568; SG CA, s 176; MY CA, s 311; IN CA, s 100.

[90] SG CA, s 157A (2); IN CA, s 179(2).

[91] HK Model Articles, art 3(1); MY CA, s 195(2) and (3).

[92] *North-West Transportation Co Ltd v Beatty* (1887) 12 App Cas 589 at 593–4.

[93] HK CO, s 473; *Raffles Town Club Pte Ltd v Lim Eng Hock Peter* [2013] 1 SLR 374 at [42]; *Teoh Peng Phe v Wan* [2001] 1 AMR 358 at 373; *Balasaraswathi Limited Tirunelveli v A Parameswara Aiyar* AIR 1957 MAD 122 at [18]; *Descon Limited v Biman Behari Sen (No. 2)* [2011] 162 Comp Cas 631.

[94] HK CO, Part 13; SG CA, Part VII; IN CA, Chapter XV; MY CA, Part III Division 7.

[95] HK CO, s 500 HK CO; SG CA, s 162; MY CA, s 224; IN CA, s 185.

[96] Regarding Singapore, see chapter 9 of the Listing Rules of the Singapore Exchange (SGX LR) on interested party transactions. Regarding Hong Kong, see chapter 14A of the

transactions;[97] voluntarily winding up the subsidiary by special resolution;[98] and inspecting the subsidiary's documents.[99]

In light of these powers wielded by the parent company over its subsidiary, it is highly questionable that the parent company can escape liability where its subsidiaries have caused uncompensated harm to innocent tort victims on the basis that it does not exercise the corporate powers (enumerated above) with the exception of appointing the subsidiary's directors. Failure to hold the parent company accountable not only allows the claims of the tort victims to remain unaddressed but, more importantly, is also likely to result in a perverse consequence and send a dangerous signal, namely, that tort law and corporate law allow companies to continue to use the group corporate structure to engage in highly risky or hazardous business operations that have a material and adverse impact on innocent third parties, without any corresponding need to bear any legal responsibility for the harm that they have caused. For these reasons, the reasoning and result in *Thompson* are highly doubtful.

One possible counterargument is that if a parent company owes a duty of care to tort victims by virtue of it having the capacity to control the subsidiary because of the corporate powers that it wields over it, then this seems to imply that a parent company owes a duty of care on this basis alone; the *Chandler* indicia is redundant as there is no need to apply it in order to decide whether a duty of care should be imposed. But this is not necessarily the case. Assuming that the first indicium is satisfied, and even if the fact that the parent company's ability to control provides the basis for satisfying the second and third indicia, there is still the fourth part, that is, the claimant must demonstrate that the parent knew or ought to have foreseen that the subsidiary or its employees would rely on it using that superior knowledge for the employees' protection. The parent company's capacity to control the subsidiary in itself does not satisfy the fourth indicium.

That said, although *Chandler* is an important and useful technique for holding the parent company liable and, thus, there is much to commend it

---

Listing Rules of the Stock Exchange of Hong Kong (HKEX LR) on connected transactions. On India, see s 188 IN CA and s 23 of the Securities and Exchange Board of India (SEBI) (Listing Obligations and Disclosure Requirements) (LODR). Regarding Malaysia, see s 228 MY CA and chapter 10 of the Main Market Listing Requirements of Bursa Malaysia (Bursa Malaysia LR).

[97] HKEX LR 14.40; SGX LR 1014(2); IN CA, s 180(1); Bursa Malaysia LR 10.07(1)(b).
[98] Hong Kong Companies (Winding Up and Miscellaneous Provisions) Ordinance (Cap 32), s 228; SG CA, s 290; MY CA, s 439; IN CA, s 304.
[99] HK CO, s 740(6); SG CA, ss 8A, 189(1), 396A; IN CA, ss 119(b), 171(1)(a), 85(2)(a), 94(2), 189(3), 190(2), 187(3), 186(10); MY CA, s 585.

to the courts in the four Asian jurisdictions, there may be three concerns with the duty of care doctrine in *Chandler*. The first is that the business of the parent company may not be the same in a relevant aspect with that of the subsidiary, such as in the case of large, decentralised MNCs or conglomerates with overseas subsidiaries containing different lines of business. If that is the case, the first indicium in *Chandler* will not be satisfied. The response to this concern is that, to begin with, the Supreme Court in *Vedanta* made it clear that the *Chandler* indicia are no more than particular examples that happened to apply to the facts in *Chandler*. Thus, failure to satisfy the first indicium in *Chandler* does not preclude the establishment of a duty of care on the part of the parent. Moreover, the fact that the parent and the subsidiary do not have the same business should not matter if it can be shown, for instance, that the former has control over, or is involved in the management of, the latter.

The second concern is that the corporate structure in *Chandler* assumes a straightforward, vertical group structure consisting of a parent company and a small number of wholly-owned or majority-owned subsidiaries. But the corporate structure of some of the listed companies in the Asian jurisdictions is more complex, consisting of horizontal group structures with a web of cross-holdings. The response to this concern is that differences in group structure should not matter. The key issue, as the court in *Vedanta* clarified, is whether the application of the ordinary, general principles of tort law in relation to the imposition of a duty of care on the parent is satisfied on the facts of the case.

The third and final concern is that *Chandler* does not cover the situation where a company circumvents liability by outsourcing risky or hazardous operations to third parties such as independent contractors that are not part of the corporate structure. In such a situation, the company does not own shares in the independent contractor but has only entered into a contract with it. The response to this concern is that it does not matter that this situation is not covered by the facts in *Chandler*. The court in *Vedanta* said that the ordinary, general principles of tort law that apply to the issue of whether a parent company owes a duty of care to a third party for the activities of the subsidiary 'are the same as would apply in relation to the question whether any third party (such as a consultant giving advice to the subsidiary) was subject to a duty of care in tort owed to a claimant dealing with the subsidiary'.[100]

---

[100] *Vedanta*, n 73 para 50, citing with approval *AAA v Unilever plc* [2018] EWCA Civ 1532 para 36.

In view of the above concerns, and in response to the concerns with the use of control as a touchstone or factor in ascribing liability to the parent company, commentators have proposed solutions. One suggested solution is to impose statutory enterprise liability such that the entire enterprise (ie all the companies in the group) is liable for the harm caused by any one company in the group.[101] This solution will address the first and second concerns as well as those related to the notion of control. The other suggested solution is to impose strict liability on a pro rata basis on all the shareholders (both corporate and personal) of the delinquent subsidiary.[102] In response to the third and final concern, one proposed solution is either to make the company vicariously liable for the wrongdoing of the independent contractor with which it has entered into a contract[103] or to impose a modified form of unlawful means of conspiracy.[104] I will analyse these proposed solutions in Sections III and IV. After that, I will put forward my proposal, which is to impose fault-based liability (subject to a reverse burden of proof) on the controlling shareholders of SOEs.

III Proposed Exceptions to Limited Liability

A Enterprise Liability

One suggested reform is statutory enterprise liability under which the victims of the tortious acts of any company in the corporate group can seek redress from the entire group.[105] In other words, the separate legal personalities of all the companies within the group are disregarded and treated as one and the same for liability purposes. This statutory enterprise liability is distinguishable from the common law doctrine of enterprise liability that has been recognised in Malaysia and India, as discussed

---

[101] See eg Meredith Dearborn, 'Enterprise Liability: Reviewing and Revitalizing Liability for Corporate Groups' (2009) 97 *California Law Review* 195 at 220–30; PI Blumberg, *The Multinational Challenge to Corporation Law: The Search for a New Corporate Personality* (Oxford University Press 1993); G Skinner, 'Rethinking Limited Liability of Parent Corporations for Foreign Subsidiaries' Violations of International Human Rights Law' (2015) 72 *Washington & Lee Law Review* 1769; Barnali Choudhury and Martin Petrin, *Corporate Duties to the Public* (Cambridge University Press 2019) at 120–3.
[102] Christian Witting, *Liability of Corporate Groups and Networks* (Cambridge University Press 2018) at 289–94.
[103] Phillip Morgan, 'Vicarious Liability for Group Companies: The Final Frontiers of Vicarious Liability?' (2015) 31 *Professional Negligence* 276.
[104] Witting, n 102 at 381–7.
[105] Choudhry and Petrin, n 101.

in Sections II(B.2) and II(B.3). Recall that in *DHN* it was found that there was an 'utter identity and community of interests'[106] among the three companies in the group. In the Malaysian decision, it was found that that the two companies constituted one integrated whole, they shared the same management, and the managing director of one company had the ultimate authority over the employees of the other company.[107] The Indian Supreme Court has accepted enterprise liability provided that the company is engaging in hazardous or inherently dangerous business.[108]

What distinguishes one version of the proposed statutory enterprise liability[109] from the common law version is that, under the former, there is no need to show any control by the company – on which liability should be imposed – over another company;[110] nor is there a need to show any overlapping interests between the companies. There is also no need to show any impropriety or fault on the part of the other companies other than the fact that the company has committed the tortious act and has caused harm to the third parties. Thus, issues of whether the parent company has exercised control or has been negligent do not pose a concern; nor do issues of whether the subsidiary in question has been at fault. As long as one company in the corporate group has committed a tort against an employee or a third party, the tort victim can bring a claim against the entire group. Another important benefit of this proposed statutory version of enterprise liability is that it is applicable to different kinds of corporate group structure ranging from typical vertical group structures comprising a parent company and its wholly-owned subsidiaries to complex web of vertical and horizontal structures that consist of multiple cross-holdings. The key justification underlying this version of statutory enterprise liability is that companies that gain the benefits from the group structure (such as lower tax rate and operational efficiency) ought to bear the cost of doing business, the latter of which should include the potential liability on the whole group for the tortious wrongdoing of any company within the group. A further benefit of enterprise liability, as compared to *Chandler*'s approach of imposing

---

[106] *DHN*, n 40 at 867.
[107] *Hotel Jaya Puri Bhd v National Union of Hotel, Bar and Restaurant Workers* [1980] 1 MLJ 109.
[108] *MC Mehta v Shriram Food and Fertilizer Industries (Oleum Gas Leak)*, AIR 1987 SC 1965.
[109] Choudhury and Petrin, n 101 at 120–3.
[110] On the problems of 'control' as a basis to impose liability, see Witting, n 102 at 282–7.

III PROPOSED EXCEPTIONS TO LIMITED LIABILITY

a duty of care on the parent company, is that as long as the claimant can show that the harm is caused by a company within the group, it is sufficient; he need not show that the parent has breached a duty of care, which can be difficult to prove in companies with complex structures, as the difficulty of gathering information that can establish a breach of duty of care is exacerbated. Another benefit of enterprise liability is that it overcomes the difficulty of judgment proofing within corporate groups where the parent company can place its key resources in subsidiaries that are different from the one which is engaging in risky operations, thereby rendering assets out of reach to the tort victims.

However, there are at least two issues with this proposed version of statutory enterprise liability. First, this version is far broader than and inconsistent with other existing versions. For example, although US courts recognise enterprise liability, they require claimants to show that the companies within the group possess a higher degree of unity such that the entire enterprise is functioning like a single entity and therefore a strict adherence to the separate legal personality will result in injustice.[111] Further, in some instances, courts have required claimants to show that the relevant persons have used the corporate structure for improper motives.[112] Moreover, US commentators who have expressed support for enterprise liability have argued that there should be economic dependency or economic integration of some sort among the companies.[113] Thus, a version of statutory enterprise liability that does not have any limitation mechanisms such as control, impropriety, undercapitalisation, or economic interdependence or integration may be open to challenge for being too expansive. The response is that imposing liability on the group for any of its members' torts has to be internalised as a cost of doing business.[114]

Second, there is uncertainty as to how an enterprise should be defined, and one definition presupposes an element of control. It has been suggested that the definition of enterprise means holding companies and their subsidiaries as defined in the companies statute.[115] For example, in the Asian jurisdictions, the holding company is one that (1) controls the

---

[111] See eg *Pan Pacific Sash & Door Co v Greendale Park, Inc.*, 166 Cal App 2d 652 (1958); *Las Palmas Association v Las Palmas Center Association* 235 Cal App 3d 1220, 1250 (1991).
[112] *Toho-Towa Co v Morgan Creek Prods Inc*, 159 Cal Rptr 3d 469, 480.
[113] Meredith Dearborn, 'Enterprise Liability: Reviewing and Revitalizing Liability for Corporate Groups' (2009) 97 *California Law Review* 195 at 252.
[114] Choudhury and Petrin, n 101 at 121–2.
[115] Ibid at 122.

composition of the other company's board of directors; (2) controls more than half of the other company's voting rights; or (3) holds more than half of the other company's issued share capital.[116] A company is a subsidiary of another company if the latter is the holding company of the former.[117] The problem with this definition is this. Suppose Company A owns 51 per cent shares in Company B. Either a Company C or an individual owns 49 per cent shares in Company B. Companies A and B are the holding company and subsidiary, respectively, both of which are part of the enterprise. But Company C or the individual who owns 49 per cent of the shares is not part of the enterprise because neither of them is a holding company under the companies statute. However, it is highly questionable why the shareholder who owns 49 per cent should not be included in the definition of enterprise and thus not subject to liability at all. If the argument is that the shareholder who owns 49 per cent should be less culpable than the one who owns 51 per cent because the latter either controls the appointment and removal of directors or is able to determine the outcome of decisions that require simple majority approval, then this implies that actual control or capacity to control or the ability to exercise substantial influence remains a relevant factor for determining whether liability should be imposed. This is not to say that the use of control as a factor is unproblematic and should be adopted. Rather, the statutory definition of a holding company and a subsidiary – relied upon by commentators for defining what an enterprise is – has a built-in notion of control which has been criticised by the same commentators who advocated for the enterprise liability approach.[118]

B Liability on Shareholders of the Wrongdoing Company

Another approach is to impose strict and pro rata liability on the shareholders – both corporate and personal – of the insolvent company that has caused physical injuries to the claimant. In other words, 'the proposed rule of modified limited liability would extend the liability of insolvent subsidiaries to their shareholders, but only in cases of unsatisfied personal injury claims'.[119] This is not only because physical interests are more deserving of protection than financial or reputational interests,

---

[116] HK CO, s 13; SG CA, s 5; MY CA, s 4; IN CA, ss 2(46), 2(87).
[117] Ibid.
[118] Witting, n 102; Choudhury and Petrin, n 101.
[119] Witting, n 102 at 288.

but also because physical injuries can also have severe consequences for the earning capacity of the victims.

There is an important similarity between this approach and the broad version of enterprise liability discussed in Section III(A). Under both approaches, liability is strict; it does not depend on the claimant proving that the defendant is at fault or that it has failed to conform to the reasonable standards of care. The rationale is that strict liability will compel the defendant to take into account all the material costs arising from its business operations.[120] Further, strict liability is more effective than fault-based liability because the latter only requires the party to take reasonable care but not to consider whether its action or omission will result in harm.[121] Moreover, fault-based liability imposes an unfair burden on the innocent victim to demonstrate that the defendant has failed to take due care, but this is particularly onerous to do in complex organisations or in MNCs where the subsidiaries and parent company are located in different jurisdictions.[122]

However, there are two important differences between this approach and that of enterprise liability. The first is that under the former, unlimited liability is imposed only on the shareholders of the insolvent subsidiary whereas under the latter, the enterprise (comprising holding companies and subsidiaries) is liable for the torts committed by any company within the group. The second difference is that under this approach, the subsidiary's shareholders are liable only for physical injuries, whereas enterprise liability theory makes no distinction between different types of tortious claim; it suffices as long as the defendant has committed a tortious act. The reason is that because the enterprise reaps the benefits of the group structure, it should be responsible for any costs that arise from using such a structure, particularly if physical harms are caused.[123]

There are three concerns arising from this approach that imposes unlimited pro rata liability only on the shareholders of the wrongdoing subsidiary. First, the shareholders of the delinquent subsidiary may be unable to, or unable to sufficiently, compensate the tort victims of the subsidiary. Yet the victims will not be able to seek redress from other companies in the group. This is unlike the case of enterprise liability under which the enterprise (ie the entire group) is liable to the claimant.

---

[120] Ibid at 290.
[121] Ibid.
[122] Ibid.
[123] Dearborn, n 101 at 200.

Second, this approach may disincentivise institutional or retail shareholders from investing in the company. These shareholders are minority investors in the majority of listed companies in the four Asian jurisdictions which are dominated by controlling shareholders. Suppose that 97 per cent of the shares of the wrongdoing subsidiary is held by a holding company, 2 per cent is held by passive institutional shareholders and the remaining 1 per cent by retail shareholders who are likely to be apathetic and will not have the resources or expertise to monitor the investee company. Under the strict liability approach, the passive institutional shareholders and retail investors will be subject to pro rata liability. The argument that strict liability compels investors to factor in all the relevant and material costs of their investment presupposes that the investors will have the expertise and resources to carefully consider these costs, which include the potential harm to third parties. While this argument can and should be applied to shareholders who are controllers or holding companies, it is questionable whether they should apply to passive institutional and particularly retail investors if they own an insignificant percentage of shares. Moreover, in light of the information asymmetry between these passive minority investors, on the one hand, and the controllers and the investee company, on the other, and in view of the free rider and collective action problems, it does not seem fair and appropriate for these passive minority investors to be subject to strict liability. But it has been said that shareholders who are worried about liability can enter into derivative contracts (such as credit default swaps) to hedge the risks of their investments.[124] This is possible for institutional shareholders, but it is doubtful that on a cost–benefit assessment, individual and retail shareholders will enter into such contracts (because of the time and resource cost incurred). Thus, the strict liability approach is likely to disincentivise them from investing.

The final concern is that it is not necessary to impose strict liability to compel shareholders and their investee companies to seriously consider the costs of their doing business; nor is this regime necessary to prevent the claimants from being unfairly burdened if they had to show that the defendant was at fault. It is possible to have a fault/negligence-based liability, but the burden of proof will be shifted to the defendant. For example, once the claimant has shown that harm has been caused to it, the law can impose liability on the parent company unless it can prove that it ought not to have known the harm or has taken all reasonable

---

[124] Witting, n 102 at 302.

actions to identify and prevent the harm. Consider the French statutory duty of vigilance under which companies are required to publish a vigilance plan showing that they have undertaken 'reasonable vigilance measures to allow for risk identification and for the prevention of severe violations of human rights and fundamental freedoms, serious bodily injury or environmental damage or health risks resulting directly or indirectly from the operations of the company and of the companies it controls ...'.[125] Thus, once the victims have shown that the defendant caused them the harm, the burden is on the defendant company to show that it complied with the duty of vigilance.

IV My Proposal

A Imposing Liability on the Controlling Shareholder

The existing academic literature as well as all the proposed exceptions to limited liability analysed in Section III seem to assume either a dispersed ownership jurisdiction or that the ownership structure of the corporate group is immaterial to the analysis. But I suggest that the fact that the four Asian jurisdictions analysed in this book are being dominated by listed companies with concentrated ownership structure that consists of controlling shareholders who are families and especially the government (or companies owned by it) has an important bearing on the issue of from whom innocent victims should seek redress for the uncompensated tortious acts committed by the subsidiary. I propose a statutory exception to limited liability which allows fault-based liability (subject to a reverse burden of proof) to be imposed on the controlling shareholder of the parent company. Thus, once the claimant has shown that any company within the corporate group has caused harm to it, liability will be imposed on the controlling shareholder unless it can discharge the burden of proving that it has exercised all reasonable care in identifying and preventing the harm. The controller consists of either the government (or a company owned by it) in SOEs or family member(s) in family-owned companies. Given that the central question in this book is whether and how the corporate mechanisms should be reformed to promote sustainability in the four Asian jurisdictions

---

[125] Art. L. 225-102-4 of the French Commercial Code (see French Corporate Duty of Vigilance Law (English Translation)) www.respect.international/french-corporate-duty-of-vigilance-law-english-translation/. The law applies to companies (and their direct or indirect subsidiaries) with at least 5,000 employees and whose head offices are located in France.

characterised by the presence of controlling shareholders especially the government in SOEs, I will focus my analysis on SOEs.

As I examined in Chapter 1, listed SOEs have social, economic and political objectives, in addition to commercial ones (ie maximisation of share price and profitability). These non-commercial objectives include, but are not limited to, job creation, income redistribution, provision and subsidisation of key goods and services, and promoting entrepreneurship. Many of the SOEs in the four Asian jurisdictions consist of the key financial, infrastructure, utilities, technological, and oil and gas companies. In short, the SOEs whose controlling shareholder is the government (or a company owned by it) control the key resources in the country and they play a critical role in the promotion and protection of the social and economic well-being of its population. The controlling shareholder is the government, which has the responsibility to act in the interests of its populace and which has the resources and the expertise to do so. The scope of responsibility should include provision of compensation to innocent victims, especially if there is physical harm and particularly if the harm is caused by a company that the government directly or indirectly controls or has the capacity to control. A strong case has even been made that the government owes fiduciary duties to those who elected it.[126] As compared to the tort victims, the government as the controller is manifestly better placed because of its superior expertise or experience and by virtue of its political and social responsibility to protect the employees of subsidiaries and the community in which they operate against tortious acts committed by its subsidiaries. In terms of risk allocation, it is efficient, fair and just that the government (or its wholly-owned company) bears the risks and costs of its business and operations.

Further and equally important, not only does the government have the capacity to control the SOEs by virtue of being the controlling shareholder, but studies have also shown that there is extensive and pervasive state intervention in the management of the SOEs.[127] This is a consequential point because courts[128] and the majority of commentators[129] have required actual control or the capacity to control as a basis for imposing liability.

---

[126] Evan J Criddle, Evan Fox-Decent, Andrew S. Gold, Sung Hui Kim and Paul B Miller (eds), *Fiduciary Government* (Cambridge University Press 2018); Ethan J Leib and Stephen R Galoob, 'Fiduciary Political Theory: A Critique' (2016) 125 *Yale Law Journal* 1820; D Theodore Rave, 'Politicians as Fiduciaries' (2013) 126 *Harvard Law Review* 671.

[127] See Chapter 1.

[128] *Chandler*, n 65.

[129] See eg Irit Mevorach, *Insolvency within Multinational Enterprise Groups* (Oxford University Press 2009); Andrew Muscat, *The Liability of the Holding Company for the Debts of Its Insolvent Subsidiaries* (Routledge 1996); Nina Mendelson, 'A Control-Based

IV MY PROPOSAL

As a matter of law, the government as the controlling shareholder has control over its companies by virtue of the significant powers that it wields over the SOEs. Its significant and wide-ranging formal powers include, but are not limited to, appointing and dismissing directors; changing the company's constitution; overruling the directors (by amending the constitution); directing directors to take certain actions or making binding recommendations; exercising management power (if provided for in the constitution); approving major transactions; and authorising or ratifying breaches of directors' duties. The government as the controller also has informal powers as it can exert pressure on directors to take or refrain from taking certain actions that will benefit itself but that are detrimental to the company and minority shareholders. Family members who are controlling shareholders also possess these formal and informal powers.

Not only do controlling shareholders have the capacity to control, ie they have formal and informal powers, but they have exercised control as evidenced in their extensive intervention in the affairs of the company. For example, in the PRC listed companies in Hong Kong, the PRC government appoints the directors and management who are connected to the government, and the politicians use the SOEs to further their own agenda.[130] Given that the directors and management in these SOEs depend on the state for promotion and other political gains, they are likely to do the bidding of the government.[131] In Malaysia, it has been said that the politicians interfere in the administration of the GLCs to advance their own interests.[132] In India, it has been found that in the

---

Approach to Shareholder Liability for Corporate Torts' (2002) 102 *Columbia Law Review* 1203; note that my suggested approach to imposing liability on the controlling shareholder of the SOEs differs from Mendelson's proposal in three key respects: first, I argue that there should be a reverse burden of proof on the controlling shareholder; second, I argue that the controlling shareholder of the parent company, and not the controlling shareholder of the delinquent company, should be held liable; and finally, my reasons for imposing liability on the controller are different from those of Mendelson as I take into account the concentrated ownership structure of the Asian jurisdictions; Cf Christopher Kutz, *Complicity: Ethics and Law for a Collective Age* (Cambridge University Press 2000); Witting, n 102 at 282–7.

[130] Lin Lin-Wen and Curtis J Milhaupt, 'We Are the (National) Champions: Understanding the Mechanisms of State Capitalism in China' (2013) 65 *Stanford Law Review* 697.

[131] Curtis J Milhaupt, 'Chinese Corporate Capitalism in Comparative Context' in Weitseng Chen (ed), *The Beijing Consensus? How China Has Changed the Western Ideas of Law and Economic Development* (Cambridge University Press 2017) at ch 11.

[132] Edmund Terence Gomez and KS Jomo, *Malaysia's Political Economy: Politics, Patronage and Profits* (2nd edn, Cambridge University Press 1999); Michael Carney and Edo Andriesse, 'Malaysia: Personal Capitalism' in Michael A Witt and Gordon Redding (eds), *The Oxford Handbook of Asian Business Systems* (Oxford University Press 2014) at 150.

SOEs, it is the government, not the board, that makes the key strategic decisions and the role of the directors is often reduced to that of implementation.[133] Other than SOEs, there is also evidence of intervention by the controlling shareholder in the listed family-owned companies in the four Asian jurisdictions.[134] After all, the controlling shareholder and/or his family members hold board and managerial positions in the company.[135] Further, in many of the family-owned companies, the chair and the CEO are the same person and he or she comes from the founder family.[136]

Finally, because the state as a controller extracts private benefits of control from SOEs, it may be said that the state should also bear the costs of being a controller, one of which is to provide compensation to the tort victims that have been harmed by the companies which are under the control of the controlling shareholder.

In sum, there are two key reasons why the controlling shareholder of SOEs should be held liable (for the harms caused by the SOEs or their subsidiaries). First, because the controlling shareholder is the government (or an entity wholly owned by it), it not only has the superior expertise and resources needed to identify and prevent the risks related to physical injuries arising from the operations of the SOEs (and their subsidiaries), but it also has the moral duty to compensate those to whom the SOEs (or their subsidiaries) have caused injuries. For the SOEs to impose externalities on society without affording its victims any effective redress is a dereliction of this basic governmental obligation. Second, because the elements of control are present, ie in view of the significant formal and informal powers wielded by the government as a controller over its investee companies, and because of its general practice of interfering in the management of the SOEs, it makes both economic and practical sense to attribute responsibility to the government for the risks posed by the business operations of the SOEs of which it has control. Thus, it is fair, just and efficient that the victims of the tortious acts committed by the SOEs (or their subsidiaries) which are unable to compensate them should be

---

[133] Jayanth Rama Varma, 'Corporate Governance in India: Disciplining the Dominant Shareholder' (1997) 9 *IIMB Management Review* 5; S Subramanian, 'A Comparison of Corporate Governance Practices in State-Owned Enterprises and Their Private Sector Peers in India' (2016) 5 *IIM Kozhikode Society & Management Review* 200.

[134] Ernest Lim, *A Case for Shareholders' Fiduciary Duties in Common Law Asia* (Cambridge University Press 2019) at 42–62.

[135] Ibid.

[136] Ibid.

allowed to seek redress from the government as the controlling shareholder. Further, these two reasons and the fact that the states in the Asian jurisdictions (especially Singapore, Malaysia and India) have a unique and critical responsibility to promote and protect the social and economic interests of their populations explain why liability should be imposed on the government as the controlling shareholder of the SOEs.

My approach of subjecting the government as the controlling shareholder to liability has three advantages over the two approaches examined earlier, namely, enterprise liability and strict liability on all the corporate and personal shareholders of the delinquent subsidiary. First, my approach avoids the problem of the definition of an enterprise that afflicts the enterprise liability approach. Second, my approach does not and need not resort to strict liability which, despite its advantages, seems severe and overreaching when there are more palatable measures such as reversing the burden of proof on the defendant.

Finally, my approach does not disincentivise institutional or retail shareholders from investing in the company given that only the controlling shareholder will be held liable. But it may be argued that imposing liability on the government as the controller may also result in the same adverse effect. However, it is doubtful whether this may happen and, if it does, it is likely that the effect will be immaterial. First, the government is no ordinary investor; as the state, it has substantially more resources than other investors to cushion the impact of payouts (if any) to tort victims. Second, because SOEs play a long-standing and pivotal role in the social, economic and political development in India, Malaysia and Singapore (and in relation to the stock market development in Hong Kong), it is unlikely that the governments in these countries will cease being controlling shareholders simply because there is a possibility of them being sued by tort victims. It can be argued that because of the possibility of being held liable, the government will proactively develop and implement measures to identify and prevent risks related to the business operations of the SOEs. The overall net effect is a significant reduction in the incidence of lawsuits and a safer working environment. And the government continues to maintain its controlling stake in the companies. Finally, as explained in Chapter 1, there are significant benefits to the government being a controlling shareholder, namely, extractions of economic and political private benefits of control. Thus, as long as the cost of the lawsuit and payouts to the tort victims do not outweigh the monitoring cost and the expropriation gains by the government, it will not be disincentivised from continuing to be a controlling shareholder.

One important legal issue is whether the government as the controlling shareholder can be sued.[137] In brief, in Singapore, because the controlling shareholder of the SOEs, Temasek Holdings Pte Ltd, is a private investment company, it can be sued under the law[138] as it is subject to the common law and all applicable legislations. In other words, the ultimate controller is the government (ie the Ministry of Finance) who interposes Temasek between itself and the SOEs.[139] In Malaysia, similar to Singapore, the government has incorporated eight different companies as controlling shareholders of the SOEs,[140] and all eight can be sued under the law.[141] In India, the controlling shareholder of the SOEs is the Union Government of India or the state government.[142] Under the Indian constitution, both the union and state governments can be sued.[143] While the doctrine of state immunity applies in India, it does so only when the government is carrying out functions related to the administration of justice, and maintenance of law and order, and not when it engages in commercial or managerial activities.[144] Thus, it is possible for the government as the controlling shareholder to be sued in India. The outlier, however, is Hong Kong. Under Hong Kong law, the controlling shareholder of the PRC SOEs, which is the PRC State Council, cannot be sued because of crown immunity,[145] although the SOEs (which of course include the parent company), when they

---

[137] Lim, n 134 at 461–6.

[138] Government Proceedings Act (Cap 121), s 4(d).

[139] Temasek, 'Why Was Temasek Established?' www.temasek.com.sg/abouttemasek/faqs# (the government transferred its holdings in the GLCs to Temasek so as 'to free the Ministry of Finance to focus on its core role of policymaking and regulations, while Temasek would own and manage investments on a commercial basis').

[140] PGC Work Team for the Government Linked Companies Transformation Program, www.pcg.gov.my/faqs#; Edmund Terence Gomez, Thirshalar Padmanabhan, Norfaryanti Kamaruddin, Sunil Bhalla and Fikri Fisal, *Minister of Finance Incorporated: Ownership and Control of Corporate Malaysia* (Springer 2017) at 96.

[141] See Lim, n 134 at Appendix 7.

[142] PSU in India, https://archive.india.gov.in/spotlight/spotlight_archive.php?id=78.

[143] Article 300 of the Constitution of India (9 November 2015) states that the 'Government of India may sue and be sued by the name of the Union of India and the Government of a State may sue or be sued by the name of the State ...'. Article 12 of the Indian Constitution defines 'State' as including the Government of India (Union Government), the state government, all local authorities, and other authorities within India or under the control of the central government.

[144] *Nagendra Rao Case In N Nagendra Rao & Co v State of AP* AIR 1994 SC 2663; *Ghaziabad Development Authority v Balbir Singh* AIR 2004 SC 2141.

[145] *Hua Tian Long (No. 3)* [2010] 3 HKC 557.

carry out commercial functions, can be sued (and can sue).[146] If that is the case, it is suggested that the enterprise liability approach, despite its flaws (examined earlier), may be adopted in Hong Kong. And with regard to Singapore, Malaysia and India, liability can and should be imposed on the controlling shareholder.

However, the concern is that the government may resist passing a legislation to permit tort victims to seek address from itself (as in the case in India) or its wholly-owned companies (as in the case in Malaysia and Singapore). The response is twofold. First, given that the government (or its wholly-owned company) as the controlling shareholder of the SOEs can already be sued under the existing law, giving innocent tort victims the right to bring a claim against the government as the controller is consistent with the existing law. It does not give the innocent tort victims any preferential treatment. But what is special is that my proposed legislation deprives the government as the controller of the protection of limited liability where the SOEs or any of their subsidiaries have committed tortious acts against innocent third parties and are unable to compensate them. And, as I have argued, as a matter of policy, the government as the controller should not enjoy limited liability in this situation. Second, there is likely to be opposition if strict liability is imposed on the government (or its wholly-owned companies), but my approach is a fault-based liability. It may be said that it will be difficult for the claimant to prove that the government as the controller has failed to take reasonable care. This concern can be addressed by reversing the burden of proof, that is, once the claimants have shown that the SOE or its subsidiary has caused harm to them, the controlling shareholder, ie the government (or its wholly-owned company), as the defendant has the burden of proving that it has taken all reasonable care in identifying and preventing the harm to the claimants. In the worst-case scenario, should the government completely oppose the proposed fault-based legislation that subjects it to liability, the fallback position is to create a statutory liability regime under which, once the claimant can show that the delinquent subsidiary has caused harm to it, the parent company and not the government as the controlling shareholder is presumed to be liable unless it can prove beyond a reasonable doubt that it has exercised all reasonable care in identifying and preventing the harm.

---

[146] *TNB Fuel Services Sdn Bhd v China National Coal Group Corp* [2017] HKEC 1184.

B Liability in Networks

The three approaches discussed earlier (ie enterprise liability, liability on shareholders of the insolvent subsidiary, and liability on the government as the controlling shareholder) apply to traditional group structures, but a supplementary approach is needed to address the externalities caused by non-traditional structures consisting of networks.[147] In networks, the companies or parties will be connected not through ownership of shares or control rights over the board but, rather, through contracts. For example, a company that belongs to the traditional group structure can enter into a contract with another party (whether corporate or individual) to produce or supply certain goods or services, the prime example of which is a supply chain agreement. Although the parties to the contract are connected not through equity holdings but only through contractual rights and obligations, they may have common economic objectives; there may be economic interdependence between them; there may be integration of operations between them; or one party may exercise control over the other. Depending on the unity of objectives, the degree of interdependence and integration, or the degree of control, it can be argued that liability should be imposed on the company (that belongs to the traditional group structure) for the wrongdoing committed by the other contractual party (that is not a member of the corporate group to which the other party to the contract belongs). Alternatively, liability can be imposed on that contractual party.

There are four possible approaches for imposing liability for the harms caused by networks. The first is to impose a duty of care on the company to a third party for the activity of the contractor using ordinary, general principles of tort law, as mentioned by the court in *Vedanta*.[148] The second is to impose vicarious liability on the company for the torts committed by the other party to the contract. The third is to reform the existing doctrine of unlawful means conspiracy. And the final one is to subject the parent company to a statutory duty of vigilance.

Regarding vicarious liability, it has been argued that the existing doctrine provides a basis for extending the law.[149] The UK Supreme Court decision of *Various Claimants v Catholic Child Welfare Society*[150] permits vicarious liability to be imposed in contexts that are akin to that between an employer and an employee. Subsequent case law has extended the

---

[147] Witting, n 102 at 3–5, 39–46.
[148] *Vedanta*, n 73 para 50.
[149] Morgan, n 103.
[150] [2013] 2 AC 1.

reasoning to other types of relationship such as by imposing liability on bishops for the sexual misconduct of their priests.[151] There is judicial[152] and academic[153] support for the view that the vicarious liability doctrine should be extended to the context of corporate groups such that the parent company should be vicariously liable for the torts committed by the subsidiary's employees. Factors that are relevant for imposing liability include whether the parent company and its subsidiaries are likely to have integrated operations; the degree of control exercised by the parent over the subsidiary; whether the parent has better resources and expertise to monitor the risks and to bear the cost of doing business. It is suggested that the vicarious liability doctrine can be extended to cover networks. The relevant factors will include, but are not limited to, the degree of economic interdependence or functional connectedness between the parties as well as which party is in a better position (by virtue, for example, of its better resources or expertise) to bear the cost of monitoring, prevention and remediation associated with the business operations.

As for the doctrine of unlawful means conspiracy, it has the potential to be applied to the context of network companies because of three advantages: first, this doctrine does not require control by one entity over another but, rather, it would suffice if there is an agreement between the entities; second, under this doctrine, liability is imposed not only on the party who has caused the harm but also on those who have entered into an agreement with it and have taken actions to further the activity that has caused the harm; and, finally, this doctrine can be used to impose liability when the torts are committed by subsidiaries in different jurisdictions if the presence of an agreement can be shown.[154] However, there are two drawbacks to this doctrine: first, it requires an intention to injure; and second, it is only restricted to financial losses. Thus, it has been argued that this doctrine should be reformed such that 'each entity having substantial commercial relations with a company acting recklessly would be deemed to have agreed to the risky activity, and would become prima facie jointly liable with the risk-taking company when personal injury ensues'.[155]

The final approach is the French statutory duty of vigilance mentioned in Section III(B). Companies have to establish and implement a vigilance

---

[151] *E v English Province of Our Lady of Charity* [2013] QB 722.
[152] *Dairy Containers Ltd v NZI Bank Ltd* [1995] 2 NZLR 30.
[153] Morgan, n 103.
[154] Witting, n 102 at 381.
[155] Ibid at 381–2.

plan which includes measures to identify risks and prevent harms that arise not only from their operations but also from the operations of their subcontractors or suppliers with whom they have a commercial relationship, when such operations are derived from this relationship.[156] The benefit of this approach as compared to the first one (vicarious liability) is that there is no need to show any interdependency or connectedness between the parties; nor the degree of control exerted by one party over the other. The advantage that this duty of vigilance has over the existing rule on unlawful means conspiracy is that the latter need not be stretched beyond its doctrinal remit merely for the sake of imposing liability on networks. It seems neater and clearer to create a new statutory rule rather than tempering with an existing common law doctrine.

However, there is one issue that has to be clarified. It is unclear whether the French statutory duty of vigilance refers to the exercise of due diligence which usually means the process undertaken by companies to identify and manage risks; or whether the duty refers to a standard of conduct against which the degree of culpability has to be assessed.[157] On the former, it is merely a procedural requirement to conduct risk assessment. On the latter, the duty is an external standard used to determine the scope of responsibility such that should reasonable care be taken, there is no breach of the duty. In other words, the former is a duty to implement and maintain internal processes of investigation and control, whereas the latter means that the parties are liable for causing harm if it stems from a failure to act with reasonable care. This distinction between these two interpretations of the duty of vigilance is important because if the former view is accepted, then it means that the company will not be liable if it has implemented risk assessment and management procedures. But if the latter view is the correct one, then the company will be treated as being legally responsible for the tortious harms that it has caused to third parties unless it can demonstrate that it exercised reasonable care. It is suggested that if the four Asian jurisdictions were to adopt the French duty of vigilance, they should make it clear that the duty encompasses both the former and the latter view. It would be remarkable if network

---

[156] Art. L. 225–102-4 of the French Commercial Code (see French Corporate Duty of Vigilance Law (English Translation)) www.respect.international/french-corporate-duty-of-vigilance-law-english-translation/.

[157] Jonathan Bonnitcha and Robert McCorquodale, 'The Concept of "Due Diligence" in the UN Guiding Principles on Business and Human Rights' (2017) 28 *European Journal of International Law* 899.

companies were required merely to set up systems or processes for monitoring and preventing risks related to their business operations.

Given that my proposed approach addresses only the harms caused by concentrated ownership companies in the four Asian jurisdictions, it is necessary to supplement it with another approach that addresses the harms caused by networks, namely, companies that are connected not through shareholdings but through contracts. It is suggested that liability should be imposed on networks using the existing principles of duty of care under tort law, the vicarious liability doctrine or an approach that is similar to the French statutory duty of vigilance.

When a company has committed a tortious act against innocent victims, not only will it be liable pursuant to claims brought by the victims, but it may also be liable for breaching certain statutory provisions to which we now turn.

V Breach of Public Interest Legislations

In all the four common law Asian jurisdictions, there are public interest legislations pertaining to the environment,[158] employee health and safety,[159] as well as operations of factories[160] that stipulate that where the company has been convicted of an offence under the statute, the directors and officers will also be liable. The central rationale for holding the directors and officers liable is to promote effective deterrence. After all, sanctioning the company by imposing fines on it, or requiring it to take certain remedial actions or to cease and desist certain activities, while necessary, are insufficient. As a result, directors and officers may be subject to fines and/or imprisonment under the statute. Two important issues arise: the first concerns the burden of proof and the second, enforcement.

---

[158] See eg Singapore Environmental Protection and Management Act (Cap 94A); Malaysian Environment Quality Act 1974 (Act 127); Indian Environment (Protection) Act 1986 (No 29 of 1986); Hong Kong Air Pollution Control Ordinance (Cap 311); Hong Kong Waste Disposal Ordinance (Cap 354); Hong Kong Water Pollution Control Ordinance (Cap.358).

[159] See eg Hong Kong Occupational Safety and Health Ordinance (Cap 509); Malaysian Occupational Safety and Health Act 1994 (Act 514); Singapore Workplace Safety and Health Act (Cap 354A); The Building and Other Construction Workers (Regulation of Employment and Conditions of Service) Act 1996 (No 27 of 1996).

[160] Indian Factories Act 1986 (No 63 of 1948); Hong Kong Factories and Industrial Undertakings Ordinance (Cap 59).

In some legislations, the authority bears the burden of proving that directors and officers are culpable. For example, s 47A(1) of the Hong Kong Air Pollution Control Ordinance provides that where the company is convicted of an offence under the statute, the directors and officers will also be guilty of the same offence if it is 'proved that the offence was committed with the consent or connivance of, or was attributable to any neglect or omission on the part of, that person'. Similarly, s 71 of Singapore's Environmental Protection and Management Act states that 'where an offence under this Act committed by a body corporate is proved (a) to have been committed with the consent or connivance of an officer; or (b) to be attributable to any act or default on his part, the officer as well as the body corporate shall be guilty of the offence . . .'.

However, in other legislations, there is a presumption that the directors and officers are liable once the authority has proven that the company has committed the offence, but the directors and officers are permitted to rebut the presumption by discharging the burden of proving that they are not culpable. The presumption of guilt coupled with the due diligence defence strikes a good balance between under- and over-deterrence. For example, s 43(1) of the Malaysian Environment Quality Act 1974 stipulates that where an offence has been committed by a company,

> any person who at the time of the commission of the offence was a director, manager, or other similar officer ... or was purporting to act in such capacity shall be deemed to be guilty of that offence unless he proves that the offence was committed without his consent or connivance and that he had exercised all such diligence as to prevent the commission of the offence as he ought to have exercised, having regard to the nature of his functions in that capacity and to all circumstances.

Another example is s 101 of the Indian Factories Act 1948 which provides that where an occupier (defined to include a director) or manager is charged with an offence, he will be exempted from liability if he proves (1) that he has used due diligence to enforce the execution of the statute; and (2) that the offence was committed without his knowledge, consent or connivance.

Imposing the burden of proof on the authority is less effective in deterring misconduct. To say the least, it is not easy for the authority to demonstrate that directors have connived, let alone consented to the commission of the offence. It is more likely that the offence committed by the company was attributable to the acts or omission of the directors and officers. But it is not easy to establish attribution because the authority has the burden of proving that there is a board resolution authorising the act, the director in question has acted with actual or apparent authority, or the director has breached his duties (specifically the duty of care, skill and diligence). It is suggested that as long as the board of a listed company has implemented effective internal systems of control and compliance taking into account all relevant circumstances, it would be difficult for the authority to prove that the offence committed by the company was attributable to the acts or omission of the director where the violations are committed by mid-level or low-level employees, unless a case can be made that the directors either have failed to monitor the actions of the relevant officers as required by the duty of care, skill and diligence or have placed unreasonable reliance on the conduct of the officers.[161]

Thus, to effectively promote deterrence, the burden of proof should be shifted to the defendant such that he is presumed to have committed the offence (once the company has been convicted) unless he can show that, first, the offence was committed without his consent or connivance and, second, he exercised due diligence to prevent the commission of the offence. A key question is what due diligence requires. It has been held that the defendants 'must establish that they exercised all reasonable care by establishing a proper system to prevent the commission of the offence and by taking all reasonable steps to ensure the effective operation of the system'.[162] Effective operation of the system includes, but is not limited to, ensuring that the officers address the concerns brought to them by government agencies or other concerned parties, and reviewing the reports provided by the officers. While directors can place reasonable reliance on those reports, they should be alert to any red flags and must raise and resolve any queries that have come, or that ought to have come, to their attention.

However, it is insufficient for promoting deterrence even if the burden of proof is shifted to the defendant. It is critical that attention is paid to enforcement. The effectiveness of public enforcement depends on both the inputs (such as the amount and quality of resources available to the authority to investigate and prosecute) and the outputs (the number and type of enforcement actions taken as well as the type and severity of

---

[161] These guidelines are drawn from *R v The Corporation of The City of Sault Ste Marie* [1978] 2 RCS 1299 (Canada Supreme Court); *R v Bata Industries Ltd* 1992 CanLII 7721.

[162] *R v The Corporation of The City of Sault Ste Marie* [1978] 2 RCS 1299; *Ministry of the Environment v Control Chem Canada Ltd* Unreported Judgment (15 March 2016), Court File No Burlington 13953701 (Ont Ct J).

sanctions imposed), while avoiding over-deterrence and under-deterrence.[163] For example, in Malaysia, the effectiveness of enforcement of environmental law has been called into question because of insufficient number of trained enforcement officers; lack of evidence in proving illegal dumping and logging due to the lack of witnesses; inadequate sanctions (ie compound summonses) being imposed; and the authority has not been doing enough to educate the relevant stakeholders about environmental protection.[164]

While there is evidence that the authorities have prosecuted companies for violating the public interest legislations, there is scant data with regard to the prosecution of directors and officers. For example, the Singapore Environmental Protection annual reports provide that there were 91 prosecutions in 2017,[165] 288 prosecutions in 2016[166] and 809 prosecutions in 2015,[167] all of which pertained to air, water and noise pollution. The data do not disclose whether any directors or officers were also prosecuted. It seems unlikely to be the case for three reasons. The Environmental Protection and Management Act imposes the burden of proof on the authority, not the defendant.[168] Second, because the prosecutions disclosed in the report are minor ones such as exceeding permissible noise limits, emission of dark smoke, discharge of trade effluent, there is less incentive from a deterrence viewpoint for the authority to prosecute officers, let alone directors. In other words, the time and resources that would be incurred in the investigation, prosecution and conviction of directors and officers would likely exceed the benefits. Finally, given that the offences are minor, there is a risk of over-deterrence if directors were to be prosecuted. Regarding the Workplace Safety and Health Act, under which the burden of proof is shifted to the defendant,[169] while officers, employers and proprietors have been

---

[163] John C Coffee, Jr, 'Law and the Market: The Impact of Enforcement' (2007) 156 *University of Pennsylvania Law Review* 229.

[164] Abdul Haseeb Ansari, 'Enforcement of Environmental Laws in Developing Countries: An Expository Study with Special Reference to Malaysia' [2007] 4 *Malayan Law Journal* liv.

[165] National Environment Agency Environmental Protection Division, Annual Report 2017 at 9, 16 and 76.

[166] National Environment Agency Environmental Protection Division, Annual Report 2016 at 10, 17 and 74–5.

[167] National Environment Agency Environmental Protection Division, Annual Report 2015 at 10, 18 and 101–2.

[168] S 71.

[169] S 48.

V BREACH OF PUBLIC INTEREST LEGISLATIONS

convicted and fined,[170] there appears to be no case law in which directors have been convicted.

In Hong Kong, pursuant to the Factories and Industrial Undertakings Ordinance (under which the burden of proof is on the authority), the regulator conducted 20 enforcement operations in 2017 in relation to workplace hazards or accident-prone workplaces, the result of which was that 1,367 prosecutions were initiated, but the data do not disclose whether directors or officers were prosecuted.[171] Regarding enforcement of environmental legislations, it was reported that there were 819 prosecutions in 2018.[172] And from 1999 to 2017, there were over fifty cases in which individuals were imprisoned, mostly under the Waste Disposal Ordinance, but the data do not disclose whether these individuals included any directors.[173] Although this particular statute imposes the burden of proof on the authority, a due diligence defence is available to the defendant such that 'if he proves that he took all reasonable precautions and exercised all due diligence to avoid the commission of the offence',[174] he will not be convicted. Given that there are a number of environment-related ordinances in Hong Kong, it is unclear why there are significantly more custodial sentences under the Waste Disposal Ordinance than under other statutes.

In each of the four common law Asian jurisdictions, there appears to be no case law showing that directors have been successfully convicted under the public interest legislations. But the absence of successful judicial proceedings, ie formal public enforcement, does not necessarily show that there has been under-deterrence provided that: there has been effective informal public enforcement such as publicised advice, warnings or reprimand (including cease and desist instructions and corrective actions) which have the potential of undermining the reputation of the company and directors, and hence providing credible deterrence. However, there appears to be no publicly disclosed information on the informal enforcement actions taken against directors and officers under the public interest legislation that provides the details of the sanctions, and the names of the directors and the companies. While there are a few cases of mid- or low-

---

[170] *Nurun Novi Saydur Rahman v Public Prosecutor* [2018] SGHC 236; *Public Prosecutor v Tay Kok Eng* [2012] SGDC 349; *Public Prosecutor v Lim Tze Fong* [2012] SGDC 96; *Public Prosecutor v Nurun Novi Saydur Rahman* [2017] SGDC 263.
[171] Hong Kong Labour Department, 2017 Annual Report www.labour.gov.hk/eng/public/iprd/2017/chapter4.html.
[172] Hong Kong, Environment Protection Department, Environmental Prosecution Statistics www.epd.gov.hk/epd/english/laws_regulations/enforcement/resource_enfor2.html.
[173] Ibid.
[174] Waste Disposal Ordinance (Cap 354), s 20G(1).

level ranking officers being convicted, the absence of publicly disclosed formal and informal enforcement actions against directors in the four Asian jurisdictions casts into doubt the effectiveness of enforcement of public interest legislations. To be clear, it is not necessarily a good thing to pursue formal enforcement actions against directors (ie convictions pursuant to judicial proceedings) because it can result in over-deterrence, among other concerns. But the seeming lack of publicly disclosed informal enforcement action against directors is not justified given that it could be an effective means of reducing future misconduct.

In short, while it is difficult to come to a definitive conclusion that there is under-deterrence with respect to prosecution of directors and officers under the public interest statutes, the available data suggest that prosecution is scarce and sporadic. This calls into question whether the existing enforcement measures, which are focused on the prosecution of companies, are adequate.

VI Conclusion

The central issue that this chapter seeks to address is this: when a subsidiary (or a company within a corporate group) has caused harm to a third party and is unable to provide compensation, whether and how an exception can be made to limited liability by requiring other companies or shareholders to provide redress to the innocent victim. This is an important question in any discussion on how corporate law should promote sustainability given that there have been numerous instances in which the business operations of companies have caused material and adverse impacts on the community and society. The existing law does not provide effective redress mechanisms for the victims of such wrongdoing. Reforms are long overdue. In addressing this question, it is important to pay attention to the concentrated ownership structure of the companies in the four Asian jurisdictions consisting of controlling shareholders, particularly the government. This chapter has critically evaluated the current and proposed redress mechanisms for victims of corporate wrongdoing including judicial piercing of the corporate veil, judicial imposition of duty of care on the parent company, statutory enterprise liability, statutory strict liability on the shareholders of the delinquent subsidiary, and liability on networks. It is recommended that a statutory fault-based liability regime (subject to a reverse burden of proof) should be created in the four Asian jurisdictions to allow claimants to seek redress from the controlling shareholder of the SOE for the

VI CONCLUSION

harms caused by the SOE or any of its subsidiaries, and in the case of family-owned companies, from the controlling shareholder of the parent company for the harms caused by the parent (or its subsidiaries). If imposing liability on the controlling shareholder (which is the government or its wholly-owned company) is opposed by the state itself, the proposed alternative is to create a statutory regime such that only the parent company is presumed to be liable unless it can discharge the burden of proving beyond a reasonable doubt that it has taken all reasonable care in identifying and preventing the harm. In other words, if the state is not willing to impose liability on itself as the controlling shareholder, then it should at the very least impose liability on the parent company.

However, having an effective redress mechanism for claimants is necessary but insufficient in deterring misconduct and promoting sustainability in the four common law Asian jurisdictions. It is important that the public interest legislations promote effective deterrence. It is suggested that the statutory provisions that impose on the authority the burden of proving guilt on the part of directors and officers should be reformed such that the latter will be presumed to be guilty (once the authority proves that the company is guilty) unless the directors and officers can discharge the burden of showing that they exercised all reasonable diligence. Further, the authorities in the four jurisdictions have to examine why there appears to be a lack of successful formal enforcement actions taken against directors and whether, going forward, prosecution and conviction of directors are warranted. Moreover, it is imperative that the authorities should actively pursue informal enforcement actions against directors by publicly disclosing the sanctions against them which can include warnings, reprimand and corrective actions. Finally, it is worth repeating that effective enforcement that avoids under- and over-deterrence depends not only on the frequency and type of enforcement actions taken and the sanctions imposed but also, crucially, on how well-resourced and well-qualified the authorities responsible for enforcement are.

8

Conclusion

This book seeks to contribute to three principal areas of research: (1) comparative sustainability/CSR; (2) comparative legal analysis of sustainability/CSR; and (3) company law and corporate governance, and sustainability/CSR.

Comparative sustainability/CSR. There are two dominant types of comparative research in this area.[1] The first is to compare companies' sustainability behaviour across different countries in relation to sustainability reporting and board gender diversity. The second is to compare the values and attitudes of stakeholders, particularly senior management and consumers, towards sustainability across different countries. The former has been termed behaviour-centred comparison and the latter, actor-centred comparison.

However, this book advances a third type of comparative research, what I call corporate mechanism-centred comparison. This research compares the corporate mechanisms that affect sustainability across different countries. This book is the first work to provide a critical and in-depth analysis of why and how the six corporate governance and corporate law mechanisms have been or can be used to promote sustainability in the four common law jurisdictions in Asia.

An important reason why there is little research on corporate mechanism-centred comparison as compared to behaviour-centred[2] and actor-

---

[1] Cynthia Williams and Ruth V Aguilera, 'Corporate Social Responsibility in a Comparative Perspective' in Andrew Crane, Dirk Matten, Abagail McWilliams, Jeremy Moon and Donald S Siegel (eds), *Oxford Handbook of Corporate Social Responsibility* (Oxford University Press 2008) at 459–67.

[2] See eg Ans Kolk, 'Sustainability, Accountability and Corporate Governance: Exploring Multinationals' Reporting Practices' (2008) 17 *Business Strategy and the Environment* 1; Petra Christmann and Glen Taylor, 'Firm Self-Regulation through International Certifiable Standards: Determinants of Symbolic versus Substantive Implementation' (2006) 37 *Journal of International Business Studies* 863.

centred[3] comparison is because these last two topics, which account for the bulk of the comparative sustainability/CSR literature, are undertaken by non-legal academics, specifically those in business, management and sociology.[4]

Comparative legal analysis of sustainability/CSR. It is widely accepted that law is one of the factors that has given rise to sustainability.[5] This claim is part of the well-established research into the drivers of sustainability, and it is well known that law together with consumer demands, institutional shareholder activism, senior management leadership and NGO pressure are some of the key reasons why sustainability exists and why sustainability varies among different countries.

However, although there is literature on the role of public international law, anti-corruption law, trade law and human rights law in supporting or undermining sustainability in different countries,[6] less has been written about the role of comparative corporate law and governance, particularly in relation to common law Asia.[7] Thus, this book advances the research on the legal analysis of sustainability by providing a framework, namely, the identification and evaluation of the role played by six key corporate governance and corporate law mechanisms in relation to sustainability.

---

[3] See eg Isabelle Maignan and David A Ralston, 'Corporate Social Responsibility in Europe and the U.S.: Insights from Businesses' Self-Presentations' (2002) 33 *Journal of International Business Studies* 497; David A Waldman et al, 'Cultural and Leadership Predictors of Corporate Social Responsibility Values of Top Management: A GLOBE Study of 15 Countries' (2006) 37 *Journal of International Business Studies* 823; Dara O'Rourke, 'Market Movements: Nongovernmental Organization Strategies to Influence Global Production and Consumption' (2005) 9 *Journal of Industry Ecology* 1; Robert V Kozinets and Jay M Handelman, 'Adversaries of Consumption: Consumer Movements, Activism, and Ideology' (2004) 31 *Journal of Consumer Research* 691.

[4] See, generally, Kiyoteru Tsutsui and Alwyn Lim (eds), *Corporate Social Responsibility in a Globalizing World* (Cambridge University Press 2015); Andreas Rasche, Mette Morsing and Jeremy Moon (eds), *Corporate Social Responsibility: Strategy, Communication, Governance* (Cambridge University Press 2017); Anders Örtenblad (ed), *Research Handbook on Corporate Social Responsibility in Context* (Edward Elgar 2016).

[5] See eg Doreen McBarnet, Aurora Voiculescu and Tom Campbell (eds), *The New Corporate Accountability: Corporate Social Responsibility and the Law* (Cambridge University Press 2007).

[6] See eg Jennifer A Zerk, *Multinationals and Corporate Social Responsibility: Limitations and Opportunities in International Law* (Cambridge University Press 2011); Adefolake O Adeyeye, *Corporate Social Responsibility of Multinational Corporations in Developing Countries: Perspectives on Anti-Corruption* (Cambridge University Press 2012); Phillip Paiement, *Transnational Sustainability Laws* (Cambridge University Press 2017).

[7] One notable exception is Beate Sjåfjell and Benjamin J Richardson (eds), *Company Law and Sustainability* (Cambridge University Press 2015).

This framework, which consists of corporate governance mechanisms (ie sustainability reporting, board gender diversity, constituency directors and stewardship codes) and corporate law mechanisms (ie directors' best interest duty, and liability on companies, shareholders and directors), can be used as a starting point to analyse other jurisdictions.[8]

Corporate law and corporate governance, and sustainability/CSR. This book contributes to the scant literature in this area in two distinct aspects. First, it engages in a critical and comprehensive analysis of the relevant corporate mechanisms. In doing so, it shows the importance of integrated and holistic analysis that is absent in the existing literature. For instance, the legal literature usually focuses on one or two developments (usually sustainability reporting, SRIs or directors' duties).[9] And the non-legal literature on CSR in Asia is predominantly about voluntary CSR reporting.[10]

Second, and crucially, this book underscores the significance of the role that controlling shareholders, particularly the government in SOEs, play in promoting or thwarting sustainability in common law jurisdictions, an issue to which little attention has been given in the literature on comparative corporate law and sustainability/CSR. This is unsurprising because the literature on sustainability/CSR in common law jurisdictions is centred on the United States and the UK, both of which are dispersed-ownership jurisdictions and not concentrated ownership jurisdictions, unlike those in common law Asia. Thus, the literature is usually not concerned with the problems of conflicts of interest involving controlling shareholders, political interference by the government in the SOEs, and lack of accountability and transparency in these companies, let alone the relationship between these problems and sustainability issues.

---

[8] Reinier Kraakman, John Armour, Paul Davies et al, *The Anatomy of Corporate Law: A Comparative and Functional Approach* (3rd edn, Oxford University Press 2017) at 92–100.

[9] See eg Jean J du Plessis, Umakanth Varottil and Jeroen Veldman (eds), *Globalisation of Corporate Social Responsibility and Its Impact on Corporate Governance* (Springer 2018); Tineke Elisabeth Lambooij, *Corporate Social Responsibility: Legal and Semi-Legal Frameworks Supporting CSR* (Kluwer 2010); Cynthia A Williams, 'Corporate Social Responsibility and Corporate Governance' in Jeffrey N Gordon and Wolf-Georg Ringe (eds), *The Oxford Handbook of Corporate Law and Governance* (Oxford University Press 2018) at ch 24.

[10] See eg Wendy Chapple and Jeremy Moon, 'Corporate Social Responsibility in Asia: A Seven Country Study of CSR Web Site Reporting' (2005) 44 *Business and Society* 415; Wendy Chapple, Christian Herzig and Rieneke Slager, 'The Dynamics of Corporate Social Responsibility in Asia: A 6 Country Study (Paper 16813)', The Academy of Management Annual Conference, Philadelphia, PA (2014).

Further, as discussed in Chapter 1, the literature on sustainability compares common law jurisdictions (exemplified by the United States and the UK) and civil law jurisdictions (in Europe), and investigates the question of whether legal origins have an impact on sustainability, concluding that civil law jurisdictions are more conducive for promoting sustainability; this is because the laws and practices in those jurisdictions are more stakeholder friendly, as compared to those in shareholder primacy jurisdictions in the UK and the United States where the shareholder-centric or friendly laws are not aligned with stakeholders' interests.

However, as I have shown, the legal origins theory does not explain the situation in common law Asia. All four Asian jurisdictions (Singapore, Malaysia, India and Hong Kong) are common law based and have corporate laws based on or derived from UK law, and yet they have pro-stakeholder practices. As I discussed in Chapter 1, a key reason is that the government as both controlling shareholder and regulator has used SOEs to advance social and economic goals. Another reason is the need for SOEs to be perceived as legitimate. A further reason lies in external economic, financial and social forces such as the rise of SRIs, competition among stock exchanges and the increased internationalisation of companies. Thus, the fact that shareholders in the four common law jurisdictions in Asia wield significant and substantial governance rights such as those in the UK is not necessarily inconsistent with stakeholder welfare. However, as I have also demonstrated, controlling shareholders can interfere in the management of the company, can extract private benefits of control, and do suffer from conflicts of interest, all of which can harm the interests of stakeholders and jeopardise the promotion of sustainability. In short, the four Asian jurisdictions, which are based on common law like the UK and the United States but which have more stakeholder-friendly practices than those in the Anglo-American jurisdictions albeit fewer than those in continental Europe, present an interesting and complex case study.

To conclude, in thinking about how regulation can be used to promote sustainability in concentrated ownership companies – which account for the vast majority of firms in the world, and which are projected to increase globally,[11] of which SOEs are major economic, social and political players[12] – a key question is how the positive effects of SOEs can be harnessed while the self-serving behaviour of their controlling shareholder is constrained. An assessment of this issue would require us to consider

---

[11] OECD, Corporate Governance Factbook 2019 at 17 (OECD Publishing 2019).
[12] See eg OECD, *The Size and Sectoral Distribution of State-Owned Enterprises* (OECD Publishing 2014).

a related but important question of how to mitigate potential opposition from the government as the controlling shareholder towards proposed legal reforms that attempt to curb its powers or to address conflicts of interest. This book takes into account these issues in its evaluation of the six corporate mechanisms. In doing so, it demonstrates that analysis of the laws and practices related to the promotion of sustainability has to be sensitive to the ownership structure of companies, the role of the state, conflicts of interest between different constituencies in different situations, and the institutional contexts in which companies operate.

APPENDIX 1

External Assurance

A1.1 Singapore

No	Company name	Code	Mkt. cap. (in S$ mm)	Government linked?	Assurance from audit firm?	Audit firm	Limited scope?
1	PRUDENTIAL PLC	K6S	73,403.80	No	No report		
2	DBS GROUP HOLDINGS LTD	D05	67,919.90	Yes	Yes	PwC	Yes
3	JARDINE MATHESON HOLDINGS LIMITED	J36	67,199.50	No	No report		
4	SINGAPORE TELECOMMUNICATIONS LIMITED	Z74	52,392.20	Yes	Yes	EY	Yes
5	OVERSEA-CHINESE BANKING CORPORATION LIMITED	O39	47,528	No	No		
6	UNITED OVERSEAS BANK LIMITED	U11	44,549.80	No	No		
7	JARDINE STRATEGIC HOLDINGS LIMITED	J37	30,180.80	No	No report		
8	HONGKONG LAND HOLDINGS LIMITED	H78	23,035.90	No	No		
9	WILMAR INTERNATIONAL LIMITED	F34	19,802	No	Yes	EY	Yes
10	THAI BEVERAGE PUBLIC COMPANY LIMITED	Y92	19,586.80	No	Yes	LRQA	Yes
11	DAIRY FARM INTERNATIONAL HOLDINGS LIMITED	D01	16,235.20	No	No report		
12	GENTING SINGAPORE LIMITED	G13	15,176.70	No	No		
13	JARDINE CYCLE & CARRIAGE LIMITED	C07	13,817.50	No	No		
14	CAPITALAND LIMITED	C31	13,141.20	Yes	Yes	Ere-S	Yes

#	Name	Code	Value			Auditor	
15	GREAT EASTERN HOLDINGS LIMITED	G07	13,129.90	No	No		
16	KEPPEL CORPORATION LIMITED	BN4	12,270.00	Yes	Yes	DNV-GL	Yes
17	SINGAPORE AIRLINES LIMITED	C6 L	11,445.30	Yes	No		
18	SINGAPORE TECHNOLOGIES ENGINEERING LTD	S63	10,483.60	Yes	No		
19	CITY DEVELOPMENTS LIMITED	C09	8,874.80	No	Yes	EY	Yes
20	ASCENDAS REAL ESTATE INVESTMENT TRUST	A17 U	8,088.00	No	No		
21	SINGAPORE EXCHANGE LIMITED	S68	7,897.40	No	No		
22	CAPITALAND MALL TRUST	C38 U	7,593.80	Yes	No		
23	OLAM INTERNATIONAL LIMITED	O32	7,100.40	Yes	No		
24	CAPITALAND COMMERCIAL TRUST	C61 U	6,437.40	Yes	No		
25	UOL GROUP LIMITED	U14	5,931.60	No	Yes	KPMG	Yes
26	SATS LTD.	S58	5,785.60	Yes	No		
27	COMFORTDELGRO CORPORATION LIMITED	C52	5,002.10	No	No		
28	SUNTEC REAL ESTATE INVESTMENT TRUST	T82 U	4,988.20	No	No		
29	FRASERS PROPERTY LIMITED	TQ5	4,950.40	No	No		
30	VENTURE CORPORATION LIMITED	V03	4,838.00	No	No		
31	SEMBCORP INDUSTRIES LTD	U96	4,681.60	Yes	Yes	PwC	Yes
32	MAPLETREE COMMERCIAL TRUST	N2IU	4,646.10	Yes	No		
33	SINGAPORE PRESS HOLDINGS LIMITED	T39	4,569.60	No	No		
34	UNITED INDUSTRIAL CORPORATION LIMITED	U06	4,512.50	No	No		
35	MAPLETREE LOGISTICS TRUST	M44 U	4,086.80	Yes	No		
36	KEPPEL REIT	K71 U	4,056.90	Yes	No		
37	MANDARIN ORIENTAL INTERNATIONAL LIMITED	M04	3,965.40	No	No		

(cont.)

No	Company name	Code	Mkt. cap. (in S$ mm)	Government linked?	Assurance from audit firm?	Audit firm	Limited scope?
38	MAPLETREE INDUSTRIAL TRUST	ME8 U	3,733.50	Yes	No		
39	YANGZIJIANG SHIPBUILDING (HOLDINGS) LTD.	BS6	3,649.80	No	No Report		
40	MAPLETREE NORTH ASIA COMMERCIAL TRUST	RW0 U	3,617.90	Yes	No		
41	GOLDEN AGRI-RESOURCES LTD	E5 H	3,565.70	No	Yes	EY	Yes
42	SIA ENGINEERING COMPANY LIMITED	S59	3,413.30	Yes	No		
43	FORTUNE REIT	F25 U	3,238.70	No	No Report		
44	SINGAPORE POST LIMITED	S08	3,121.50	Yes	No		
45	HUTCHISON PORT HOLDINGS TRUST	NS8 U	3,036.60	No	No		
46	NETLINK NBN TRUST	CJLU	3,020.20	Yes	No		
47	HAW PAR CORPORATION LIMITED	H02	2,994.30	No	No		
48	FRASER AND NEAVE, LIMITED	F99	2,983.10	No	No		
49	STARHUB LTD	CC3	2,959.50	Yes	Yes	KPMG	Yes
50	YANLORD LAND GROUP LIMITED	Z25	2,839.40	No	No		

Source: SGX website: www.sgx.com/wps/portal/sgxweb/home/company_disclosure/stockfacts (accessed 1 August 2018)

A1.2 Malaysia

No	Company name	Code	Mkt. cap. (in RM)	Government linked?	Basis of report	Assurance from audit firm?	Audit firm	Limited scope?
1	MALAYAN BANKING BHD	1155	107.591B	Yes	GRI-G4	Yes	Sirim Qas	No
2	PUBLIC BANK BHD	1295	93.792B	No	Bursa Listing Req	No		
3	TENAGA NASIONAL BHD	5347	87.558B	Yes	GRI-G4	No		
4	PETRONAS CHEMICALS GROUP BHD	5183	72.24B	Yes	Bursa Listing Req	No		
5	CIMB GROUP HOLDINGS BERHAD	1023	54.228B	Yes	GRI-G4	No		
6	IHH HEALTHCARE BERHAD	5225	48.644B	Yes	GRI-G4	No		
7	MAXIS BERHAD	6012	44.398B	No	Bursa Listing Req	No		
8	HONG LEONG BANK BHD	5819	41.447B	No	GRI-G4	Yes	Sirim Qas	No
9	AXIATA GROUP BERHAD	6888	39.181B	Yes	GRI-G4	Yes	Deloitte	Yes
10	PETRONAS GAS BHD	6033	37.754B	Yes	Bursa Listing Req	No		
11	SIME DARBY PLANTATION BERHAD	5285	35.772B	Yes	GRI-G4	No		
12	DIGI.COM BHD	6947	35.61B	No	Bursa Listing Req	Yes	KPMG	No
13	NESTLE (M) BHD	4707	34.542B	No	GRI-G4	Yes	PwC	Yes
14	GENTING BHD	3182	33.565B	No	GRI-G4	No		
15	GENTING MALAYSIA BERHAD	4715	30.225B	No	GRI-G4	No		
16	MISC BHD	3816	29.015B	Yes	GRI-G4	No		
17	IOI CORPORATION BHD	1961	28.783B	No	GRI-G4	No		
18	PETRONAS DAGANGAN BHD	5681	26.625B	Yes	GRI-G4	No		
19	KUALA LUMPUR KEPONG BHD	2445	26.346B	No	GRI-G4	No		
20	HAP SENG CONSOLIDATED BHD	3034	24.349B	No	Bursa Listing Req	No		
21	PPB GROUP BHD	4065	23.53B	No	GRI-G4	No		

(cont.)

No	Company name	Code	Mkt. cap. (in RM)	Government linked?	Basis of report	Assurance from audit firm?	Audit firm	Limited scope?
22	RHB BANK BERHAD	1066	21.855B	Yes	GRI-G4	No		
23	HONG LEONG FINANCIAL GROUP BHD	1082	20.816B	No	Bursa Listing Req	No		
24	HARTALEGA HOLDINGS BHD	5168	20.396B	No	Bursa Listing Req	No		
25	DIALOG GROUP BHD	7277	19.069B	Yes	Bursa Listing Req	No		
26	PRESS METAL ALUMINIUM HOLDINGS BERHAD	8869	18.184B	No	Bursa Listing Req	No		
27	SIME DARBY BHD	4197	17.342B	Yes	Bursa Listing Req	Yes	PwC	Yes
28	MALAYSIA AIRPORTS HOLDINGS BHD	5014	16.26B	Yes	GRI-G4	Yes	Sirim Qas	No
29	YTL CORPORATION BHD	4677	14.729B	No	GRI-G4	No		
30	TELEKOM MALAYSIA BHD	4863	13.829B	Yes	GRI-G4	Yes	Sirim Qas	No
31	FRASER & NEAVE HOLDINGS BHD	3689	13.769B	No	GRI-G4	No		
32	TOP GLOVE CORPORATION BHD	7113	12.802B	No	Bursa Listing Req	No		
33	WESTPORTS HOLDINGS BERHAD	5246	12.788B	No	GRI-G4	No		
34	AMMB HOLDINGS BHD	1015	12.057B	No	GRI-G4	No		
35	LOTTE CHEMICAL TITAN HOLDING BERHAD	5284	11.885B	No	Bursa Listing Req	No		
36	AIRASIA GROUP BERHAD	5099	11.663B	No	GRI-G4	No		

37	SP SETIA BHD	8664	11.586B	Yes		Bursa Listing Req	No
38	YTL POWER INTERNATIONAL BHD	6742	10.116B	No		GRI-G4	No
39	IOI PROPERTIES GROUP BERHAD	5249	9.911B	No		GRI-G4	No
40	QL RESOURCES BHD	7084	9.718B	No		Bursa Listing Req	No
41	BRITISH AMERICAN TOBACCO (M)	4162	9.708B	No	EY	GRI-G4	Yes
42	ASTRO MALAYSIA HOLDINGS BERHAD	6399	9.594B	Yes		GRI-G4	No
43	GAMUDA BHD	5398	9.576B	No		GRI-G4	No
44	SIME DARBY PROPERTY BERHAD	5288	9.181B	Yes	PwC	Bursa Listing Req	Yes
45	SUNWAY BERHAD	5211	7.774B	No		GRI-G4	No
46	GENTING PLANTATIONS BERHAD	2291	7.64B	No		GRI-G4	No
47	INARI AMERTRON BERHAD	0166	7.576B	No		Bursa Listing Req	No
48	BATU KAWAN BHD	1899	7.568B	No		Bursa Listing Req	No
49	UMW HOLDINGS BHD	4588	6.986B	Yes		GRI-G4	No
50	IJM CORPORATION BHD	3336	6.981B	No		GRI-G4	No

Source: Tradingview website: www.tradingview.com/markets/stocks-malaysia/market-movers-large-cap/ (accessed 1 August 2018)

A1.3 Hong Kong

No	Company name	Code	Mkt. cap. (in HK$)	SOE?	Assurance from audit firm?	Audit firm	Qualification of assurance?
1	TENCENT	700	3,342.30B	No	No		
2	CCB	939	1,670.90B	Yes	Yes	PwC	No
3	HSBC HOLDINGS	5	1,465.59B	No	No		
4	CHINA MOBILE	941	1,413.83B	Yes	Yes	EY	Yes
5	AIA	1299	802.46B	No	Yes	PwC	Yes
6	CNOOC	883	553.62B	Yes	No		
7	PING AN	2318	519.46B	No	Yes	Deloitte	No
8	ICBC	1398	496.46B	Yes	Yes	KPMG	No
9	PRU	2378	464.46B	No	Yes	LRQA	Yes
10	BOC HONG KONG	2388	389.60B	Yes	No		
11	HANG SENG BANK	11	388.48B	No	Yes	HKQAA	No
12	XIAOMI-W	1810	384.27B	No	No report		
13	SHK PPT	16	344.18B	No	Yes	British Standards Institution	Yes
14	CKH HOLDINGS	1	324.43B	No	No		
15	CITIC	267	314.75B	Yes	No		
16	BANK OF CHINA	3988	301.04B	Yes	Yes	EY	Yes
17	SANDS CHINA LTD	1928	300.58B	No	No		
18	CHINA UNICOM	762	290.07B	Yes	No		
19	MANULIFE-S	945	283.52B	No	No		
20	HKEX	388	278.27B	No	Yes	HKQAA	Yes

					Report in Chinese		
21	EVERGRANDE	3333	272.51B	No	Yes		
22	MTR CORPORATION	66	259.09B	No	No	Deloitte	Yes
23	CHINA OVERSEAS	688	258.01B	Yes	No		
24	GALAXY ENT	27	246.84B	No	No		
25	HK & CHINA GAS	3	240.64B	No	Yes	HKQAA	No
26	COUNTRY GARDEN	2007	239.00B	No	No		
27	STANCHART	2888	228.82B	No	Yes	The Carbon Trust	Yes
28	CLP HOLDINGS	2	221.69B	No	Yes	PwC	Yes
29	CK ASSET	1113	214.82B	No	No		
30	BANKCOMM	3328	193.61B	Yes	Yes	PwC	Yes
31	CHINA RES LAND	1109	186.78B	Yes	No		
32	SINOPEC CORP	386	186.75B	Yes	No		
33	HENDERSON LAND	12	183.31B	No	No		
34	SWIREPROPERTIES	1972	173.45B	No	Yes	PwC	Yes
35	WHARF REIC	1997	170.63B	No	No		
36	HANERGY TFP	566	164.78B	No	No		
37	CHINA GAS HOLD	384	157.12B	No	No		
38	CKI HOLDINGS	1038	153.07B	No	No		
39	GEELY AUTO	175	149.39B	No	No		
40	CHINA LIFE	2628	140.78B	Yes	No		
41	SHENZHOU INTL	2313	137.92B	No	No		
42	CM BANK	3968	134.97B	Yes	Yes	PwC	Yes
43	SUNNY OPTICAL	2382	133.06B	No	No		
44	SINO BIOPHARM	1177	129.91B	No	No		

(cont.)

No	Company name	Code	Mkt. cap. (in HK$)	SOE?	Assurance from audit firm?	Audit firm	Qualification of assurance?
45	CSPC PHARMA	1093	123.23B	No	No		
46	LONGFOR GROUP	960	122.16B	No	no		
47	PETROCHINA	857	119.84B	Yes	No		
48	POWER ASSETS	6	117.70B	No	No		
49	FOSUN INTL	656	116.08B	No	No		
50	AAC TECH	2018	115.84B	No	Yes	HKQAA	No

Source: HKEX website: www.hkex.com.hk/Market-Data/Securities-Prices/Equities?sc_lang=en (accessed 1 August 2018)

A1.4 India

No	Company name	Code	Mkt. cap. (in cr.)	Government linked?	Basis of report	Assurance from audit firm?	Audit firm	Limited scope?
1	TATA CONSULTANCY SERVICES LTD	532540	757,043.31	No	SEBI	No		
2	RELIANCE INDUSTRIES LTD	500325	745,782.95	No	GRI G4	Yes	KPMG	No
3	HDFC BANK LTD	500180	560,634.32	No	SEBI	No		
4	HINDUSTAN UNILEVER LTD	500696	380,856.49	No	SEBI	No		
5	ITC LTD	500875	371,153.10	No	SEBI	No		
6	HOUSING DEVELOPMENT FINANCE CORP LTD	500010	333,714.86	No	SEBI	No		
7	INFOSYS LTD	500209	297,936.80	No	SEBI	Yes	DNV GL	Yes
8	MARUTI SUZUKI INDIA LTD	532500	277,561.73	No	GRI G4	Yes	DNV GL	Yes
9	STATE BANK OF INDIA	500112	266,488.18	Yes	GRI G4	No		
10	KOTAK MAHINDRA BANK LTD	500247	249,575.74	No	SEBI	No		
11	OIL AND NATURAL GAS CORPORATION LTD	500312	214,058.36	Yes	SEBI	No		
12	ICICI BANK LTD	532174	196,060.40	No	SEBI	No		
13	LARSEN & TOUBRO LTD	500510	181,027.10	No	SEBI	No		
14	COAL INDIA LTD	533278	172,876.35	Yes	GRI G4	Yes	SR Asia	No
15	INDIAN OIL CORPORATION LTD	530965	163,789.67	Yes	SEBI	No		

(cont.)

No	Company name	Code	Mkt. cap. (in cr.)	Government linked?	Basis of report	Assurance from audit firm?	Audit firm	Limited scope?
16	BAJAJ FINANCE LIMITED	500034	154,887.97	No	SEBI	No		
17	BHARTI AIRTEL LTD	532454	149,782.58	No	SEBI	Yes		
18	AXIS BANK LTD	532215	147,492.54	No	SEBI	No		
19	SUN PHARMACEUTICAL INDUSTRIES LTD	524715	140,321.03	No	SEBI	No		
20	ASIAN PAINTS LTD	500820	135,376.38	No	SEBI	No		
21	HCL TECHNOLOGIES LTD	532281	134,429.91	No	SEBI	No		
22	NTPC LTD	532555	129,000.29	Yes	SEBI	No		
23	WIPRO LTD	507685	125,835.54	No	GRI G4	Yes	DNV GL	Yes
24	INDUSIND BANK LTD	532187	121,049.02	No	SEBI	No		
25	HINDUSTAN ZINC LTD	500188	119,323.01	No	SEBI	No		
26	ULTRATECH CEMENT LTD	532538	114,664.6	No	SEBI	No		
27	MAHINDRA & MAHINDRA LTD	500520	114,323.99	No	SEBI	No		
28	BAJAJ FINSERV LTD	532978	110,299.01	No	SEBI	No		
29	AVENUE SUPERMARTS LTD	540376	102,889.69	No	SEBI	No		
30	NESTLE INDIA LTD	500790	994,36.42	No	SEBI	No		
31	POWER GRID CORPORATION OF INDIA LTD	532898	99,190.94	Yes	SEBI	No		
32	HDFC STANDARD LIFE INSURANCE COMPANY LTD	540777	98,271.24	No	SEBI	No		

#	Company	Code	Market Cap					
33	GODREJ CONSUMER PRODUCTS LTD	532424	90,487.37	No		SEBI		No
34	GAIL (INDIA) LTD	532155	87,496.75	Yes		SEBI		No
35	BHARAT PETROLEUM CORPORATION LTD	500547	86,976.19	Yes		GRI G4	KPMG	Yes
36	YES BANK LTD	532648	85,899.64	No		SEBI		No
37	BANDHAN BANK LTD	541153	83,180.25	No		SEBI		No
38	ADANI PORTS AND SPECIAL ECONOMIC ZONE LTD	532921	82,786.3	No		GRI G4	BSI	No
39	VEDANTA LIMITED	500295	82,466.01	No		No report		No report
40	TITAN COMPANY LIMITED	500114	81,525.4	No		SEBI		No
41	JSW STEEL LTD	500228	81,327.38	No		GRI G4	Deloitte	Yes
42	BAJAJ AUTO LTD	532977	77,800.66	No		SEBI		No
43	DABUR INDIA LTD	500096	77,079.78	No		SEBI		No
44	BRITANNIA INDUSTRIES LTD	500825	76,781.43	No		SEBI		No
45	TATA MOTORS LTD	500570	74,710.15	No		SEBI		No
46	EICHER MOTORS LTD	505200	73,539.94	No		SEBI		No
47	SBI LIFE INSURANCE COMPANY LTD	540719	69,130.00	Yes		SEBI		No
48	GRASIM INDUSTRIES LTD	500300	66,283.89	No		SEBI		No
49	TECH MAHINDRA LTD	532755	64,929.91	No		SEBI		No
50	MOTHERSON SUMI SYSTEMS LTD	517334	64,881.27	No		SEBI		No

Source: BSE Website: www.bseindia.com/markets/equity/EQReports/TopMarketCapitalization.aspx?expandable=3 (accessed 1 August 2018)

APPENDIX 2

Top Fifty Listed Companies in Each of the Four Jurisdictions

A2.1 Singapore

No	Company name	Code	Mkt. cap. (in S$ mm)	Government linked?
1	PRUDENTIAL PLC	K6S	73,403.80	No
2	DBS GROUP HOLDINGS LTD	D05	67,919.90	Yes
3	JARDINE MATHESON HOLDINGS LIMITED	J36	67,199.50	No
4	SINGAPORE TELECOMMUNICATIONS LIMITED	Z74	52,392.20	Yes
5	OVERSEA-CHINESE BANKING CORPORATION LIMITED	O39	47,528.00	No
6	UNITED OVERSEAS BANK LIMITED	U11	44,549.80	No
7	JARDINE STRATEGIC HOLDINGS LIMITED	J37	30,180.80	No
8	HONGKONG LAND HOLDINGS LIMITED	H78	23,035.90	No
9	WILMAR INTERNATIONAL LIMITED	F34	19,802.00	No
10	THAI BEVERAGE PUBLIC COMPANY LIMITED	Y92	19,586.80	No
11	DAIRY FARM INTERNATIONAL HOLDINGS LIMITED	D01	16,235.20	No
12	GENTING SINGAPORE LIMITED	G13	15,176.70	No
13	JARDINE CYCLE & CARRIAGE LIMITED	C07	13,817.50	No
14	CAPITALAND LIMITED	C31	13,141.20	Yes
15	GREAT EASTERN HOLDINGS LIMITED	G07	13,129.90	No
16	KEPPEL CORPORATION LIMITED	BN4	12,270.00	Yes

(cont.)

No	Company name	Code	Mkt. cap. (in S$ mm)	Government linked?
17	SINGAPORE AIRLINES LIMITED	C6 L	11,445.30	Yes
18	SINGAPORE TECHNOLOGIES ENGINEERING LTD	S63	10,483.60	Yes
19	CITY DEVELOPMENTS LIMITED	C09	8,874.80	No
20	ASCENDAS REAL ESTATE INVESTMENT TRUST	A17 U	8,088.00	No
21	SINGAPORE EXCHANGE LIMITED	S68	7,897.40	No
22	CAPITALAND MALL TRUST	C38 U	7,593.80	Yes
23	OLAM INTERNATIONAL LIMITED	O32	7,100.40	Yes
24	CAPITALAND COMMERCIAL TRUST	C61 U	6,437.40	Yes
25	UOL GROUP LIMITED	U14	5,931.60	No
26	SATS LTD.	S58	5,785.60	Yes
27	COMFORTDELGRO CORPORATION LIMITED	C52	5,002.10	No
28	SUNTEC REAL ESTATE INVESTMENT TRUST	T82 U	4,988.20	No
29	FRASERS PROPERTY LIMITED	TQ5	4,950.40	No
30	VENTURE CORPORATION LIMITED	V03	4,838.00	No
31	SEMBCORP INDUSTRIES LTD	U96	4,681.60	Yes
32	MAPLETREE COMMERCIAL TRUST	N2IU	4,646.10	Yes
33	SINGAPORE PRESS HOLDINGS LIMITED	T39	4,569.60	No
34	UNITED INDUSTRIAL CORPORATION LIMITED	U06	4,512.50	No
35	MAPLETREE LOGISTICS TRUST	M44 U	4,086.80	Yes
36	KEPPEL REIT	K71 U	4,056.90	Yes
37	MANDARIN ORIENTAL INTERNATIONAL LIMITED	M04	3,965.40	No
38	MAPLETREE INDUSTRIAL TRUST	ME8 U	3,733.50	Yes
39	YANGZIJIANG SHIPBUILDING (HOLDINGS) LTD.	BS6	3,649.80	No
40	MAPLETREE NORTH ASIA COMMERCIAL TRUST	RW0 U	3,617.90	Yes
41	GOLDEN AGRI-RESOURCES LTD	E5 H	3,565.70	No
42	SIA ENGINEERING COMPANY LIMITED	S59	3,413.30	Yes
43	FORTUNE REIT	F25 U	3,238.70	No

(cont.)

No	Company name	Code	Mkt. cap. (in S$ mm)	Government linked?
44	SINGAPORE POST LIMITED	S08	3,121.50	Yes
45	HUTCHISON PORT HOLDINGS TRUST	NS8 U	3,036.60	No[1]
46	NETLINK NBN TRUST	CJLU	3,020.20	Yes[2]
47	HAW PAR CORPORATION LIMITED	H02	2,994.30	No
48	FRASER AND NEAVE, LIMITED	F99	2,983.10	No
49	STARHUB LTD	CC3	2,959.50	Yes
50	YANLORD LAND GROUP LIMITED	Z25	2,839.40	No

Source: SGX website: www.sgx.com/wps/portal/sgxweb/home/company_disclosure/stockfacts (accessed 1 August 2018)

A2.2 Malaysia

No	Company name	Code	Mkt. cap. (in RM)	Government linked?
1	MALAYAN BANKING BHD	1155	107.591B	Yes
2	PUBLIC BANK BHD	1295	93.792B	No
3	TENAGA NASIONAL BHD	5347	87.558B	Yes
4	PETRONAS CHEMICALS GROUP BHD	5183	72.240B	Yes
5	CIMB GROUP HOLDINGS BERHAD	1023	54.228B	Yes
6	IHH HEALTHCARE BERHAD	5225	48.644B	Yes
7	MAXIS BERHAD	6012	44.398B	No
8	HONG LEONG BANK BHD	5819	41.447B	No
9	AXIATA GROUP BERHAD	6888	39.181B	Yes
10	PETRONAS GAS BHD	6033	37.754B	Yes
11	SIME DARBY PLANTATION BERHAD	5285	35.772B	Yes
12	DIGI.COM BHD	6947	35.610B	No
13	NESTLE (M) BHD	4707	34.542B	No
14	GENTING BHD	3182	33.565B	No

[1] Temasek has 20 per cent shareholdings but CK Hutchinson has 80 per cent.
[2] (Tier 2) SingTel owns 24 per cent.

(*cont.*)

No	Company name	Code	Mkt. cap. (in RM)	Government linked?
15	GENTING MALAYSIA BERHAD	4715	30.225B	No
16	MISC BHD	3816	29.015B	Yes
17	IOI CORPORATION BHD	1961	28.783B	No
18	PETRONAS DAGANGAN BHD	5681	26.625B	Yes
19	KUALA LUMPUR KEPONG BHD	2445	26.346B	No
20	HAP SENG CONSOLIDATED BHD	3034	24.349B	No
21	PPB GROUP BHD	4065	23.530B	No
22	RHB BANK BERHAD	1066	21.855B	Yes
23	HONG LEONG FINANCIAL GROUP BHD	1082	20.816B	No
24	HARTALEGA HOLDINGS BHD	5168	20.396B	No
25	DIALOG GROUP BHD	7277	19.069B	Yes
26	PRESS METAL ALUMINIUM HOLDINGS BERHAD	8869	18.184B	No
27	SIME DARBY BHD	4197	17.342B	Yes
28	MALAYSIA AIRPORTS HOLDINGS BHD	5014	16.260B	Yes
29	YTL CORPORATION BHD	4677	14.729B	No
30	TELEKOM MALAYSIA BHD	4863	13.829B	Yes
31	FRASER & NEAVE HOLDINGS BHD	3689	13.769B	No
32	TOP GLOVE CORPORATION BHD	7113	12.802B	No
33	WESTPORTS HOLDINGS BERHAD	5246	12.788B	No
34	AMMB HOLDINGS BHD	1015	12.057B	No
35	LOTTE CHEMICAL TITAN HOLDING BERHAD	5284	11.885B	No
36	AIRASIA GROUP BERHAD	5099	11.663B	No
37	SP SETIA BHD	8664	11.586B	Yes
38	YTL POWER INTERNATIONAL BHD	6742	10.116B	No
39	IOI PROPERTIES GROUP BERHAD	5249	9.911B	No
40	QL RESOURCES BHD	7084	9.718B	No
41	BRITISH AMERICAN TOBACCO (M)	4162	9.708B	No
42	ASTRO MALAYSIA HOLDINGS BERHAD	6399	9.594B	Yes
43	GAMUDA BHD	5398	9.576B	No
44	SIME DARBY PROPERTY BERHAD	5288	9.181B	Yes
45	SUNWAY BERHAD	5211	7.774B	No

(cont.)

No	Company name	Code	Mkt. cap. (in RM)	Government linked?
46	GENTING PLANTATIONS BERHAD	2291	7.64B	No
47	INARI AMERTRON BERHAD	0166	7.576B	No
48	BATU KAWAN BHD	1899	7.568B	No
49	UMW HOLDINGS BHD	4588	6.986B	Yes
50	IJM CORPORATION BHD	3336	6.981B	No

Source: Tradingview website: www.tradingview.com/markets/stocks-malaysia/market-movers-large-cap/ (accessed 1 August 2018)

A2.3 Hong Kong

No	Company name	Code	Mkt. cap. (in HK$)	SOE?
1	TENCENT	700	3,342.30B	No
2	CCB	939	1,670.90B	Yes
3	HSBC HOLDINGS	5	1,465.59B	No
4	CHINA MOBILE	941	1,413.83B	Yes
5	AIA	1299	802.46B	No
6	CNOOC	883	553.62B	Yes
7	PING AN	2318	519.46B	No
8	ICBC	1398	496.46B	Yes
9	PRU	2378	464.46B	No
10	BOC HONG KONG	2388	389.60B	Yes
11	HANG SENG BANK	11	388.48B	No
12	XIAOMI-W	1810	384.27B	No
13	SHK PPT	16	344.18B	No
14	CKH HOLDINGS	1	324.43B	No
15	CITIC	267	314.75B	Yes
16	BANK OF CHINA	3988	301.04B	Yes
17	SANDS CHINA LTD	1928	300.58B	No
18	CHINA UNICOM	762	290.07B	Yes
19	MANULIFE-S	945	283.52B	No
20	HKEX	388	278.27B	No
21	EVERGRANDE	3333	272.51B	No
22	MTR CORPORATION	66	259.09B	No

(cont.)

No	Company name	Code	Mkt. cap. (in HK$)	SOE?
23	CHINA OVERSEAS	688	258.01B	Yes
24	GALAXY ENT	27	246.84B	No
25	HK & CHINA GAS	3	240.64B	No
26	COUNTRY GARDEN	2007	239.00B	No
27	STANCHART	2888	228.82B	No
28	CLP HOLDINGS	2	221.69B	No
29	CK ASSET	1113	214.82B	No
30	BANKCOMM	3328	193.61B	Yes
31	CHINA RES LAND	1109	186.78B	Yes
32	SINOPEC CORP	386	186.75B	Yes
33	HENDERSON LAND	12	183.31B	No
34	SWIREPROPERTIES	1972	173.45B	No
35	WHARF REIC	1997	170.63B	No
36	HANERGY TFP	566	164.78B	No
37	CHINA GAS HOLD	384	157.12B	No
38	CKI HOLDINGS	1038	153.07B	No
39	GEELY AUTO	175	149.39B	No
40	CHINA LIFE	2628	140.78B	Yes
41	SHENZHOU INTL	2313	137.92B	No
42	CM BANK	3968	134.97B	Yes
43	SUNNY OPTICAL	2382	133.06B	No
44	SINO BIOPHARM	1177	129.91B	No
45	CSPC PHARMA	1093	123.23B	No
46	LONGFOR GROUP	960	122.16B	No
47	PETROCHINA	857	119.84B	Yes
48	POWER ASSETS	6	117.70B	No
49	FOSUN INTL	656	116.08B	No
50	AAC TECH	2018	115.84B	No

Source: HKEX website: www.hkex.com.hk/Market-Data/Securities-Prices/Equities?sc_lang=en (accessed 1 August 2018)

A2.4 India

No	Company name	Code	Mkt. cap. (in cr.)	Government linked?
1	TATA CONSULTANCY SERVICES LTD	532540	757,043.31	No
2	RELIANCE INDUSTRIES LTD	500325	745,782.95	No
3	HDFC BANK LTD	500180	560,634.32	No
4	HINDUSTAN UNILEVER LTD	500696	380,856.49	No
5	ITC LTD	500875	371,153.10	No
6	HOUSING DEVELOPMENT FINANCE CORP LTD	500010	333,714.86	No
7	INFOSYS LTD	500209	297,936.80	No
8	MARUTI SUZUKI INDIA LTD	532500	277,561.73	No
9	STATE BANK OF INDIA	500112	266,488.18	Yes
10	KOTAK MAHINDRA BANK LTD	500247	249,575.74	No
11	OIL AND NATURAL GAS CORPORATION LTD	500312	214,058.36	Yes
12	ICICI BANK LTD	532174	196,060.40	No
13	LARSEN & TOUBRO LTD	500510	181,027.10	No
14	COAL INDIA LTD	533278	172,876.35	Yes
15	INDIAN OIL CORPORATION LTD	530965	163,789.67	Yes
16	BAJAJ FINANCE LIMITED	500034	154,887.97	No
17	BHARTI AIRTEL LTD	532454	149,782.58	No
18	AXIS BANK LTD	532215	147,492.54	No
19	SUN PHARMACEUTICAL INDUSTRIES LTD	524715	140,321.03	No
20	ASIAN PAINTS LTD	500820	135,376.38	No
21	HCL TECHNOLOGIES LTD	532281	134,429.91	No
22	NTPC LTD	532555	129,000.29	Yes
23	WIPRO LTD	507685	125,835.54	No
24	INDUSIND BANK LTD	532187	121,049.02	No
25	HINDUSTAN ZINC LTD	500188	119,323.01	No
26	ULTRATECH CEMENT LTD	532538	114,664.6	No
27	MAHINDRA & MAHINDRA LTD	500520	114,323.99	No
28	BAJAJ FINSERV LTD	532978	110,299.01	No
29	AVENUE SUPERMARTS LTD	540376	102,889.69	No
30	NESTLE INDIA LTD	500790	99,436.42	No
31	POWER GRID CORPORATION OF INDIA LTD	532898	99,190.94	Yes

(cont.)

No	Company name	Code	Mkt. cap. (in cr.)	Government linked?
32	HDFC STANDARD LIFE INSURANCE COMPANY LTD	540777	98,271.24	No
33	GODREJ CONSUMER PRODUCTS LTD	532424	90,487.37	No
34	GAIL (INDIA) LTD	532155	87,496.75	Yes
35	BHARAT PETROLEUM CORPORATION LTD	500547	86,976.19	Yes
36	YES BANK LTD	532648	85,899.64	No
37	BANDHAN BANK LTD	541153	83,180.25	No
38	ADANI PORTS AND SPECIAL ECONOMIC ZONE LTD	532921	82,786.30	No
39	VEDANTA LIMITED	500295	82,466.01	No
40	TITAN COMPANY LIMITED	500114	81,525.40	No
41	JSW STEEL LTD	500228	81,327.38	No
42	BAJAJ AUTO LTD	532977	77,800.66	No
43	DABUR INDIA LTD	500096	77,079.78	No
44	BRITANNIA INDUSTRIES LTD	500825	76,781.43	No
45	TATA MOTORS LTD	500570	74,710.15	No
46	EICHER MOTORS LTD	505200	73,539.94	No
47	SBI LIFE INSURANCE COMPANY LTD	540719	69,130.00	Yes
48	GRASIM INDUSTRIES LTD	500300	66,283.89	No
49	TECH MAHINDRA LTD	532755	64,929.91	No
50	MOTHERSON SUMI SYSTEMS LTD	517334	64,881.27	No

Source: BSE Website: www.bseindia.com/markets/equity/EQReports/TopMarketCapitalization.aspx?expandable=3 (accessed 1 August 2018)

APPENDIX 3

Qualitative Assessment of Sustainability Reports

Hong Kong

The companies are classified as follows:

Telecommunication and internet services	Energy, oil and gas	Investments	Manufacturing and consumer products	Property development and management	Pharmaceutical	Financial institutions
Tencent	CNOOC	CKH Holdings	Xiaomi	Sun Hung Kai Properties	Sino Biopharm	CCB
China Mobile	HK & China Gas	CITIC	Geely Auto	China Evergrande	CSPC Pharma	HSBC Holdings
China Unicom	Sinopec Corp	Fosun Intl	Shenzhou Intl	China Overseas		AIA
	Hanenergy TFP		Sunny Optical	Country Garden		Ping An
	China Gas Holdings		AAC Tech	MTR Corporation		ICBC
	Petrochina			CK Asset		Prudential
	CLP Holdings			China Res Land		BOC Hong Kong
	Power Assets			Henderson Land		Hang Seng Bank
				Swire Properties		Bank of China
				Wharf REIC		Manulife
				Longfor Group		HKEX
				Sands China Ltd		Standard Chartered
				Galaxy Ent		Bank of Communications
				CKI Holdings		China Life
						CM Bank

Ranking/Assessment of ESG Reports

Telecommunications and internet services

Rank	Name	Notes
1	China Mobile	China mobile stands out in that it has a standard way of presenting its information for all aspects that require disclosure: (1) 'Challenges and Priorities' gives context to the aspect; (2) 'Management Approach' highlights its qualitative policies and strategies; and (3) 'Progress in 2017' is for purposes of accountability and keeping shareholders up to date. All in all, it is a comprehensive and in-depth disclosure. Disclosure is also specific; environmental and social standards and certifications attained are disclosed. Further, each part comes with well-organised data sets with previous years for ease of reference. China Mobile laid out its 'Achievements in 2017' and 'Goals for 2018' in the beginning to aid shareholders in understanding its ESG efforts. Customer data and privacy issues are at the forefront of the investor's mind given the nature of the business. With its three-step approach, China Mobile's disclosure regarding its customer privacy and data protection policy is well presented and informative.
2	China Unicom	Good use of temporal (ie time frame) comparison throughout ESG. Goals for next year and achievements for the present year are laid out for each segment before delving into the specifics. Disclosure not as comprehensive or specific as China Mobile.
3	Tencent	Tencent's disclosure on its strategies and practices is specific enough for shareholders to have a good understanding and/or to do further research on its policies. The social aspects relating to employment, health and safety, and labour standards are poorly addressed, with only vague statements about how Tencent is in compliance with all applicable laws and regulations. There are no statistics presented on wages, age, gender, race, diversity, etc. Other than a brief and vague mention of Tencent's overall environment and social direction, the ESG report is lacking in terms of future plans and goals for shareholders to hold Tencent accountable to. It is also lacking in temporal data for comparison – there was no quantitative reporting of emissions data in the previous years for shareholders to compare Tencent's progress in this area.

Energy, oil and gas

Rank	Name	Notes
1	HK and China Gas	Specific and comprehensive exposition on policies adopted by the company for all relevant KPIs. There is a good focus on 'how' the policies are effected rather than just 'what' they are.
		Targets achieved and goals for the next year for each of the relevant segments of disclosure are disclosed. This is a good show of accountability which builds trust in investors.
		Data sets fulfil all KPI requirements, and where data are missing, sufficient explanation is given. Further, the data sets presented allow for extensive temporal comparison (2013–17).
2	CNOOC	Comprehensive exposition of the company's environmental policies (which is arguably the most important KPI for disclosure for companies in the energy, oil and gas industry) and projects undertaken (case studies) in fulfilment of such policies. Data include previous years for comparison.
		CNOOC's disclosure on safety measures is also comprehensive. Exposition on its safety culture, safety drills performed, safety steps taken during work gives a further insight into how operations at the oil plants are conducted. This is definitely an important aspect for investors to take note of where a company is involved with dangerous and volatile substances.
3	Sinopec Corp	Data relating to the production of hazardous and non-hazardous waste are missing from the ESG report. The explanations are inadequate.
		Exposition on policies relating to the KPIs is sufficiently comprehensive. Company touches on both the 'what' and the 'how' and uses relevant case studies to put disclosures in perspective.
4	Petrochina	Data relating to greenhouse gas produced and hazardous waste produced are lacking. Explanation is inadequate.
		Exposition on policies relating to the KPIs is sufficiently comprehensive. Company touches on both the 'what' and the 'how'.

(cont.)

Rank	Name	Notes
5	CLP Holdings	Overall, a vague and not very in-depth exposition on its policies relating to the disclosure KPIs.
6	Hanenergy TFP	Environmental data are missing without explanation. Even the policies disclosed merely state the fact of their compliance with laws and imposition of relevant (energy/resource/emissions savings/reductions) policies within the company; there is no exposition on how it was achieved.
		However, exposition on issues relating to employment, labour and training is significantly better. There is an in-depth review of case studies and how the company carries out its objectives.
7	China Gas	The majority of the environmental data are missing without explanation.
8	Power Assets Holdings	Environmental data are provided but poorly represented. A lot of percentage values are given but they do not provide much information about how the company is doing compared to its competitors. No temporal comparison is available.
		The company has not published any data relating to employment, labour, training, etc.
		Exposition on each KPI is brief. The company does not delve into the 'how' aspect of carrying out its policies. Case studies, when listed, are similarly brief and do not add value.
		Given that Power Assets operates in the energy industry, investors would expect that the company is in a position to provide a higher level of environmental disclosure. This is unfortunately not the case in the ESG.

APPENDIX 3

Investment

Rank	Name	Notes
1	Fosun Intl	Data sets for environmental disclosure are split between the different business arms. Data sets also allow for temporal comparison.
		Disclosure for different KPIs is in-depth and both the 'what' and the 'how' are addressed adequately across the different business arms.
		Policies and case studies are also split up and disclosed according to the various business arms, which allows investors to have a more nuanced view of the various working parts of the holding company.
2	CITIC	Data sets for environmental disclosure are not split between the different business arms and are lacking in temporal comparison.
		Data relating to employment and labour are not present in the ESG.
		However, disclosures are comprehensive and in-depth, with relevant case studies that add value to investors' review of the company's policies.
		Like Fosun Intl, policies and case studies are split up and disclosed according to the various business arms.
3	CKH Holdings	Qualitative disclosure is not in-depth. The disclosure for various KPIs touches only on the 'what', rather than the 'how'.
		Employment, labour and operational data sets are not available.
		Environmental data sets do not provide for temporal comparison.
		Given the vast amount of investments that CKH Holding possesses (port developer and operator, retail, energy, telecommunications, infrastructure), the general, broad disclosure on its 'Overall Business' does not help investors make informed decisions. It would be better if CKH were to address each of its specific business arms separately in its ESG report.
		However, CKH jumps back and forth between different business arms for different areas of disclosure. Overall, it is a confusing way of presenting information.

Manufacturing and consumer products

Rank	Name	Notes
1	AAC Tech	Comprehensive data sets are provided. Temporal comparisons are available.
		What sets this ESG report apart from the rest is the quality of its disclosure. For all of the relevant KPIs, AAC Tech's disclosure is specific as well as comprehensive. It addresses the 'what' and the 'how' – utilising relevant case studies to supplement its exposition on its policies.
		Disclosure on its supply management is done well, better than the rest of the companies in the industry. This disclosure is especially important for investors seeking to make decisions in the manufacturing industry.
2	Shenzhou Intl	Data sets provided go above and beyond the requirements of HKEX Appendix 27. Temporal comparisons are also available.
3	Geely Auto	Disclosure for KPIs is not comprehensive. There is a lot on the 'what' but not on the 'how'.
4	Sunny Optical	There is no temporal comparison of data.
		There is a lot on the 'what' but not on the 'how'.
5	Xiaomi	The IPO was only in July 2018, so no ESG report is available.

Property development and management

Rank	Name	Notes
1	MTR Corporation	Policies disclosed for all KPIs are specific and in-depth. The 'what' and 'how' aspects of the disclosures are well addressed. Case studies, where appropriate, add value to the disclosure.
		It has a 'Target and Performance' section under the safety disclosure and is comprehensive on the aspect of customer and occupational safety, which might be expected due to the nature of the company.
		Data sets disclosed have multiple years for temporal comparison and go above and beyond the requirements of HKEX Appendix 27.

(cont.)

Rank	Name	Notes
2	Swire Properties	Temporal comparisons are available for the data sets. The 2020 KPIs are identified and disclosed, along with the company's progress for 2017, for both the environmental and economic portions of the disclosure. Policies disclosed are specific as well as in-depth. The policies are generally elaborated upon and relevant case studies are also provided.
3	Sun Hung Kai Properties	Disclosure of policies relating to the KPIs is specific and in-depth. Data sets cover most of the KPIs and allow for temporal comparison.
4	Sands China	Qualitative information for environmental issues is specific and comes with case studies. Data sets are comprehensive and allow for temporal comparison. Employment, health and safety, and labour issues also have comprehensive data sets that hit all the KPIs; however, there is no temporal comparison. The company has set 2020 goals for itself for shareholders to hold it accountable.
5	China Overseas Holdings	Disclosure relating to development and training, and health and safety is specific but lacks depth – for example: (1) the company lists the names of all of its programmes, but fails to mention their content; and (2) it mentions the safety guide it formulated to provide employees with a safe and healthy work environment, but neglects to mention what guidelines it abides by. Disclosure relating to the environment is both specific and in-depth. Environmental data sets have multiple years for comparison. Data sets relating to employment, labour, training and development, and health and safety do not have temporal comparisons.
6	Henderson Land	KPI disclosures are both specific and in-depth. Case studies given are comprehensive and help investors to better understand the policies in place. Data sets for all KPIs are comprehensive, with temporal comparisons available.

(cont.)

Rank	Name	Notes
7	Country Garden	KPI disclosures are both specific and in-depth. However, case studies are not as well fleshed out.
		Data sets for KPIs are comprehensive with temporal comparisons available.
8	Longfor Group	KPI disclosures are both specific and in-depth. Case studies, when given, are relevant and add value.
		What is lacking are data for the KPIs relating to employment, labour, health and safety, and training and development.
9	CR Land	KPI disclosures are generally specific and in-depth. Some KPIs, however, are inadequately addressed. For example, the disclosure on environmental management measures focuses on the 'what' rather than the 'how'.
10	CK Asset	CK Asset structured its ESG report to closely follow HKEX Appendix 27 reporting requirements.
		Disclosures are both sufficiently specific and in-depth (examples are given as to how policies are effected). However, no case studies are given.
		There is a lack of data for the employment, labour, health and safety, and training and development KPIs.
		No temporal comparisons are available for the data provided.
11	Galaxy Ent	Disclosure for KPIs in general is not comprehensive. There is a lot on the 'what' but not the 'how'.
		A large part of the ESG report is dedicated to disclosure of charitable activities.
		No temporal comparisons are available for the environmental data set.
12	CKI Holdings	Overall, it is a barebones ESG report.
		Temporal data for the environmental disclosure are not available.
		Data sets for disclosures relating to employment, labour, training and development, and health and safety are not available.
		Qualitative disclosure of policies is vague and shallow. It comes in the form of announcing that there are indeed policies in place relating to the KPIs. No case studies are given and detail on 'how' policies are executed is missing.

APPENDIX 3 319

(cont.)

Rank	Name	Notes
13	Wharf REIC	The ESG reporting for Wharf REIC is sparse. Many of the KPIs are unfulfilled with no explanations given. No data sets relating to KPIs are disclosed. Qualitative disclosure of policies is vague and shallow. It comes in the form of announcing that there are indeed policies in place relating to the KPIs. No case studies are given and detail on 'how' policies are executed is missing.
14	China Evergrande	Unfortunately, the ESG report is available only in Chinese; thus, I was unable to properly review the ESG report.

Pharmaceutical

Rank	Name	Notes
1	CSPC Pharma	Disclosure on policies is comprehensive and in-depth. There is a lot of exposition on how things are done, rather than just what is done. Data provided are sparse, but not as bad as Sino Biopharm. Temporal comparison of data is unavailable. Of note is the in-depth supply chain disclosure – given CSPC Pharma's line of business in dealing with pharmaceutical products, how its supply chain is being managed is definitely an important aspect which investors would like to be privy to.
2	Sino Biopharm	This is a sparse ESG report. Many of the KPIs listed in HKEX Appendix 27 have not been satisfied – quantitative data on employment, labour, health and safety, and training and development are not present. Disclosure for various KPIs mostly focuses on 'what the company does' rather than 'how the company does it'. Case studies are provided but are often sparse and do not add much value.

Financial institutions

Rank	Name	Notes
1	Ping An	Ping An's thirty years milestone summary at the front of the ESG report was an impressive way of getting shareholders (especially new shareholders) up to speed on Ping An's CSR commitments.
		Ping An's ESG report has a 'Response and Outlook' section that clearly lays out its targets for 2017, responses (to the targets) in 2017, and outlook for 2018. It is mostly qualitative information, but it allows shareholders to easily hold Ping An accountable to its moderately specific set of goals.
		The report's presentation of data for both environmental and social disclosure is comprehensive, providing relevant and specific breakdowns for data where possible and also comparison with previous years. This gives shareholders a clear picture of how the company is managing such issues.
2	Hang Seng Bank	In-depth explanation of social policies and initiatives relating to employment is provided in the report. The data set provided is comprehensive and also allows for temporal comparisons.
		There is in-depth and specific disclosure on the company's operating practices, but no relevant quantitative data sets are provided.
		Detailed examples are given of how the company has done its part for the environment over the years and in 2017. There is specific disclosure of the technical environment-related certifications that the company has obtained. Temporal comparisons for environment data are available. Future plans – 2020 goals – are laid out.
3	HSBC Holdings	A big part of the ESG report is devoted to how the company has responded to customer feedback and made its business more customer friendly. This goes above and beyond the requirements of Appendix 27, but is still relevant for investors

(cont.)

Rank	Name	Notes
		seeking to make decisions regarding the company. HSBC Holdings is open about its future plans and policies. Under each aspect addressed by the company, there is a short section on future goals and implementations. Further, the ESG report also states what HSBC Holdings has achieved during the past year, giving shareholders the impression of a timeline and a company that is actively making improvements. There are clear and comprehensive quantitative data for disclosures relating to employment, training and development, health and safety, and labour. Previous years' data are included for comparison. One commendable aspect of this ESG report is the relevant case studies provided alongside data which help shareholders to put the data into context. Where the ESG report is lacking is in its presentation of data relating to the environment. There are no quantitative data on the breakdown of emissions or waste management. However, HSBC Holdings' ESG report does provide a vague indicator of both its 2020 goals and its progress in achieving them.
4	HKEX	This has good disclosure in terms of specificity and comprehensiveness, with the 'what' and the 'how' for each KPI adequately addressed. Case studies are also provided for some of the KPIs. Data sets include previous years for temporal comparison. Of note are the 'CSR Plans and Progress Update' sections at the end of each disclosure segment. These give investors a bird's-eye view of what the company has been working on with regard to ESG over the past year and also help investors to hold it accountable for the next year.

(cont.)

Rank	Name	Notes
5	China Life	Overall, this is a comprehensive disclosure of company policies relating to the KPIs. Both the 'what' and the 'how' are addressed.
		One if its more impressive case studies for its environmental disclosure is the blueprint of the 'China Life Science and Technology Park' with all its resource and energy saving properties outlined.
		Data sets are comprehensive and hit most of the KPIs. Data which are missing are explained adequately.
6	China Merchants Bank (CM Bank)	Data sets provided have multiple years for temporal comparison.
7	Bank of Communications	Similar to China Merchants Bank, data sets provided have multiple years for temporal comparison.
		The generous use of case studies puts disclosed policies into perspective for investors.
8	CCB	Disclosed environmental data have multiple years for temporal comparison. Data relating to employment, labour, and health and safety do not.
		Of note are the case studies disclosed by the company. Where possible, the case studies are of a personal nature, giving investors a clear insight into the everyday ground operations of the company. An example is the case study on 'Providing Professional and Conscientious Services, Protecting Customers' Financial Assets'.
9	BOC Hong Kong	Both qualitative information and quantitative data are adequate. However, there is no temporal comparison available for data relating to disclosures on employment, labour, health and safety, etc. There are no future plans laid out for investors to hold the company accountable to.
		Detailed examples are given of how the company has done its part for the environment

APPENDIX 3

(cont.)

Rank	Name	Notes
		over the years and in 2017. There is also specific disclosure of all the technical environment-related certifications that the company has obtained. Temporal comparisons for environment data are available, but no future plans are laid out.
10	Prudential	Data sets for environmental disclosure are average. Qualitative information regarding policies and initiatives is vague.
		Qualitative information on policies and initiatives for disclosure on KPIs relating to employment, labour, training, etc is comprehensive with examples and case studies given. However, there is a lack of data sets in this section. Shareholders are unable to view the substantive impact of the policies put in place without data to compare with previous years.
11	AIA	Disclosure is specific but shallow. AIA includes specifications and certifications for environmental-related disclosure. However, most of the policies that are disclosed are focused on the 'what' rather than the 'how'.
12	Bank of China	This has a lot of case studies, but they are focused on the company's charitable endeavours.
		The report seems more data-centric and less focused on the qualitative information/policies implemented.
		The data sets, when provided, have temporal comparisons.
13	Manulife	Manulife's disclosure manages to fulfil most of the qualitative KPIs. However, the disclosure itself is shallow. Much of the focus is on 'what' the company is doing, rather than 'how' the company is doing it.
		Case studies are also vague and do not add much value.
		Much of the data-based KPIs have not been fulfilled.

(cont.)

Rank	Name	Notes
14	ICBC	Waste statistics are presented by item (pieces of printers, servers, laptop, etc) and not by genus (hazardous, non-hazardous) – which may lead shareholders into thinking that the company is deliberately under-reporting its waste statistics. There are data for greenhouse gas emissions, but no comparison with other years. Qualitative information about the company's environmental policy is sparse and vague. ICBC's qualitative disclosure in its policies regarding labour and employment is vague. The content is mostly on how relevant laws are abided by. There are no statistical data sets under ICBC's disclosure on employment, labour, or training and development. The sections relating to the above contain mostly qualitative information about the company's initiatives. Numbers are mostly used to prove a point and not for comparison.
15	Standard Chartered	Data sets are provided, but there is little in terms of explanations or case studies on the company's policies. It would be hard for shareholders to tell how the figures in the data were achieved. Granted, the company claims that further information is available in its 'position statements', such as on climate change (available on its website); however, these statements are also vague and do not add much value. There is a lot of 'what the company wants to achieve', but little on 'how'.

Singapore

The companies are classified as follows:

Telecommunication, information technology and internet services	Industrial services and consumer services providers	Investments and diversified conglomerates	Manufacturing and consumer products	Property development and management	Financial institutions
Singapore Telecommunications	Singapore Airlines	Jardine Matheson Holdings	Wilmar International	Hongkong Land Holdings	Prudential Plc
NetLink NBN Trust	Singapore Technologies Engineering	Jardine Strategic Holdings	Thai Beverage	Genting Singapore	DBS Group Holdings
StarHub	Singapore Exchange	Jardine Cycle and Carriage	Dairy Farm International Holdings	Capitaland	OCBC
	Sembcorp Industries	Keppel Corporation	Venture Corporation	City Developments limited	UOB
	Singapore Press Holdings Limited	Ascendas REIT	Yangzijiang Shipbuilding (Holdings)	UOL Group	Great Eastern Holdings Limited
	SIA Engineering Company Limited	Capitaland Mall Trust	Golden Agri-Resources Ltd	Frasers Property	
	Singapore Post Limited	Capitaland Commercial Trust	Haw Par Corporation	United Industrial Corporation	
	SATs	Suntec REIT	Fraser and Neave	Mandarin Oriental International	
		Mapletree Commercial Trust Mapletree Logistics Trust Keppel REIT Mapletree Industrial Trust Mapletree North Asia Commercial Trust Fortune REIT Hutchison Port Holdings Trust	Olam International	Yanlord Land Group	

Ranking/Assessment of sustainability statements:

Telecommunication, information technology and internet services

Rank	Name	Notes
1	Singapore Telecommunications	Analysis of both Singapore Telecommunications and Starhub: both sustainability reports are well prepared. Both reports disclose the reasons for and the process of selecting the material ESG factors (stakeholder engagements, consultations, etc). Under these factors, the companies' policies are well discussed, often explaining the rationale for the policies in the context of the telecommunication industries. In-depth and specific case studies and examples (practices) are given to back up the policies discussed. And quantitative facts (performance) with comprehensive breakdowns (especially in the environmental and employee welfare and training segments) and temporal comparisons are also disclosed for accountability and to give context to the examples. What puts Singapore Telecommunications ahead of Starhub is its quantifiable target setting. Singapore Telecommunications sets quantifiable targets in terms of numbers with a specific deadline, as opposed to Starhub which merely sets general sustainability objectives without any specific deadlines.
2	Starhub	See above.
*	Netlink NBN Trust	Sustainability report not published.

APPENDIX 3

Industrial services and consumer services providers

Rank	Name	Notes
1	Singapore Airlines Holdings	The report clearly discloses the reasons for and the process of selecting the material ESG factors.
		The safety of the business is likely to be the top concern of any investor. In this regard, Singapore Airlines displays an understanding of possible investor concerns with a detailed and comprehensive disclosure on the different safety policies – flight, operations and food. Case studies and examples are given where relevant. Relevant statistics are also provided, albeit without temporal comparison.
		Quantifiable targets for ESG factors are set with deadlines provided for accountability. Data sets provided are also comprehensive (eg greenhouse gas emissions are broken down by different fleets) with temporal comparisons.
2	SIA Engineering Company	The report discloses the reasons for and the process of selecting the material ESG factors in a comprehensive and detailed manner.
		Clear and quantifiable future targets are set for ESG factors where relevant, including reiteration of previous targets and disclosure of progress towards meeting them.
		Policies and practices are sufficiently in-depth and specific.
		Data sets for employee demographics and turnover are comprehensive with temporal comparisons available. Unfortunately, environmental data are sparse in comparison.
3	SATs	The report discloses the reasons for and the process of selecting the material ESG factors.
		Clear and quantifiable future targets are set for ESG factors where relevant, including reiteration of previous targets and disclosure of progress towards meeting them.
		Policies and practices are sufficiently in-depth and specific.

(cont.)

Rank	Name	Notes
		Data sets for environmental and employee demographics and turnover are comprehensive with temporal comparisons available.
4	Singapore Press Holdings	See above for SATs.
5	Singapore Exchange	See above for SATs.
6	Comfortdelgro	See above for SATs.
7	Sembcorp Industries	See above for SATs.
8	Singapore Technologies Engineering	This report does not disclose the reasons for or the process of selecting the material ESG factors. However, clear and quantifiable future targets are set for ESG factors where relevant, including reiteration of previous targets and disclosure of progress towards meeting them. Policies and practices are sufficiently in-depth and specific. Data sets for environmental and workplace safety are comprehensive with temporal comparisons available. Temporal comparisons are unavailable for employee turnover and training data.
9	Singapore Post	See above for SATs.

Investments and diversified conglomerates

Rank	Name	Notes
1	Keppel Corporation	The report discloses the reasons for and the process of selecting the material ESG factors. Clear and quantifiable future targets are set for ESG factors where relevant, including reiteration of previous targets and disclosure of progress towards meeting them. Policies and practices are especially in-depth and specific. Explanation and breakdown of Keppel Corporation's policies and practices

(cont.)

Rank	Name	Notes
		in place are done in a clear and understandable manner.
		Data sets are detailed and comprehensive with temporal comparisons available.
		*Generally, the reports are satisfactory. What put Keppel Corporation ahead was its extra-detailed qualitative exposition on its policies and practices in place.
2	Ascendas REIT	This report discloses the reasons for and the process of selecting the material ESG factors.
		Clear and quantifiable future targets are set for ESG factors where relevant, including reiteration of previous targets and disclosure of progress towards meeting them.
		Policies and practices are sufficiently in-depth and specific.
		Data sets for environmental and employee demographics and turnover are comprehensive with temporal comparisons available.
3	Capitaland Commercial Trust	See above for Ascendas REIT.
4	Suntec REIT	See above for Ascendas REIT.
5	Capitaland Mall Trust	See above for Ascendas REIT.
6	Mapletree Industrial Trust	The report discloses the reasons for and the process of selecting the material ESG factors.
		Clear and quantifiable future targets are set for ESG factors where relevant, including reiteration of previous targets and disclosure of progress towards meeting them.
		Policies and practices are sufficiently in-depth and specific.
		Data sets for environmental sustainability are especially comprehensive, with breakdowns from different types of building under the trust. This is important information to investors, given the industry.

(*cont.*)

Rank	Name	Notes
7	Mapletree North Asia Commercial Trust	Data sets for employee demographics are present with temporal comparisons available. See above for Ascendas REIT.
8	Mapletree Logistics trust	The report discloses the reasons for and the process of selecting the material ESG factors. Clear and quantifiable future targets are set for ESG factors where relevant, including reiteration of previous targets and disclosure of progress towards meeting them. Policies and practices are sufficiently in-depth and specific. Data sets for environmental sustainability are comprehensive with temporal comparisons available. This information is likely to be important to investors, given that the trust manages many buildings. Data for employee health and training are sparse. However, this may not prove to be as important to investors.
9	Keppel REIT	Report disclosed the reasons for and process of selecting the material ESG factors. Clear and quantifiable future targets set for ESG factors where relevant. Reiterated previous targets set and disclosed progress for previous targets. Policies and practices were sufficiently in-depth and specific. Data sets for environmental sustainability are comprehensive with temporal comparisons available. This information is likely to be important to investors, given that the trust manages many buildings. Data for employee health and training are sparse. However, this may not prove to be as important to investors.
10	Hutchinson Port Holding Trust	The report discloses the reasons for and the process of selecting the material ESG factors.

(cont.)

Rank	Name	Notes
11	Jardine Cycle and Carriage	No quantifiable targets are set, only broad objectives. No deadlines are set. Policies and practices are sufficiently in-depth and specific. Data sets lack temporal comparison. The report discloses the reasons for and the process of selecting the material ESG factors. No quantifiable targets are set, only broad objectives. No deadlines are set. Policies and practices are sufficiently in-depth and specific. Data sets lack temporal comparison.
12	Mapletree Commercial Trust	The report discloses the reasons for and the process of selecting the material ESG factors. Clear and quantifiable future targets are set for ESG factors where relevant. However, there is no information on current progress with regard to previous targets set. Policies and practices are sufficiently in-depth and specific. Environmental data sets with comprehensive breakdowns and temporal comparisons are unavailable. This is unacceptable given that the trust has many buildings under its portfolio. Employee turnover and training data sets are unavailable.
*	Fortune REIT	Singapore sustainability report unavailable. The only sustainability report available is written in accordance with SEHK Appendix 27.
*	Jardine Matheson Holdings	Sustainability report not published.
*	Jardine Strategic Holdings	Sustainability report not published.

Manufacturing and consumer products

Rank	Name	Notes
1	Wilmar International	The report discloses the reasons for and the process of selecting the material ESG factors.
		Policies and practices relating to the environment and employee welfare/safety are sufficiently in-depth and specific.
		There is a detailed breakdown of environmental (resource consumption and waste emission) and employee data by region.
		Temporal comparisons are available.
		Clear, quantifiable targets are set, as are objective targets where quantifiability is not applicable. Deadlines are also set. The report makes reference to previous targets and the company's current progress. The company is candid in admitting that it is behind schedule in completing 15 methane capture facilities (it is 1 short) as part of its environmental sustainability policy.
		It is candid in admitting fault such as fire incidents and incidents relating to fatalities – attributed to lack of training, malfunctioning equipment, as well as oversight of the company. The report also highlights instances resulting in employee health and safety concerns (such as workers using herbicide containers to store drinking water). However, what is lacking is disclosure of detailed steps or examples of how the company has tried to deal with such issues. At present, only vague declarations of better future practices are made.
2	Thaibev	The report discloses the reasons for and the process of selecting the material ESG factors.
		Environmental and employee policies and practice are detailed with supporting quantitative data.
		Of note is the company's detailed breakdown on its waste management initiatives – as part of its environmental sustainability policies and practice.

(cont.)

Rank	Name	Notes
3	Olam International	Clear quantifiable targets are set, as are objective targets where quantifiability is not applicable. Deadlines are also set.
		The report discloses the reasons for and the process of selecting the material ESG factors.
		Clear and quantifiable future targets are set for ESG factors where relevant, including reiteration of previous targets and disclosure of progress towards meeting them.
		Environmental and employee policies and practice are detailed with supporting quantitative data. Temporal comparison is available.
4	Fraser and Neave	The report discloses the reasons for and the process of selecting the material ESG factors.
		Clear and quantifiable future targets are set for ESG factors where relevant, including reiteration of previous targets and disclosure of progress towards meeting them.
		Environmental and employee policies and practice are detailed with supporting quantitative data. No temporal comparison is available for the data.
5	Golden Agri Resources	The report discloses the reasons for and the process of selecting the material ESG factors.
		Clear and quantifiable future targets are set for ESG factors where relevant, including reiteration of previous targets and disclosure of progress towards meeting them.
		Environmental policies and practice are detailed with supporting quantitative data. However, there is an inconsistent availability of temporal comparison for environmental data.
6	Haw Par Corporation	The report discloses the reasons for and the process of selecting the material ESG factors.
		No targets relating to identified ESG factors are set. There is also no disclosure of previous targets set or progress made. The explanation given – 'The process of developing a range of measurable, time-bound

(cont.)

Rank	Name	Notes
		sustainability targets for our Material Issues [is] in the works, which we will share and report against in forthcoming sustainability reports' – is unsatisfactory.
		Environmental disclosure is sparse – the only disclosure is about how the company has switched to electronic communications and its support of wildlife conservation. There are no instances in which environmental policies or practices are disclosed that relate to the company's actual business of manufacturing consumer goods.
		When considering a manufacturing company, investors are likely to consider data relating to resource consumption as important. The company unfortunately did not disclose any data in this regard.
7	Venture Corporation	The report discloses the reasons for and the process of selecting the material ESG factors.
		No targets relating to identified ESG factors are set. There is also no disclosure of previous targets set or progress made. No explanations are given for failure to include this compulsory component.
		Policies and practices relating to identified ESG factors (environmental sustainability, employment) are disclosed in a brief manner. No data are available to give investors context or to serve as a point of comparison.
*	Dairy Farm International Holdings	Sustainability report not published.
*	Yangzijiang Shipbuilding (Holdings)	Sustainability report not published.

APPENDIX 3

Property development and management

Rank	Name	Notes
1	CapitaLand	The report discloses the reasons for and the process of selecting the material ESG factors. Clear, quantifiable and comprehensive future targets are set for ESG factors where relevant. Current performance for targets is disclosed. The report provides a concisely written framework that allows investors to understand the context behind the company's targets as well as its detailed plans for fulfilling them. Policies, practice and performance for the top three sustainability factors that investors are likely to be concerned with – resource consumption, emissions and workplace safety – are disclosed. Data sets are comprehensive, and temporal comparisons are available. Data relating to employee training and demographics are also comprehensive, with temporal comparisons available.
2	City Developments Singapore	The report discloses the reasons for and the process of selecting the material ESG factors. Clear and quantifiable future targets are set for ESG factors where relevant, including reiteration of previous targets and disclosure of progress towards meeting them. Polices, practice and performance for the top three sustainability factors that investors are likely to be concerned with – resource consumption, emissions and workplace safety – are disclosed. Data sets are comprehensive – for example, environmental data for different aspects of the business (corporate office, commercial and industrial buildings, construction sites) are

(*cont.*)

Rank	Name	Notes
		displayed separately. Temporal comparisons are available.
		Data relating to employee training and demographics are also comprehensive, with temporal comparisons available.
3	Genting Singapore	The report discloses the reasons for and the process of selecting the material ESG factors.
		Clear and quantifiable future targets are set for ESG factors where relevant, including reiteration of previous targets and disclosure of progress towards meeting them.
		Polices, practice and performance for the top three sustainability factors that investors are likely to be concerned with – resource consumption, emissions and workplace safety – are disclosed. Data sets are comprehensive, and temporal comparisons are available.
		Data relating to employee training and demographics are also comprehensive, with temporal comparisons available.
		Geographic breakdown of where the company procures its resources provided in the report is an added bonus.
4	UOL Group	The report discloses the reasons for and the process of selecting the material ESG factors.
		Clear and quantifiable future targets are set for ESG factors where relevant, including reiteration of previous targets and disclosure of progress towards meeting them.
		Polices, practice and performance for the top three sustainability factors that investors are likely to be concerned with – resource consumption, emissions and workplace safety – are disclosed. Temporal comparison for data is available.
5	United Industrial Corporation	See above for UOL Group.

APPENDIX 3

(cont.)

Rank	Name	Notes
6	Frasers Property	See above for UOL Group.
7	Mandarin Oriental International	See above for UOL Group.
8	Hong Kong Land	The report discloses the reasons for and the process of selecting the material ESG factors.
		Clear and quantifiable future targets are set for ESG factors where relevant, including reiteration of previous targets and disclosure of progress towards meeting them.
		Polices, practice and performance for the top three sustainability factors that investors are likely to be concerned with – resource consumption, emissions and workplace safety – are disclosed. However, temporal comparison for data is unavailable.
9	Yanlord Land Group	The report discloses the reasons for and the process of selecting the material ESG factors. However, the process of selecting material ESG factors is poorly explained.
		Of the ESG factors identified, only the section titled 'Caring for Our Customers' has targets set. Further, no quantifiable targets are set, only broad objectives. No deadlines are set.
		There is no disclosure relating to employee training or demographics. Employee safety has been disclosed; however, there are no temporal comparisons available.
		There is no environmental disclosure. This is unacceptable for a property developer, as investors are likely to be interested in resource consumption and emission of waste/GHG and ways to reduce such. The lack of data and policies in this aspect thus stands out.

Financial institutions

Rank	Name	Notes
1	DBS	The report discloses the reasons for and the process of selecting the material ESG factors.
		Future targets set for ESG factors are mostly objective based. However, this is the only sustainability report in this industry that reiterates previous targets and discloses progress towards meeting them.
		Quantitative data for employee training and demographics are comprehensive with detailed breakdowns. Temporal comparisons are available.
2	Great Eastern Holdings	The report discloses the reasons for and the process of selecting the material ESG factors.
		Targets set for ESG factors are very unclear. No timelines/deadlines are set. Progress updates are available, but there is no discussion on what previously set targets were.
		Quantitative data for employee training and demographics are comprehensive with detailed breakdowns. Temporal comparisons are available.
3	OCBC	See above for Great Eastern Holdings.
4	UOB	The report discloses the reasons for and the process of selecting the material ESG factors.
		No quantifiable targets are set for ESG factors, only broad objectives. No timelines/deadlines are set. There is no progress update provided for previously set targets.
		Quantitative data for employee training and demographics are comprehensive with temporal comparisons available.
*	Prudential plc	Sustainability report not published.

Malaysia

The companies are classified as follows:

Telecommunication, information technology and internet services	Natural resources, energy, oil and gas	Industrial services and consumer services providers	Investments and diversified conglomerates	Manufacturing and consumer products	Property development and management	Financial institutions
Maxis	Tenaga Nasional	IHH Healthcare	Genting	Sime Darby Plantation	Genting Malaysia	Malayan Banking
Axiata Group	Petronas Chemicals	Misc	IOI Corporation	Nestle (M)	Malaysia Airports Holdings	Public Bank
Digi.com	Petronas Gas	Dialog Group	PPB Group	Petronas Dagangan	SP Setia	CIMB Group Holdings
Telekom Malaysia	Press Metal Aluminium Holdings	Westports Holdings	Sime Darby	Kuala Lumpur Kepong	IOI Properties Group	Hong Leong Bank
Astro Malaysia Holdings	YTL Power		YTL Corporation	Hartalega Holdings	Gamuda	RHB Bank
			Sunway	Fraser and Neave Holdings	Sime Darby Property	Hong Leong Financial Group
			Batu Kawan	Top Glove Corporation		AMMB Holdings
			IJM Corporation	Lotte Chemical Titan		
			Hap Seng Consolidated	QL Resources		
				British American Tobacco (M)		
				Genting Plantations		
				Inari Amertron		
				UMW Holdings		

Ranking/Assessment of Sustainability Statements:

Telecommunication, information technology and internet services

Rank	Name	Notes
1	Maxis	How the company arrived at the issues deemed material to the company and stakeholders is discussed only in broad terms. Methodologies for both company level and stakeholder level inquiries as to materiality of issues are missing. Qualitative and quantitative data on data and privacy issues are not disclosed. Considering the industry, this seems to be an issue of import to stakeholders, company and investors, and should have been part of the report. Maxis performs better with regard to employee training disclosure, providing data on training hours etc to support its disclosure on training policies. Digi.com does not.
2	Digi.com	Similar to Maxis, how the company arrived at the issues deemed material to the company and stakeholders is discussed only in broad terms. Methodologies for both company level and stakeholder level inquiries as to materiality of issues are missing. Policies on data and privacy issues are discussed briefly, but no quantitative data are disclosed.
*	Axiata Group	The report is produced based on the GRI-G4 standards, exempt from Bursa Malaysia Listing Requirements Practice Note 9 paras 6.2–6.3. No comparison is made.
*	Telekom Malaysia	See above for Axiata Group.
*	Astro Malaysia Holdings	See above for Axiata Group.

APPENDIX 3

Natural resources, energy, oil and gas

Rank	Name	Notes
1	Petronas Chemicals	Steps taken and the methodology behind the steps for distilling sustainability issues at both company and stakeholder levels are disclosed clearly.
		Environmental and employee training and safety reporting are both in-depth and specific – diagrams detailing environmentally friendly technology have been included, and case studies for both issues are comprehensive. Data sets are also provided with temporal comparisons.
		The company is candid about reporting poor environmental performance (greenhouse gas emissions) in 2017 as compared to 2016 – it also provides reasons why. Environmentally friendly technologies and policies adopted are disclosed. However, despite the poorer performance in 2017, no improvement goals for the future are elaborated upon.
		The company is also candid about the fatality suffered in 2017, as compared to no fatalities in 2014 and 2015. It is candid about what occurred and has detailed steps to prevent future occurrences.
2	Petronas Gas	Steps taken and the methodology behind the steps for distilling sustainability issues at both company and stakeholder levels are disclosed clearly.
		Environmental disclosure is comprehensive, but disclosure relating to employee training and safety pales in comparison.
3	Press Metal Aluminium Holdings	The report discusses both stakeholder engagement and the company-level approach to distilling sustainability issues. Stakeholder engagement is sufficiently in-depth and detailed. Disclosure on the company level sufficiently elaborates on 'what' has been done to assess material issues. However, disclosure on 'how' (such as methodology and approach), while provided, is poor.
		A thing of note – the company's stakeholder prioritisation matrix gives further insight into the methodology of how the material issues based on stakeholder engagement are formed.

(cont.)

Rank	Name	Notes
		Given the industry, environmental issues are likely to be at the top of an investor's concerns. Data regarding resource consumption and environmental impact disclosure are provided. However, there is a lack of elaboration on current policies in place to improve the situation, as well as a lack of elaboration on future planned improvements.
*	YTL Power	The report is produced based on the GRI-G4 standards, exempt from Bursa Malaysia Listing Requirements Practice Note 9 paras 6.2–6.3. No comparison is made.
*	Tenaga Nasional	See above for YTL Power.

Industrial services and consumer services providers

Rank	Name	Notes
1	Dialog Group	The report discloses 'what' the company does to determine material sustainability issues. But disclosure of 'how' is not done beyond broad principles – for example, the content and methodology of the 'material assessment workshop with the management team' (the company's means of determining materiality) are not disclosed.
		There are specific and detailed disclosures relating to material issues identified. Data provided are detailed with temporal comparisons.
		Specificity – disclosure of the company's international certifications and training schemes is comprehensively presented in the sustainability report.
*	IHH Healthcare	The report is produced based on the GRI-G4 standards, exempt from Bursa Malaysia Listing Requirements Practice Note 9 paras 6.2–6.3. No comparison is made.
*	Misc	See above for IHH Healthcare.
*	Westports Holdings	See above for IHH Healthcare.

APPENDIX 3

Investments and diversified conglomerates

Rank	Name	Notes
1	Hap Seng Consolidated	The report discusses both stakeholder engagement and the company-level approach to distilling sustainability issues. Stakeholder engagement is sufficiently in-depth and detailed. Disclosure on the company level sufficiently elaborates on 'what' has been done to assess material issues, but disclosure on the 'how' aspect is poor. Detailed quantitative data with temporal comparisons are provided for environmental disclosure, across the holding company's subsidiaries. Policies for environmental sustainability across the holding company's subsidiaries are also disclosed. The company does not fall into the trap of overly focusing on one subsidiary company.
2	Sime Darby	Disclosure is satisfactory, but there is poor discussion of the methodology (both stakeholder and company level) for determining the current material sustainability issues. The company admits that its materiality assessment is still based around its core plantation business. However, the company does go on to further explain that consultations with KPMG were in order to develop a new set of material sustainability issues taking into account the other segments of its business. The company is candid with its disclosure – it highlights the fact that there was a fatality in its motor division and promises to prevent such issues from occurring in the future. Disclosure of environmental issues relating to its business division is not well organised and feels haphazard. Disclosure of what the holding company does at the shareholder level is lacking. Instead, only bits and pieces of the policies that the subsidiaries adopt are disclosed.
3	Batu Kawan	This report fails to discuss the material sustainability issues identified or how they were identified. The report seems to be overly focused on one subsidiary – Kuala Lumpur Kepong.

(cont.)

Rank	Name	Notes
*	Sunway	As an investment holding company, it focuses too much on regurgitating its main subsidiary's sustainability approach. There is little to no exposition on how it deals with material sustainability issues as a shareholder across all of its investments/businesses. The report is produced based on the GRI-G4 standards, exempt from Bursa Malaysia Listing Requirements Practice Note 9 paras 6.2–6.3. No comparison is made.
*	IJM Corporation	See above for Sunway.
*	Genting	See above for Sunway.
*	IOI Corporation	See above for Sunway.
*	PPB Group	See above for Sunway.
*	YTL Corporation	See above for Sunway.

Manufacturing and consumer products

Rank	Name	Notes
1	Lotte Chemical Titan	The 'what' and the 'how' for identifying material issues are both sufficiently disclosed at company and stakeholder levels. The methodology for determining the relative importance of each material issue is not disclosed. Policies disclosed are in-depth and specific with data sets and temporal comparisons used to back any assertions where relevant. Environmental and employee-related disclosure is especially in-depth and specific. Data sets are generally comprehensive. Disclosure of qualitative policies adopted is well elaborated upon.
2	Inari Amertron	'What' has been done to identify material issues is disclosed. However, disclosure on 'how' (such as methodology and approach), while provided, is poor.

(cont.)

Rank	Name	Notes
3	Top Glove Corporation	Policies disclosed are in-depth and specific with data sets and temporal comparisons used to back any assertions where relevant. Data sets are relatively more comprehensive. 'What' has been done to identify material issues is disclosed. However, disclosure on 'how' (such as methodology and approach), while provided, is poor. Policies disclosed are in-depth and specific with data sets and temporal comparisons used to back any assertions where relevant.
4	Hartalega Holdings	See above for Top Glove Corporation.
5	QL Resources	'What' has been done to identify material issues is disclosed. However, disclosure on 'how' (such as methodology and approach), while provided, is poor. Minimal quantitative data are provided. No temporal comparisons for data are available.
*	Sime Darby Plantation	The report is produced based on the GRI-G4 standards, exempt from Bursa Malaysia Listing Requirements Practice Note 9 paras 6.2–6.3. No comparison is made.
*	Nestle (M)	See above for Sime Darby Plantation.
*	Petronas Dagangan	See above for Sime Darby Plantation.
*	Kuala Lumpur Kepong	See above for Sime Darby Plantation.
*	Fraser and Neave Holdings	See above for Sime Darby Plantation.
*	British American Tobacco (M)	See above for Sime Darby Plantation.
*	Genting Plantations	See above for Sime Darby Plantation.
*	UMW Holdings	See above for Sime Darby Plantation.

Property development and management

Rank	Name	Notes
1	Sime Darby Property	The company reports based on its own proprietary sustainability index. However, it does not explain how the index was conceived of or its relevance to Bursa Malaysia's Listing Requirements Practice Note 9 paras 6.2–6.3. Ultimately, it fails to explain how it arrived at its material sustainability issues for disclosure. There is in-depth and specific disclosure on occupational safety issues. Examples of initiatives are provided along with quantitative data with temporal comparisons available. Policies and quantitative data relating to environmental impact are also comprehensively disclosed. Reduction targets are provided for added accountability.
2	SP Setia	This report discloses how it engaged stakeholders to develop its set of material issues for disclosure. However, it does not elaborate on the methodology of its 'internal assessment' or why the issues identified are relevant to the company. As a property developer, fatality and injury rates are likely to be of concern to the prospective investor. Policies and issues relating to such are also likely to be material to its business. Unfortunately, this issue is not addressed in the report. Disclosure relating to environmental impact is sparse (only office electricity and water consumption are disclosed) when compared to Sime Darby Property. Data relating to property development works would have been more relevant to investors, but are, unfortunately, not disclosed.
*	Genting Malaysia	This report is produced based on the GRI-G4 standards, exempt from Bursa Malaysia Listing Requirements Practice Note 9 paras 6.2–6.3. No comparison is made.
*	Malaysia Airports Holdings	See above for Genting Malaysia.
*	IOI Properties Group	See above for Genting Malaysia.
*	Gamuda	See above for Genting Malaysia.

APPENDIX 3

Financial institutions

Rank	Name	Notes
1	Public Bank	Public Bank's disclosure is generally in-depth and specific, especially its disclosure on how it conducts business responsibly and how it develops its employees. The company also specifically discloses the certifications it encourages its employees to attain, which is a nice touch, given that these service providers form the backbone of the company.
		The company provides a lot of quantitative data to support its qualitative assertions, whether they be initiatives it has put in place or the effects of the initiatives themselves. Temporal comparisons are also often available.
		The company has determined the material issues based solely on the interests of the stakeholders. It does not explain how the issues identified are material in terms of business operations such that they reflect the listed issuer's significant economic, environmental and social impacts. The company also does not provide its methodology or/thought process behind ranking the relative importance of the material issues identified.
2	Hong Leong Financial Group	Quantitative data sets provided by Hong Leong Financial Group are much more sparse when compared to the data sets provided by Public Bank. Examples are the data on resources consumption, social initiatives and, of more importance (to investors), human resources.
		The company does give many case studies of the initiatives it has adopted – but only qualitatively and without quantitative data to support its assertions, which pales in comparison with Public Bank's disclosure.
*	Malayan Banking	The report is produced based on the GRI-G4 standards, exempt from Bursa Malaysia Listing Requirements Practice Note 9 paras 6.2–6.3. No comparison is made.
*	CIMB Group Holdings	See above for Malayan Banking.
*	Hong Leong Bank	See above for Malayan Banking.
*	RHB Bank	See above for Malayan Banking.
*	AMMB Holdings	See above for Malayan Banking.

India

The companies are classified as follows:

Telecommunication, information technology and internet services	Natural resources, energy, oil and gas	Investments	Manufacturing and consumer products	Property development and management	Pharmaceutical	Financial institutions
Tata Consultancy services	Oil and Natural Gas Corporation	Reliance Industries	Hindustan Unilever	Larsen and Toubro	Sun Pharmaceutical	HDFC Bank
Infosys	Coal India		ITC	Avenue Supermarts		Housing Development Finance Corporation
Bharti Airtel	Indian Oil Corporation		Maruti Suzuki	Adani Ports		State Bank of India
HCL Tech	NTPC		Asian Paints			Kotak Mahindra Bank
Wipro	Hindustan Zinc		Ultratech Cement			ICICI Bank
Tech Mahindra	Power Grid Corporation of India		Mahindra & Mahindra			Bajaj Finance
	Gail (India)		Nestle India			Axis Bank
	Bharat Petroleum		Godrej Consumer Products			Indusind Bank
			Titan Company			Bajaj Finserv
			JSW Steel			HDFC Standard Life Insurance Company
			Bajaj Auto			Yes Bank
			Britannia Industries			Bandhand Bank
			Tata Motors			SBI Life Insurance Company
			Eicher Motors			
			Grasim Industries			
			Motherson Sumi Systems			
			Dabur			

APPENDIX 3

Ranking/Assessment of BRRs

Telecommunication, information technology and internet services

Rank	Name	Notes
1	HCL Technology	The Section E disclosure is in-depth and specific. Particularly, disclosure on issues relating to Principles 2 and 3 (environmental and employee treatment) goes above and beyond the requirements. Issues relating to employee health and training are also likely to be of concern to investors. Principle 2 – environmental initiatives (reducing carbon footprint) and the results of the initiatives are published. Generally, there is in-depth and specific disclosure of the steps taken to reduce environmental impact. Principle 3 – this goes beyond the requirements by going into in-depth qualitative description of employee initiatives. Principle 6 – beyond answering the questions provided, future goals relating to environmental protection are disclosed. There are no temporal comparisons.
2	Bharti Airtel	The Section E disclosure is generally in-depth and specific, citing specific examples and case studies to back up its assertions. Principle 2 – there is in-depth qualitative disclosure on its various environmental initiatives but no data to back it up. Only the waste management initiative has data on how much waste is recycled. Principle 3 – this addresses the base questions required, but there is no qualitative disclosure on employee initiatives. Principle 6 – there is brief description of the existence of environmental protection initiatives, but no data are provided. There are no temporal comparisons.
3	Infosys	Principle 2 – disclosure is generally about how the company does have environmental initiatives in place, but it does not elaborate on what these initiatives are or provide any data.

(cont.)

Rank	Name	Notes
		Principle 3 – there is a detailed breakdown of complaints relating to employee grievances, and employee training data are available. Employee training data also have temporal comparisons available.
		Principle 6 – this answers the questions posed by the SEBI guidelines, but it is only a surface-level disclosure and does not elaborate beyond stating the existence of compliance.
4	Tech Mahindra	The Section E disclosure is generally brief and not much qualitative or quantitative disclosure is published.
		Principle 2 – the disclosure is generally about how the company does have environmental initiatives in place, but it does not elaborate on what these initiatives are or provide any data.
		Principle 3 – this answers all the queries, but does not go further to discuss any employee-related initiatives.
		Principle 6 – this answers the questions posed by the SEBI guidelines, but it is only a surface-level disclosure and does not elaborate beyond stating the existence of compliance.
5	Tata Consultancy Services	This gives minimum disclosure for Section E. There is no elaboration beyond what is required in the questions.
		Principles 2, 3 and 6 – the questions in the SEBI guidelines are briefly answered, but there is no further elaboration beyond this.
		There are no temporal comparisons.
*	Wipro	SEBI requirements are mapped to an independent sustainability report prepared according to GRI G4 standards instead.
		Reports produced according to GRI G4 standards are of a much higher quality than those produced according to SEBI requirements.

Natural resources, energy, oil and gas

Rank	Name	Notes
1	NTPC	The Section E disclosure is both in-depth and specific. Principle 2 – there is a detailed breakdown on energy and water consumption. Temporal comparisons for resource consumption are also available, which is important given the nature of the industry that NTPC is in. Principle 3 – employee training and safety data are available. However, beyond that there is a lack of qualitative elaboration on training and safety-related initiatives. Principle 6 – there is in-depth and specific disclosure of renewable energy and energy efficiency initiatives. Data relating to the company's progress with regard to this principle are provided. However, they give only a snapshot and there is no temporal comparison. No temporal comparison is available other than for Principle 2
2	Indian Oil Corporation	Principle 2 – qualitative descriptions and quantitative data are provided. Qualitative descriptions are in-depth and specific with case studies. Principle 3 – there are no additional data or qualitative disclosure regarding initiatives beyond the questions asked under the SEBI guidelines. Principle 6 – qualitative disclosure regarding initiatives towards global environmental issues is vague and no quantitative data are provided. However, qualitative and quantitative disclosures on initiatives for clean technology are in-depth and specific with data provided. There are no temporal comparisons.
3	Gail (India)	Principle 2 – there is in-depth and specific qualitative disclosure. However, no additional data are provided beyond what are required by the questions. Principle 3 – no additional data or qualitative disclosure regarding initiatives are provided beyond the questions asked under the SEBI guidelines. Principle 6 – qualitative disclosure is generally in-depth and specific. Case studies are provided. No data

(*cont.*)

Rank	Name	Notes
		beyond what are required by the questions are provided. There are no temporal comparisons.
4	Power Grid Corporation of India	Principles 2 and 3 – no additional data or qualitative disclosure regarding initiatives are provided beyond the questions asked under the SEBI guidelines. Principle 6 – qualitative disclosure is generally in-depth and specific. Case studies are provided. No data beyond what are required by the questions are provided.
5	Hindustan Zinc	Elaboration is sparse; there is little elaboration beyond the answering of the guiding questions. This provides for temporal comparison when applicable in certain parts.
6	Oil and Natural Gas Corporation	Bare minimum answers are provided for a large portion of the Section E disclosure. There are no temporal comparisons.
*	Coal India	This does not have a BRR written according to SEBI's published guidelines. Instead, it includes a mapping index back to the SEBI principles in a standalone sustainability report based on the GRI G4. Mapping is difficult for investors interested in BRR metrics to navigate. Nevertheless, it provides much more in-depth and comprehensive information than is required. This is unable to be ranked in comparison with other BRRs. If ranked, it would undoubtedly be in first place. It is hard to tell the effectiveness of SEBI's guidelines in these cases.
*	Bharat Petroleum	The report is prepared according to GRI G4 standards instead. Reports produced according to GRI G4 standards are of a much higher quality than those produced according to SEBI requirements.

APPENDIX 3

Investments

Rank	Name	Notes
*	Reliance Industries	This does not directly answer the BRR mandated disclosures. It has mapped requirements to various parts of its annual report and the company's CSR report.

Manufacturing and consumer products

Rank	Name	Notes
1	Mahindra & Mahindra	Principle 2 – this is generally in-depth and specific, especially the details relating to the resource use per unit of product, which is well broken down with temporal comparisons. Principle 2 is likely to be an investor's top concern regarding this industry, given that the company is in the business of consumer goods. Principle 3 – no additional data or qualitative disclosure regarding initiatives are provided beyond the questions asked under the SEBI guidelines. Principle 6 – case studies are provided on top of the required disclosure under the SEBI guidelines.
2	Godrej Consumer Products	Principle 2 – in-depth and specific disclosure as well as relevant data on the environmental impact of products are provided. There are no temporal comparisons. Principle 3 – this has in-depth and specific disclosure, with employee-related initiatives disclosed as case studies. However, there are no data to support the case studies provided. Principle 6 – this has generally in-depth and specific disclosure with case studies and data provided. It also lays out future goals for addressing global environmental issues.
3	Titan Company	Principle 2 – qualitative disclosure about the environmental friendliness of the product is sparse. However, data in terms of resources expended for production are comprehensive.

(cont.)

Rank	Name	Notes
		Principle 6 – this has generally in-depth and specific disclosure with case studies and data provided. Principle 9 – as a producer of consumer goods, it is good that the company is candid with its disclosure of data relating to complaints received. There are no temporal comparisons.
4	Tata Motors	Principle 2 – this has generally in-depth and specific qualitative disclosures. However, it lacks data to support qualitative disclosures. Principle 3 – there is brief disclosure on safety policies beyond just answering what is required under the SEBI guidelines. Principle 6 – this has generally in-depth and specific disclosure of environmental initiatives. No data are provided. There are no temporal comparisons.
5	Eicher Motors	This does not follow the SEBI Q&A style. Nevertheless, qualitative disclosures for the principles are generally in-depth and specific, with case studies and examples. Quantitative data are provided for Principles 1–6 to back up the qualitative disclosures. However, there are no temporal comparisons available.
6	ITC	This does not follow the SEBI Q&A style. Nevertheless, qualitative disclosures for the principles are generally in-depth and specific, with case studies and examples. However, data outside of the company's charitable initiatives are sparse and there are no temporal comparisons available.
7	Hindustan Unilever	This does not follow the SEBI Q&A style. Nevertheless, qualitative disclosures for the principles are generally in-depth and specific, with case studies and examples. In addition, under Principles 3 and 6, percentage improvements over the years from a 2008 baseline are provided. The report, however, does not provide raw data for comparison.

(cont.)

Rank	Name	Notes
8	Asian Paints	This does not follow the SEBI Q&A style. Nevertheless, qualitative disclosures for the principles are generally in-depth and specific, with case studies and examples. However, it lacks quantitative data to back up case studies and examples. Minimal quantitative data are provided relating to company demographics and employee training. No temporal comparisons are available.
9	Ultratech Cement	Principle 2 – this gives generally in-depth and specific disclosure with case studies. However, no data are provided to back up examples. Principle 3 – the breakdown of data relating to employee training is comprehensive. However, there are no additional data or qualitative disclosure provided beyond the minimum required to answer the questions asked under the SEBI guidelines. Principle 6 – no additional data or qualitative disclosure regarding initiatives are provided beyond the minimum required to answer the questions asked under the SEBI guidelines. There are no temporal comparisons.
10	Grasim Industries	Principles 2, 3 and 6 – no additional data or qualitative disclosure regarding initiatives are provided beyond the minimum required to answer the questions asked under the SEBI guidelines. There are no temporal comparisons.
11	Motherson Sumi Systems	See above for Grasim Industries.
12	Dabur	See above for Grasim Industries.
13	Britannia Industries	See above for Grasim Industries.
14	Bajaj Auto	See above for Grasim Industries.
15	Nestle India	There is sparse disclosure. Principle 2 – on whether the design of products incorporates social/environmental concerns, risks and/or opportunities are especially unsatisfactorily disclosed.

(cont.)

Rank	Name	Notes
*	JSW Steel	There are no temporal comparisons. Section E for the BRR not produced. SEBI requirements are mapped to an independent sustainability report prepared according to GRI G4 standards instead. Reports produced according to GRI G4 standards are of a much higher quality than those produced according to SEBI requirements.
*	Maruti Suzuki	Adequate reasons are given for some options selected in Section D. Section E for the BRR not produced. SEBI requirements are mapped to an independent sustainability report prepared according to GRI G4 standards instead. Reports produced according to GRI G4 standards are of a much higher quality than those produced according to SEBI requirements.

Property development and management

Rank	Name	Notes
1	Avenue Supermarts	Principle 3 – specific and in-depth workforce disclosure is given. The company gives various examples of its ongoing education programmes and their content. The data breakdown for employee training is comprehensive. Principle 6 – no additional data or qualitative disclosure regarding initiatives are provided beyond the minimum required to answer the questions asked under the SEBI guidelines. There are no temporal comparisons.
2	Larsen & Toubro	This does not follow the SEBI Q&A style. Nevertheless, qualitative disclosures for the principles are generally in-depth and specific, with case studies and examples. It lacks real data to back up examples. Otherwise, data provided are only in the vague ballpark range (Principles 3 and 6).

(*cont.*)

Rank	Name	Notes
*	Adani Ports	BRR not produced.
		SEBI requirements are mapped to an independent sustainability report prepared according to GRI G4 standards instead.
		Reports produced according to GRI G4 standards are of a much higher quality than those produced according to SEBI requirements.

Financial Institutions

Rank	Name	Notes
1	Kotak Mahindra Bank	Principle 3 – this has in-depth and specific qualitative disclosure with many case studies of employee-related initiatives (diversity, talent development, health and safety, equality). However, it lacks data relating to the effects of such initiatives. With regard to employee training data, there is a comprehensive breakdown – however, no temporal comparisons are available.
		Principle 6 – this has in-depth and specific qualitative disclosure relating to the bank's environmental initiatives. Further, there is a comprehensive breakdown of energy expenditure data, along with temporal comparison.
2	Indusind Bank	Principle 3 – this has a specific and in-depth breakdown relating to employee training initiatives. Data relating to initiatives are provided. However, no temporal comparisons are available.
		Principle 6 – this has specific and in-depth disclosure relating to environmental initiatives. The company also goes above and beyond to provide a breakdown of data relating to resources saved from each initiative.
3	HDFC Standard Life Insurance Company	Principles 3 and 6 – no additional data or qualitative disclosure regarding initiatives are provided

(cont.)

Rank	Name	Notes
		beyond the minimum required to answer the questions asked under the SEBI guidelines. There are no temporal comparisons.
4	Axis Bank	See above for HDFC Standard Life Insurance Company.
5	SBI Life Insurance Company	See above for HDFC Standard Life Insurance Company.
6	Yes Bank	See above for HDFC Standard Life Insurance Company.
7	ICICI Bank	See above for HDFC Standard Life Insurance Company.
8	Housing Development Finance Corp	See above for HDFC Standard Life Insurance Company.
9	HDFC Bank	Principles 3 and 6 – no additional data or qualitative disclosure regarding initiatives are provided beyond the minimum required to answer the questions asked under the SEBI guidelines. Principle 3 – this, arguably, does not satisfactorily disclose on complaints relating to child labour, forced labour, involuntary labour and sexual harassment. There are no temporal comparisons.
10	Bajaj Finserv	Principle 3 – no additional data or qualitative disclosure regarding initiatives are provided beyond the minimum required to answer the questions asked under the SEBI guidelines. There is poor Principle 6 disclosure, which only partially addresses the SEBI guideline questions. It arguably does not fulfil the SEBI Section E guidelines. The company uses the fact that it is a holding company as an excuse/reason.
11	Bajaj Finance	Principle 3 – no additional data or qualitative disclosure regarding initiatives are provided beyond the minimum required to answer the questions asked under the SEBI guidelines. There is poor Principle 6 disclosure, which only partially addresses the SEBI guideline questions. It arguably does not fulfil the EBI Section E guidelines.

(*cont.*)

Rank	Name	Notes
12	Bandhan Bank	There is poor Section E disclosure, which fails to answer the SEBI guideline questions. It arguably does not fulfil the SEBI Section E guidelines.
*	State Bank of India	BRR not produced. SEBI requirements are mapped to an independent sustainability report prepared according to GRI G4 standards instead. Reports produced according to GRI G4 standards are of a much higher quality than those produced according to SEBI requirements.

APPENDIX 4

Good Examples of Diversity Policy Disclosure

Singapore
Singapore Telecommunications
2018 Annual Report at 69

BOARD DIVERSITY
Singtel is committed to building a diverse, inclusive and collaborative culture. Singtel recognises and embraces the benefits of diversity on the Board, and views diversity at the Board level as an essential element in supporting the attainment of its strategic objectives and its sustainable development. The Board's Diversity Policy provides that, in reviewing Board composition and succession planning, the CGNC will consider the benefits of all aspects of diversity, including diversity of skills, experience, background, gender, age, ethnicity and other relevant factors. These differences will be considered in determining the optimum composition of the Board and when possible should be balanced appropriately. All Board appointments are made based on merit, in the context of the skills, experience, independence and knowledge which the Board as a whole requires to be effective. Diversity is a key criterion in the instructions to external search consultants. The Board is of the view that gender is an important aspect of diversity and will strive to ensure that (a) any brief to external search consultants to search for candidates for appointment to the Board will include a requirement to present female candidates, (b) female candidates are included for consideration by the CGNC whenever it seeks to identify a new Director for appointment to the Board, (c) the Board appoints at least one female Director to the CGNC, and (d) there is significant and appropriate female representation on the Board, recognising that the Board's needs will change over time taking into account the skills and experience of the Board. Reflecting the focus of the Group's business in the region, three of Singtel's nine Directors are from, and have extensive experience in, jurisdictions outside Singapore, namely, the Chairman, Mr Simon Israel, and non-executive Directors, Messrs Venky Ganesan and Peter Mason AM. In relation to gender diversity, approximately 33% of the Singtel Board, or three out of the nine Board members, are female. Other than the Group CEO, none of the Directors is a former or current employee of the Company or its subsidiaries.

Comment: Singtel's diversity policy not only echoes the sentiment of meritocracy in DBS's diversity policy, but also goes further to offer ways to increase the number of females within the purview of the selection committee appointing directors. This thoughtfulness indicates that Singtel has put significant effort into understanding the problems behind and importance of gender diversity, recognising that one of the largest obstacles to female directorship is the fact that potential female directors rarely come within the purview of the selection committee.

Hong Kong
CK Infrastructure Holdings
2018 Annual Report at 163

IN THE BOARD DIVERSITY POLICY:

1 The Company recognises the benefits of having a Board that has a balance of skills, experience and diversity of perspectives appropriate to the requirements of the Company's businesses.
2 The Company maintains that appointments to the Board should be based on merit that complements and expands the skills and experience of the Board as a whole, and after due regard to factors which include but not limited to gender, age, cultural and educational background, and/or professional experience, and any other factors that the Board may consider relevant and applicable from time to time towards achieving a diverse Board.
3 The full Board of the Company is responsible for reviewing the structure, size and composition of the Board and the appointment of new directors of the Company from time to time to ensure that it has a balanced composition of skills and experience appropriate to the requirements of the Company's businesses, with due regard to the benefits of diversity on the Board. The Board as a whole is also responsible for reviewing the succession plan for the directors of the Company, in particular, for the Chairman and the Group Managing Director.

Selection of Board members is based on a range of diversity perspectives, including but not limited to gender, age, cultural and educational background, ethnicity, professional experience, skills, knowledge and other factors that the Board may consider relevant and applicable from time to time. The ultimate decision is based on merit and contribution that the selected Board members could bring to the Board.

The Board has, from time to time, reviewed and monitored the implementation of the policy to ensure its effectiveness. It will at appropriate time set measurable objectives for achieving diversity on the Board.

Comment: What is commendable about this diversity policy is that it provides for a revision of the board of directors from time to time to ensure that it is sufficiently diverse in numerous aspects, gender included. While gender remains an important consideration in the appointment of directors, the policy also emphasises that the merit of the candidates must be subsequently considered. This ensures that women who do get appointed as directors can and will be seen as being able to contribute to the company not only by virtue of their gender but also in other ways.

Malaysia
UMW Holdings Berhad
2017 Annual Report at 73

BOARD COMPOSITION

The Board believes that a truly diverse and inclusive Board will leverage on the differences in thought, perspective, knowledge, skills and industry experience, as this will ensure that the Group retains its competitive edge. Diversity is a critical attribute of a well-functioning leadership team.

In this regard, the NRC is empowered to identify and recommend to the Board nominees qualified to serve on the Board (including the PGCEO) and Board Committees. Nominations may come from a wide variety of sources, including Directors' pool, senior employees of the Group, shareholders, industry associations, recruiting firms and others.

The key responsibilities of the NRC are to identify and make recommendations to the Board on new candidates for appointment to the Board and its subsidiaries and associated companies, and to review and make recommendations to the Board on the appointment of Directors to fill seats on Board Committees. The NRC is entrusted to annually review the required mix of skills, experience and other qualities of the Board including gender diversity, ethnicity and age where appropriate, and core competencies, which NEDs should bring to the Board.

We believe that gender diversity policies will only bring about desired outcomes if there is firm commitment and promotion of a corporate culture that embraces diversity. In line with the Government's aspiration to have at least 30% women representation in decision-making positions of Malaysian public companies, UMW now has four (4) women Directors on the Board of eleven (11) members and achieved beyond the 30% level. The Board had earlier achieved 45% women representation in 2017 before the resignation of Rohaya Mohammad Yusof on 1 January 2018.

In 2017, UMW was recognised as one of the companies in the top 15 of the 100 public-listed companies with more than 30% women on the Board. The recognition marks the Group's strong advocacy towards supporting and advancing the Government's agenda of promoting boardroom diversity.

Whilst the Board recognises gender diversity as one of the key drivers to enhance Board effectiveness, appointments to the Board are ultimately made based on merit as the overriding principle in order to achieve a high-performance Board. Other competencies such as individual skills, background, industry knowledge and experience, amongst other factors, will be taken into consideration.

Comment: This is arguably the most commendable diversity policy amongst all those in the Malaysian companies. It fulfils all the laudable points of the abovementioned diversity policies and, more importantly, it recognises that gender diversity policies are effective only if there is a strong corporate culture that embraces diversity. This is an important point not raised by many other companies, but it is probably the cornerstone of an effective diversity policy. Further, it emphasises that appointments to the board are ultimately made based on merit, meaning that women who do get appointed as directors of the company will be able to command the same amount of respect as their male counterparts since they would have achieved their position based on merit rather than simply their gender. It is also no surprise that this company has one of the highest numbers of women directors amongst all fifty Malaysian companies.

India
HCL Technologies
2017–18 Annual Report at 19

DIVERSITY
As an organization, we believe diversity brings innovative thoughts and when leveraged constructively can lead to sustained innovation in the workplace. HCL prides itself as an organization with an open, transparent and inclusive culture. We focus on creating and sustaining a nurturing environment for employees with diverse backgrounds. We have embedded and strengthened our diversity and inclusion focus in our policies and processes across all key workforce practices. HCL has taken a three-tiered approach to improve gender diversity and inclusion outcomes, which has helped us sustain our overall gender diversity rate at 24%. The key elements of HCL gender diversity strategy involve: 1 Building shared leadership of diversity & inclusion at all levels 2 Leadership commitment and extensive ongoing advocacy to nurture and promote an inclusive thinking culture 3 On-boarding multiple stakeholders and driving the agenda based on diversity and inclusion goals of the respective unit, wherein the framework is global, but the implementation is to suit varied business and location needs 4 Facilitate Developmental initiatives for mid and senior women leaders enabling career progression, retaining talent and maximizing their potential. Two enabling programs for women leadership development which are based on formal mentoring are: o ASCEND is the key diversity initiative which provides a platform to women leaders for their career development through range of experiential learning, powering up the network, and creating visibility in the leadership forums. The program's key elements include Creation of DAPs, Mentoring by Senior Leaders, Peer Mentoring, Action Learning Projects, and Leadership Webinar Series.

(Cont.)

- o The second program is called 'Stepping Stones', which is a focused career development program to enable mid-level women employees to realize their career aspirations and potential to help them in their developmental journey.
5. Hundred Steps Journey: An initiative by our CEO launched on Women's Day to provide us an opportunity to pause, refocus and reaffirm our commitment to keep moving forward on an important journey. The journey of ensuring our women colleagues to reach their full potential. Employees across the globe shared their ideas on accelerating the gender diversity agenda and the hundreds of small steps that each of us need to take to empower and enable our women colleagues on an everyday basis.
6. HCL has also launched 'iBelieve – HCL's Second Career Program for Women' a platform for women to restart their tech careers after a break. The program was launched in Chennai recently, though HCL will be extending this program to other locations too. The program focuses on refreshing the candidates' existing skills and provides training on new age technologies to make them future ready. To be eligible, applicants must have had a career break of 2 to 6 years after a minimum of 2 years of work experience. Women who meet the eligibility criteria will undergo a rigorous selection process where they are assessed on their current knowledge and are allocated a suitable job role & salary commensurate to their previous experience. The training period varies from 1 month to 3 months depending on the candidate's skill proficiency assessed during the selection process.
7. Focused advocacy campaigns to build diverse perspectives: 'iMotivate', 'Feminspiration', 'Women Connect', 'BlogHer' wherein successful women leaders address the aspiring young leaders, help HCLites gain insight into successful leadership as well as understand perspectives on gender matters.

Comment: Clearly, a significant amount of thought has been put into encouraging gender diversity in the workplace. This is commendable as it shows that the company not only believes in the importance of gender diversity but is taking specific steps to reach this goal. The language used in the diversity policy is also extremely inclusive, using terms such as 'our women colleagues', whilst referring to other women who may not be working in the company currently but are aspiring young leaders. All these women have been covered in the diversity policy of this company, implying a genuine care for gender diversity.

APPENDIX 5

Proportion of Female Directors

Proportion of female directors to male directors in Singapore, Malaysia, India and Hong Kong

Proportion of female directors to male directors in the top 50 companies in Singapore (by market capitalisation as of 2018)

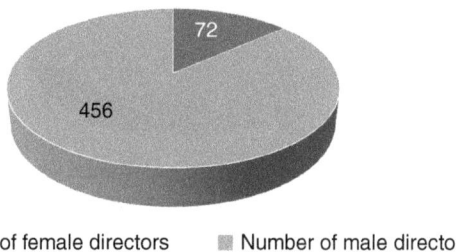

■ Number of female directors   ■ Number of male directors

Figure A5.1(a) Singapore

Proportion of female directors to male directors in the top 50 companies in Malaysia (by market capitalisation as of 2018)

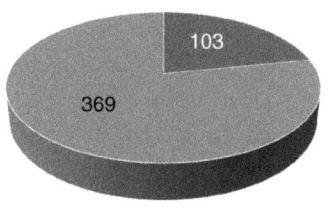

■ Number of female directors   ■ Number of male directors

Figure A5.1(b) Malaysia

Proportion of female directors to male directors in the top 50 companies in India (by market capitalisation as of 2018)

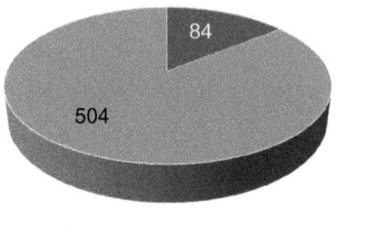

■ Number of female directors ■ Number of male directors

Figure A5.1(c) India

Proportion of female directors to male directors in the top 50 companies in Hong Kong (by market capitalisation as of 2018)

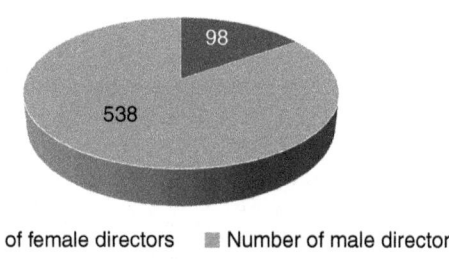

■ Number of female directors ■ Number of male directors

Figure A5.1(d) Hong Kong

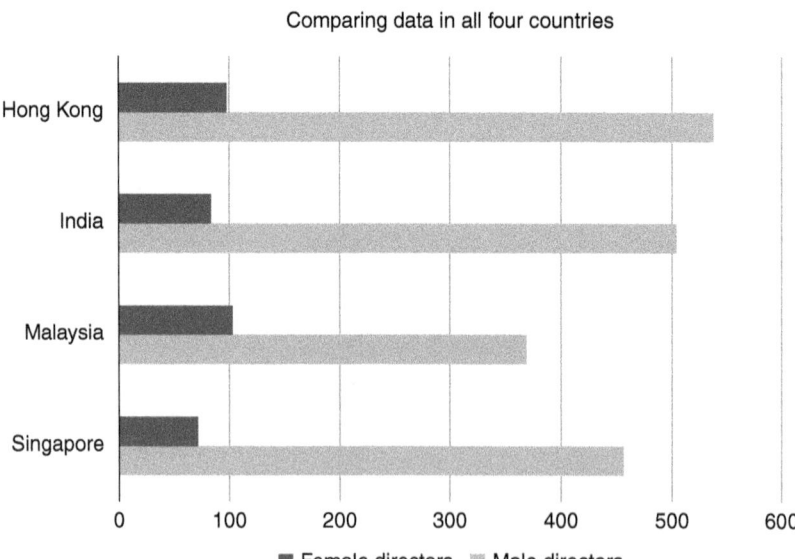

Comparing data in all four countries

APPENDIX 5 367

Proportion of female directors to male directors in the SOEs/GLCs in Singapore, Malaysia, India and Hong Kong

Proportion of female directors to male directors in the top 50 government-linked companies in Singapore (by market capitalisation as of 2018)

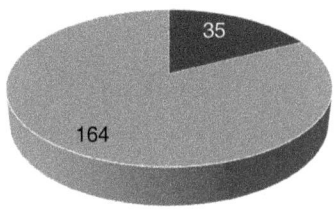

■ Number of female directors   ■ Number of male directors

Figure A5.2(a)   Singapore

Proportion of female directors to male directors in the top 50 government-linked companies in Malaysia (by market capitalisation as of 2018)

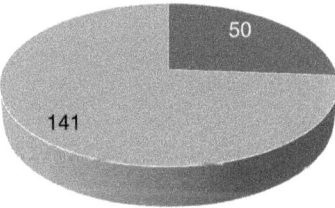

■ Number of female directors   ■ Number of male directors

Figure A5.2(b)   Malaysia

Proportion of female directors to male directors in the top 50 state-owned enterprises in India (by market capitalisation as of 2018)

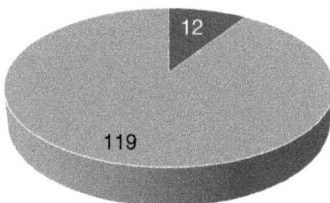

■ Number of female directors   ■ Number of male directors

Figure A5.2(c)   India

Proportion of female directors to male directors in the top 50 state-owned enterprises in Hong Kong (by market capitalisation as of 2018)

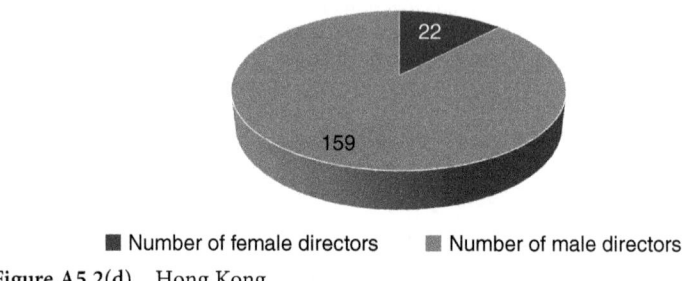

Figure A5.2(d) Hong Kong

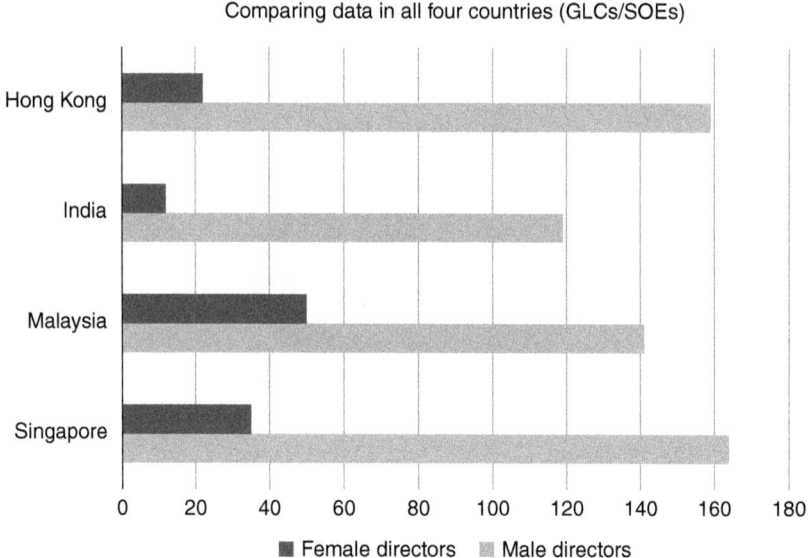

APPENDIX 5 369

Proportion of female directors to male directors in the non-SOEs/GLCs in Singapore, Malaysia, India and Hong Kong

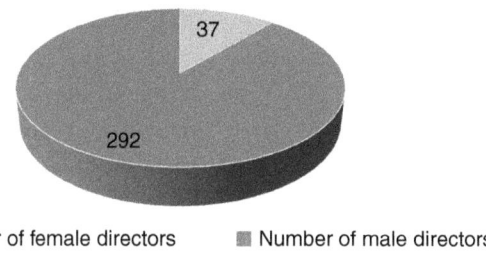

Figure A5.3(a)   Singapore

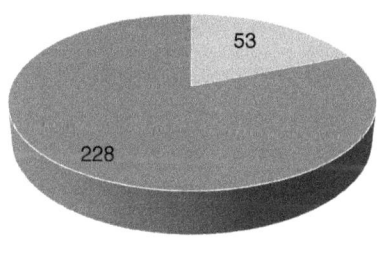

Figure A5.3(b)   Malaysia

Proportion of female directors to male directors in the top 50 non state-owned enterprises in India (by market capitalisation as of 2018)

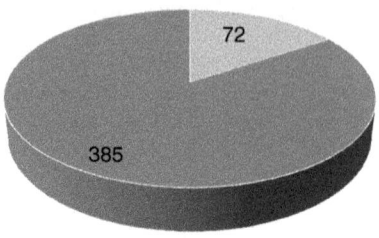

Figure A5.3(c) India

Proportion of female directors to male directors in the top 50 non state-owned enterprises in Hong Kong (by market capitalisation as of 2018)

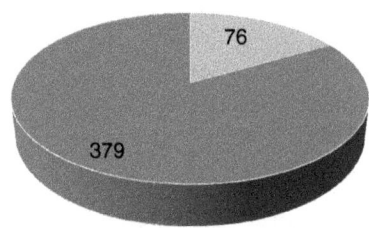

Figure A5.3(d) Hong Kong

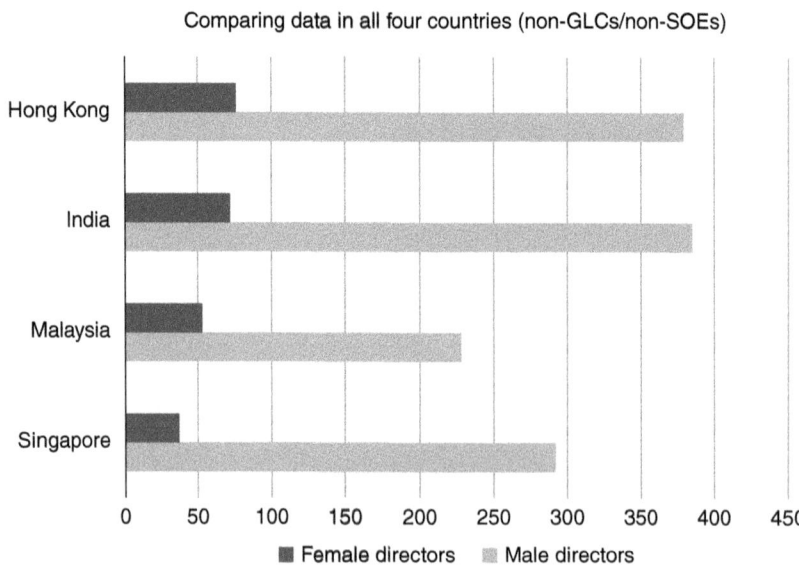

BIBLIOGRAPHY

Adams, RB, 'Women on Boards: The Superheroes of Tomorrow' (2016) 27 *Leadership Quarterly* 371.

Adams, RB and Ferreira, D, 'Women in the Boardroom and Their Impact on Governance and Performance' (2009) 94 *Journal of Financial Economics* 291.

Adams, RB and Funk, P, 'Beyond the Glass Ceiling: Does Gender Matter?' (2012) 58 *Management Science* 219.

Adams, RB and Kirchmaier, T, 'Barriers to Boardrooms' (2015), ECGI – Finance Working Paper No 347/2013, https://papers.ssrn.com/sol3/papers.cfm?abstract_id=2192918.

Adams, RB and Ragunathan, V, 'Lehman Sisters' (1 August 2015), FIRN Research Paper, https://ssrn.com/abstract=2380036.

Addison, JT, Teixeira, P, Evers, K and Bellmann, L, 'Collective Bargaining and Innovation in Germany: A Case of Cooperative Industrial Relations?' (2017) 56 *Industrial Relations* 73.

Adeyeye, AO, *Corporate Social Responsibility of Multinational Corporations in Developing Countries: Perspectives on Anti-Corruption* (Cambridge University Press 2012).

Adhikari, BK, Agrawal, A and Malm, J, 'Do Women Managers Keep Firms out of Trouble? Evidence from Corporate Litigation and Policies' (2019) 67 *Journal of Accounting and Economics* 202.

Adnan, SM, Van Staden, CJ and Hay, D, 'The Legitimacy of Institutional Theory: The Case of CSR Reporting in Cross-Cultural Settings' (18 September 2014), https://papers.ssrn.com/sol3/papers.cfm?abstract_id=2498257.

Aerts, W and Cormier, D, 'Media Legitimacy and Corporate Environmental Communication' (2009) 34 *Accounting, Organisations and Society* 1.

Afsharipour, A, 'Corporate Social Responsibility and the Corporate Board: Assessing the Indian Experiment' in Du Plessis, JJ, Varottil, U and Veldman, J (eds), *Globalisation of Corporate Social Responsibility and Its Impact on Corporate Governance* (Springer 2018).

Afsharipour, A and Rana, S, 'The Emergence of New Corporate Social Responsibility Regimes in China and India' (2014) 14 *UC Davis Business Law Journal* 175.

Ahern, KR and Dittmar, AK, 'The Changing of the Boards: The Impact on Firm Valuation of Mandated Female Board Representation' (2012) 127 *Quarterly Journal of Economics* 137.

Alagappa, M (ed), *Political Legitimacy in Southeast Asia: The Quest for Moral Authority* (Stanford University Press 1995).

Allaire, Y and Dauphin, F, *'Activist' Hedge Funds: Creators of Lasting Wealth? What Do the Empirical Studies Really Say?* (Institute for Governance and Public Organizations 2014).

Allen, F, Carletti, E and Marquez, R, 'Stakeholder Governance, Competition and Firm Value' (2015) 19 *Review of Finance* 1315.

Amira, K and Muzere, ML, 'Competition among Stock Exchanges for Equity' (2011) 35 *Journal of Banking and Finance* 2355.

Amran, A and Devi, SS, 'The Impact of Government and Foreign Affiliate Influence on Corporate Social Reporting: The Case of Malaysia' (2008) 23 *Managerial Auditing Journal* 386.

Amran, A and Nabiha, AKS, 'Corporate Social Reporting in Malaysia: A Case of Mimicking the West or Succumbing to Local Pressure' (2009) 5 *Social Responsibility Journal* 358.

Amutha, D, 'The Roots of Gender Inequality in India' (27 January 2017), https://ssrn.com/abstract=2906950.

Ang, JS and Ding, DK, 'Government Ownership and the Performance of Government-Linked Companies: The Case of Singapore' (2006) 16 *Journal of Multinational Financial Management* 64.

Ansari, AH, 'Enforcement of Environmental Laws in Developing Countries: An Expository Study with Special Reference to Malaysia' (2007) 4 *Malayan Law Journal* liv.

Arcot, S and Bruno, V, 'In Letter but Not in Spirit: An Analysis of Corporate Governance in the UK' (May 2006), http://ssrn.com/abstract=819784.

Arcot, S, Bruno, V and Faure-Grimaud, A, 'Corporate Governance in the UK: Is the Comply or Explain Approach Working?' (2010) 30 *International Review of Law and Economics* 193.

Arcot, SR and Bruno, VG 'One Size Does Not Fit All, After All: Evidence from Corporate Governance' (2007) 4 *Journal of Empirical Legal Studies* 1041.

Argenti, J, 'Stakeholders: The Case Against' (1997) 30 *Long Range Planning* 442.

Aschenfelter, O and Card, D (eds), *Handbook of Labor Economics* (vol. 3B, Elsevier 1999).

Ashraf, R, Jayaraman, N and Ryan, HE, 'Do Pension-Related Business Ties Influence Mutual Fund Proxy Voting? Evidence from Shareholder Proposals on Executive Compensation' (2012) 47 *Journal of Financial and Quantitative Analysis* 567.

Atan, R and Mohd Razali, N, 'CSR Reporting by Government Linked Companies and Their Corporate Attributes' (2013) 7 *Australian Journal of Basic and Applied Sciences* 163.

Attig, N, Boubakri, N and Ghoul, SE, 'Firm Internationalization and Corporate Social Responsibility' (2016) 134 *Journal of Business Ethics* 171.

Bainbridge, SM and Henderson, MT, *Limited Liability: A Legal and Economic Analysis* (Edward Elgar 2016).

Batra, R and Reio, TGJ, 'Gender Inequality Issues in India' (2016) 18 *Advances in Developing Human Resources* 1.

Bebchuk, LA, Cohen, A and Hirst, S, 'The Agency Problems of Institutional Investors' (2017) 31 *Journal of Economic Perspectives* 89.

Bebchuk, LA, Cohen, A and Wang, CCY, 'Learning and the Disappearing Association between Governance and Returns' (2013) 108 *Journal of Financial Economics* 323.

Bebchuk, LA and Hamdani, A, 'Independent Directors and Controlling Shareholders' (2016) 165 *University of Pennsylvania Law Review* 1271.

Bebchuk, LA and Hirst, S, 'Index Funds and the Future of Corporate Governance: Theory, Evidence, and Policy' (2019) 119 *Columbia Law Review* (forthcoming).

Bebchuk, LA and Neeman, Z, 'Investor Protection and Interest Group Politics' (2010) 23 *Review of Financial Studies* 1089.

Bebchuk, LA and Roe, MJ, 'A Theory of Path Dependence in Corporate Ownership and Governance' (1999) 52 *Stanford Law Review* 127.

Beck, C, Frost, G and Jones, S, 'CSR Disclosure and Financial Performance Revisited: A Cross-Country Analysis' (2018) 43 *Australian Journal of Management* 517.

Belinfanti, T and Stout, L, 'Contested Visions: The Value of Systems Theory for Corporate Law' (2018) 166 *University of Pennsylvania Law Review* 579.

Bénabou, R and Tirole, J, 'Individual and Corporate Social Responsibility' (2010) 77 *Econometrica* 1.

Berger, AN, Kick, T and Schaeck, K, 'Executive Board Composition and Bank Risk Taking' (2014) 28 *Journal of Corporate Finance* 48.

Berle, AA, 'For Whom Corporate Managers Are Trustees: A Note' (1932) 45 *Harvard Law Review* 1365.

Bertrand, M, 'New Perspectives on Gender' in Ashenfelter, O and Card, D, *Handbook of Labor Economics*, vol 4B (Elsevier 2011).

Bertrand, M, Goldin, C and Katz, LF, 'Dynamics of the Gender Gap for Young Professionals in the Financial and Corporate Sectors' (2010) 2 *American Economic Journal: Applied Economics* 228.

Bilimoria, D, 'Building the Business Case for Women Corporate Directors' in Burke, RJ and Mattis, MC (eds), *Women on Corporate Boards of Directors: International Challenges and Opportunities* (Kluwer Academic Publishers 2000).

Blair, M and Roe, MJ (eds), *Employees and Corporate Governance* (Brookings Institution Press 1999).

Blumberg, PI, *The Multinational Challenge to Corporation Law: The Search for a New Corporate Personality* (Oxford University Press 1993).

Boeger, N and Villiers, C (eds), *Shaping the Corporate Landscape* (Hart 2018).
Bogg, A, Costello, C, Davies, ACL and Prassl, J (eds), *The Autonomy of Labour Law* (Hart Publishing 2015).
Bøhren, Ø and Staubo, S, 'Mandatory Gender Balance and Board Independence' (2016) 22 *European Financial Management* 3.
Bolton, P, Scheinkman, J and Xiong, W, 'Executive Compensation and Short-Termist Behaviour in Speculative Markets' (2006) 73 *Review of Economic Studies* 577.
Bonnitcha, J and McCorquodale, R, 'The Concept of "Due Diligence" in the UN Guiding Principles on Business and Human Rights' (2017) 28 *European Journal of International Law* 899.
Bower, JL and Paine, LS, 'The Error at the Heart of the Corporate Leadership' (2017) *Harvard Business Review* https://hbr.org/2017/05/managing-for-the-long-term.
Boze, B, Krivitski, M, Larcker, DF, Tayan, B and Zlotnicka, E 'The Business Case for ESG' (23 May 2019) Rock Center for Corporate Governance at Stanford University Closer Look Series: Topics, Issues and Controversies in Corporate Governance No CGRP-77 https://ssrn.com/abstract=3393082.
Brammer, SJ, Pavelin, S and Porter, LA, 'Corporate Social Performance and Geographical Diversification' (2006) 59 *Journal of Business Research* 1025.
Brav, A, Jiang, W and Kim, H, 'The Real Effects of Hedge Fund Activism: Productivity, Asset Allocation, and Labor Outcomes' (2015) 28 *Review of Financial Studies* 2723.
Brest, P, Gilson, RJ and Wolfson, MA, 'How Investors Can (and Can't) Create Social Value' (March 2018) http://ssrn.com/abstract_id=3150347.
Burkart, M, Gromb, D and Panunzi, F, 'Large Shareholders, Monitoring, and Fiduciary Duty' (1997) 112 *Quarterly Journal of Economics* 112.
Burke, RJ and Mattis, MC (eds), *Women on Corporate Boards of Directors: International Challenges and Opportunities* (Kluwer Academic Publishers 2000).
Byrnes, JP, Miller, DC and Schafer, WD, 'Gender Differences in Risk Taking: A Meta-Analysis' (1999) 125 *Psychological Bulletin* 367.
Campbell, T, 'The Normative Grounding of Corporate Social Responsibility: A Human Rights Approach' in McBarnet, D, Voiculescu, A and Campbell, T (eds), *The New Corporate Accountability: Corporate Social Responsibility and the Law* (Cambridge University Press 2007).
Carney, M and Andriesse, E, 'Malaysia: Personal Capitalism' in Witt, MA and Redding, G (eds), *The Oxford Handbook of Asian Business Systems* (Oxford University Press 2014).
Carney, RW, 'Singapore: Open State-Led Capitalism' in Witt, MA and Redding, G (eds), *The Oxford Handbook of Asian Business Systems* (Oxford University Press 2014).
Cassels, J, 'Outlaws: Multinational Corporations and Catastrophic Law' (2001) 31 *Cumberland Law Review* 311.

Chapple, W, Herzig, C and Slager, R, 'The Dynamics of Corporate Social Responsibility in Asia: A 6 Country Study' (Paper 16813) The Academy of Management Annual Conference, Philadelphia, PA (2014).

Chapple, W and Moon, J, 'Corporate Social Responsibility (CSR) in Asia: A Seven Country Study of CSR Website Reporting' (2005) 44 *Business and Society* 415.

Cheffins, B and Black, B, 'Outside Director Liability across Countries' (2006) 84 *Texas Law Review* 1385.

Chen, CJP and Jaggi, B, 'Association between Independent Non-Executive Directors, Family Control and Financial Disclosures in Hong Kong' (2000) 19 *Journal of Accounting and Public Policy* 285.

Chen, W (ed), *The Beijing Consensus? How China Has Changed the Western Ideas of Law and Economic Development* (Cambridge University Press 2017).

Cheng, IH, Hong, HG and Shue, K, 'Do Managers Do Good with Other Peoples' Money?' Chicago Booth Research Paper No 12–47 https://ssrn.com/abstract= 1962120.

Cheung, YL, Connelly, JT, Limpaphayom, P and Zhou, L, 'Do Investors Really Value Corporate Governance? Evidence from the Hong Kong Market' (2007) 18 *Journal of International Financial Management & Accounting* 86.

Cheung, YL, Kong, D, Tan, W and Wang, W, 'Being Good When Being International in an Emerging Economy: The Case of China' (2015) 130 *Journal of Business Ethics* 805.

Cheung, YL, Rau, PR and Stouraitis, A, 'Tunnelling, Propping, and Expropriation: Evidence from Connected Party Transactions in Hong Kong' (2006) 82 *Journal of Financial Economics* 343.

Cheung, YL, Tan, W, Ahn, HJ and Zhang, Z, 'Does Corporate Social Responsibility Matter in Asian Emerging Markets' (2010) 92 *Journal of Business Ethics* 401.

Chiu, I, 'Operationalising a Stakeholder Conception in Company Law' (2016) 10 *Law and Financial Markets Review* 173.

Choudhury, B, 'New Rationales for Women on Boards' (2014) 34 *Oxford Journal of Legal Studies* 511.

Choudhury, B and Petrin, M, *Corporate Duties to the Public* (Cambridge University Press 2019).

Christmann, P and Taylor, G, 'Firm Self-Regulation through International Certifiable Standards: Determinants of Symbolic versus Substantive Implementation' (2006) 37 *Journal of International Business Studies* 863.

Clark, GL, Feiner, A and Viehs, M, 'From the Stockholder to the Stakeholder: How Sustainability Can Drive Financial Outperformance' (2015) http://papers.ssrn.com/sol3/papers.cfm?abstract_id=2508281.

Clarkson, MBE, 'A Stakeholder Framework for Analyzing and Evaluating Corporate Social Performance' (1995) 20 *Academy Management Review* 92.

Coen, D, Grant, W and Wilson, G (eds), *Oxford Handbook of Business and Government* (Oxford University Press 2011).

Coffee, JC, 'Racing towards the Top: The Impact of Cross-Listing and Stock Market Competition on International Corporate Governance' (2002) 102 *Columbia Law Review* 1757.

Coffee, JCJ, 'Law and the Market: The Impact of Enforcement' (2007) 156 *University of Pennsylvania Law Review* 229.

Coffee, JCJ and Palia, D, 'The Wolf at the Door: The Impact of Hedge Fund Activism on Corporate Governance' (2016) 1 *Annals of Corporate Governance* 1.

Cox, JD and Thomas, RS, 'Common Challenges Facing Shareholder Suits in Europe and the United States' (2009) 6 *European Company and Financial Law Review* 348.

Crane, A, Matten, D, McWilliams, A, Moon, J and Siegel, DS (eds), *The Oxford Handbook of Corporate Social Responsibility* (Oxford University Press 2008).

Cremers, M, Pareek, A and Sautner, Z, 'Short-Term Investors, Long-Term Investments, and Firm Value' (14 March 2017) https://papers.ssrn.com/sol3/papers.cfm?abstract_id=2720248.

Cremers, M and Sepe, SM, 'The Shareholder Value of Empowered Boards' (2016) 68 *Stanford Law Review* 1.

Criddle, EJ, Fox-Decent, E, Gold, AS, Kim, SH and Miller, PB (eds), *Fiduciary Government* (Cambridge University Press 2018).

Croson, R and Gneezy, U, 'Gender Differences in Preferences' (2009) 47 *Journal of Economic Literature* 1.

Cvijanović, D, Dasgupta, A and Zachariadis, KE, 'Ties that Bind: How Business Connections Affect Mutual Fund Activism' (2016) 71 *Journal of Finance* 2933.

Dahlerup, D, *Women, Quotas and Politics* (Routledge 2006).

Datar, AP and Balasubramanian, S, *A Ramaiya Guide to the Companies Act* (18th edn, Lexis Nexis 2014).

Davies, P, 'Efficiency Arguments for the Collective Representation of Workers' in Bogg, A, Costello, C, Davies, ACL and Prassl, J (eds), *The Autonomy of Labour Law* (Hart Publishing 2015).

Davies, P, Hopt, K, Nowak, R and Solinge, G (eds), *Corporate Boards in Law and Practice* (Oxford University Press 2013).

Davis, GF and Kim, EH, 'Business Ties and Proxy Voting by Mutual Funds' (2007) 85 *Journal of Financial Economics* 552.

De Bakker, FGA, Groenewegen, P and Den Hond, F, 'A Bibliometric Analysis of 30 Years of Research and Theory on Corporate Social Responsibility and Corporate Social Performance' (2005) 44 *Business and Society* 283.

Dearborn, M, 'Enterprise Liability: Reviewing and Revitalizing Liability for Corporate Groups' (2009) 97 *California Law Review* 195.

Deegan, C, Rankin, M and Voght, P, 'Firms' Disclosure Reactions to Major Social Incidents: Australian Evidence' (2000) 24 *Accounting Forum* 101.

DeHaan, E, Larcker, D and McClure, C, 'Long-Term Economic Consequences of Hedge Fund Activist Interventions' (3 October 2018) https://papers.ssrn.com/sol3/papers.cfm?abstract_id=3260095.

Deng, X et al, 'Corporate Social Responsibility and Stakeholder Value Maximization: Evidence from Mergers' (2013) 110 *Journal of Financial Economics* 87.

Dhanesh, GS, 'Why Corporate Social Responsibility? An Analysis of Drivers of CSR in India' (2015) 29 *Management Communication Quarterly* 114.

Dharmapala, D and Khanna, V, 'The Impact of Mandated Corporate Social Responsibility: Evidence from India's Companies Act of 2013' (8 September 2018) University of Chicago, Public Law Working Paper No 601 https://ssrn.com/abstract=2862714.

Dimson, E, 'Active Ownership' (2015) 28 *Review of Financial Studies* 3225.

Dixit, A, 'Incentives and Organizations in the Public Sector: An Interpretative Review' (2002) 37 *Journal of Human Resources* 696.

Djankov, S, Porta, RL, Lopez-de-Silanes, F and Shleifer, A, 'The Law and Economics of Self-Dealing' (2008) 88 *Journal of Financial Economics* 430.

Dodd, EMJ, 'Is Effective Enforcement of the Fiduciary Duties of Corporate Managers Practicable?' (1934) 2 *University of Chicago Law Review* 194.

Doldor, E, Vinnicombe, S, Gaughan, M and Sealy, R, 'Gender Diversity on Boards: The Appointment Process and the Role of Executive Search Firms' (2012) Equality and Human Rights Commission Research Report 85.

Donald, DC, Wang, J and VanderWolk, JP, *A Financial Center for Two Empires: Hong Kong's Corporate, Securities and Tax Laws in Its Transition from Britain to China* (Cambridge University Press 2014).

Donaldson, T and Preston, LE, 'The Stakeholder Theory for the Corporation: Concepts, Evidence, Implications' (1995) 20 *Academy Management Review* 6.

Dowling, J and Pfeffer, J, 'Organizational Legitimacy: Social Values and Organizational Behavior' (1975) 18 *Pacific Sociological Review* 122.

Du Plessis, JJ, Varottil, U and Veldman, J (eds), *Globalisation of Corporate Social Responsibility and Its Impact on Corporate Governance* (Springer 2018).

Dworkin, R, *Sovereign Virtue: The Theory and Practice of Equality* (Harvard University Press 2000).

Dyck, A, Lins, KV, Roth, L and Wagner, HF, 'Do Institutional Investors Drive Corporate Social Responsibility? International Evidence' (2019) 131 *Journal of Financial Economics* 693.

Eagly, AH and Karau, SJ, 'Role Congruity Theory of Prejudice toward Female Leaders' (2002) 109 *Psychological Review* 573.

Easterbrook, F, 'Two-Agency Cost Explanation of Dividends' (1984) 74 *American Economic Review* 650.

Easterbook, F and Fischel, D, 'Limited Liability and the Corporation' (1985) 52 *University of Chicago Law Review* 89.

Eastman, MT, Rallis, D and Mazzucchelli, G, 'MSCI, The Tipping Point: Women on Boards and Financial Performance' (2016) Women on Boards Report.

Eckbo, BE, Nygaard, K and Thorburn, KS, 'Does Gender-Balancing the Board Reduce Firm Value?' (March 2016) CEPR Discussion Paper No DP11176 https://ssrn.com/abstract=2766471.

Edmans, A, 'Does the Stock Market Fully Value Intangibles? Employee Satisfaction and Equity Prices' (2011) 101 *Journal of Financial Economics* 621.

Eger, T, 'Opportunistic Termination of Employment Contracts and Legal Protection against Dismissal in Germany and the USA' (2004) 23 *International Review of Law and Economics* 381.

Eng, LL and Mak, YT, 'Corporate Governance and Voluntary Disclosure' (2003) 22 *Journal of Accounting and Public Policy* 325.

Engelstad, F and Teigen, M (eds), *Firms, Boards and Gender Quotas: Comparative Perspectives* (Emerald Group Publishing Ltd 2012).

Esa, E and Mohd Ghazali, NA, 'Corporate Social Responsibility and Corporate Governance in Malaysian Government-Linked Companies' (2012) 12 *Corporate Governance* 292.

Faccio, M, 'Politically Connected Firms' (2006) 96 *American Economic Review* 369.

Fauver, L and Fuerst, ME, 'Does Good Corporate Governance Include Employee Representation? Evidence from German Corporate Boards' (2006) 82 *Journal of Financial Economics* 673.

Ferran, E, 'Corporate Mobility and Company Law' (2016) 79 *Modern Law Review* 813.

Ferrell, A, Liang, H and Renneboog, L, 'Socially Responsible Firms' (2016) 122 *Journal of Financial Economics* 585.

FitzRoy, F and Kraft, K, 'Co-determination, Efficiency and Productivity' (2005) 43 *British Journal of Industrial Relations* 233.

Flammer, C and Kacperczk, A, 'The Impact of Stakeholder Orientation on Innovation: Evidence from a Natural Experiment' (2014) http://papers.ssrn.com/sol3/papers.cfm?abstract_id=2353076.

Francis, N and Wong, W, 'The Legal Essentials of Trade Unions in Hong Kong' (2010) 16 *China Staff; Hong Kong* 35.

Franks, J, Mayer, C and Renneboog, L, 'Who Disciplines Management in Poorly Performing Companies?' (2001) 10 *Journal of Financial Intermediation* 209.

Freeman, RE, *Strategic Management: A Stakeholder Approach* (Pitman/Ballinger 1984).

French, KR, 'Presidential Address: The Cost of Active Investing' (2008) 63 *Journal of Finance* 1537.

Freshfields Bruckhaus Deringer, *A Legal Framework for the Integration of Environmental, Social and Governance Issues into Institutional Investment* (2005).

Frick, B and Lehman, E, 'Corporate Governance in Germany: Ownership, Codetermination and Firm Performance in a Stakeholder Economy' in Gospel, H and Pendleton, A (eds), *Corporate Governance and Labour Management* (Oxford University Press 2006).

Frostick, X, 'Is There a Duty to Act in the Best Interests of the Beneficiaries?' (2000) 83 *Pension Lawyer* 2.

Gainet, C, 'Exploring the Impact of Legal Systems and Financial Structures on CR' (2010) 95 *Journal of Business Ethics* 195.

Garg, P, 'CSR and Corporate Performance: Evidence from India' (2016) 43 *Decision* 333.
Gary, SN, 'Best Interests in the Long Term: Fiduciary Duties and ESG Integration' (2019) 90 *University of Colorado Law Review* 731.
Gary, SN, 'Values and Value: University Endowments, Fiduciary Duties, and ESG Investing' (2016) 42 *Journal of College and University Law* 247.
Gelter, M, 'The Dark Side of Shareholder Influence: Managerial Autonomy and Stakeholder Orientation in Comparative Governance' (2009) 50 *Harvard International Law Journal* 129.
Gelter, M, 'Why Do Shareholder Derivative Suits Remain Rare in Continental Europe?' (2012) 37 *Brooklyn Journal of International Law* 843.
Gilson, RJ, 'Controlling Shareholders and Corporate Governance: Complicating the Comparative Taxonomy' (2006) 119 *Harvard Law Review* 1641.
Gilson, RJ, Hansmann, H and Pargendler, M, 'Regulatory Dualism as a Development Strategy: Corporate Reform in Brazil, the United States, and the European Union' (2011) 63 *Stanford Law Review* 475.
Global Sustainable Investment Alliance, '2016 Global Sustainable Investment Review' (2016) www.gsi-alliance.org/wp-content/uploads/2017/03/GSIR_Review2016.F.pdf.
Glynn, TP, 'Beyond "Unlimiting" Shareholder Liability: Vicarious Tort Liability for Corporate Officers' (2004) 57 *Vanderbilt Law Review* 329.
Gomez, ET and Jomo, KS, *Malaysia's Political Economy: Politics, Patronage, and Profits* (2nd edn, Cambridge University Press 1999).
Gomez, ET, Padmanabhan, T, Kamaruddin, N, Bhalla, S and Fisal, F, *Minister of Finance Incorporated: Ownership and Control of Corporate Malaysia* (Springer 2017).
Gompers, P and Kovvali, S, 'The Other Diversity Dividend' (2018) July–August *Harvard Business Review* 72.
Gond, JP, Kang, N and Moon, J, 'The Government of Self-Regulation: On the Comparative Dynamics of Corporate Social Responsibility' (2011) 40 *Economy and Society* 640.
Gond, JP and Moon, J (eds), *Corporate Social Responsibility: A Reader*, vol 1 (Routledge 2011).
Gond, JP and Moon, J, 'Corporate Social Responsibility in Retrospect and Prospect: Exploring the Life-Cycle of an Essentially Contested Concept' in Gond, JP and Moon, J (eds), *Corporate Social Responsibility: A Reader*, vol 1 (Routledge 2011).
Gopalan, S and Kamalnath, A, 'Mandatory Corporate Social Responsibility as a Vehicle for Reducing Equality: An Indian Solution for Piketty and the Millennials' (2015) 10 *Northwestern Journal of International Law and Business* 34.
Gordon, JN and Ringe, WG (eds), *The Oxford Handbook of Corporate Law and Governance* (Oxford University Press 2018).

Gorton, G and Schmid, FA, 'Capital, Labor and the Firm: A Study of German Codetermination' (2004) 2 *Journal of the European Economic Association* 863.

Gosepath, S, 'Equality' (2001) Stanford Encyclopedia of Philosophy https://plato.stanford.edu/entries/equality/.

Gospel, H and Pendleton, A (eds), *Corporate Governance and Labour Management* (Oxford University Press 2006).

Gourevitch, PA and Shinn, J, *Political Power and Corporate Control: The New Global Politics of Corporate Governance* (Princeton University Press 2005).

Grewal, J, Riedl, EJ and Serafeim, G, 'Market Reaction to Mandatory Nonfinancial Disclosure' (2019) 65 *Management Science* 2947.

Gul, FA, 'Auditors' Response to Political Connections and Cronyism in Malaysia' (2006) 44 *Journal of Accounting Research* 931.

Gupta, S and Goldar, B, 'Do Stock Markets Penalize Environment-Unfriendly Behavior? Evidence from India' (2005) 52 *Ecological Economics* 81.

Haji, AA, 'Corporate Social Responsibility Disclosures over Time: Evidence from Malaysia' (2013) 28 *Managerial Auditing Journal* 647.

Halpern, P, Tebilcock, MJ and Turnbull, SM, 'An Economic Analysis of Limited Liability' (1980) 30 *University of Toronto Law Journal* 117.

Hamdani, A and Yafeh, Y, 'Institutional Investors as Minority Shareholders' (2013) 17 *Review of Finance* 691.

Hamid, FZA, Atan, R and Md Saleh, MS, 'A Case Study of Corporate Social Responsibility by Malaysian Government Link Company' (2014) 164 *Procedia – Social and Behavioral Sciences* 600.

Hampton-Alexander Review, 'FTSE Women Leaders: Improving Gender Balance in FTSE Leadership' (2017).

Hamrouni, A, Miloudi, A and Benkraiem, R, 'Signaling Firm Performance through Corporate Voluntary Disclosure' (2015) 31 *Journal of Applied Business Research* 609.

Haniffa, RM and Cooke, TE, 'The Impact of Culture and Governance on Corporate Social Reporting' (2005) 24 *Journal of Accounting and Public Policy* 391.

Hansmann, H and Kraakman, R, 'The Essential Role of Organization Law' (2005) 119 *Harvard Law Review* 1335.

Hansmann, H and Kraakman, R, 'Towards Unlimited Shareholder Liability for Corporate Torts' (1991) 100 *Yale Law Journal* 1879.

Hansmann, H, Kraakman, R and Squire, R, 'Law and the Rise of the Firm' (2006) 119 *Harvard Law Review* 1333.

Hart, O and Zingales, L, 'Companies Should Maximize Shareholder Welfare Not Market Value' (2017) 2 *Journal of Law, Finance, and Accounting* 247.

Heard, JE and Sherman, HD, *Conflicts of Interest in the Proxy Voting System* (Investor Responsibility Research Center 1987).

Heidenreichat, V, 'Why Gender Quotas in Company Boards in Norway – and Not in Sweden?' in Engelstad, F and Teigen, M (eds), *Firms, Boards and Gender Quotas: Comparative Perspectives* (Emerald Group Publishing Ltd 2012).

Heng, PK, 'The New Economic Policy and the Chinese Community in Peninsula Malaysia' (1997) 35 *Developing Economies* 262.

Hernan, RE, *This Borrowed Earth: Lessons from the Fifteen Worst Environmental Disasters around the World* (Macmillan Science 2010).

Higgins, C and Debroux, P, 'Globalization and CSR in Asia' (2009) 8 *Asian Business and Management* 125.

Hill, J, 'Good Activist/Bad Activist: The Rise of International Stewardship Codes' (2018) 41 *Seattle University Law Review* 497.

Hill, JG, 'Images of the Shareholder' in Hill, JG and Thomas, RS (eds), *Research Handbook on Shareholder Power* (Edward Elgar 2015).

Hill, JG and Thomas, RS (eds), *Research Handbook on Shareholder Power* (Edward Elgar 2015).

Hillman, AJ, Cannella, AAJ and Harris, IC, 'Women and Racial Minorities in the Boardroom: How Do Directors Differ?' (2002) 28 *Journal of Management* 747.

Hillman, AJ and Dalziel, T, 'Board of Directors and Firm Performance: Integrating Agency and Resource Dependence Perspectives' (2003) 28 *Academy Management Review* 383.

Hofman, PS, Moon, J and Wu, B, 'Corporate Social Responsibility under Authoritarian Capitalism: Dynamics and Prospects of State-Led and Society-Driven CSR' (2017) 56 *Business & Society* 651.

Hu, M and Loh, L, 'Board Governance and Sustainability Disclosure: A Cross-Sectional Study of Singapore-Listed Companies' (2018) 10 *Sustainability* 1.

Hulme, SEK, 'The Basic Duty of Trustees of Superannuation Trusts: Fair to One, Fair to All?' (2000) 14 *Trust Law International* 130.

Hung, M, Wong, TJ and Zhang, T, 'Political Considerations in the Decision of Chinese SOEs to List in Hong Kong' (2012) 53 *Journal of Accounting and Economics* 435.

Huse, M and Solberg, AG, 'Gender-Related Boardroom Dynamics: How Scandinavian Women Make and Can Make Contributions on Corporate Boards' (2006) 21 *Women Management Review* 113.

Hwang, S, Shivdasani, A and Simintzi, E, 'Mandating Women on Boards: Evidence from the United States' (13 October 2018) Kenan Institute of Private Enterprise Research Paper No 18–34 https://ssrn.com/abstract=3265783.

Ioannou, I and Serafeim, G, 'The Consequences of Mandatory Corporate Sustainability Reporting' (1 May 2017) Harvard Business School Research Working Paper No 11–100 https://ssrn.com/abstract=1799589.

Ioannou, I and Serafeim, G, 'Corporate Sustainability: A Strategy?' (1 January 2019) Harvard Business School Accounting & Management Unit Working Paper No 19–065 https://ssrn.com/abstract=3312191.

Jacobs, BW, Singhal, VR and Subramanian, R, 'An Empirical Investigation of Environmental Performance and the Market Value of the Firm' (2010) 28 *Journal of Operations Management* 430.

Jain, R and Winner, LH, 'CSR and Sustainability Reporting Practices of Top Companies in India' (2016) 21 *Corporate Communications: An International Journal* 36.

Jain, S, Blackford, B, Dabney, D and Small, J, 'What Is the Optimal Balance in the Relative Roles of Management, Directors, and Investors in the Governance of Public Corporations?' (11 March 2014) https://ssrn.com/abstract=2407716.

Jensen, M, 'Value Maximisation, Stakeholder Theory and the Corporate Objective Function' (2010) 22 *Journal of Applied Corporate Finance* 32.

Johnson, S and Mitton, T, 'Cronyism and Capital Controls: Evidence from Malaysia' (2003) 67 *Journal of Financial Economics* 351.

Kagel, J and Roth, AE (eds), *Handbook of Experimental Economics*, vol 2 (Princeton University Press 2016).

Kang, J, 'The Relationship between Corporate Diversification and Corporate Social Performance' (2013) 34 *Strategic Management Journal* 94.

Kang, N and Moon, J, 'Institutional Complementarity between Corporate Governance and Corporate Social Responsibility: A Comparative Institutional Analysis of Three Capitalisms' (2012) 10 *Socio-Economic Review* 85.

Kansal, M, Joshi, M, Babu, S and Sharma, S, 'Reporting of Corporate Social Responsibility in Central Public Social Enterprises: A Study of Post Mandatory Regime in India' (2018) 151 *Journal of Business Ethics* 813.

Katelouzou, D, 'Shareholder Stewardship: A Case of (Re)-Embedding the Institutional Investors and the Corporation?' in Sjåfjell, B and Bruner, CM (eds), *Cambridge Handbook of Corporate Law, Corporate Governance and Sustainability* (Cambridge University Press 2019).

Kay, J, *The Kay Review of UK Equity Markets and Long-Term Decision-Making, Final Report* (Department of Business, Innovation and Skills 2012).

Keay, A, 'Ascertaining the Corporate Objective: An Entity Maximisation and Sustainability Theory' (2008) 71 *Modern Law Review* 663.

Keay, A, 'Comply or Explain in Corporate Governance Codes: In Need of Greater Regulatory Oversight?' (2014) 34 *Legal Studies* 279.

Kelly, G and Parkinson, J, 'The Conceptual Foundations of the Company: A Pluralist Approach' in Parkinson, J, Kelly, G and Gamble, A (eds), *The Political Economy of the Company* (Hart 2001).

Kershaw, D, *Company Law in Context: Text and Materials* (2nd edn, Oxford University Press 2012).

Khan, M, Serafeim, G and Yoon, A, 'Corporate Sustainability: First Evidence on Materiality' (2016) 91 *Accounting Review* 1697.

Khong, CO, 'Singapore: Political Legitimacy through Managing Conformity' in Alagappa, M (ed), *Political Legitimacy in Southeast Asia: The Quest for Moral Authority* (Stanford University Press 1995).

Kim, EH, Maug, E and Schneider, C, 'Labor Representation in Governance as an Insurance Mechanism' (2018) 22 *Review of Finance* 1251.

Kirkpatrick, G (Consultant for OECD Secretariat), *Managing State Assets to Achieve Development Goals: The Case of Singapore and Other Countries in the Region* (OECD Workshop on State-Owned Enterprises in the Development Process 2014).

Klein, A and Zur, E, 'The Impact of Hedge Fund Activism on the Target Firm's Existing Bondholders' (2011) 24 *Review of Financial Studies* 1735.

Knudsen, JS and Moon, J, *Visible Hands: Government Regulation and International Business Responsibility* (Cambridge University Press 2017).

Kolk, A, 'Sustainability, Accountability and Corporate Governance: Exploring Multinationals' Reporting Practices' (2008) 17 *Business Strategy and the Environment* 1.

Kozinets, RV and Handelman, JM, 'Adversaries of Consumption: Consumer Movements, Activism, and Ideology' (2004) 31 *Journal of Consumer Research* 691.

Kraakman, R, Armour, J, Davies, P et al, *The Anatomy of Corporate Law: A Comparative and Functional Approach* (2nd edn, Oxford University Press 2009).

Kraakman, R, Armour, J, Davies, P et al, *The Anatomy of Corporate Law: A Comparative and Functional Approach* (3rd edn, Oxford University Press 2017).

Kramer, VW, Konrad, AM and Erkut, S, 'Critical Mass on Corporate Boards: Why Three or More Women Enhance Governance' (2006) Wellesley Center Report 74.

Kroes, N, 'Good for Women and Good for Ireland' Speech at 'Women for Europe', Dublin (16 July 2009) http://europa.eu/rapid/pressReleasesAction.do?reference=SPEECH/09/344&format=HTML&aged=0&language=EN &guiLanguage=en.

Krueger, AO, 'Government Failures in Development' (1990) 4 *Journal of Economic Perspectives* 9.

Kubler, F, Schmidt, W and Simitis, S, *Mitbestimmungsproblem als Gesetzgebungspolitische Aufgabe* (Nomos Verlagsgesellschaft 1978).

Kumar, NS and Rao, US, 'Guidelines for Value Based Management in Kautilya's Arthashastra' (1996) 15 *Journal of Business Ethics* 415.

Kutz, C, *Complicity: Ethics and Law for a Collective Age* (Cambridge University Press 2000).

Kytle, B and Ruggie, J, 'Corporate Social Responsibility as Risk Management: A Model for Multinationals' (2005) Corporate Social Responsibility Initiative Working Paper No 10, Harvard University, Cambridge.

Lambooij, TE, *Corporate Social Responsibility: Legal and Semi-Legal Frameworks Supporting CSR* (Kluwer 2010).

Lau, CM, Lu, Y and Liang, Q, 'Corporate Social Responsibility in China: A Corporate Governance Approach' (2016) 136 *Journal of Business Ethics* 73.

Leebron, DW, 'Limited Liability, Tort Victims, and Creditors' (1991) 91 *Columbia Law Review* 1565.

Leib, EJ and Galoob, SR, 'Fiduciary Political Theory: A Critique' (2016) 125 *Yale Law Journal* 1820.

Levi, M, Li, K and Zhang, F, 'Director Gender and Mergers and Acquisitions' (2014) 28 *Journal of Corporate Finance* 185.

Leyens, PC, 'Corporate Social Responsibility in European Union Law: Foundations, Developments, Enforcement' in Du Plessis, JJ, Varottil, U and Veldman, J (eds), *Globalisation of Corporate Social Responsibility and Its Impact on Corporate Governance* (Springer 2018).

Liang, H and Renneboog, L, 'Corporate Donations and Shareholder Value' (2017) 33 *Oxford Review of Economic Policy* 278.

Liang, H and Renneboog, L, 'On the Foundations of Corporate Social Responsibility' (2017) 72 *Journal of Finance* 853.

Liebman, BL and Milhaupt, CJ, 'Reputational Sanctions in China's Securities Market' (2008) 108 *Columbia Law Review* 929.

Lim, E, *A Case for Shareholder's Fiduciary Duties in Common Law Asia* (Cambridge University Press 2019).

Lin, LW and Milhaupt, CJ, 'We Are the (National) Champions: Understanding the Mechanisms of State Capitalism in China' (2013) 65 *Stanford Law Review* 697.

Lindblom, CK, 'The Implications of Organizational Legitimacy for Corporate Social Performance and Disclosure' (2010) Paper Presented at the Critical Perspectives on Accounting Conference, New York NY.

Lliev, P, Lins, KV, Miller, DP and Roth, L, 'Shareholder Voting and Corporate Governance around the World' (2015) 28 *Review of Financial Studies* 2167.

Lo, KY and Kwan, CL, 'The Effect of Environmental, Social, Governance and Sustainability Initiatives on Stock Value: Examining Market Response to Initiatives Undertaken by Listed Companies' (2017) 24 *Corporate Social Responsibility and Environmental Management* 606.

Lo, SHC and Qu, CZ, *Law of Companies in Hong Kong* (2nd edn, Sweet & Maxwell 2015).

Loh, L, Nguyen TP, Sim, I, Thomas, T and Wang, Y, 'Sustainability Reporting in ASEAN: State of Progress in Indonesia, Malaysia, Singapore and Thailand' (2015) https://bschool.nus.edu.sg/cgio/wp-content/uploads/sites/7/2018/10/ACN-CGIO-Sustainability-Reporting-in-ASEAN-2016.pdf.

Loh, L, Thomas, T and Wang, Y, 'Sustainability Reporting and Firm Value: Evidence from Singapore-Listed Companies' (2017) *Sustainability* 1.

LoPucki, ML, 'The Death of Liability' (1996) 106 *Yale Law Journal* 1.

Lord Nicholls, 'Trustees and Their Broader Community: Where Duty, Morality and Ethics Converge' (1996) 70 *Australian Law Journal* 205.

Low, KCP and Ang, S, 'Confucian Ethics, Governance and Corporate Social Responsibility' (2013) 8 *International Journal of Business and Management* 30.

Low, KCP, Idowu, SO and Ang, SL (eds), *Corporate Social Responsibility in Asia: Practice and Experience* (Springer 2014).

Lund, DS, 'The Case against Passive Shareholder Voting' (2018) 43 *Journal of Corporation Law* 101.
Ma, SY, 'Role of the State in Chinese Enterprises Listed in Hong Kong' (2002) 15 *Pacific Review* 279.
Magill, M, Quinzii, M and Rochet, JC, 'A Theory of the Stakeholder Corporation' (2015) 83 *Econometrica* 1685.
Maignan, I and Ralston, DA, 'Corporate Social Responsibility in Europe and the U.S.: Insights from Businesses' Self-Presentations' (2002) 33 *Journal of International Business Studies* 497.
Majumdar, AB, 'India's Journey with Corporate Social Responsibility: What Next?' (2015) 33 *Journal of Law and Commerce* 165.
Malcolmson, JM, 'Individual Employment Contracts' in Aschenfelter, O and Card, D (eds), *Handbook of Labor Economics*, vol 3B (Elsevier 1999).
Masulis, RW and Reza, SW, 'Agency Problems of Corporate Philanthropy' (2015) 28 *Review of Financial Studies* 592.
Matsa, DA and Miller, AR, 'A Female Style in Corporate Leadership? Evidence from Quotas' (2013) 5 *American Economic Journal: Applied Economics* 136.
Matten, D and Moon, J, '"Implicit" and "Explicit" CSR: A Conceptual Framework for a Comparative Understanding of Corporate Social Responsibility' (2008) 33 *Academy of Management Review* 404.
Mayer, C, 'Who's Responsible for an Irresponsible Business? An Assessment' (2017) 33 *Oxford Review of Economic Policy* 157.
McBarnet, D, Voiculescu, A and Campbell, T (eds), *The New Corporate Accountability: Corporate Social Responsibility and the Law* (Cambridge University Press 2007).
McGaughey, E, 'The Codetermination Bargains: The History of German Corporate and Labour Law' (2016) 23 *Columbia Journal of European Law* 135.
McIrnerney-Lacombe, N, Bilimoria, D and Salipante, PF, 'Championing the Discussion of Tough Issues: How Women Corporate Directors Contribute to Board Deliberations' in Vinnicombe, S, Singh, V, Burke, RJ, Bilimoria, D and Huse, M (eds), *Women on Corporate Boards of Directors: International Research and Practice* (Edward Elgar Publishing 2008).
Mendelson, N, 'A Control-Based Approach to Shareholder Liability for Corporate Torts' (2002) 102 *Columbia Law Review* 1203.
Menon, J, 'Government-Linked Companies: Impacts on the Malaysian Economy' (December 2017) Policy IDEAS No 45.
Mevorach, I, *Insolvency within Multinational Enterprise Groups* (Oxford University Press 2009).
McGhee, J (ed), *Snell's Equity* (18th edn, Sweet & Maxwell 2012).
Milhaupt, CJ, 'Chinese Corporate Capitalism in Comparative Context' in Chen, W (ed), *The Beijing Consensus? How China Has Changed the Western Ideas of Law and Economic Development* (Cambridge University Press 2017).

Million, D, 'Corporate Social Responsibility and Environmental Sustainability' in Sjåfjell, B and Richardson, BJ (eds), *Company Law and Sustainability: Legal Barriers and Opportunities* (Cambridge University Press 2015).

Mitchell, RK, Agle, BR and Wood, DJ, 'Toward a Theory of Stakeholder Identification and Salience: Defining the Principle of Who and What Really Counts' (1997) 22 *Academy Management Review* 853.

Moe, TM, 'The New Economics of Organization' (1984) 28 *American Journal of Political Science* 739.

Mohamed Ghazali, NA, 'Ownership Structure and Corporate Social Responsibility Disclosure: Some Malaysian Evidence' (2007) 7 *Corporate Governance* 251.

Moon, J, Kang, N and Gond, JP, 'Corporate Social Responsibility and Government' in Coen, D, Grant, W and Wilson, G (eds), *Oxford Handbook of Business and Government* (Oxford University Press 2011).

Moore, JD, *Varieties of Capitalism in Southeast Asia* (Springer 2017).

Morgan, P, 'Vicarious Liability for Group Companies: The Final Frontiers of Vicarious Liability?' (2015) 31 *Professional Negligence* 276.

Muchlinski, P, 'Limited Liability and Multinational Enterprises: A Case for Reform?' (2010) 34 *Cambridge Journal of Economics* 915.

Muller-Jentsch, W, 'Germany: From Collective Voice to Co-management' in Rogers, J and Streek, W (eds), *Works Councils* (University of Chicago Press 1995).

Muniapan, B, 'The Roots of Indian Corporate Social Responsibility (CSR) Practice from a Vedantic Perspective' in Low, KCP, Idowu, SO and Ang, SL (eds), *Corporate Social Responsibility in Asia: Practice and Experience* (Springer 2014).

Musacchio, A and Lazzarini, SG, 'Leviathan in Business: Varieties of State Capitalism and Their Implications for Economic Performance' (2012) https://papers.ssrn.com/sol3/papers.cfm?abstract_id=2070942.

Musacchio, A and Lazzarini, SG, *Reinventing State Capitalism: Leviathan in Business, Brazil and Beyond* (Harvard University Press 2014).

Muscat, A, *The Liability of the Holding Company for the Debts of Its Insolvent Subsidiaries* (Routledge 1996).

Naniwadekar, M and Varottil, U, 'The Stakeholder Approach towards Directors' Duties under Indian Company Law: A Comparative Analysis' (11 August 2016) https://papers.ssrn.com/sol3/papers.cfm?abstract_id=2822109.

Nariman, A, Sulaiman, M and Othman, E, *Malaysia Company Law: Principles and Practices* (Wolters Kluwer 2015).

Niederle, M, 'Gender' in Kagel, J and Roth, AE (eds), *Handbook of Experimental Economics*, vol 2 (Princeton University Press 2016).

Nielsen, S and Huse, M, 'The Contribution of Women on Boards of Directors: Going beyond the Surface' (2010) 18 *Corporate Governance* 136.

Nutzinger, HG and Backhaus, J (eds), *Codetermination: A Discussion of Different Approaches* (Springer 2000).

Nutzinger, HG, 'Codetermination in West Germany: Institutions and Experiences' in Nutzinger, HG and Backhaus, J (eds), *Codetermination: A Discussion of Different Approaches* (Springer 2000).

O'Rourke, D, 'Market Movements: Nongovernmental Organization Strategies to Influence Global Production and Consumption' (2005) 9 *Journal of Industry Ecology* 1.

Oberfichtner, M, 'Works Council Introductions in Germany: Do They Reflect Workers' Voice?' (2019) 40 *Economic and Industrial Democracy* 301.

OECD, 'SOEs in India's Economic Development' in *State-Owned Enterprises in the Development Process* (OECD Publishing 2015).

OECD, *Corporate Governance Factbook 2019* (OECD Publishing 2019).

OECD, *State-Owned Enterprises and Corruption: What Are the Risks and What Can Be Done?* (OECD Publishing 2018).

OECD, *The Role of Institutional Investors in Promoting Good Corporate Governance* (OECD Publishing 2011).

OECD, *The Size and Sectoral Distribution of State-Owned Enterprises* (OECD Publishing 2014).

Olson, M, *The Rise and Decline of Nations* (Yale University Press 1982).

Örtenblad, A (ed), *Research Handbook on Corporate Social Responsibility in Context* (Edward Elgar 2016).

Paiement, P, *Transnational Sustainability Laws* (Cambridge University Press 2017).

Pande, R and Ford, D, 'Gender Quotas and Female Leadership: A Review' (2012) Background paper for the World Development Report on Gender Equality and Development https://openknowledge.worldbank.org/handle/10986/9120.

Pargendler, M, 'State Ownership and Corporate Governance' (2011) 80 *Fordham Law Review* 2917.

Pargendler, M, 'The Corporate Governance Obsession' (2016) 42 *Journal of Corporation Law* 359.

Pargendler, M, Musacchio, A and Lazzarini, SG, 'The Puzzle of Private Investment in State Controlled Firms' (2013) Harvard Business School WP 13–071 https://papers.ssrn.com/sol3/papers.cfm?abstract_id=2217627.

Parkinson, J, Kelly, G and Gamble, A (eds), *The Political Economy of the Company* (Hart 2001).

Peloza, J, 'The Challenge of Measuring Financial Impacts from Investments in Corporate Social Performance' (2009) 35 *Journal of Management* 1518.

Peloza, J, 'Using Corporate Social Responsibility as Insurance for Financial Performance' (2006) 48 *California Management Review* 52.

Phillips, A, 'Defending Equality of Outcome' (2004) 12 *Journal of Political Philosophy* 1.

Pistor, K, 'Codetermination: A Sociopolitical Model with Governance Externalities' in Blair, M and Roe, MJ (eds), *Employees and Corporate Governance* (Brookings Institution Press 1999).

Pogach, J, 'Short-Termism of Executive Compensation' (2018) 148 *Journal of Economic Behavior and Organization* 150.

Porta, RL, Lopez-de-Silanes, F and Shleifer, A, 'The Economic Consequence of Legal Origins' (2008) 46 *Journal of Economic Literature* 285.

Puchniak, DW, 'Multiple Faces of Shareholder Power in Asia: Complexity Revealed' in Hill, JG and Thomas, RS (eds), *Research Handbook on Shareholder Power* (Edward Elgar 2015).

Puchniak, DW and Lan, LL, 'Independent Directors in Singapore: Puzzling Compliance Requiring Explanation' (2017) 65 *American Journal of Comparative Law* 265.

Rajan, RG and Zingales, L, 'The Great Reversals: The Politics of Financial Development in the Twentieth Century' (2003) 69 *Journal of Financial Economics* 5.

Ramirez, CD and Tan, LH, 'Singapore, Inc. Versus the Private Sector: Are Government-Linked Companies Different?' (2003) IMF Working Paper WP/03/156 www.imf.org/external/pubs/ft/wp/2003/wp03156.pdf.

Ramsay, I, 'Allocating Liability in Corporate Groups: An Australian Perspective' (1999) 13 *Connecticut Journal of International Law* 329.

Rasche, A, Morsing, M and Moon, J (eds), *Corporate Social Responsibility: Strategy, Communication, Governance* (Cambridge University Press 2017).

Rave, DT, 'Politicians as Fiduciaries' (2013) 126 *Harvard Law Review* 671.

Rawls, J, *A Theory of Justice* (revised edn, Harvard University Press 1999).

Rawls, J, *Political Liberalism* (Columbia University Press 1993).

Redding, G, Wong, GYY and Leung, WK, 'Hong Kong: Hybrid Capitalism as Catalyst' in Witt, MA and Redding, G (eds), *The Oxford Handbook of Asian Business Systems* (Oxford University Press 2014).

Reisberg, A, 'The UK Stewardship Code: On the Road to Nowhere?' (2015) 15 *Journal of Corporate Law Studies* 217.

Ribstein, LE, 'Limited Liability and Theories of the Corporation' (1991) 50 *Maryland Law Review* 80.

Richardson, B, 'Financial Markets and Socially Responsible Investing' in Sjåfjell, B and Richardson, BJ (eds), *Company Law and Sustainability: Legal Barriers and Opportunities* (Cambridge University Press 2015).

Riedl, A and Smeets, P, 'Why Do Investors Hold Socially Responsible Mutual Funds?' (2017) 72 *Journal of Finance* 2505.

Ringe, WG, 'Shareholder Activism: A Renaissance' in Gordon, JN and Ringe, WG (eds), *The Oxford Handbook of Corporate Law and Governance* (Oxford University Press 2018).

Roe, MJ, 'Stock Market Short-Termism's Impact' (25 May 2018) https://ssrn.com/abstract=3171090.

Roe, MJ, 'The Shareholder Wealth Maximization Norm and Industrial Organization' (2011) 149 *University of Pennsylvania Law Review* 2063.
Roemer, JE, *Equality of Opportunity* (Harvard University Press 1998).
Rogers, J and Streek, W (eds), *Works Councils* (University of Chicago Press 1995).
Roth, M, 'Corporate Boards in Germany' in Davies, P, Hopt, K, Nowak, R and Solinge, G (eds), *Corporate Boards in Law and Practice* (Oxford University Press 2013).
Safari, N and Gelter, M, 'British Home Stores Collapse: The Case for an Employee Derivative Claim' (2019) 19 *Journal of Corporate Law Studies* 43.
Saito, K, 'Social Preferences under Risk: Equality of Opportunity versus Equality of Outcome' (2013) 103 *American Economic Review* 3084.
Schanzenbach, MM and Sitkoff, RH, 'Reconciling Fiduciary Duty and Social Conscience: The Law and Economics of ESG Investing by a Trustee' (2020) 72 *Stanford Law Review* (forthcoming).
Scherer, AG and Palazzo, G, 'The New Political Role of Business in a Globalized World: A Review of a New Perspective on CSR and Its Implications for the Firm, Governance, and Democracy' (2011) 48 *Journal of Management Studies* 899.
Schwartz-Ziv, M, 'Does the Gender of Directors Matter?' (2 May 2013) https://papers.ssrn.com/sol3/papers.cfm?abstract_id=2257867.
Segall, S, *Equality and Opportunity* (Oxford University Press 2013).
Seidl, D, Sanderson, P and Roberts, J, 'Applying "Comply-or-Explain": Conformance with Codes of Corporate Governance in the UK and Germany' (June 2009) Centre for Business Research, University of Cambridge, Working Paper 389 www.cbr.cam.ac.uk/fileadmin/user_upload/centre-for-business-research/downloads/working-papers/wp389.pdf.
Shabbir, A, 'To Comply or Not to Comply: Evidence on Changes and Factors Associated with the Changes in Compliance with the UK Code of Corporate Governance' (18 March 2008) http://papers.ssrn.com/sol3/papers.cfm?abstract_id=1101412.
Shamsul, AB, 'The Economic Dimension of Malay Nationalism: The Socio-Historical Roots of the New Economic Policy and Its Contemporary Implications' (1997) 35 *Developing Economies* 240.
Shleifer, A and Vishny, RW, 'A Survey of Corporate Governance' (1997) 52 *Journal of Finance* 737.
Shleifer, A and Vishny, RW, *The Grabbing Hand: Government Pathologies and Their Cures* (Harvard University Press 2002).
Shleifer, A and Wolfenzon, D, 'Investor Protection and Equity Markets' (2002) 66 *Journal of Financial Economics* 3.
Simerly, RL and Li, M, 'Corporate Social Performance and Multinationality: A Longitudinal Study' (2000) www.westga.edu/~bquest/2000/corporate.html.
Simerly, RL, 'Corporate Social Performance and Multinationality: An Empirical Examination' (1997) 14 *International Journal of Management* 699.

Singh, S, Holvoet, N and Pandey, V, 'Bridging Sustainability and Corporate Social Responsibility: Culture of Monitoring and Evaluation of CSR Initiatives in India' (2018) 10 *Sustainability* 1.

Sjåfjell, B, 'Dismantling the Legal Myth of Shareholder Primacy: The Corporation as a Sustainable Market Actor' (2017) University of Oslo Faculty of Law Research Paper No 2017–03 https://papers.ssrn.com/sol3/papers.cfm?abstract_id=2912141.

Sjåfjell, B, 'Dismantling the Legal Myth of Shareholder Primacy: The Corporation as a Sustaintable Market Actor' in Boeger, N and Villiers, C (eds), *Shaping the Corporate Landscape* (Hart 2018).

Sjåfjell, B and Bruner, CM (eds), *Cambridge Handbook of Corporate Law, Corporate Governance and Sustainability* (Cambridge University Press 2019).

Sjåfjell, B, Johnston, A, Anker-Sorensen, L and Millon, D, 'Shareholder Primacy: The Main Barrier to Sustainable Companies' in Sjåfjell, B and Richardson, BJ (eds), *Company Law and Sustainability* (Cambridge University Press 2015).

Sjåfjell, B and Richardson, BJ (eds), *Company Law and Sustainability: Legal Barriers and Opportunities* (Cambridge University Press 2015).

Skinner, G, 'Rethinking Limited Liability of Parent Corporations for Foreign Subsidiaries' Violations of International Human Rights Law' (2015) 72 *Washington & Lee Law Review* 1769.

Snape, E and Chan, AW, 'Whither Hong Kong's Unions: Autonomous Trade Unionism or Classic Dualism?' (1997) 35 *British Journal of Industrial Relations* 39.

Sternberg, E, 'The Defects of Stakeholder Theory' (1997) 5 *Corporate Governance* 3.

Sternberg, E, 'Stakeholding: Betraying the Corporation's Objectives' (1998) London Social Affairs Unit Research Paper No 27.

Stout, LA, 'New Thinking on "Shareholder Primacy"' (2012) 2 *Accounting, Economics and Law* 1.

Stout, LA, *The Shareholder Value Myth: How Putting Shareholders First Harms Investors, Corporations, and the Public* (Berrett-Koehler Publishers 2012).

Streeck, W, 'Codetermination: The Fourth Decade' in Wilpert, B and Sorge, A (eds), *International Perspectives on Organizational Democracy* (John Wiley 1984).

Strine, LEJ, 'The Dangers of Denial: The Need for a Clear-Eyed Understanding of the Power and Accountability Structure Established by the Delaware General Corporation Law' (2015) University of Pennsylvania Law School Institute for Law and Economics Research Paper No 15–08 http://ssrn.com/abstract=2576389.

Strine, LJ, 'Corporate Power Is Corporate Purpose II: An Encouragement for Future Consideration from Professors Johnson and Million' (2017) 74 *Washington & Lee Law Review* 1165.

Subramanian, S, 'A Comparison of Corporate Governance Practices in State-Owned Enterprises and Their Private Sector Peers in India' (2016) 5 *IIM Kozhikode Society & Management Review* 200.

Sukhtankar, S and Vaishnav, M, 'Corruption in India: Bridging Research Evidence and Policy Options' (2014–15) 11 *India Policy Forum* 193.

Tan, CH, Puchniak, DW and Varottil, U, 'State-Owned Enterprises in Singapore: Historical Insights into a Potential Model for Reform' (2015) 28 *Columbia Journal of Asian Law* 61.

Tan, J, 'Rent-Seeking and Money Politics in Malaysia' in Weiss, ML (ed), *Routledge Handbook of Contemporary Malaysia* (Routledge 2014).

Teck, AKY, 'The Role of the NTUC in Singapore' (2001) Dissertation, National University of Singapore.

Teigen, M, 'Gender Quotas on Corporate Boards' in Engelstad, F and Teigen, M (eds), *Firms, Boards and Gender Quotas: Comparative Perspectives* (Emerald Group Publishing 2012).

Temasek, *Temasek Review* (2017).

Thompson, RB, 'The Power of Shareholders in the United States' in Hill, JG and Thomas, RS (eds), *Research Handbook on Shareholder Power* (Edward Elgar 2015).

Tilba, A and Reisberg, A, 'Fiduciary Duty under the Microscope: Stewardship and the Spectrum of Pension Fund Engagement' (2019) 82 *Modern Law Review* 456.

Tilling, MV and Tilt, CA, 'The Edge of Legitimacy: Voluntary Social and Environmental Reporting in Rothmans' 1956–1999 Annual Reports' (2010) 23 *Accounting, Auditing and Accountability Journal* 55.

Tjio, H, Koh, P and Woan, LP, *Corporate Law* (Academy Publishing 2016).

Torii, T, 'The New Economic Policy and the United Malays National Organisation, with Special Reference to the Restructuring of the Malaysian Society' (2007) 35 *Developing Economies* 209.

Tsutsui, K and Lim, A (eds), *Corporate Social Responsibility in a Globalizing World* (Cambridge University Press 2015).

Tucker, L, Le Poidevin, N and Brightwell, J, *Lewin on Trusts* (18th edn, Sweet & Maxwell 2012).

UK Law Commission, *Fiduciary Duties of Investment Intermediaries* (Law Commission No 350) (1 July 2014).

UK Law Commission, *Pension Funds and Social Investment* (Law Com No 374) (12 June 2017).

UNEP Finance Initiative, *A Legal Framework for the Integration of Environmental, Social and Governance Issues into Institutional Investment* (2005).

UNEP Finance Initiative, *Fiduciary Duty in the 21st Century* (2015).

Varma, JR, 'Corporate Governance in India: Disciplining the Dominant Shareholder' (1997) 9 *IIMB Management Review* 5.

Varottil, U, 'Analysing the CSR Spending Requirements under Indian Company Law' in Du Plessis, JJ, Varottil, U and Veldman, J (eds), *Globalisation of Corporate Social Responsibility and Its Impact on Corporate Governance* (Springer 2018).

Veasey, EN and DiGuglielmo, CT, 'What Happened in Delaware Corporate Law and Governance from 1992–2004? A Retrospective on Some Key Developments' (2005) 153 *University of Pennsylvania Law Review* 1399.

Vinnicombe, S, Singh, V, Burke, RJ, Bilimoria, D and Huse, M (eds), *Women on Corporate Boards of Directors: International Research and Practice* (Edward Elgar Publishing 2008).

Vithiatharan, V and Gomez, ET, 'Politics, Economic Crises and Corporate Governance Reforms: Regulatory Capture in Malaysia' (2014) 44 *Journal of Contemporary Asia* 599.

Waldman, DA et al, 'Cultural and Leadership Predictors of Corporate Social Responsibility Values of Top Management: A GLOBE Study of 15 Countries' (2006) 37 *Journal of International Business Studies* 823.

Watchman, P, Anstee-Wedderburn, J and Shipway, L, 'Fiduciary Duties in the 21st Century: A UK Perspective' (2005) 19 *Trust Law International* 127.

Weiss, ML (ed), *Routledge Handbook of Contemporary Malaysia* (Routledge 2014).

Williams, C and Aguilera, RV, 'Corporate Social Responsibility in a Comparative Perspective' in Crane, A, Matten, D, McWilliams, A, Moon, J and Siegel, DS, *The Oxford Handbook of Corporate Social Responsibility* (Oxford University Press 2008).

Williams, CA, 'Corporate Social Responsibility and Corporate Governance' in Gordon, JN and Ringe, WG (eds), *The Oxford Handbook of Corporate Law and Governance* (Oxford University Press 2018).

Wilpert, B and Sorge, A (eds), *International Perspectives on Organizational Democracy* (John Wiley 1984).

Witt, MA and Redding, G (eds), *The Oxford Handbook of Asian Business Systems* (Oxford University Press 2014).

Witt, MA and Redding, G, 'China: Authoritarian Capitalism' in Witt, MA and Redding, G (eds), *The Oxford Handbook of Asian Business Systems* (Oxford University Press 2014).

Witting, C, *Liability of Corporate Groups and Networks* (Cambridge University Press 2018).

Wong, CYS, 'The State of Governance at State-Owned Enterprises' (2018) Private Sector Opinion, Issue 40, IFC Corporate Governance Knowledge Publication www.ifc.org/wps/wcm/connect/b1adde06-267d-4d79-bfaf-62f17de51f4a/ PSO40.pdf?MOD=AJPERES&CVID=m7T0xLQ.

Wong, FMK, 'Shareholder Engagement and Activism under the Radar: Empirical Evidence from Hong Kong (2003–15): Rethinking Disclosure of Interests Regime' (23 June 2017) https://papers.ssrn.com/sol3/papers.cfm?abstract_id=2725318.

World Commission on Environment and Development, *Our Common Future* (Oxford University Press 1987).

Wyman, O and AVPN, *Driving ESG Investing in Asia: The Imperative for Growth* (Marsh & McLennan Companies' Asia Pacific Risk Center 2018).

Yatim, P, Kent, P and Clarkson, P, 'Governance Structures, Ethnicity, and Audit Fees of Malaysian Listed Firms' (2006) 21 *Managerial Auditing Journal* 757.

Zaidi, A and Low, KCP, 'The Koranic Discourse on Corporate Social Responsibility' in Low, KCP, Idowu, SO and Ang, SL (eds), *Corporate Social Responsibility in Asia: Practice and Experience* (Springer 2014).

Zerk, JA, *Multinationals and Corporate Social Responsibility: Limitations and Opportunities in International Law* (Cambridge University Press 2011).

INDEX

Adams v Cape Industries plc, 246–7
agency, limited liability and role of, 252
Air Pollution Control Ordinance (Hong Kong), 277–82
alter ego principle, Singapore companies' liability and, 247–9
apply or explain an alternative approach, gender diversity and, 116–18, 120–4
Arthashastra, 10–11
auditing firms
  comply or explain mechanisms in sustainability reporting and, 63–7
  oversight of sustainability reporting and, 97–9

bargaining power, German co-determination model, 149–52
best interests of company, duty to act in, 2–4
  in common law jurisdictions, 217–28
  constituency directors and, 231–2
  corporate governance mechanisms and, 228–32
  corporate law and, 52–3
  directors' duties doctrine, 17–18
  fiduciary duties and, 196–8
  in Hong Kong, 220–3
  in India, 217–20
  long-term value and viability and, 215–17
  in Malaysia, 225–6
  shareholder primacy theory and, 208–12
  in Singapore, 223–5
  stakeholder value theory and, 212–15
  stewardship code and, 229–31
  sustainability and, 206–8, 232–4
  sustainability reporting and, 228–9

binary structure, Business and Responsibility Reports, 77–80
BlackRock, 74–5, 131–2, 172–4, 189–93
boards of directors. *See also* best interests of company, duty to act in; constituency directors
  apply or explain an alternative approach to gender diversity on, 120–4
  equality of outcomes and gender diversity, 110–11
  gender diversity on, 14–15, 105–6, 360–4
  German co-determination model, 143–62
  legal origin theory and, 18–22
  sanctions and oversight of, 99–102
  in Singapore, 83–4
  state-owned enterprises, absence of female directors in, 137
  women as repeat players on, 139–40
Bombay Stock Exchange, 33–5
Brundtland Report, 6
burden of proof
  breach of public interest legislation and, 277–82
  liability cases and, 235–7
Bursa Malaysia, 33–5
  materiality of ESG factors in reporting rules, 69–72
  Sustainability Guide for, 71–2
  sustainability reporting requirements, 57, 96
  target indicators in reporting rules, 73–7
business case for sustainability, 7–10

394

Business Responsibility Reports (BRR) (India), 4n.10, 57, 77–80, 96–7
   CSR board committee and, 161–7

Cadbury Report, 58–9
capital, business case for sustainability and access to, 8
Carbon Disclosure Project, 8
Chandler v Cape plc, 252–61
civil law origin, common law jurisdictions (Asia) and, 18–22
Code on Corporate Governance (Malaysia) (MCCG), 84–5
   gender diversity in boards of directors in, 14–15, 120–4
Code on Corporate Governance (Singapore), gender diversity in boards of directors in, 14–15, 123–4
co-determination constituency directors model, 143–62
   benefits, 149–52
   best interests of company duties and, 231–2
   common law jurisdictions and adoption of, 152–3
   costs of, 145–9
   CSR board committee *vs.*, 168–9
   in Hong Kong, 159–61
   Indian CSR board committee and, 161–7
   in Malaysia, 156–9
   in Singapore, 153–6
common law jurisdictions (Asia)
   best interests of company, duty to act in, 217–28, 231–4
   breach of public interest legislation and, 277–82
   comply or explain mechanisms in sustainability reporting and, 59–61
   constituency directors requirements in, 15–16, 231–2
   corporate governance and law and, 2–4
   corporate social responsibility in, 4–6
   directors' duties doctrine in, 17–18
   duty of care, parent companies breach of, 252–61
   enterprise liability and, 261–4
   female to male director ratios in, 365–9
   gender diversity in, 14–15, 51–2, 106–8, 133–40
   German co-determination model adoption in, 152–3
   institutional context in, 22–5
   internationalisation of companies and, 35–6
   legal origins theory and, 18–22
   liability for controlling shareholders in, 267–73
   monitoring of gender diversity in, 124–30
   qualitative evaluation of sustainability reporting in, 89–97
   recent legal developments in, 12–18
   socially responsible investment in, 36–9
   socio-economic development agendas in, 25–33
   state intervention in, 20–1
   state-owned enterprises gender diversity in, 133–40
   stewardship codes in, 16–17
   stock exchange rules in, 33–5
   sustainability reporting in, 12–14, 55–7, 83–97
   target indicators in sustainability reporting and, 73–7
comparative sustainability research, 3, 284–5
compliance issues
   Indian CSR 2 per cent expenditure requirement in sustainability reporting, 82–3, 163–7
   stewardship codes, 180–4
comply or explain mechanisms, sustainability reporting
   absence of third party/independent assessment for, 63–7
   barriers to accountability and, 62–3

comply or explain mechanisms (cont.)
  concentrated ownership
    jurisdictions, 59–61
  gender diversity and, 122–3
  lack of guidelines for, 61–2
  sustainability reporting, 58–67
concentrated ownership model, best
  interests of company and, 226–8
conflicts of interest
  best interests of company duty and,
    232–4
  controlling *vs.* institutional
    shareholders, 194–6
  CSR board committee and, 163–7
  German co-determination model,
    149–52
  government as regulator and
    shareholder, 41–3
  oversight of sustainability reporting
    and, 97–9
Confucianism, sustainability practices
  and, 10–11
constituency directors, 2–4
  best interests of company duties and,
    231–2
  in common law jurisdictions, 15–16
  German co-determination model
    for, 143–62
  government as regulator and
    shareholder, conflicts of
    interest, 41–3
  Indian sustainability and, 29–32
  overview of, 142–3
  sustainability and, 52
content requirements for sustainability
  reporting, 69–83
  India Business Responsibility
    Reports, 77–80
  Indian CSR 2 per cent expenditure
    requirement, 80–3
  indicators, 73–7
  materiality of ESG factors in, 69–72
controlling shareholders
  best interests of company duty and,
    232–4
  comply or explain mechanisms in
    sustainability reporting and,
    59–61
  conflicts of interest with institutional
    shareholders, 194–6
  formal power of, 189–93
  German co-determination model
    and, 148–52
  government as regulator and
    shareholder, conflicts of interest
    between, 41–3
  in India, duties of, 217–20
  informal power of, 193–4
  institutional shareholder
    disincentivise and, 189–93
  liability of, 235–7, 267–73
  limited liability and, 237–42
  in Malaysian GLCs, 156–9
  Malaysian sustainability initiatives
    and, 27–9
  PRC SOEs in Hong Kong as, 159–61
  private benefits extraction and, 43–5
  public benefits of, 46
  sanctions and oversight duties,
    99–102
  in Singapore, 83–4
  stewardship codes and, 42–3, 52,
    188–96
  sustainability mechanisms and, 2–4,
    39–40, 286–8
corporate governance
  Asian common law jurisdictions
    and, 2–4
  best interests of company duties and,
    228–34
  Cadbury Report on, 58–9
  comparative legal analysis of, 285–6
  corporate law and, 286–8
  enterprise liability and, 261–4
  gender diversity and, 105–6, 115–20
  government as regulator and
    shareholder, conflicts of
    interest, 41–3
  in India, 85–6
  limited liability and, 237–42
  in Malaysia, 84–5
  network liability and, 274–7
  parent company breach of duty of
    care and, 260
  public benefits of, 46
  in Singapore, 83–4

Singapore sustainability initiatives and, 25–7
stewardship codes and, 172–4
sustainability reporting and characteristics of, 83–6
corporate law
　Asian common law jurisdictions and, 2–4
　comparative analysis in, 285–6
　corporate governance and, 286–8
　directors' best interest duty and, 52–3
corporate social responsibility (CSR)
　comparative legal analysis of, 285–6
　Indian CSR 2 per cent expenditure requirement in sustainability reporting, 80–3, 163–7
　research on, 3
　terminology and definitions, 4–6
corruption
　in India, 29–32
　in Malaysia, 27–9
　Singapore sustainability initiatives and absence of, 27
Council for Board Diversity (Singapore), 104–5, 135–6
　monitoring procedures at, 124–30
Cowan v Scargill, 197n.106, 198n.112
creditors
　limited liability and monitoring by, 237–42
　separate legal personality and, 243–6
crony capitalism index, 44n.166
　gender quota requirements and, 116–18
CSR Board Committee (India)
　benefits and limitations of, 161–7
　German co-determination model *vs.*, 168–9
CSR Ltd v Wren, 256–7

decision-making process
　German co-determination model and, 145–9
　sustainability considerations in, 199–202
developing countries, sustainability in, 3

Development Bank of Singapore, 25–7
DHN Food Distributors Ltd v Tower Hamlets London Borough Council, 246–7
directors' duties doctrine
　in common law jurisdictions (Asia), 17–18
　corporate law and, 52–3
disclosure requirements
　CSR board committee, 163–7
　gender diversity and, 124–30
　in-depth *vs.* shallow disclosure, variations in, 91–2
　sustainability reporting, 57–69
diversification of investment, limited liability and, 237–42
Diversity Action Committee (DAC) (Singapore), 124–30, 135–6
due diligence defence
　breach of public interest legislation and, 277–82
　liability cases and, 235–7
duty of care
　network liability and, 274–7
　parent companies breach of, 252–61

Ecomagination Initiative, 7
efficiency, stakeholder value and, 214
Employee Provident Fund, 27–9
employees and employment
　German co-determination model and, 146–8
　in Hong Kong, 159–61
　in Malaysia, 156–9
　parent company breach of duty of care and, 252–4
　in Singapore, 153–6
employment, Singapore sustainability initiatives and, 25–7
enterprise liability
　of controlling shareholders, 271–3
　parent company breach of duty of care and, 261
　proposals for, 261–4
　shareholders and, 264–7
entity shielding, separate legal personality and, 243–6

Environmental, Social and Governance (ESG) factors
  adoption of, 6
  decision-making process and, 199–202
  defined, 6n.19
  fiduciary duties and, 196–8
  German co-determination constituency directors model and, 143–62
  key performance indicators and, 73–7
  materiality of, 69–72
  socio-economic development and, 25–7
  stock exchange rules and, 33–5
  sustainability reporting requirements and, 12–14
Environmental, Social and Governance (ESG) Reporting Guide (Hong Kong), 4n.9
environmental factors
  Indian CSR 2 per cent expenditure requirement in sustainability reporting, 80–3
  as target indicators, 75–6
Environmental Protection and Management Act (Singapore), 277–82
Environment Quality Act (Malaysia), 277–82
equality
  gender diversity as justification for, 108–14
  of outcomes, 110–11
  of resources and opportunity, 111–14
ethics, sustainability strategies and, 10–11
EU Directive 2014, sustainability reporting, 12
European company law, stakeholder value theory and, 22–5
European Union (EU), constituency directors in, 15–16
EU Shareholder Rights Directive, 16–17
ex ante rules, legal origin theory and, 18–22

ex post sanctions, legal origin theory and, 18–22
expropriation, best interests of company duty and, 232–4
external assurance
  Hong Kong, 298
  India, 300
  Malaysia, 294
  Singapore, 292

Factories and Industrial Undertakings Ordinance (Hong Kong), 281
fairness, stakeholder value and, 213–14
family-owned companies
  controlling shareholders in, 2n.2
  institutional theory and, 22–5
  stewardship codes and, 187
fault-based liability
  government conflicts of interest and, 42–3
  of shareholders, 264–7
fiduciary duties
  decision-making and input of, 199–202
  ESG factors and, 196–8
  institutional shareholders, 196–203
  liability of controlling shareholders and, 267–73
  required sustainability factors and, 202–3
financial capital, long-term value and viability and, 215–17
firm-specific investments, German co-determination model, 149–52
firm value
  business case for sustainability and, 8–9
  CSR board committee and, 163–7
  gender diversity and, 106–8, 115–20
  gender quotas and, 116–18
  German co-determination model and, 149–52
foreign direct investment
  gender diversity and influence of, 132–3
  sustainability and, 35–6
formal power, stewardship codes and, 189–93

INDEX 399

Fortune Global 500, 3
free rider problem, stewardship codes
  and, 189–93

gender diversity
  apply or explain an alternative
    approach, 120–4
  on board of directors, 14–15
  comply or explain approach to,
    122–3
  corporate governance and, 105–6
  disclosure monitoring and
    'name and shame' approaches
    to, 124–30
  equality justifications, 108–14
  equality of outcomes and, 110–11
  examples of policies, 360–4
  female to male director ratios and,
    365–9
  firm value and, 106–8
  government connections of women
    and, 137–9
  historical trends in, 103–4
  institutional shareholders influence
    on, 131–2
  instrumental justifications for, 140–1
  internationalisation of companies
    and rates of, 132–3
  mechanisms for, 2–4
  political interference in goal of, 45
  promotion mechanisms and, 115–33
  quota requirements and, 51–2,
    115–20
  rationales for, 51–2, 104–14
  repeat players as tools for, 139–40
  in state-owned enterprises (SOEs),
    133–40
  target setting strategies for, 130–3
General Electric, 7
German co-determination
  constituency directors model,
    143–62
  benefits, 149–52
  best interests of company duties and,
    231–2
  common law jurisdictions and
    adoption of, 152–3
  costs of, 145–9

CSR board committee *vs.*, 168–9
  in Hong Kong, 159–61
  Indian CSR board committee and,
    161–7
  in Malaysia, 156–9
  in Singapore, 153–6
Germany, constituency directors in,
  15–16
Global Gender Gap Report,
  113–14
globalisation, sustainability of
  companies and, 35–6
Global Report Initiative (GRI-G4)
  Guidelines, 86–7
government
  best interests of company duty and
    role of, 232–4
  liability of, 235–7, 267–73
  Malaysian GLCs and, 156–9
  as regulator and shareholder,
    conflicts of interest, 41–3
  state-owned enterprises and
    legitimacy of, 46–50
  sustainability mechanisms and role
    of, 2–4
  women directors and connections to,
    137–9
government-linked companies (GLCs).
  See also state-owned enterprises
  (SOEs)
  German co-determination model
    and, 153–9
  in Malaysia, 27–9, 84–5
  in Singapore, 25–7, 83–4
  Singapore best interests of company
    duties and, 223–5
  stewardship codes and, 188–9
green stocks and bonds, increased
  demand for, 38–9

hedge funds
  Hong Kong, best interest duties and,
    220–3
  shareholder primacy theory and
    sustainability and, 210–11
  stewardship codes and, 193
Hinduism, Indian sustainability
  practices and, 10–11

Hong Kong
  absence of mandatory sustainability reporting requirements in, 67–9
  best interests of company duties in, 220–3
  breach of public interest legislation in, 277–82
  business case for sustainability in, 8–9
  company classification in, 311
  comply or explain approach to gender diversity in, 122–3
  corporate social responsibility in, 4–6
  directors' duties doctrine in, 17–18
  disclosure extent and quality, sustainability reporting, 88–9
  ESG initiatives and market reactions in, 63–7
  external assurance, 298
  female directors statistics in, 116–18
  gender diversity in boards of directors and, 103–4, 130–3
  gender diversity in state-owned enterprises of, 136–7
  German co-determination model in, 159–61
  green stocks and bonds in, 38–9
  institutional shareholder influence on gender diversity in, 131–2
  key performance indicators in, 73–7
  lifting the corporate veil in, 247–9
  materiality of ESG factors in reporting rules, 69–72
  monitoring of gender diversity in, 124–30
  political interference and private benefits extraction in, 43–5
  socio-economic development in, 32–3
  state-owned enterprises in, 20–1n.83
  stewardship code in, 16–17, 172–4, 180, 182–3, 229–30
  sustainability reporting in, 13, 55–7, 92–4
  top listed companies in, 306
  women directors' government connections in, 137–9

Hong Kong Principles of Responsible Ownership (HKPRO), 16–17, 229–30
  scope of, 185–7
  stewardship codes and, 180
human rights, business violations of, 235–7

IHH Healthcare, 120–2, 128
independent assessment, comply or explain mechanisms and lack of, 63–7
India
  best interests of company, duty to act in, 217–20
  business responsibility reports in, 77–80
  company classification in, 348
  constituency directors in, 16, 231–2
  controlling shareholder liability and, 272–3
  corporate social responsibility in, 4–6, 85–6
  crony capitalism in, 44n.166
  CSR 2 per cent expenditure requirement in sustainability reporting, 80–3, 163–7
  CSR Board Committee in, 161–7
  disclosure extent and quality, sustainability reporting, 87–8
  enterprise liability in, 261–4
  equality of resources and opportunity and, 113–14
  ESG initiatives and market reactions in, 63–7
  external assurance, 300
  female directors statistics in, 116–18
  foreign direct investment in, 35–6
  gender diversity in boards of directors and, 14–15, 103–4
  gender diversity in state-owned enterprises of, 136
  gender quota requirements and, 115–20
  government intervention in, 22–5
  legal origin theory and laws of, 20–1
  lifting the corporate veil in, 250–2

INDEX 401

mandatory sustainability reporting
  requirements in, 67–9
socio-economic development in,
  29–32
stewardship codes in, 16–17
sustainability reporting in, 13–14,
  55–7, 96–7
top listed companies in, 308
women directors' government
  connections in, 137–9
Indian Companies Act 2013,
  best interests of company, duty to act
    in, 217–20
  constituency directors in, 16
  CSR 2 per cent expenditure
    requirement in sustainability
    reporting, 80–3
  CSR Board Committee and, 161–7
  directors' duties doctrine in, 17–18
  gender diversity in boards of
    directors in, 14–15
  oversight of sustainability reporting
    in, 97–9
  sustainability reporting
    requirements, 13–14, 57
indicators, in sustainability
  reporting, 73–7
indigenous Malays, socio-economic
  development in Malaysia and, 27–9
information asymmetry, German
  co-determination model, 146–8
innovation, business case for
  sustainability and, 7–10
institutional shareholders
  conflicts of interest with controlling
    shareholders, 194–6
  controlling shareholder
    disincentivise and, 189–93
  decision-making process and,
    199–202
  dissent voting patterns
    for, 192–3
  fiduciary duties of, 196–203
  gender diversity of directors and,
    131–2
  liability issues and, 271–3
  Malaysian stewardship codes and,
    176–80

required sustainability factors and
  fiduciary duties, 202–3
risk-adjusted returns and
  sustainability and, 202
stewardship codes and, 172–4
institutional theory, in common law
  jurisdictions (Asia), 22–5
internationalisation of companies
  gender diversity and, 132–3
  institutional theory and, 24–5
  sustainability and, 35–6
investors. *See also* foreign direct
  investment
  business case for sustainability
    and, 7–10
  German co-determination model,
    149–52
  limited liability and, 237–42
Islam, sustainability practices and,
  10–11

judgment-proofing, limited liability
  and, 240–1
justice, stakeholder value and, 214

key performance indicators (KPI)
  ESG factors and, 73–7
  in Hong Kong, 92–4

labour
  German co-determination model
    and, 145–9
  in Malaysia, 156–9
  Singapore regulation of, 153–6
  as target indicator, 74
Lee v Lee's Air Farming Ltd, 243–6
legal origins theory, sustainability and,
  18–22, 286–8
legitimacy theory, sustainability and,
  46–50
Lehman crisis, 105–6
liability. *See also* limited liability
  controlling shareholders, 235–7,
    267–73
  government conflicts of interest
    and, 42–3
  legislative imposition of, 53–4
  in networks, 274–7

402   INDEX

liability (cont.)
　parent company breach of duty of
　　care and, 252–61
　of shareholders, 264–7
　structure of, 235–7
lifting the corporate veil
　exceptions to limited liability and,
　　246–52
　in Hong Kong, 247–9
　in India, 250–2
　in Malaysia, 249–50
　separate legal personality and,
　　243–52
　in Singapore, 247–9
　subsidiaries and corporate
　　governance and, 237–42
limited liability. *See also* liability
　breach of duty of care by parent
　　companies and, 252–61
　enterprise liability proposals and,
　　261–4
　exceptions to, 242–61
　government imposition
　　of, 53–4
　legal personality and, 243–6
　piercing the corporate veil and,
　　246–52
　rationales for, 237–42
liquidation protection rule, 243–6
long-term value and viability
　best interests of company duty and,
　　206–8, 232–4
　corporate law and, 52–3
　Hong Kong, best interest duties and,
　　220–3
　shareholder primacy theory and
　　sustainability, 208–12
　Singapore best interests of company
　　duties and, 223–5
long-term value and viability and,
　sustainability and, 215–17

Mahabharata, 10–11
Malay affirmative action, 156–9
Malaysia, 14–15
　apply or explain an alternative
　　approach to gender diversity in,
　　120–4

best interests of company, duty to act
　in, 225–6
company classification in, 339–48
controlling shareholder liability and,
　272–3
corporate social responsibility in,
　4–6, 84–5
crony capitalism in, 44n.166
directors' duties doctrine in, 17–18
disclosure extent and quality,
　sustainability reporting, 86–7
enterprise liability in, 261–4
equality of resources and
　opportunity and, 113–14
external assurance in, 294
female directors statistics in, 116–18
gender diversity in state-owned
　enterprises of, 133–40
gender diversity on boards of
　directors in, 14–15, 103–4, 124–33
German co-determination model in,
　156–9
government intervention in, 22–5
lifting the corporate veil in, 249–50
long-term value and viability, 52–3
mandatory sustainability reporting
　requirements in, 67–9
shareholder primacy theory in, 20–1
socio-economic development
　in, 27–9
state legitimacy and sustainability in,
　46–50
stewardship code in, 16–17, 172–4,
　176–80, 230–1
sustainability reporting in, 55–7, 96
sustainability strategies in,
　13–14, 27–9
top listed companies in, 304
women directors' government
　connections in, 137–9
Malaysian Code for Institutional
　Investors (MCII), 16–17, 176–83
　controlling shareholders and, 188–9
　scope of, 185–7
Malaysian Companies Act, best
　interests of company in, 225–6
Malaysian Corporate Governance
　Code, 109, 110–11

Malaysian Securities Commission (MSC), gender diversity monitoring and, 124–30
mandatory sustainability reporting requirements, 67–9
market forces, comply or explain mechanisms and, 63–7
Ministry of Corporate Affairs (MCA) (India), CSR Board Committee and, 161–7
Minority Shareholders Watch Group (MSWG), 176–80
multinational corporations
  limited liability and, 240–1
  in Malaysia, 156–9
  parent company breach of duty of care and, 259–60
  in Singapore, 153–6
  Singapore sustainability initiatives and, 27

name and shame approach, gender diversity and, 124–30
National Stock Exchange of India, 33–5
National Voluntary Guidelines on Social, Environmental, and Economic Responsibilities of Business (India), 10–11
National Voluntary Guidelines on Social, Environmental and Economic Responsibilities of Business (India CSR Board Committee), 161–7
nepotism, gender quota requirements and, 116–18
networks, liability in, 274–7
New Economic Policy (Malaysia), 27–9
NGOs
  comply or explain mechanisms and, 63–7
  gender diversity and influence of, 132–40
non-interventionist policies, Hong Kong and, 159–61
non-shareholders
  directors' duties doctrine and, 17–18
  institutional theory and, 24–5
  sustainability guidelines and, 5–6

normative component principle, parent company breach of duty of care and, 257–61
Norwegian quota system, 115–20

opportunistic behaviour, German co-determination model and, 149–52
opportunity, equality of, 111–14
outsourcing of hazardous operations, parent company breach of duty of care and, 260
overseas shareholders
  gender diversity and influence of, 132–3
  Indian liability issues and, 250–2
oversight of sustainability reporting, 97–9
owner shielding, limited liability and, 245–6

parent company
  breach of duty of care by, 252–61
  enterprise liability and, 261–4
  Indian liability issues and, 250–2
  lifting the corporate veil on, 246–52
  limited liability and, 237–42
  statutory duty of vigilance and, 274–7
patriarchal norms, gender diversity and, 108, 115–20
pension funds, Malaysian socio-economic development and, 27–9
People's Republic of China
  Hong Kong socio-economic development and, 32–3
  SOEs in Hong Kong from, 159–61
Petronas Chemical, 120–2, 128
political goals
  gender quotas and, 119–20
  of state-owned enterprises, 20–1
political interference
  in state-owned enterprises, 43–5
  women directors' government connections and, 137–9
Prest v Petrodel, 247–9
Principles of Responsible Investments (PRI) (UN), 36–9

private benefits extraction
  German co-determination model and, 149–52
  in Malaysian GLCs, 156–9
  sustainability and, 43–5
private entities, sustainability reporting using, 42–3, 97–9
private market outcomes, legal origin theory and, 18–22
product responsibility indicator, 74
profit maximisation, Singapore sustainability initiatives and, 25–7
promotion mechanisms, gender equality and, 115–33
property development companies, materiality of ESG factors in reporting rules, 71
public interest legislation, breaches of, 277–82
public sector undertakings (PSUs) (India), 29–32

qualitative evaluation
  common law jurisdictions (Asia) sustainability reporting, 89–97
  Hong Kong sustainability reporting, 88–9
  Indian sustainability reporting, 87–8
  Malaysia sustainability reporting, 86–7, 96
  Singapore sustainability reporting, 86–7, 94–5
  of sustainability reporting requirements, 83–97
quota systems
  equality of outcomes and gender diversity, 110–11
  gender diversity in directors and, 51–2, 140–1
  promotion of female directors and, 115–20

Rawls, John, 111–14
related-party transactions, in state-owned enterprises, 43–5
resources, equality of, 111–14
retail shareholders, liability issues and, 271–3
reverse causality, gender diversity and, 108
risk-taking, shareholder primacy theory and sustainability and, 208–12

sanctions
  gender quota requirements and, 116–18
  sustainability reporting oversight and, 99–102
Securities and Exchange Board of India (SEBI)
  Business and Responsibility Reports, 77–80
  CSR board committee and, 161–7
  listing rules, 57
  sustainability reporting in, 96–7
Securities Commission Malaysia, stewardship code and, 176–80
securities markets, limited liability and, 237–42
separate legal personality
  enterprise liability proposals and, 261–4
  lifting the corporate veil and, 246–52
  Singapore and Hong Kong liability issues and, 247–9
separate legal personality doctrine
  limited liability and, 243–6
  long-term value and viability and, 215–17
shareholder primacy theory
  best interests of company duty and, 206–8, 232–4
  common law jurisdictions and, 226–8
  comply or explain mechanisms in sustainability reporting and, 59–61
  corporate law and, 52–3
  German co-determination model and, 146–8
  in Hong Kong, best interest duties and, 220–3
  in India, best interests duties and, 217–20
  legal origins and, 18–22

Malaysian best interests of company duties and, 225-6
in Singapore best interests of company duties, 223-5
stewardship codes and, 172-4, 185-7
sustainability and, 208-12
sustainability reporting rules, 228-9
shareholders
legal origin theory, 18-22
liability of, 264-7
limited liability for, 237-42
litigation by, 21-2
separate legal personality and, 243-6
sustainability reporting to, 12-14
share price
comply or explain mechanisms and shifts in, 63-7
gender quotas and, 115-20
Hong Kong, best interest duties and, 220-3
shareholder primacy theory and sustainability and, 208-12
short-termism
shareholder primacy theory and sustainability and, 208-12
stewardship codes and, 172-4
significant financial detriment principle, shareholder decision-making and, 199-201
Singapore
absence of mandatory sustainability reporting requirements in, 67-9
best interests of company, duty to act in, 223-5
breach of public interest legislation in, 277-82
company classification in, 325-39
comply or explain approach to gender diversity in, 122-3
controlling shareholder liability and, 272-3
corporate social responsibility in, 4-6, 83-4
crony capitalism in, 44n.166
directors' duties doctrine in, 17-18
disclosure extent and quality, sustainability reporting, 86-7

equality of resources and opportunity and, 113-14
external assurance in, 292
female directors statistics in, 116-18
foreign investment in, 35-6
gender diversity in boards of directors in, 14-15
gender diversity in state-owned enterprises of, 133-40
German co-determination model in, 153-6
government intervention in, 22-5
green stocks and bonds in, 38-9
lifting the corporate veil on companies in, 247-9
long-term value and viability, 52-3
monitoring of gender diversity in, 124-30
public benefits of control in, 46
shareholder primacy theory in, 20-1
socio-economic development in, 25-7
state-owned enterprises in, 44n.166
stewardship code in, 16-17, 175-6, 230
sustainability reporting in, 13, 55-7, 94-5
top listed companies in, 302
women directors' government connections in, 137-9
Singapore Airlines, 25-7, 125-6
Singapore Code of Corporate Governance, 109
Singapore Companies Act, best interests of company in, 223-5
Singapore Diversity Action Committee, 104-5
Singapore Exchange
materiality of ESG factors in reporting rules, 69-72
sustainability reporting rules, 57
target indicators in reporting rules, 73-7
Singapore Stewardship Principles for Responsible Investors (SSP), 16-17, 175-6
contents, 180-3
controlling shareholders and, 188-9
scope of, 185-7

single economic unit doctrine
  corporate liability and, 235–7, 246–52
  Indian liability issues and, 250–2
  limited liability and, 237–42
  Malaysian liability issues and, 249–50
  in Singapore and Hong Kong, 247–9
social factors
  business externalities, impact of, 235–7
  gender quotas and, 119–20
  as target indicators, 74–5, 76
social governance, German co-determination model, 143–62
socialist government, in India, 29–32
socially responsible investment
  institutional theory and, 24–5
  sustainability and, 36–9
socio-economic development
  in Hong Kong, 32–3
  in India, 29–32
  in Malaysia, 27–9
  in Singapore, 25–7
  sustainability and, 25–33
soft law, stewardship codes as, 183–4
stakeholders
  business case for sustainability and, 7–10
  civil law origin and, 18–22
  sustainability reporting to, 12–14
stakeholder value theory
  best interests of company duty and, 206–8, 232–4
  common law jurisdictions and, 226–8
  corporate law and, 52–3
  European company law and, 22–5
  in Hong Kong, best interest duties and, 220–3
  in India, best interests duties and, 217–20
  Indian sustainability and, 29–32
  Malaysian best interests of company duties and, 225–6
  Malaysian stewardship codes and, 176–80
  shareholder primacy theory and sustainability and, 211–12

in Singapore best interests of company duties, 223–5
sustainability and, 212–15
sustainability reporting rules and, 228–9
state intervention
  civil law origin and, 18–22
  comply or explain mechanisms in sustainability reporting and, 61
  institutional theory and, 22–5
state legitimacy, state-owned enterprises and, 46–50
State-Owned Assets Supervision and Administration Commission (SASAC), 43–5
state-owned enterprises (SOEs). *See also* government-linked companies (GLCs)
  absence of female directors in, 137
  barriers to accountability for, 62–3
  best interests of company duty and, 232–4
  comply or explain mechanisms in sustainability reporting and, 59–61
  gender diversity in, 133–40
  government as regular and shareholder, conflicts of interest, 41–3
  in Hong Kong, 32–3, 92–4
  in India, 29–32, 85–6
  legal origin theory and, 20–1
  liability for controlling shareholders in, 267–73
  in Malaysia, 96, 156–9
  political interference in, 43–5
  PRC SOEs in Hong Kong, 159–61
  private benefits extraction from, 43–5
  public benefits of, 46
  sanctions against, 99–102
  in Singapore, 94–5
  state legitimacy and, 46–50
  sustainability mechanisms and, 2–4, 39–40
statutory duty of vigilance, network liability and, 274–7
statutory enterprise liability

INDEX 407

parent company breach of duty
    and, 261
proposals for, 261–4
Stewardship Asia Center, 188–9
stewardship codes, 2–4
    best interests of company duties and,
        229–31
    in common law jurisdictions (Asia),
        16–17
    compliance, 180–4
    conflicts of interest, controlling vs.
        institutional shareholders, 194–6
    controlling shareholders and, 42–3,
        52, 188–96
    emergence of, 172–4
    fiduciary duties of institutional
        shareholders, 196–203
    formal power, 189–93
    Hong Kong, 180
    institutional shareholder
        disincentivise and, 189–93
    Malaysia, 16–17, 172–4, 176–80, 230–1
    political interference in, 45
    proposed reforms, 204–5
    rationales for, 175–80
    scope of, 185–7
    Singapore, 16–17, 175–6
    sustainability and, 16–17, 52, 175–87
Stewardship Principles for Family
    Businesses (SPFB) (Singapore),
    187, 230
Stock Exchange of Hong Kong
    (SEHK), 33–5
    barriers to accountability for, 62–3
    comply or explain approach to
        gender diversity on, 122–3
    disclosure extent and quality,
        sustainability reporting, 88–9
    gender diversity and, 104–5, 130–3
    gender diversity in state-owned
        enterprises and, 136–7
    key performance indicators in, 73–7
    materiality of ESG factors in
        reporting rules, 69–72
    oversight of sustainability reporting
        and, 97–9
    sustainability reporting rules, 57,
        228–9

stock exchange rules
    comply or explain mechanisms in
        sustainability reporting and, 63–7
    Malaysia, 96
    materiality of ESG factors and, 69–72
    opt-out option for, 89–90
    Singapore sustainability reporting
        and, 94–5
    sustainability promotion and,
        24–5, 33–5
    target indicators in, 73–7
strategic benefits of sustainability
    promotion, 7–10
strict liability
    of controlling shareholders, 271–3
    government conflicts of interest
        and, 42–3
    of shareholders, 264–7
subsidiaries
    corporate liability for, 235–7
    enterprise liability and, 261–4
    Indian liability issues and, 250–2
    lifting the corporate veil on, 246–52
    limited liability and, 237–42
    Malaysian liability issues and,
        249–50
    parent company breach of duty of
        care and, 252–61
    shareholders liability and, 264–7
    Singapore and Hong Kong liability
        issues and, 247–9
superior knowledge principle, parent
    company breach of duty of care
    and, 257–61
supermajority requirements, civil law
    countries and, 18–22
suppliers, German co-determination
    model and, 149–52
sustainability. See also comparative
    sustainability research
    best interests of company duty and,
        206–8, 232–4
    business case for, 7–10
    business wrongdoing and, 235–7
    CSR board committee and
        promotion of, 163–7
    decision-making process and,
        199–202

sustainability (cont.)
  ethical reasons for pursuing, 10–11
  fiduciary duties and, 196–8
  German co-determination model and, 145–9
  government as regulator and shareholder, conflicts of interest, 41–3
  Indian socio-economic development and, 29–32
  institutional theory and, 22–5
  internationalisation of companies and, 35–6
  legal origin theory and, 18–22
  long-term value and viability and, 215–17
  political interference and private benefit extraction, 43–5
  problems and effects of, 39–40
  shareholder primacy theory and, 208–12
  socially responsible investment and, 36–9
  socio-economic development agendas and, 25–33
  stakeholder value theory and, 212–15
  state legitimacy and, 46–50
  stewardship codes and, 16–17, 52, 175–87
  stock exchange rules and, 33–5
  terminology and definitions, 4–6
sustainability reporting
  best interests of company duties and, 228–9
  comply or explain mechanisms, 58–67
  content requirements, 69–83
  corporate characteristics and, 83–6
  differences in emphasis in, 90
  disclosure extent and quality, 86–9
  evaluation methodologies, 90–1
  mandatory requirements, 67–9
  oversight mechanism, 97–9
  qualitative evaluation of, 83–97
  requirements, 2–4, 12–14, 50–1, 55–7
  sanctions and, 99–102
  structural requirements, 57–69
  suggested reforms for, 97–102

sustainable investment market, growth of, 8
sustainable value concept, Malaysian stewardship codes and, 176–80

Tata Consultancy Ltd, Business and Responsibility Reports for, 77–80
Temasek Holdings Pte Ltd, 25–7, 46, 153–6, 188–9, 223–5, 226–8, 272–3
Temasek Management Services Group, 188–9
third party entities
  comply or explain mechanisms and lack of, 63–7
  sustainability reporting using, 42–3
Thompson v The Renwick Group plc, 255–6
tort claims
  enterprise liability in, 261–4
  liability of controlling shareholders and, 267–73
  limited liability and, 237–42
  network liability and, 274–7
  parent company breach of duty of care and, 257–61
trade unions
  absence in Hong Kong of, 159–61
  German co-determination model and, 145–52
  in Singapore, 155–6

UK Committee on the Financial Aspects of Corporate Governance Report, 58–9
UK Companies Act, directors' duties doctrine in, 17–18, 207n.4
UK Corporate Governance Code, 168–9
United Kingdom (UK)
  comply or explain approach to gender diversity in, 122–3
  gender diversity in boards of directors in, 14–15
  sustainability reporting in, 12
UK Stewardship Code, 16–17, 172–4, 183–4

United States
  comply or explain mechanisms and shifts in share prices in, 63–7
  shareholder primacy approach in, 22–5
unlawful means conspiracy, network liability and, 274–7
UN Principles for Responsible Investment, 8

Vanguard, 131–2, 172–4, 189–93
Various Claimants v Catholic Child Welfare Society, 274–7
Vedanta Resources Plc v Lungowe, 254–5
vicarious liability, 274–7
victims of business wrongdoing
  enterprise liability and claims by, 261–4
  exceptions to limited liability and, 243
  Indian liability law and, 250–2
  lack of compensation for, 235–7
  parent company breach of duty of care and, 257–61
  remedies and redress for, 235–7
Voluntary Guidelines for Corporate Social Responsibility, 161–7

Waste Disposal Ordinance (Hong Kong), 281
women directors
  absence in state-owned enterprises of, 137
  in common law companies, 14–15
  equality of outcomes and, 110–11
  female to male director ratios, 365–9
  government connections of, 137–9
  promotion mechanisms for, 115–33
  quota requirements for, 115–20
  rationales for, 104–14
  as repeat players, 139–40
World Economic Forum, 113–14

Ingram Content Group UK Ltd.
Milton Keynes UK
UKHW020739290523
422439UK00029B/223